THE DOCTRINE
OF THE TRINITY

Christianity's Self-Inflicted Wound

THE DOCTRINE OF THE TRINITY

Christianity's Self-Inflicted Wound

Anthony F. Buzzard
and
Charles F. Hunting

International Scholars Publications
Lanham · New York · Oxford

Copyright © 1998 by
Anthony F. Buzzard and Charles F. Hunting

International Scholars Publications
4720 Boston Way
Lanham, Maryland 20706

12 Hid's Copse Rd.
Cumnor Hill, Oxford OX2 9JJ

Library of Congress Cataloging-in-Publication Data

Buzzard, Anthony
The doctrine of the Trinity : Christianity's self-inflicted wound /
Anthony F. Buzzard and Charles F. Hunting
p.   cm
Includes bibliographical references and index.
1. Trinity—Controversial literature. 2. Trinity—History of
doctrines. I. Hunting, Charles F. II. Title.
BT115.B88   231'.044—21   98-3870 CIP

ISBN 1-57309-309-2 (pbk. : alk. ppr.)

♾™ The paper used in this publication meets the minimum
requirements of American National Standard for Information
Sciences—Permanence of Paper for Printed Library Materials,
ANSI Z39.48—1984

*These chapters are dedicated to
the memory of those noble-minded
students of Scripture who,
having discovered the God of the Bible,
died for the conviction that He is One.*

TABLE OF CONTENTS

"In the year 317, a new contention arose in Egypt with consequences of a pernicious nature. The subject of this fatal controversy which kindled such deplorable divisions throughout the Christian world, was the doctrine of three Persons in the Godhead, a doctrine which in the three preceding centuries had happily escaped the vain curiosity of human researches."[1]

"When we look back through the long ages of the reign of the Trinity...we shall perceive that few doctrines have produced more unmixed evil."[2]

"Christological doctrine has never in practice been derived simply by way of logical inference from the statements of Scripture...The Church has not usually in practice (whatever it may have claimed to be doing in theory) based its Christology exclusively on the witness of the New Testament."[3]

"The Greeks distorted the concept of Jesus' legal agency to ontological identity, creating an illogical set of creeds and doctrines to cause confusion and terror for later generations of Christians."[4]

"Nowhere does the New Testament *identify* Jesus with God."[5]

"Because the Trinity is such an important part of later Christian doctrine, it is striking that the term does not appear in the New Testament. Likewise, the developed concept of three coequal partners in the Godhead found in later creedal formulations cannot be clearly detected within the confines of the canon."[6]

"How shall we determine the nature of the distinction between the God who became man and the God who did not become man, without destroying the unity of God on the one hand or interfering with Christology on the other? Neither the Council of Nicea nor the Church Fathers of the fourth century satisfactorily answered this question."[7]

"The adoption of a non-biblical phrase at Nicea constituted a landmark in the growth of dogma; the Trinity is *true*, since the Church — the universal Church speaking by its Bishops — says so, though the Bible does not!...We have a formula, but what does that formula contain? No child of the Church dare seek to answer."[8]

---

[1] J.L. Mosheim, *Institutes of Ecclesiastical History* (New York: Harper, 1839), 1:399.

[2] Andrews Norton, *A Statement of Reasons for Not Believing the Doctrine of the Trinitarians Concerning the Nature of God and the Person of Christ* (Hilliard, Gray & Co., 1833), 287.

[3] Maurice Wiles, *The Remaking of Christian Doctrine* (London: SCM Press, 1974), 54-55.

[4] Professor G.W. Buchanan, from correspondence, 1994.

[5] William Barclay, *A Spiritual Autobiography* (Grand Rapids: Eerdmans, 1975), 50.

[6] "Trinity," in *The Oxford Companion to the Bible* (Oxford University Press, 1993), 782.

[7] I.A. Dorner, *The History of the Development of the Doctrine of the Person of Christ* (Edinburgh: T & T Clark, 1882), Div. I, 2:330.

[8] "Dogma, Dogmatic Theology," in *Encyclopedia Britannica*, 14th edition (1936), 7:501, 502.

FOREWORD

I could not read *Christianity's Self-Inflicted Wound* without becoming excited again about the primitive Christian (and Jewish) doctrine that "God is One." If there are any Nicene encrustations in one's mind and life, this book should sweep them all away.

It is a pleasing experience to read Anthony Buzzard's and Charles Hunting's clear explanations of key passages of Scripture usually seen before through a Trinitarian prism. At the same time it is a delight to read concise statements which are certain to etch themselves upon the reader's mind. An example is the explanation of Thomas's great confession in John 20:28. Thomas recognized in the risen Jesus the one appointed to be "God" of the coming age, replacing Satan, the "God" of the present age. However, Thomas' words "Lord" and "God" are simply Messianic titles analogous with the divine title given in the Old Testament to the angel of the Lord as God's representative. The previously doubting Apostle did not suddenly adopt the Nicene or the Athanasian Creed and see his Lord as "very God of very God." The Gospel of John must not be forced to conform to much later speculation by Greek theologians.

No apparent Trinitarian or preexistence passage is left unchallenged. (This includes the enigmatic saying of Jesus in John 8:58 which must be balanced by the many other parallel Christological statements in John and by the rest of Scripture.) It is a major point and basis of the book that the assertion of Christ's preexistence as God the Son placed a strain on the truth of his humanity, in theological thinking, which it was unable to bear. .

In this connection Buzzard and Hunting advance a most interesting thesis: John's epistles are his answer to those Gnostic heretics who misused his Gospel. John labels their treatment of his Gospel as very "antichrist."

But the authors of *Christianity's Self-Inflicted Wound* are not content to settle for explanations of the critical texts of Scripture. They are usually followed by the confirmatory words of prominent theologians in Europe and North America. Their familiarity with the entire field of theological opinion, especially on the subject of the Trinity, is obvious and impressive.

There is a pleasing element of humor in this book which elevates it above the genre of textbook and tome. Professor Buzzard and Charles Hunting point out that one of the great marvels of Christian history has been the ability of post-biblical theologians to convince Christian people that three Persons are really One God. Paul preached the whole counsel of God (Acts 20:28). Why did he not explain the Trinity?

In discussing Jesus' use of the word "only" in John 17:3 ("the only true God") the authors write that we would be suspicious of anyone who claimed he had "only one wife" if his household consisted of three separate women, all of whom he claimed were his *one* wife!

Paul explained to the Corinthians "that there is no God but One," defining that One God as the Father only. He went on to say that "not all have this knowledge." The authors add: "We are tempted to think that not much has changed since the first century."

Finally, in this regard, the doctrine of the Trinity is an adult theological myth. Christianity condemns the world for imposing the unproved theory of evolution on mankind. But orthodoxy imposes something equally problematic: a multiple-person God.

It is a familiar criticism of the Protestant Reformation that it only went back to the Council of Nicea. There it encountered a roadblock, in this instance a barricade built of politics, philosophy, bigotry, envy, and intrigue. The authors of this book are not deterred by any such roadblock — Nicea, Chalcedon or otherwise.

Christianity's Self-Inflicted Wound does not attempt to hurdle the early church councils, nor does it detour around them. It meets them head on, drives through them, and arrives at the more authoritative "decrees" of Jesus and the Apostles. If Jesus evidently was not a Trinitarian, why should his followers be?

Readers will be intrigued by the title of this book. It is most appropriate for the authors' thesis. As far as the pristine Jewish Christianity of Jesus and the Apostles is concerned, the wound has been nearly fatal. The patient's life has been spared by the scriptural principle that God always has His remnant.

To express it another way (the illustration is mine, not the authors'), the dogma of the Trinity is that potion of hemlock which Gnostically-inclined theologians deliberately chose to drink, mixing the pure stream of Hebrew doctrine with the poison of Greek philosophy. Then they forced the mixture on their disciples. The penalty for refusal would be eternal damnation.

If there is a key text to the book, it is John 17:3, "And this is life eternal, that they might know You, the only true God, and Jesus Christ whom You have sent." In this connection the authors make much of the fact that Jesus was the Son of God from conception, not from eternity (Luke 1:35). He came into the world *en sarki*, a human being, not *into* a human body (cp. 1 John 4:2; 2 John 7).

Trinitarianism has long had a field day in charging that non-Trinitarian believers are not really Christians. The Athanasian Creed is renowned for its damnatory clauses. The authors counter this charge by pointing out that "eternal life" (the life of the coming Kingdom) is linked with knowledge of the truth about God and Jesus (John 17:3; 1 Tim. 2:4, 5). It is the Trinitarians who should be on the defensive, not the biblical unitarians. The latter group has had its heroic exponents and the authors give us much of their little-known history.

This book is a telling indictment of the central dogma of historic or mainstream Christianity — that version of the faith which, unknown to many, stems from the councils and the creeds. Christianity still prostrates itself before the low wrought-gold throne of Constantine. Its dogma has produced tragic and bloody episodes in history. Something is askew.

At the same time, however, the message and purpose of *Christianity's Self-Inflicted Wound* is positive. It does not condemn but attempts to tell the patient about the wound to his body-ecclesiastic and then offers the healing balm of Jesus' own unifying creed. Its very object is to propose ways of believing that more accurately conform to what Jesus believed and taught about God and about himself. Let us pray that this message does not go unheeded.

— Sidney A. Hatch, B.A. (UCLA),
M. Div. (American Baptist Seminary of the West),
Th. M. (Dallas Theological Seminary)

ACKNOWLEDGMENTS

Special thanks are due to Professor George Buchanan for invaluable suggestions; to Jeff, Harry, Mark, Lorraine, Sarah, Claire, Heather, Jack, Aaron, Jason, Lisa, Amy, Wendy, Barbara, Martha and Don, whose skills have left their mark on this manuscript; and to many others for their enthusiastic support.

INTRODUCTION

"Nowhere in the New Testament is there...a text with 'God' which has unquestionably to be referred to the Trinitarian God as a whole existing in three Persons." — Karl Rahner

This book is concerned with a single question. Does the Bible teach that God is one unique person, the sole creator of the universe, or is the Godhead composed of two or three coequal partners? The authors formerly subscribed to the prevailing understanding that Jesus is coequal and coeternal with his Father. We taught this view for twenty years. We are fully aware of the verses in the New Testament which might appear to support the traditional doctrine of the Trinity. But prolonged research in the Scriptures and the history of doctrine has brought us to the settled conviction that the case for the Trinity rests on questionable treatment of the biblical documents. It ignores the massive evidence for *unitary* monotheism — belief in One God as a single person, the Father of Jesus Christ — and relies heavily on inference from a few select verses. It isolates certain texts and forgets that their context is the whole of Scripture.

Biblical doctrines must be established by the plain, straightforward texts which bear directly on the subject in question. When the Bible's creedal declarations are taken at face value, according to the ordinary rules of language, they present a doctrine about God which cannot be reconciled with traditional belief systems. As we probed the question about the biblical creed, we were encouraged in our research by a number of contemporary studies by prominent biblical experts. Many scholars now admit that Trinitarianism cannot be documented in the Bible. It is a Gentile distortion of the Bible arising in post-biblical times.

Perhaps the most significant of all admissions about the
attempt to base the Trinity on the Bible comes from a leading
Trinitarian theologian of this century. Leonard Hodgson informs
us that in the seventeenth- and eighteenth-century debates
between unitarians and Trinitarians, both parties "accepted the
Bible as containing revelation given in the form of propositions."
He then concludes that "on the basis of argument which both
sides held in common, *the unitarians had the better case*."[1] This
observation deserves careful consideration by all Trinitarians.

Our desire is that the reader will examine the evidence
presented with an open mind. We realize that this may be asking
a great deal from anyone trained and perhaps entrenched in a
different theological viewpoint. Once a belief has been accepted
both intellectually and emotionally as truth, any challenge to that
cherished tenet is liable to almost automatic rejection. The very
human desire of all of us to conform to the group which has
nourished us and the lifetime patterns of thought learned from
sincere teachers we trusted and respected tends to create barriers
which secure us against all objections and can blind us to the
most obvious truths. When those deeply held beliefs are
challenged, we naturally feel threatened and defensive. Robert
Hall, a 19th-century writer on religion, observed wisely that:

> Whatever holds back a spirit of inquiry is favorable to
> error, whatever promotes it, to truth. But nothing, it will
> be acknowledged, has a greater tendency to obstruct the
> spirit of inquiry, than the spirit and feeling of party. Let
> a doctrine, however erroneous, become a party
> distinction, and it is at once entrenched in interests and

---

[1] *The Doctrine of the Trinity* (Nisbet, 1943), 220, 223, emphasis added.
The "unitarian" understanding of the nature of God which we propose
in the following chapters should not be confused with contemporary
Unitarian Universalist theology.

attachments which make it extremely difficult for the most powerful artillery of reason to dislodge it.[2]

The concepts developed in the following chapters, although largely hidden from public view in this century, are not novel. They were the cornerstone of the first-century apostolic Church and (initially, at least) the unopposed beliefs of that dynamic, struggling group. It may be surprising to some, but church historians record that believers in God as a single person — unitarian Christians — were "at the beginning of the third century still forming the large majority."[3]

Though quickly assaulted by competing Greek philosophy and Roman political ambition and subsequently replaced by a tri-personal God, belief in a single person, One God and Creator, has never been totally obliterated. It has been forced to cling tenaciously to the fringes of Christianity as a small but persistent voice, appealing to the conscience of any who would listen.

Much of the confusion which obstructs clear thinking about the Godhead may be traced to a prime cause. We have not reckoned with changes in the meaning of words, effected by time, as language is transplanted from one culture to another. A foremost example of this is the term "Son of God," which most today unconsciously translate as "God, the Son," a meaning which it cannot possibly bear in the original Christian documents. "Son of God" is the title which identifies the principal actor in the Christian drama, Jesus, the Messiah. "Son of God" is a name given in the Bible to representatives of God, principally His chosen king. A distortion of the meaning of that title will have a disastrous effect on our understanding of the original faith. True Christianity must be shaped by the ideas and concepts which circulated in their first-century apostolic environment, now viewed by us at a distance of 1900 years. The passage of time alienates us from the thought-world of the

---

[2] "Terms of Communion," *Works*, 1:352, cited by John Wilson in *Unitarian Principles Confirmed by Trinitarian Testimonies* (Boston: American Unitarian Association, 1848), 156.

[3] *Encyclopedia Britannica*, 11th ed, Vol. 23, 963.

apostolic Bible writers. A very different picture of what they
taught emerges if we examine our Scriptures against the
linguistic, cultural and religious background of those historic
first-century believers.

You may be persuaded, as we have been, that the final irony
of this century's fundamental Christianity, which claims so
fervently to believe in the inerrancy of Scripture, is that it simply
never came to believe Christ's summary statement about the way
to salvation: "This is eternal life, that they may know You, *the
only true God*, and Jesus Christ whom You sent" (John 17:3).
Could our generation of Christians have become insensitive to
the warning issued by Jesus when he said, "In vain they worship
me, teaching as doctrines the precepts of men"? (Matt. 15:9).
Could we have fallen under the spell of theological leaders,
mainly from the second- to the fifth-century Gentile world,
whose Greek philosophical backgrounds led them to corrupt the
Hebrew thought and theology which formed the basis of the
apostolic Christian Church?

Following in the steps of those who have begged to differ
with Trinitarian theology, it is our intention to show that neither
the Old Testament nor the New Testament offer substantial
evidence for the doctrine of the Trinity as it is popularly
believed. We believe that the reader can establish this fact by a
careful, open-minded examination of the sacred documents.
There is no passage of Scripture which asserts that God is three.
No authentic verse claims that the One God is three persons,
three spirits, three divine, infinite minds, or three anything. No
verse or word of the Bible can be shown to carry the meaning
"God in three Persons." Any claim that there are three who
compose the Deity must be based on inference, rather than plain
statements. The Trinitarian concept relies upon sophisticated and
often tortured logic which lacks solid support in the earliest
Christian writings. Our impression is that most Trinitarians
approach the New Testament as if it were a document en route to
Trinitarianism. They overlook the primary fact that no New
Testament writer on any occasion can be shown to mean "the
Triune God" when he says "God." They then ransack the
documents for evidence that the Apostles provide the materials

for the later creation of the doctrine of the Trinity. The fact that none of them arrives at Trinitarianism does not deter them.

There was a time when it was required by religious leaders that one accept as biblical fact that the earth is the center of the universe and that it is flat. To hold otherwise branded one a heretic, in spite of Copernicus' revolutionary discovery. The present situation in regard to the doctrine of the Trinity may turn out to be strikingly parallel.

If we believe that God reveals Himself through the words of the Bible, it must be incumbent upon everyone who claims the name of Jesus to examine the evidence in the Scriptures to determine who the God of the Bible is. A truth-seeking Christian is personally responsible for carefully sifting the various relevant texts, as the enthusiastic Bereans did. They were acclaimed for their refreshing but rare nobility of mind (Acts 17:11). They dared to see "if these things were so." The result was that they became true believers.

Many of us may think that the doctrine of the Trinity is a baffling mystery best left to the deliberations of learned theologians. But can we safely leave such a crucial question to them? Even such an astute observer as Thomas Jefferson (third President of the United States [1800-1809] and author of the Declaration of Independence) remarked that the Trinity is "an unintelligible proposition of Platonic mysticisms that three are one and one is three; and yet *one is not three and three are not one.*" He goes on to say, "I never had sense enough to comprehend the Trinity, and it appeared to me that comprehension must precede assent."[4]

Nevertheless, it is not uncommon for religious leaders to insist that you must believe in the Trinity to be a Christian, or be branded a cultist. To be a member of the World Council of Churches, for instance, requires assent to the doctrine of the Trinity.

---

[4] C.B. Sanford, *The Religious Life of Thomas Jefferson* (University Press of Virginia, 1987), 88.

Paraphrasing Thomas Jefferson's remarks, we ask the question: How can one be expected to agree with something that can neither be explained nor understood? Is it fair to ask the Christian community to accept this doctrine "on faith" — a doctrine which is never mentioned by name and, on the admission of some Trinitarians, never discussed in the pages of the New Testament? Should we not expect somewhere in Scripture a precise, clear formulation of the strange proposition that God is "three-in-one"?

If our suspicions are well founded, what we know as Christianity today may unwittingly be at variance with the instructions of its founder, Jesus, the Messiah. The faith as we know it seems to have adopted a doctrine of God that Jesus would not have recognized.

Church history shows that the concept of even two equal persons in the Godhead — the Father and Son — did not receive formal approval in the Christian community until three hundred years after the ministry of Jesus, at the Council of Nicea in 325 AD, and this under circumstances confused with political agitation. What was true in the fourth and fifth centuries must also have been true in the first century. If Jesus were ranked as God in the first century, why did it take so long for the Church to declare formally a Godhead of two persons, and later of three persons — and then only under great political pressure? Following Nicea, thousands of Christians died at the hands of other Christians because they sincerely believed that God was a single person.

Trinitarian dogma is one of the great enigmas of our time. The fact that it defies both conventional logic and rational explanation does not seem to diminish the Trinitarian's desire to protect at all costs his complex theological formula. We are puzzled at the agitation that is created when the Trinity is questioned. This seems to point to a lack of confidence in what is claimed to be the unquestionable party line of virtually all Christian ministers. The common branding of all objectors as unbelievers does nothing to reassure us.

The overwhelming majority's acceptance of a religious idea neither vindicates or validates its truthfulness. Is the earth flat or the center of our solar system? All Christendom was once required to believe this as an article of faith and great was the penalty for disbelief. It was still false dogma notwithstanding.

A further question must be asked: Was the apostolic Church made up of brilliant, sophisticated theologians? With the exception of the Apostle Paul, in the leadership of the early Church we see a cross-section of humanity represented — ordinary workers, businessmen and civil servants. Would they not have been every bit as mystified as we over the idea that God was two or three persons, and yet somehow still one being? Such an innovation would have required the most careful and repeated explanation for men and women who had been steeped from birth in the belief that God was one person only. It is undeniable that the idea of a sole, unique creator God was the most sacred tenet of Israel's national heritage. Their cardinal belief in One God could not have been quickly or easily dispelled. In fact, belief in the Trinitarian God would have been the most revolutionary and explosive concept ever to have rocked the first-century Church. Yet of that revolution, if it ever occurred, the New Testament gives us not one hint.

Many of us may be innocently unaware that the unresolved controversy over the Trinity has raged for almost two thousand years. Thousands have been tortured and slaughtered as parties to this disagreement. Nevertheless, at the risk of being branded with labels such as "liberal," "heretic," "cultist," and forced into isolation by "established" religion, today a growing number of Catholic and Protestant theologians, with high regard for the sacred Scriptures and with everything to lose by leaving the mainstream of Christianity, question whether this most fundamental of all beliefs — the Trinity — can be found in the Bible.

Theological tradition has divided into three camps in the matter of defining God. Belief has been expressed in a Trinitarian God (three persons — Father, Son, and Holy Spirit), a Binitarian God (two persons — Father and Son) and a one-person God, the Father, uncreated and unique in all the universe (unitarianism).[5] Any doctrine which has caused such hostility among professed believers in Christ deserves careful analysis.

In our examination of the Trinity we have used the Bible and recorded history as our sources. We are not concerned with the various controversies concerning whether or not the Bible is the revealed word of God. We ignore the charge that the Bible is outmoded and no longer relevant in modern society. Our primary concern is the question: What did the words spoken by Jesus and the Apostles mean to those Christians who formed the first-century Church? If the Christian religion is founded on what the Bible says, then the Bible must be our source for authentic Christian faith.

We do not, of course, challenge the sincerity of Trinitarian faith. We insist, however, that sincerity does not make belief true. We do not underestimate the extraordinary power of tradition in forming theological convictions and the almost limitless capacity of teachers of religion to believe that what they teach has the authority of Scripture to back it.

The purpose of this book is to help break down the barriers which time and tradition have erected between us and the first-century Church founded by Jesus. We are persuaded that a new concept of God emerged under the influence of Greek philosophy and imposed itself on the original faith. We think this was a mistake, not a legitimate cultural development.

We are greatly indebted to the many scholars who have helped to clarify the meanings of biblical words in their original environment. We are the richer for their lifelong studies in this most important field. We have been constantly encouraged by those interpreters who aim at telling us what a text says, not what it ought to say. We are impressed with the method of Alexander Reese who, while searching out the truth on a different issue, drew on "the great exegetes [interpreters]...trusting that the average educated reader will see that a natural interpretation, backed by scholars of the highest standing, is preferable to a

---

[5] Another view of God is held by the United Pentecostal Church. Their "oneness" conception of the Deity is that God and Jesus are the same Person.

freak one backed by dogmatism and the requirements of a system."[6]

We have borrowed from the treasury of ideas of numerous writers of the past and present without stopping to give credit in all instances. Their works appear in the list of source material at the conclusion of this book. We have sometimes included extended quotations from the works of distinguished experts in the field of biblical studies. We wanted the full force of their insights to be included in the dialogue.

At the outset we should question the common claims of Trinitarians and Binitarians that unless Jesus is "very God," no appropriate atonement has been made for man's sins. Our challenge to them is: If this is true, then where can it be documented in the Bible? Is God not at liberty to save the world by whomever He chooses? The discovery that Scripture is not the source of this classic Trinitarian argument is as startling as the fact that the word "God" in the New Testament never describes a tripersonal God. Almost without exception the New Testament means the Father when it says "God." We appeal to Trinitarians to take stock of a glaring difference between the Bible and themselves in this regard.

It is important to state what we are *not* saying in this book. We do not believe that Jesus was "just a good man," or one of a series of prophets. Our faith is in him as God's unique, chosen and sinless agent for the salvation of men and women everywhere. To say in contemporary English that he *is* God, however, misrepresents the Christian Scriptures. It is sufficient, and fully biblical, to believe that he is the Messiah, Son of God. We are not intimidated by the popular argument that Jesus must be either "mad, bad or God." To force a choice upon us between accepting him as lunatic, liar or God himself, cleverly diverts us from the truth about his real identity. There is another option — one that satisfies the scriptural description accurately.

---

6 *The Approaching Advent of Christ* (Grand Rapids: International Publications, rep. 1975), xii.

On a technical point, we want to declare our conscious decision to speak of God and Jesus as "persons," without the use of a capital "P." We are aware that well-instructed Trinitarians express their belief in three "Persons," and that by "Person" they do not mean what we now normally understand by that word. Since, however, it seems quite obvious that *in the Bible* the Father and Jesus are presented as persons, i.e., distinct individuals, in the modern sense, we object to the confusing procedure of trying to explain the Bible by introducing the unbiblical notion of "Person." Thoughtful Trinitarians have been unable to define what they mean by "Person" in the Godhead. The obscure terms "distinction" or "subsistence" do nothing to ease their predicament. Augustine, the famous Latin Church Father, apologized for using the term "Person" when speaking of the members of the Trinity. As he admitted, the best that could be argued for "Person" was that it was preferable to total silence.[7] For the writers of the Bible, however, no such special terminology was needed to define the relationship of God and Jesus. One was the Father and the other His Son.

As for the attempt of some to define God as one "what" in three "who's," we find this devoid of biblical support. A moment's thought reveals that in Scripture the God of Israel is never described as a "what" or in any way impersonal. Singular personal pronouns inform us that the One God is definitely a "who." To make Him three "who's" demonstrably violates the consistent testimony of the Bible. Should anyone confess that the Trinitarian idea of God as both three and one cannot be comprehended, we suggest that such an admission points only to the weakness of the whole Trinitarian concept.

Finally, we do not deny the existence of "mystery" in religion. We do not refuse to accept any doctrine which we cannot fully explain. But mystery and contradiction are two different things. There is much that we do not understand about the second coming of Jesus, but when Christ declared that he did not know the time of his return to the earth, it is plainly an error

---

[7] Augustine, *On the Trinity*, Book V, ch. 9.

to say that he was omniscient. It is an abuse of language to say with Charles Wesley, "'Tis mystery all; the immortal dies." Bankruptcy of thought occurs when words become unintelligible. Our complaint about the doctrine of the Trinity is that it is a shibboleth without clear meaning. One of the strongest arguments against it is that it cannot be expressed without abandoning biblical language. There is a further major objection: By many it is conceived in terms of three equal "Gods," since that is the only way they can imagine three persons who are all God.

We start by considering the most crucial question to be answered by any Christian, if he claims to believe that the Bible is the authoritative word of the Supreme Being: What did the founder of Christianity mean when, addressing the Father, he said, "This is eternal life, that they may know You, *the only true God*, and Jesus Christ whom You sent?" (John 17:3).

I. THE GOD OF THE JEWS

*"We know whom we worship, for salvation comes
from the Jews." — Jesus Christ*

The depth of Jewish feeling about monotheism was formed
by centuries of experience. As long as the nation had clung to its
central conviction about the One God, it had prospered. Terrible
suffering had been the penalty for any defection into polytheism.
The result was that the celebrated "Hear, O Israel, the Lord our
God is one Lord" (Deut. 6:4, RSV; cp. Mark 12:29)[1], defining
Israel's national creed, was spoken by every pious Israelite
throughout his life and in the hour of death. To sense the fervor
which surrounded Jewish belief in One God we should think of
our own deepest commitments: love of liberty and country, home
and family.

Had you been born a Jew of orthodox religious parents in
first-century Palestine, you would have held the unshakable
conviction that there is one, and only one, supreme creator God
worthy of worship in the universe. This creed was inextricably
woven into the fabric of Jewish life. The national holidays, the
agricultural calendar, as well as the hope of national liberation
from the Roman oppressor and promise of future greatness, were
all founded on the revelation of the one-person God contained in
the pages of the writings we call the Old Testament. The Jew's
religious literature defined the believer's relationship with that
One God and provided instruction for dealing with his fellow
human beings. Much of the Old Testament is a history,

---

[1] The Nash Papyrus, the oldest known specimen of Hebrew biblical
text, probably from the second century, ends the Shema with the words
"one Lord is He."

sometimes positive, sometimes tragic, of the One God's dealings with His chosen nation, Israel. In addition, the sacred writings predicted a glorious future for the nation and the world, a day when everyone on earth would recognize and serve the one true God of Israel (Zech. 14:9).

It was into this deeply committed and distinctive religious community that Jesus was born. The origins of the faithful community's devotion to monotheism were rooted in the covenant made with Abraham as the father of the faithful. Judaism's cardinal tenet that God is One Lord was strenuously instilled in the people by Moses. Subsequently some apostate Israelites had reverted to belief in the gods of their pagan neighbors. The representatives of these powerful ancient gods espoused temple prostitution, the burning of children to the god Molech, and mutilation of the body — to mention some of their more notable rites.

The story recorded in the first five books of Israel's ancient literature describes a nation divinely chosen to be separate from a polytheistic world. By a powerful divine intervention, first at the call of Abraham and later at the Exodus, a whole nation was introduced to a being who claimed not only to be the sole creator of all that existed, but the only *true* God in existence. His message to His people Israel was unequivocal. Through Moses He said: "But the Lord has taken you, and brought you out of the iron furnace, from Egypt, to be a people for His own possession as today...To you it was shown, that you might know that the Lord, He is God; *there is no other besides Him*" (Deut. 4:20, 35).

It is certain that the nation of Israel, to whom these grand declarations about the Deity were given, knew nothing about a duality or Trinity of persons in the Godhead. No fact could be more firmly established, once their national literature is taken as a guide, and if language has any stable meaning.

One thing is indisputable: the nations surrounding Israel were under no illusion about Israel's belief in One God. This creed was partly responsible for the age-lasting persecution of the religious Jew, who refused to accept any other object of worship than his One God. Crusaders, those valiant 11th-century Christian warriors, relished the task of expelling "infidel," monotheistic Moslems from the Holy Land. Their fervor led them likewise to the slaughter of helpless European Jews in one community after another. Three centuries later neither the unitarian Jew or Christian nor a Protestant Trinitarian could survive the persecutions of the Spanish Inquisition without renouncing his religious beliefs and accepting Roman Catholicism or fleeing to some less hostile part of the world. It may come as a shock to many, but thousands of Christians, who also believed in the one-person God of the Jew, were able to escape the same cruel fate at the hands of the Church only by flight.

Belief in a unipersonal God conferred on Israel a world view which separated her from all other philosophies, religions, cultures and nations. She retains her special understanding of God to this day. By contrast, the broad spectrum of Christianity holds to the idea of the three-person God of the Trinity (Father, Son and Holy Spirit), with a minority claiming to believe in a two-person God (Father and "Word"),[2] both persons existing from eternity. Oriental religions admit to more than one god, or at least personal intermediate beings between the Supreme God and the creation, as did much of the Greek world by which the early Christian Church was influenced shortly after the death of its founder, Jesus, the Messiah. Large numbers today are finding their theological roots in the Oriental concept of many gods — the creed that all of us are gods awaiting self-discovery and, somewhat confusingly, that all is God. It is hard not to observe that religious anarchy inevitably ensues when every person is a god in his own right, determining his own creed and conduct.

In order to emphasize the oneness of God to national Israel, so that there could be no chance of mistake or misunderstanding, God repeated through Moses: "Know therefore this day, and lay it to heart, that the Lord is God in heaven above and on the earth beneath; *there is none other*" (Deut. 4:39). On the strength of this text, and many like it, we can fully sympathize with Jewish

---

[2] The Worldwide Church of God, founded by Herbert Armstrong, held this "binitarian" view. Doctrinal changes in favor of Trinitarianism took place in 1995.

devotion to the unipersonal God. The statement appears to be proof against all possibility of misinterpretation. The Jews understood "one" to mean "one" and were never in doubt about the expression "no other." A leading contemporary Jewish spokesman, Pinchas Lapide, emphasizes the persistence with which Jews guard the heart of their faith:

> In order to protect the oneness of God from every multiplication, watering down, or amalgamation with the rites of the surrounding world, the people of Israel chose for itself that verse of the Bible to be its credo which to this very day belongs to the daily liturgy of the synagogue but also is impressed as the first sentence of instruction upon the five-year-old school child. This is the confession which Jesus acknowledged as "the most important of all the commandments."[3]

As Lapide recognizes, when Jesus was explaining the foundation of his belief, he repeated the words spoken by Moses to the nation of Israel: "Hear, O Israel: the Lord our God is *one Lord*: and you shall love the Lord your God with all your heart, and with all your soul, and with all your might" (Deut. 6:4, 5; Mark 12:29, 30). From Jesus' confirmation of the words of Moses recorded in the book of Deuteronomy, we are forced to conclude that he must have understood and believed whatever Moses believed these words to mean. If it had been otherwise, or if some radical change had occurred to negate Moses' definitive "One God" statement, the New Testament writers utterly fail to supply any equally unambiguous declaration to reverse or revise this linchpin of the Jewish faith.

A further confirmation of the persistence of Judaism's cardinal creed is found in the conversation of Jesus with the Samaritan woman. He told her forthrightly, "You worship that which you do not know; we [Jews] worship that which we know, for salvation is from the Jews. But the hour is coming, and now is, when the true worshippers shall worship the Father in spirit

---

[3] *Jewish Monotheism and Christian Trinitarian Doctrine* (Philadelphia: Fortress Press, 1981), 27.

and in truth" (John 4:22, 23). Not once do we find Jesus criticizing his fellow countrymen for holding an inadequate understanding of the number of persons in the Godhead. Nor indeed did Paul recognize any God other than the God of Israel. He expected Gentiles to be grafted into Israel and to worship that same God: "Is God the God of the Jews only? Is He not the God of the Gentiles also?" (Rom. 3:29; cp. 11:17). The God known to the Jew Paul was concisely defined by him in Galatians 3:20, in the words of the Amplified Translation of the New Testament which reads: "God is [only] one person."

Early in his ministry Jesus strongly confirmed the divine revelation given to Moses: "Do not think that I came to abolish the Law or the Prophets; I did not come to abolish, but to fulfill" (Matt. 5:17). The first principle of the great summary of Israel's Law given in the Torah through Moses provided the national creed: "You shall have no other gods besides Me" (Exod. 20:1-3).

If there were one, sole, unique, all-powerful being in the universe wanting to reveal to His creation the fact that He alone was God, and that there was no other, just how could this have been stated without any possibility of error? What could have been said to ensure not the slightest chance of misunderstanding? How would any one of us express the absolute uniqueness of God, if it were our responsibility to make that message clear to an entire nation? Would we not have said, as Moses reports God saying, "See now that I, I am He, and there is no God besides Me"? (Deut. 32:39). Israel, to this day, in response to these categorical declarations, will accept none but the one-person God of Moses as a result of these words. Regardless of any other religious differences, the oneness of God remains the binding thread which unites the Jewish community.

The Hebrew Bible and the New Testament contain well over twenty thousand singular pronouns and verbs describing the One God. Language has no clearer or more obvious way of providing a testimony to Israel's and Jesus' unitary monotheism.

The being revealed in Israel's Torah was a God to be sharply distinguished from the pagan gods of Egypt. By an act of power He had rescued an enslaved nation from captivity. He was a God of awesome power and yet personal and approachable — a God to be loved, of whom it was said, "the Lord used to speak to Moses face to face, as a man speaks to his friend" (Exod. 33:11). He was a person with whom David communed: "You have said, 'Seek My face.' My heart says to Thee, 'Thy face, Lord, do I seek'" (Ps. 27:8). At the Exodus the Jews knew that for the first time in history a whole nation was brought into intimate contact with the creator God through His constituted representative. This unparalleled event was to be embedded in the national consciousness forever. To be banished from their worship were the gods of the world around them. Tragically, superstitious fears and the desire to be like the other nations sometimes tempted Israel to embrace the multiple gods of paganism. For this they suffered disastrously. Shortly after their flight out of Egypt, at fearful cost to themselves they built a golden calf as an object of worship.

The nation needed continually to be reminded of its unique creed: "Listen, Israel: Yahweh our God is the one, the only Yahweh" (Deut. 6:4, New Jerusalem Bible). Through the prophet Isaiah, Israel was once again made aware of its national identity: "You are My witnesses…and understand that I am He. Before Me there was *no God* formed, and there will be *none* after Me" (Isa. 43:10). Theologies which promise their followers that they will one day become "God" seem not to grasp the exclusive prerogative claimed by the one who insists that there has been *no God formed prior to Him* and there will be *none after Him*.

Isaiah's continued emphasis on the oneness of God is pointed and clear. He quotes God as saying, "I am the first, I am the last, and there is *no God besides Me*" (Isa. 44:6). The question is repeated: "Is there any God besides Me, or is there any other Rock? I know of none" (Isa. 44:8). This exclusive claim was an integral part of the religious instruction with which Jesus was nurtured. It was a creed which he held in common with every young Jew. His repeated reference to the prophet Isaiah, indeed to the entire Old Testament, during his public ministry demonstrates how significantly his theology had been formed by the Hebrew Scriptures. The God whom Jesus served had announced Himself as a single person, never Triune.

We should not be surprised at the tenacity with which the Jews preserved the concept of one, single, unique creator God. Their persistence was encouraged by Isaiah's continued repetition of the most important of all religious facts. The prophet again speaks of Israel's God: "I, the Lord, am the Maker of all things, stretching out the heavens *by Myself* and spreading out the earth *all alone* [or 'who was with Me?']" (Isa. 44:24). Few statements could be better calculated to banish forever from the Jewish mind the idea that *more than one person* had been responsible for the creation.

The emphasis is even more striking when this same writer, in seven separate verses in the 45th chapter of his book, records the following: "I am the Lord, there is no other; besides Me there is no God" (Isa. 45:5). These statements were designed to fix forever in Israel's mind the idea that God is one. The same One God continued through Isaiah to say: "It is I who made the earth, and created man upon it" (Isa. 45:12).

It is widely taught that the one who is supposed to have become Jesus, the Son of God of the New Testament, was responsible for the work of creation. How, on the basis of what we have read, could such an idea be conceived? Would not the writings of Isaiah prevent such a notion from entering the Jewish mind? "Surely God is with you, and there is none else, no other God" (Isa. 45:14). And again, "For thus says the Lord, who created the heavens (He is God who formed the earth and made it; He established it and did not create it a waste place, but formed it to be inhabited), 'I am the Lord, and there is no other'" (Isa. 45:18).

Two further passages challenged Israel to faithful devotion to the One God: "Who has announced this from of old? Who has long since declared it? Is it not I, the Lord? And there is *no other God besides Me*. A righteous God and a Savior; there is none except Me. Turn to Me and be saved, all the ends of the earth; for I am God and there is *none other*" (Isa. 45:21, 22). Some have confused the use of the word "Savior" in this text with the frequent references of the same word to Jesus, the Messiah. He is quite obviously also called Savior in the New Testament (as are the judges in the book of Judges and as also Josephus called Vespasian).[4] We note the distinction drawn in Jude 25, where both Jesus and God are named at the close of the book: "to the *only* God our Savior, through Jesus Christ our Lord, be glory, majesty, dominion and authority, before all time and now and forever." Quite clearly the Jewish concept of a one-person God is not disturbed by this New Testament writer. In fact, there can be no clearer statement made than this — that there is "only" one person in the Godhead. Both God the Father and Jesus Christ are mentioned in the same sentence, but Jesus is obviously distinguished from the "only God." Other New Testament writers make equally unambiguous statements. The Father of Jesus is the only absolute Savior. Others than He can function as savior in a subordinate and delegated sense.

It was into this Jewish culture with its deeply entrenched belief in the One God that Jesus was born. Nineteen centuries later an Orthodox Israeli Jew, Pinchas Lapide, faculty member of Bar Ilan University in Israel (whom we cited earlier), shows that Jews were forbidden to deviate from belief in the oneness of God: "From the Hebrew word *echad* (meaning one) we learn not only that there is none outside of the Lord, but also that the Lord is one and that therefore the Lord cannot be viewed as something put together which would be divisible into various properties or attributes."[5] No wonder that according to the biblical record, when Israel chose to embrace other gods, chaos ensued, the nation divided, and the threatening prophecies of Isaiah came to pass. National captivity was the penalty for their defection into polytheism. It may well be that the confusion and fragmentation we witness in the history of Christianity is to be traced to exactly the same defection from the original belief that God was one person.

---

[4] Judges 3:9, 15, where the word "deliverer" is elsewhere rendered "savior."

[5] *Jewish Monotheism and Christian Trinitarian Doctrine*, 31.

The concept of the one-person God was not limited to the prophet Isaiah. Hosea reports Israel's God as saying: "Yet I have been the Lord your God since the land of Egypt; and you were not to know any god except Me, for there is no Savior besides Me" (Hos. 13:4). Moreover, the unique status of the One God was not limited to those ancient days. We receive the clear impression from the prophet Joel, speaking of a future Israel after it has achieved its promised greatness, that the nation would still, and forever, be tied to the One God: "Thus you will know that I am in the midst of Israel, and that I am the Lord your God and *there is no other*" (Joel 2:27). Joel lets us know that whatever or whoever the God of the Jews of the Old Testament was, He was to remain their God in perpetuity.

The Jewish mind was convinced that the One God, the creator, was also the Father of the nation. So says the prophet Malachi: "Do we not all have *one Father*? Has not *one God* created us?" (Mal. 2:10).[6] Nothing could be clearer than that the One God of Jewish monotheism, on which Jesus' heritage was founded, was the Father. This unique being is very frequently described as God and Father in the New Testament. Indeed He is the "God and Father of our Lord Jesus Christ,"[7] His Son. Highly significant is the fact that Jesus even as "Lord" is still subordinate to his God. The Messianic title "Lord" therefore does not mean that Jesus is God.

The Hebrew Word *Elohim*
With little authority from those trained in the Hebrew language, Trinitarians and Binitarians sometimes advance the statement in Genesis 1:26 as proof (in contradiction of the evidence of thousands of singular pronouns denoting the One God) that a plurality of persons in the Godhead was responsible for the creation. "Then God said, 'Let Us make man in Our image, according to Our likeness.'" This argument is precarious. Modern scholars no longer take the Hebrew phrase, "Let Us" or

---

[6] See also 1 Chron. 29:10, where the God of Israel is also "our Father."

[7] Rom. 15:6; 2 Cor. 1:3; 11:31; 1 Pet. 1:3.

the word *elohim* (God) to mean a plurality of God persons as creator. It is most likely that the plural pronoun "us" contains a reference to the One God's attendant council of angels,[8] who themselves had been created in the image of God and had been witnesses to the creation of the universe (Job 38:7). It is fanciful to imagine that this verse supports the idea that God was speaking to the Son and the Holy Spirit. Where in Scripture does God ever speak to His own Spirit? The text says nothing at all about an eternal Son of God, the second member of a coequal Trinity. Moreover, the "us" of the text gives no indication of *two* other equal partners in the Godhead. If God is a single person, His use of the word "us" means that He is addressing someone other than Himself, i.e., other than God.

A Hebrew lexicon of the Bible will confirm that the word *elohim* (God) is not a "uniplural" word, meaning that two or more persons make up the Godhead (or, as some have thought, the "God-family"). The peculiarities of any language must be reckoned with if we are to gain a proper sense of its meaning. This, we will discover, is indispensable in our search for true understanding.

The recognized facts of the Hebrew language will not support a case for multiple persons as God. We note what the *Gesenius' Hebrew Grammar*, a standard authority, has to say about the word *elohim*:

> The plural of majesty...sums up the several characteristics belonging to the idea, besides posing the secondary sense of an intensification of the original

---

[8] See 1 Kings 22:19-22, and note the strong statement of the Trinitarian commentator G. J. Wenham: "Christians have traditionally seen this verse [Gen. 1:26] as adumbrating [foreshadowing] the Trinity. It is now universally admitted that this was not what the plural meant to the original author" (*Genesis 1-15, Word Biblical Commentary*, ed. David A. Hubbard and Glenn W. Barker, Waco, TX: Word Books, 1987, 27). See also the note in the *NIV Study Bible* (Grand Rapids: Zondervan, 1985), 7: "God speaks as the Creator-King, announcing his crowning work to the members of his heavenly court (see 3:22; 11:7; Isa. 6:8; see also 1 Ki 22:19-23; Job 15:8; Jer 23:18)."

idea...That the language has entirely rejected the idea of a numerical plurality in *elohim* (whenever it denotes one God), is proved especially by its being almost invariably joined with a singular attribute.[9]

We must respect the fact that the Jews' familiarity with their own language had never led them to conclude that a plurality of persons in the Godhead was remotely hinted at in this creation chapter of Genesis. In the event that we might feel the Jews missed something from their own Bible, we should note in the succeeding verses (vv. 27-31) that the singular pronoun is always used with the word God: "in His [not Their] own image, in the image of God He [not They] created them" (v. 27). One would be hard-pressed to conclude from this verse, where the personal pronoun describing God (His) is singular, that a plurality of beings was intended. Note further: "Look, I [not We] have given you every plant yielding seed...for food...and God saw all that He [not They] had made, and it was very good" (vv. 29-31).[10]

---

[9] *Gesenius' Hebrew Grammar*, ed. E. Kautzsch (Oxford: Clarendon Press, 1910), 398. 399. See also the standard authority, *Hebrew and English Lexicon of the Old Testament*, by Brown, Driver and Briggs (Oxford: Clarendon Press, 1968), 43, 44. Gesenius lists many examples of Hebrew words with plural endings which are not plural in meaning. For example, *panim* = face. *Elohim* is modified by a singular adjective in Ps. 7:10.

[10] An occasional grammatical anomaly cannot possibly offset the evidence of thousands of occurrences in which the Divine Name and titles take singular verbs. Where a plural verb is found with *elohim* in 2 Sam. 7:23, the parallel passage in 1 Chron. 17:21 replaces the plural with a singular verb. This shows that the very exceptional plural was of no significance. *Elohim* in Gen. 31:24 may be rendered (as Calvin and others thought) as angels, as for example also in Ps. 8:5 and its quotation in Heb. 2:7. Yahweh and *Adonai* ("the Lord") invariably take a singular verb. The singular *El* and *Eloah* (God) confirm that God is one person. It is amazing that some continue to advance, against the evidence of thousands of texts in which God is described by singular pronouns and verbs, the four "us" verses, as a hint that God is Triune!

A study of the Hebrew word for God (*elohim*) lends no support to the persistent idea that "God" in Genesis 1:1 includes both God, the Father as well as His Son and Spirit. We should not miss the obvious difficulty of such an interpretation. If *elohim* implies more than one person in this text, how is one going to explain that the identical word, *elohim*, refers to Moses: "And the Lord said to Moses, 'See I make you God [*elohim*] to Pharaoh, and Aaron your brother shall be your prophet'" (Exod. 7:1)? Surely no one would claim plurality for the one person Moses. The single pagan god Dagon is called *elohim* (God): "The ark of the God [*elohim*] of Israel must not remain with us, for His hand is severe on us and on Dagon our god [*elohim*]" (1 Sam. 5:7). Similarly the word *elohim* is used to describe the god of the Amorites: "Will you not possess what Chemosh your god [*elohim*] gives you to possess?" (Judges 11:24). Furthermore, the Messiah himself is addressed as *elohim* (Ps. 45:6; Heb. 1:8). No one would contend that the Messiah is more than a single person.

From this evidence we conclude that the Jews, in whose language the Old Testament is recorded, did not employ the word *elohim*, used of the true God, to mean more than one person. Those who attempt to read the Trinity or Binity into Genesis 1:26, or into the word *elohim*, are involved in a forced interpretation. *Elohim* is plural in form but singular in meaning. When it refers to the One God it is followed by a singular verb. No one before the twelfth century imagined that plurality in the Godhead was in any way indicated by the Hebrew title for God. Many Trinitarians have themselves long since ceased to argue for the Trinity from Genesis 1:1 or Genesis 1:26.

It is reasonable to put this question to those Trinitarians who say that *Elohim* is a real plural: Why do they not put an "s" on God? In English plurals are marked by a final "s." If the plural pronoun "us" in Genesis 1:26 describes a plural Godhead, then the Godhead ought regularly to be referred to as "they" and "them." Trinitarians are unhappy with this, showing that their notion of the Godhead defies the laws of language and logic. If God really is plural, why not instead translate the opening verse of Genesis 1: "In the beginning Gods..."? The latent polytheism of much Trinitarian thinking would then be clearly exposed.

The Hebrew Word for One — *Echad*

It is untrue to say that the Hebrew word *echad* (one) in Deuteronomy 6:4 points to "compound unity." A recent defense of the Trinity[11] argues that when "one" modifies a collective noun like "bunch" or "herd," a plurality is implied in *echad*. The argument is fallacious. The sense of plurality is derived from the collective noun (herd, etc.), not from the word "one." *Echad* in Hebrew is the numeral "one." "Abraham was one [*echad*]" (Ezek. 33:24; "only one man," NIV). Isaiah 51:2 also describes Abraham as "one" (*echad*; "alone," KJV; "the only one," NJB), where there is no possible misunderstanding about the meaning of this simple word. *Echad* appears in translation as the numeral "one," "only," "alone," "entire, undivided," "one single."[12] Its normal meaning is "one and not two" (Ecc. 4:8). "God is one Lord" (Deut. 6:4, cited by Jesus in Mark 12:29, NASV), hence obviously *one person only* and distinct from the "Lord Messiah" mentioned in the same passage (Mark 12:36). The One God is identified with the Father in Malachi 1:6 and 2:10 and is constantly in the New Testament distinguished from Jesus, the Son of God, who is presented as a separate individual. In the Hebrew Bible "the Lord's anointed" (literally "christ") is the King of Israel. This agent of the Lord God is on no occasion confused with God.

The claim that "one" really means "compound oneness" is an example of argument by assertion without logical proof. Robert Morey holds that *echad* does not mean an absolute one but a compound one.[13] The argument involves an easily detectable linguistic fallacy. *Echad* appears some 960 times in

---

[11] Robert Morey, *The Trinity: Evidence and Issues* (World Publishing, 1996).

[12] *Theological Dictionary of the Old Testament* (Grand Rapids: Eerdmans, 1974), 1:194.

[13] Morey, 88.

the Hebrew Bible and in no case does the word itself carry a hint of plurality. It means strictly "one and not two or more." *Echad* is a numerical adjective and naturally enough is sometimes found modifying a collective noun — one family, one herd, one bunch. But we should observe carefully that the sense of plurality resides in the compound noun and not in the word *echad* (one).

Early in Genesis we learn that "the two will become one flesh" (Gen. 2:24). The word "one" here means precisely one and no more (one flesh and not two "fleshes"!). One bunch of grapes is just that — one and not two bunches. Thus when God is said to be "one Lord" (Deut. 6:4; Mark 12:29, NASV) He is a single Lord and no more.

Imagine that someone claimed that the word "one" meant "compound one" in the words "one tripod." Suppose someone thought that "the one United States of America" implied that "one" was really plural in meaning. The specious reasoning is obvious: the idea of plurality belongs to the words "tripod" and "States," *not to the word "one."* It is a subterfuge to transfer to "one" the plurality which belongs only to the following noun. It would be similar to saying that "one" really means "one hundred" when it appears in the combination "one centipede"!

Our point can be confirmed in any lexicon of biblical Hebrew. The lexicon by Koehler and Baumgartner gives as the fundamental meaning of *echad*, "one single."[14] When the spies returned with evidence of the fruitfulness of the Promised Land they carried "a single [*echad*] cluster of grapes" (Num. 13:23, NRSV). *Echad* is often rendered "a single," or "only one."[15] Thus when it comes to the matter of Israel's creed, the text informs us (as do the multiple singular pronouns for God) that Israel's supreme Lord is "one single Lord," "one Lord alone."

---

[14] *Hebrew and Aramaic Lexicon of the Old Testament* (Leiden: E.J. Brill, 1967).

[15] See RSV, Exod. 10:19, "a single locust"; Exod. 33:5, "a single moment"; Deut. 19:15, "a single witness," etc.

It has been necessary to belabor our point because the recent defense of the Trinity makes the astonishing assertion that *echad* always implies a "compound unity." The author then builds his case for a multi-personal God on what he thinks is a firm foundation in the Hebrew Bible. The linguistic fact is that *echad* never means "compound one," but strictly a "single one." The fact that "many waters were gathered to one [*echad*] place" (Gen. 1:9) provides no data at all for a compound sense for one, much less for a plurality in the Godhead.[16]

Since the strange argument about a so-called "plurality" in the word one is so widespread and has apparently been accepted uncritically, we add here the comments of a Trinitarian professor of theology who concedes that the popular argument from the word *echad* (one) is as frail as the argument from the word *elohim.* No case for a multi-personal God can be based on the fact that "one" in Hebrew and English may sometimes modify a collective term:

> Even weaker [than the argument from *Elohim*] is the argument that the Hebrew word for "one" (*echad*) used in the *Shema* ("Hear O Israel, the Lord our God is one Lord") refers to a unified one, not an absolute one. Hence, some Trinitarians have argued, the Old Testament has a view of a united Godhead. It is, of course, true that the meaning of the word may in some contexts denote a unified plurality (e.g. Gen. 2:24, "they shall become one flesh"). But this really proves nothing. An examination of the Old Testament usage reveals that the word *echad* is as capable of various meanings as is

---

16 In Genesis 1, 2 alone, we have examples of "one day," "one place," "one of his ribs," "one of us." If according to Trinitarian theory "us" means a Triune Godhead, "one" would presumably mean "one single member of the three."

our English word one. The context must determine
whether a numerical or unified singularity is intended.[17]

It has sometimes been argued that God would have been
described as *yachid*, i.e. "solitary, isolated, the only one," if there
were only one person in the Godhead. The use of *echad* ("one
single"), however, is quite sufficient to indicate that the One
Person comprises the Deity. *Yachid* is rare in biblical Hebrew. It
carries in the Bible the meaning "beloved," "only-begotten" or
"lonely" and would be inappropriate as a description of the
Deity.[18] There is another Hebrew word *bad*, "alone, by oneself,
isolated," which does in fact describe the One God.
Deuteronomy 4:35 states that "there is no one else besides Him."
The absolute singularity of the One God is similarly emphasized
when He is addressed: "You are Jehovah alone" (Neh. 9:6),
"You are God alone, the God of all the Kingdoms of the earth"
(2 Kings 19:15), "You alone are God" (Ps. 86:10). The One God
of Israel is a single person, unrivaled and in a class of His own.
He is One, with all the mathematical simplicity implied by that
word.[19]

With these facts before us, it would be difficult not to
sympathize with the first-century Jew, possessing the Old
Testament as his guide, for maintaining with unrelenting tenacity

---

[17] Gregory Boyd, *Oneness Pentecostals and the Trinity* (Baker Book
House, 1995), 47, 48. It is not strictly true that *echad denotes* a unified
plurality. It may modify a compound noun.

[18] *Yachid* is in fact found as a description of the One God in the
Pseudepigrapha.

[19] Cp. the remarks on "the Old Testament name for God" (in the
*Theological Dictionary of the New Testament, Abridged in One
Volume,* 489): "The name Yahweh is distinguished by a specific
content. God is not just any deity but a distinct divine person...Behind
statements like 'the Lord is God' (1 Kings 18:39) or 'the Lord is his
name' (Ex. 15:3) stand the more specific expressions 'Yahweh (or
Yahweh of hosts) is his name.' There is encounter here with the
definite person of God." There is no suggestion here that God is three
persons.

a belief in One God, consisting of one person. A search of the Hebrew Scriptures for any sign of a duality or Trinity of divine persons active in the creation will prove fruitless.[20] To propose a Godhead of more than one person would require us to cast aside the rules of language and grammar. Responsible historians, both secular and religious, agree that the Jews of Jesus' time held firmly to faith in a unipersonal God. It is one of the great ironies of history that Christian theologians have denied the Jews the right to explain the meaning of God in their own Scriptures. The Jewish voice on this matter needs urgently to be heard again:

> The Old Testament is strictly monotheistic. God is a single personal being. The idea that a Trinity is to be found there or even in any way shadowed forth, is an assumption that has long held sway in theology, but is

---

[20] The following statements from standard authorities confirm the weakness of any attempt to base the Trinity on the Old Testament: "There is in the Old Testament no indication of distinctions in the Godhead; it is an anachronism to find either the doctrine of the Incarnation or that of the Trinity in its pages" ("God," in the *Encyclopedia of Religion and Ethics*, T&T Clark, 1913, 6:254). "Theologians today are in agreement that the Hebrew Bible does not contain a doctrine of the Trinity" (*The Encyclopedia of Religion*, ed. Mircea Eliade, Macmillan Publishing Company, 1987, 15:54)."The doctrine of the Trinity is not taught in the Old Testament" (*New Catholic Encyclopedia*, Pub. Guild., 1967, 14:306)."The Old Testament tells us nothing explicitly or by necessary implication of a Triune God who is Father, Son and Holy Spirit...*There is no evidence that any sacred writer even suspected the existence of a [Trinity] within the Godhead*...Even to see in the Old Testament suggestions or foreshadowings or 'veiled signs' of the Trinity of persons, is to go beyond the words and intent of the sacred writers" (Edmund J. Fortman, *The Triune God*, Baker Book House, 1972, xv, 8, 9). "The Old Testament can scarcely be used as authority for the existence of distinctions within the Godhead. The use of 'us' by the divine speaker (Gen. 1:26; 3:32; 11:7) is strange, but it is perhaps due to His consciousness of being surrounded by other beings of a loftier order than men (Isa. 6:8)" (A.B. Davidson, "God," *Hastings Dictionary of the Bible*, Charles Scribner's Sons, 1911, 2:205).

utterly without foundation. The Jews, as a people, under its teachings became stern opponents of all polytheistic tendencies, and they have remained unflinching monotheists to this day. On this point there is no break between the Old Testament Scriptures and the New. The monotheistic tradition is continued. Jesus was a Jew, trained by Jewish parents in the Old Testament Scriptures. His teaching was Jewish to the core; a new gospel indeed, but not a new theology.[21]

Judaism is not as devoid of dogmatic formulas as one often supposes...Judaism has its own creeds and articles of faith. The *Shema Israel* (Deut. 6:4) is not only a liturgical formula and a commandment; it is also a confession of faith, and considered as more important than the historical Jewish creeds. As a confession of faith, the *Shema* is the affirmation of the unity and uniqueness of God. It constitutes the highest expression of the "Jewish monotheism": "*Adonai*[22] is our God; *Adonai* is one..." The Christian symbols of faith — the Apostles' Creed, the Nicaean-Constantinopolitan Creed, the Athanasian Creed, to quote only the main ones — are considered by the Jews as being in flat contradiction to this fundamental assertion of Jewish monotheism. Claude Montefiore has put it in the clearest way: "As to the nature of God, all Jews maintain that the doctrines of the divinity of Christ, of the Trinity, of the Eternal Son,

---

[21] L.L. Paine, *A Critical History of the Evolution of Trinitarianism* (Boston and New York: Houghton Mifflin and Co., 1902), 4.

[22] *Adonai* means "the (supreme) Lord" and is found in the Hebrew Bible (449 times) as well as the divine name YHVH. Jews today substitute *Adonai* for the sacred name when reading Scripture and in prayer.

of the personality of the Holy Spirit, are infractions of
the divine Unity and false."[23]

The belief that God is made up of several personalities
such as the Christian belief in the Trinity is a departure
from the pure conception of the unity of God. Israel has
throughout the ages rejected everything that marred or
obscured the conception of pure monotheism it has given
to the world, and rather than admit any weakening of it,
Jews are prepared to wander, to suffer, to die.[24]

Trinitarian theologians have struggled with the obvious
problem of how to reconcile the Trinity with the fact that
Christianity's matrix was unitarian. The Trinitarian theologian
Leonard Hodgson wrote:

[Christianity] arose within Judaism and the monotheism
of Judaism was then, as it is still, unitarian. How was the
Christian church to state a theology adequate to express
the new knowledge of God which had come to it through
Jesus Christ?...Could the monotheism be revised so as
to include the new revelation without ceasing to be
monotheistic?[25]

Jesus was a Jew committed to the creed of Israel (Mark
12:28ff.). This fact alone should persuade us that a departure
from Jesus' Jewish creed has occurred somewhere in the history
of the faith. For the moment we must emphasize that Judaism
was unitarian, never Trinitarian. It was under the tutelage of this
Jewish school of thought, and empowered by belief in Israel's
One God, that the promised Messiah reached maturity and
entered his unique ministry.

[23] Lev Gillet, *Communion in the Messiah: Studies in the Relationship
between Judaism and Christianity* (Lutterworth Press, 1968), 75, 76.

[24] Chief Rabbi J.H. Hertz, *Pentateuch and Haftorahs* (London:
Soncino Press, 1960), 770.

[25] *Christian Faith and Practice, Seven Lectures* (Oxford: Blackwell,
1952), 74.

Can it be demonstrated that Jesus upheld and taught belief in this same One God of the Jews throughout his career? To answer this question, it is only reasonable that we consult his own words, faithfully recorded by those who accompanied him as he proclaimed the saving Gospel of the coming Kingdom of God in Palestine (Mark 1:14, 15; Luke 4:43, etc.)

II. JESUS AND THE GOD OF THE JEWS

"Those who worship God must worship Him in spirit and truth."
— *Jesus Christ*

The sharp-eyed guardians of fundamental Judaism were highly agitated by the growing competition and threat presented to the religious community by the troublesome Galilean, Jesus. His ever-increasing following, attracted by his miracles, a quick intellect and candid, outspoken observations exposing the hypocrisy of religious leadership, had created a climate of fear and antagonism among the establishment.

From the beginning of recorded history, fear of religious competition has normally produced a thinly-veiled state of belligerency on the part of official custodians of the faith. In that atmosphere there seems little room for calm, open discussion of differences. It is appropriate to ask ourselves how we view any threat, imagined or real, to our own cherished convictions. The ideal response to challenge is a humble, inquiring attitude, eager to consider the merits or faults of whatever is put before us for examination. Unfortunately, traditional religious systems often meet any threat to the status quo with hostility and intransigence. They have dealt harshly with the nonconformist.

In the case of Jesus, an intolerant clergy exposed their fears by conspiring to end the threat presented by the upstart teacher's influence over the minds of the truth-seeking members of his audience. The Gospel of Mark records the story of an ongoing theological battle in which representatives of two competing religious factions cooperated by sending "the Pharisees and Herodians to him, in order to trap him in a statement" (Mark 12:13). Their initial flattery aimed at catching Jesus in their web: "Teacher, we know that you are truthful and defer to no one; for

you are not partial to any, but teach the way of God in truth"
(Mark 12:14). This opening gambit was followed by questions
designed to discredit Jesus in the eyes of his audience. His
perceptive answers to these difficult questions, however, gained
him the admiration of at least one of the more open-minded
scribes.

The scribe (or biblical scholar) decided to pose his own
question. His approach was straightforward, devoid of trickery or
sham. Paraphrased in modern language it would read like this:
"What is the core, the central idea, of what you believe and
teach? What is the single most important tenet of your
theology?" Mark reports the question as follows: "What
commandment is the first commandment?" Or, as other
translators catch the flavor of the inquiry: "What commandment
is the foremost of all?" (Mark 12:28).

Jesus' reply bypassed the Ten Commandments and quoted
directly from a later divine statement, the so-called *Shema*:
"Hear, O Israel! The Lord our God is one Lord; and you shall
love the Lord your God with all your heart, and with all your
soul, and with all your mind, and with all your strength" (Deut.
6:4, 5; Mark 12:29, 30). Students of the Bible should consider
whether they have grasped the implications of Jesus' basic
Christian response. He evidently treats the Old Testament words
of Moses as a repository of divine truth. His definition of God
relies for its authority on what both Jesus and his audience knew
to be a primary revelation. Jesus simply restated with complete
clarity the fundamental tenet of the Jewish religious system,
confirming beyond all argument that the true God is one Lord —
and thus one person.

The conversation which followed reveals the critical nature
of the question. Few exchanges could be more enlightening, as
we hear Jesus himself laying the groundwork of all true faith and
understanding. Here were two religious Jews in conversation
about the question most crucial to spiritual life. An incorrect
answer would have destroyed the credibility of Jesus with the
Jewish community. The answer Jesus gave, however,
immediately struck a responsive chord with the thoroughly
monotheistic scribe. His enthusiasm for the historic creed of

Israel is shown by his warm reaction: "Right, teacher, you have truly stated that He is one; and there is no one else besides Him" (Mark 12:32).

In the mind of this or any other orthodox Jew, Jesus' reference could only have been to the one-person God of the Old Testament. The celebrated *Shema* ("Hear, O Israel") declared that "The Lord our God is one Lord" (Deut. 6:4).

God is *one*, Jesus affirmed, and He is one Lord! (Mark 12:29). This simplest and clearest of all creeds permeates the Old Testament: "For who is God besides the Lord?...There is no one holy like the Lord. Indeed, there is no one besides You, nor is there any rock like our God" (2 Sam. 22:32; 1 Sam. 2:2).

Could there have been lurking in the consciousness of Jesus the idea that he himself was another, coequal person in the Godhead, and therefore also fully God? It is beyond our imagination that any such notion could possibly be detected here or in anything else reported about Jesus by Mark. There was no disagreement whatever between the orthodox Jewish theologian and Jesus, the pioneer of the Christian faith. God is one and only one. He is one Lord. This is Christ's central statement about the nature of the Deity. Coming from Christ himself, it must also automatically stand as the central Christian creed.

Jesus' closing comment confirms the understanding he held in common with the scribe: "And when Jesus saw that he had answered intelligently, he said to him, 'You are not far from the Kingdom of God'" (Mark 12:34). From this remark we would deduce that without this intelligent belief in the One God of the Jews, one would be far from the Kingdom of God. Jesus' open declaration about the foundation of true religion should invite us to compare our own thinking with his, on this most basic of all issues.

It is important to note that this conversation took place at a late date in Jesus' ministry. If he were to introduce a shattering, radical change in Judaism's understanding about God, this would have been an obvious opportunity. Some modern theologians have attempted to account for the absence from Jesus' teaching of any new statement about the nature of God. One Trinitarian commentator, Loraine Boettner, remarked:

> That a doctrine [of the Trinity], which to us is so
> difficult, should even in the hands of a people who had
> become fiercely monotheistic, take its place silently and
> imperceptibly among accepted Christian truths without
> struggle and without controversy, is certainly one of the
> most remarkable phenomena in the history of human
> thought...At the time of the New Testament books the
> Trinity was already common property.[1]

This is a striking, if problematic, observation. First there is
the frank acknowledgment that the Jewish people — and this
would include the original twelve disciples, who were all Jews
— were "fiercely monotheistic." As for the statements that the
Trinitarian idea "took its place silently and imperceptibly among
Christian truths" and "at the time of the New Testament books
the Trinity was already common property," where is the
evidence for this, in view of the plain teaching of Jesus recorded
by Mark? Jesus evidently knows nothing at all of any Trinity. He
introduces no new idea of God. He agrees with the Old
Testament, the Jewish scribe and millions of Jews ever since that
God is one person. What does this imply about traditional
Christianity, which has so long proclaimed a definition of the
Godhead *different from the one on which Jesus insisted*?

Boettner's assertion seems to overlook the fact that Mark's
Gospel represents the Christian faith as the Church understood it
when he wrote, perhaps as late as 80 AD. Boettner attributes to
the first-century Church a doctrine of God which did not become
fully formulated as part of the Church's official creed until the
fourth century, and even then under great protest. His conclusion
that Trinitarianism was already at home in the circle of Jesus'
disciples does not allow for the extreme sensitivity of the Jewish
majority which constituted the membership of the primitive
Church, to whom the idea of a Triune God would have been
alien, not to say blasphemous.

The earliest recorded history of the Church, the book of
Acts, reports a whole conference held to decide such questions

---

[1] *Studies in Theology* (Grand Rapids: Eerdmans, 1957), 95.

as Gentile circumcision, eating food containing blood, and the eating of meat from strangled animals. If these physical matters were considered worthy of formal discussion, how much more would a conference be necessary to discuss the explosive change from belief in the single-person God to that of a Triune God, among those fiercely monotheistic Jews, leaders of the early Christian community?

What seems even more extraordinary in view of all Jesus' controversy with his chief critics is this: Never was there the slightest trace of any argument concerning the Trinity. This is not to ignore the controversy that came about as a result of Jesus' claim to be the "Son of God." But that claim should not be confused with the much later assertion by the Church that he was "God, the Son." It remains a fact that the doctrine of the Trinity was never defended in the whole of the New Testament. This could simply be because it was unheard of. The Messiah is seen in the New Testament documents as the unique, legal representative of God, not as the second member of the Trinity.

Boettner's observation seems also to ignore the second- and third-century debates that ensued over the nature of God and Christ and the violent controversy at the time of the Council of Nicea itself, as Christians were forced to accept belief in a preexistent, second person of the Godhead, identified with Jesus. The *Encyclopedia Americana*, speaking of the conflict between the believers in the one-person God and those in the two- and three-person God, makes this important comment:

> Unitarianism as a theological movement began much earlier in history; indeed it antedated Trinitarianism by many decades. Christianity derived from Judaism, and Judaism was strictly Unitarian. *The road which led from Jerusalem to [the Council of] Nicea was scarcely a straight one. Fourth-century Trinitarianism did not reflect accurately early Christian teaching regarding the nature of God; it was on the contrary a deviation from*

> *this teaching. It therefore developed against constant*
> *Unitarian, or at least anti-Trinitarian opposition.*[2]

A statement by the *Encyclopedia Britannica* shows how wide of the mark is the suggestion that Trinitarianism was the settled creed of the earliest believers: "the Trinitarians and the Unitarians continued to confront each other, the latter at the beginning of the third century still forming the large majority."[3]

In view of this documented evidence, it is not reasonable to claim that the doctrine of the Trinity took "its place silently and imperceptibly among accepted Christian truths without a struggle and without controversy."[4] Boettner's assessment seems not to accord with the development of the doctrine over three centuries.

There are other equally unambiguous statements confirming Jesus' belief in the God of Judaism. There is no hint of the introduction of a second person into the Godhead in the farewell prayer Jesus offered at the conclusion of his ministry. Shortly before his death he prayed to his Father on behalf of the disciples whom he left behind to carry on the work he had begun. Summarizing the true faith, he declared, "And this is eternal life, that they may know You, the *only true God*, and Jesus Christ whom You have sent" (John 17:3).

We note the remarkable comment of a celebrated Church Father. It was so difficult for Augustine to harmonize this original Christian creed with the Trinitarian dogma known to him in the fifth century, that this immensely influential church leader actually restructured Jesus' words to accommodate both Father and Son in the Godhead. Augustine, in his *Homilies on John*, boldly asserts that John 17:3 means: "This is eternal life, that they may know Thee *and Jesus Christ*, whom Thou hast

---

[2] (1956), 27:2941, emphasis added.

[3] 11th ed., 23:963.

[4] Boettner, *Studies in Theology*, 95.

sent, as the only true God."[5] This daring alteration of the Holy Scripture seriously distorts the words given to us by Jesus. Jesus defines his own position as the *Messiah*, distinct from the Godhead, which consists of the Father alone. The wise believer will distance himself from such violence to the Bible. Such forcing of the text merely exposes Augustine's desperation to find his creed in the Scriptures.

The original statement of Jesus needs little clarification. It is straightforward and clear. Jesus is a person separate and distinct from his Father, the only true God. Jesus has not been incorporated into the Godhead. The importance of Jesus' own creed cannot be overemphasized. The word "only" in the Greek language is *monos*, a term which has several equivalents in English. Its meaning is "only," "alone," "solitary." The word "true" in the Greek is *alethinos*, meaning true in the sense of genuine or real. Putting the two Greek words *monos* and *alethinos* together, we see that Jesus describes his Father as the only real or genuine God.

Consider further Jesus' use of the word "only." There is no doubt about the meaning of the word or the accuracy of its translation in John 17:3. "Only" is a word which limits and excludes. Whatever is described as "only" is in a class of its own — completely unique. All other things are excluded. If something is "the only..." automatically there can be nothing

---

[5] Tractate CV, ch. 17. Cp. the remarks of H.A.W. Meyer (*Commentary on John*, New York: Funk & Wagnalls, 1884, 462). Despite his own insistence on the deity of Jesus he admits that it was "a perversion of the passage and running counter to the strict monotheism of John, when Augustine, Ambrose, Hilary, Beda, Thomas, Aretius, and several others explained [John 17:3] as if the language were 'that they may know you and Jesus Christ as the only true God.' Only one, the Father, can absolutely be termed the only true God (comp. 'the one who is over all God,' Rom. 9:5), not at the same time Christ (who is not even in 1 John 5:20 'the true God'), since His divine entity stands in relation of *genetic* subsistence to the Father, John 1:18, although He, in unity with the Father, works as His commissioner, 10:30, and is His representative, 14:9, 10." It is hard to see how a unitarian could possibly disagree with this fine statement.

besides it. To see its usage in another text of the Bible, we note
Paul's words to the Philippian church: "No church shared with
me in the giving and receiving, but you only" (Phil. 4:15). All
other churches were excluded from Paul's reference. In another
passage, speaking of the Second Coming, Jesus said: "Of that
day and hour no one knows, not the angels of heaven, nor the
Son, but the Father *only*" (Matt. 24:36; Mark 13:32). Only the
Father knew; no one else had this knowledge.

We do not require an army of expert theologians or linguists
to help us understand these statements. We have all used similar
language involving "only" since we learned to speak. We all
know what "only" means. Jesus described the Father as the "only
true God." No one disagrees that the Father is the *true* God. But
note carefully: not only is the Father "the true God," He is the
"*only* true God." We would be suspicious of anyone who claims
he has "only one wife" if his household consisted of three
separate women, each of whom he claimed was his *one* wife. As
"the only true God," or as we might equally well say, "the only
one who is truly God," the Father of Jesus holds a unique and
unrivaled position.

Another statement of Jesus, recorded by John, provides the
strongest evidence of his continuing belief in the unipersonal
God of the Jews. To the Pharisees he said, "How can you
believe, when you receive glory from one another, and you do
not seek the glory that is from *the one and only God*?" (John
5:44).[6] The NRSV translates Jesus' words as "the one who alone
is God." A more transparently simple unitarian statement would
be hard to imagine. "The one who alone is God" recalls a
number of monotheistic statements found in the documents of
Jesus' heritage. It was the God of Israel who "alone knows the
hearts of men," "the only one who knows the hearts of men" (1
Kings 8:39). Hezekiah had prayed to God with these words: "O

---

[6] Standard commentaries recognize that Jesus subscribed unreservedly
to his Jewish heritage. For example, G.R. Beasley-Murray says, "The
only God [John 5:44] reflects the Jewish confession of faith, rooted in
the *Shema* in Deut. 6:4" (*John, Word Biblical Commentary,* Waco, TX:
Word Books, 1987, 70).

Lord, the God of Israel, You who are enthroned above the cherubim, You are God alone of all the kingdoms of the earth. You made heaven and earth" (2 Kings 19:15). The psalmist had appealed to "You, alone, whose name is Yahweh, the Most High over all the earth" (Ps. 83:18) and to "You the great and only God" (Ps. 85:10, LXX). Jesus echoed these brilliant testimonies to Israel's unique privilege as guardians of monotheism. It was his Father to whom the words "only God" and "the one who alone is God" were applied. Jesus makes this clear in the statement immediately following his reference to "the one who alone is God" (John 5:44). The Pharisees were not to think that Jesus would accuse them before *the Father* (John 5:45). Moses' own words condemned them for their failure to see in Jesus the promised Messiah. On the other hand Jesus always sought honor from "the one who sent him" (John 7:18). Indeed the Messiah was the one on whom "the Father, namely God," has set His seal (John 6:27).

John portrays Jesus as a loyal Jew faithful to the strict monotheism of his people and able to speak in harmony with them of "the one who alone is God," "the only true God," and the God who had placed His seal of approval on His unique Son. If the Father of Jesus is "the only one who is God,"[7] it is obvious that no one else belongs in that class. John's Jesus subscribes unequivocally to Israel's unitary monotheism.

Jesus as Son of God

Despite Jesus' definitive creedal statements, which show him to be a true son of Israel, some present-day theologians are determined to justify the much later creed formulated in the fourth and fifth centuries. They maintain that Jesus, after all, *did* claim to be God because he did not deny that he was the "Son of

---

[7] Cp. Walter Bauer, *A Greek Lexicon of the New Testament and Other Early Christian Literature,* 527, who renders "the only master" (Jude 4) as "the only one who is master." Jesus' reference to "the only God" (John 5:44) likewise designates the Father as "the only one who is God."

God." The repeated equation of "Son of God" with "God" in Trinitarian writings needs to be examined.

Klaas Runia is typical of a contemporary school of thought which asserts that the term Son of God leads naturally to the developed orthodox dogma that Jesus is God the Son. What does it mean, however, *in the Bible* to be Son of God?

Runia examines the title Son of God in his book on Christology and states categorically that for theologians to take the term "Son of God" in its Old Testament meaning "runs entirely contrary to what the Gospels tell us."[8] He maintains that the title "Son of God," as used in the New Testament, is a clear indication that Jesus was preexistent Deity.

No evidence is presented to show that the New Testament abandons its own roots in the Old Testament and ascribes to the title "Son of God" a meaning never hinted at in the Hebrew Bible. The Old Testament meaning of "Son of God" is devastating to the Trinitarian cause. "Son of God" was used in various ways — to describe the nation of Israel, its king, and, in the plural, even angels. In none of these instances does the title imply Deity in a Trinitarian sense. A much more sensitive treatment of this question appears in an article by another biblical scholar, James R. Brady, who says:

> When the Scriptures talk of Jesus as the Messiah, probably *the* most significant title they use is "Son of God." In passages such as Matthew 16:16 and 26:63 it is clear that these two titles — Messiah and Son of God — stand in apposition [one defines the other]. *The title Son of God undoubtedly stems from Old Testament texts such as 2 Sam. 7:14 and Psalm 2:7, in its association with the Davidic King.*[9]

Runia offers Mark 2:7 and John 5:18 as proof that Jesus' claims to forgive sins and that God was his own Father mean that

---

[8] *The Present-Day Christological Debate* (InterVarsity Press, 1984), 93.

[9] "Do Miracles Authenticate the Messiah?" *Evangelical Review of Theology* 13 (1989): 101, emphasis added.

he thought of himself as God. When Jesus said he was the "Son of God," we are asked to believe that he was claiming to be God. Rather than siding with the hostile Pharisees in their hasty criticism of Jesus' claims, it would be wise to consider Jesus' own response to the charge of blasphemy.

It is critically important not to lose sight of the Old Testament usage of the term "Son of God." It would be fatal to lift this title out of its biblical context and give it a meaning not found in Scripture. Jesus habitually appealed to the Old Testament to support his teaching. This technique, on another occasion, as we shall see, demolished the arguments of the Jewish religious leaders, when they falsely accused him of usurping the prerogatives of God. Jesus complained that they had misunderstood their own sacred writings.

Let us first examine both texts advanced by Runia. According to Mark Jesus said to the paralytic, "My son, your sins are forgiven." Some of the scribes said to themselves, "This fellow blasphemes. Who can forgive sins but God alone?" (Mark 2:5, 7). Jesus' claim to be able to forgive sins seemed to place him on a par with God. By way of clarification and to silence criticism, which Jesus attributed to malicious intent, he said to them, "But in order that you may know that the Son of Man has authority on earth to forgive sins" — he said to the paralytic — "I say to you, rise, take up your bed, and go home" (Mark 2:10, 11). The authority to forgive sins had been bestowed on Jesus *as God's representative*. This did not make him God, but a human being vested with extraordinary powers as God's legal agent. The point was not lost on the crowds. They did not believe that Jesus had claimed to be God, but that God had given exceptional authority to *a man*. Matthew reports that "when the multitudes saw this, they were filled with awe and glorified God who had *given such authority to men*" (Matt. 9:8).

Nothing in the account suggests that the crowds understood that Jesus was claiming to be God. There is no indication that the monotheism of the Old Testament was in any way disturbed. Indeed, the subject of Old Testament monotheism was not at issue. Jesus' opponents took offense at his claim to be the uniquely authorized agent of God. His is a functional equality with God which has nothing to do with a claim to be a coequal, coeternal member of the Godhead. Jesus was careful to point out that the Son can do nothing of himself (John 5:19). On a later occasion he invested the Apostles with the right to forgive sins — a responsibility which did not include them in the Godhead (John 20:23).

We are much heartened by the statement of a distinguished Professor of Systematic Theology at Fuller Seminary and general editor of the prestigious *New International Dictionary of New Testament Theology.* In an illuminating discussion of issues relating to the Trinity, he says: "The crux of the matter is how we understand the term 'Son of God'…The title Son of God is not in itself a designation of personal deity or an expression of metaphysical distinctions within the Godhead. Indeed, to be a 'Son of God' one has to be a being who is *not* God! It is a designation for a creature indicating a special relationship with God. In particular, it denotes God's representative, God's vice-regent. It is a designation of kingship, identifying the king as God's Son."[10] Theologians who simply assert, without proof, that "Son of God" means "God the Son" are in Brown's words laboring under "a systematic misunderstanding of Son of God language in Scripture."

The Messiah Is Not God, but God's Agent

Could it be that today's Trinitarians inadvertently, and in sincerity desiring to exalt Jesus, fall into the trap of ascribing to the Messiah a position as God which he never claimed for himself? A claim to be Deity in the Trinitarian sense would actually be blasphemous by Jesus' own standards, since he repeatedly affirmed that his Father was the *only* true God.

Runia insists that Jesus did claim he was God, and was understood to have done so by some of the Jewish leaders in John 5:18, but he has read a much later Trinitarian controversy back into these first-century accounts, to the confusion of the

[10] Colin Brown, "Trinity and Incarnation: In Search of Contemporary Orthodoxy," *Ex Auditu,* 1991, 87-88.

whole issue. In the fourth Gospel Jesus is an uncompromising advocate of the unipersonal monotheism of his Jewish heritage.[11] As "Son of God" Jesus recognized that he possessed no inherent power apart from the Father. His was a derived authority. He always sought the will of Him who had commissioned him, meaning that he was totally dependent on the One God. His exchange with the Pharisees ended with Jesus affirming belief in the One who alone is God (John 5:44). He upholds the monotheism of his Jewish heritage.

A subsequent charge of blasphemy by the Pharisees gave Jesus the opportunity to show his opponents how poorly they understood their own Scriptures. The episode is recorded in John 10:32-36. On this occasion, Jesus asked the question, "For which good work are you stoning me?" "The Jews answered him, 'For a good work we do not stone you, but for blasphemy; and because you, being a man, make yourself out to be God.'"[12] Jesus dealt with the accusation by citing the Old Testament, showing that the Hebrew Scriptures were still the supreme authority able to clarify his Messianic claim: "Has it not been written in your Law, 'I said, *you are gods*'? If he called them gods, to whom the word of God came...do you say of him [Jesus] whom the Father sanctified and sent into the world, 'You are blaspheming,' because I said, 'I am *the Son of God*'?"

Jesus seized the opportunity to define once again his position in relation to God. Quoting Psalm 82:6, he pointed out that the word "God" could be legitimately used of human beings who enjoyed special positions as divinely commissioned agents. "God" in the case of the judges of Israel certainly did not mean God, the Almighty. No one would claim Deity in that sense for

---

11 John 17:3; 5:44; cp. Mark 12:28-30. Jesus did indeed claim an "equality" with God (John 5:18), but it is not the equality expressed by Trinitarianism. Jesus functioned on behalf of the One God as His representative. In that sense he may be said to be "equal with God." It is an abuse of these texts to pretend that Jesus had any knowledge of a Godhead of three persons.

12 The Greek is ambiguous and could also be rendered "a god."

these human leaders of Israel. The "gods" described in Psalm 82 were probably administrators authorized to act for God. Jesus based his argument for a correct understanding of "Son of God" on this Psalm, where "gods" are defined as "sons of God": "I said, 'You are gods, and all of you are *sons of the Most High.*' Nevertheless you will die like men" (Ps. 82:6, 7).

It would be unreasonable to maintain that Jesus changed this special Old Testament meaning of the word "god," equivalent to the phrase "Son of God" ("Sons of the Most High"), when he expressly appealed to Psalm 82 to clarify his own right to the title "Son of God." In countering the charge of blasphemy, Jesus laid claim to a unique position as divine agent. He is the supreme example of a human ruler invested with divine powers. He went on record to declare his true status: "I said, 'I am the Son of God'" (John 10:36). But this provides no basis at all for the later Trinitarian assertion that "Son of God" is equivalent to "God the Son." Thus Jesus' defense of his own status explicitly contains the claim *not* to be Almighty God. Trinitarians frequently pass over John 10:34-36 in silence.

Old Testament Expectation about the Messiah

Jesus was thoroughly schooled in the Hebrew Scriptures and could have made no claims about himself which contradicted the divine records to which he constantly appealed. A critically important prophecy in Deuteronomy 18:15, applied to Jesus by Peter and Stephen in the book of Acts (3:22; 7:37), describes the expected "greater Moses." The important point is that this prophet would be, as Moses said, "a *prophet like me* from among *your brothers.*" Moses and his brothers were evidently fully human, all members of the tribes of Israel. No stronger indication could be given that the one who was to fulfill the prophecy would be equally human and mortal. Moses would have been shocked to learn that the prophet "like me" already preexisted as God and did not really originate in the human family. Moreover, God consented to Israel's request that God's agent, *and not God Himself*, would address them.[13] To read John's Gospel as if Jesus claimed to *be* God would therefore be in direct conflict with this important Christological text in Deuteronomy as well as with Jesus' own declarations about who he was. Moreover the Apostles claimed to have found "the one of whom Moses in the Law, and the prophets wrote, Jesus of Nazareth" (John 1:45). That predicted Messiah was not God, but God's ultimate human spokesman. To claim, therefore, that John intended to present Jesus as *God* would throw his own testimony into hopeless contradiction.

Had a knowledge of a Deity of two or three persons ever filtered down through the centuries, it entirely escaped the notice of the Jewish people. We cite again the words of the contemporary orthodox Jewish theologian, Lapide:

> The confession that Jesus acknowledged "as the most important of all commandments," and which is spoken by every child of Israel as a final word in the hour of death [was]: "Hear, O Israel! The Lord our God is one" (Deut. 6:4). What the "Shema Israel" has meant for the inner life and survival of Judaism can only with difficulty be understood from without. As orthodox, liberal, or progressive as one might be in one's religiosity, the oneness of God raises faith to a central height before which all other questions shrink to secondary ones. Whatever might separate the Jew on the fringe from the Jew at the center, the oneness of the common God makes secure the oneness of religious consciousness.[14]

Psalm 110:1

Though the Jews could find nothing of an already existing, much less eternal, Son of God in the Old Testament, this has not prevented large numbers of contemporary students of the Bible

---

13 See Deut. 18:15-20 where the promised prophet, the Messiah, is specifically said *not to be God!*

14 *Jewish Monotheism and Christian Trinitarian Doctrine*, 27, 28.

from confidently proving the preexistence of Jesus, and thus at least a duality in God, from Psalm 110:1: "The Lord says to my lord: 'Sit at My right hand, until I make your enemies a footstool for your feet.'" Both the Pharisees and Jesus recognized that the second lord of this verse described the promised Messiah. Jesus advanced this text as a divine oracle demonstrating his view of the Messiah as both the son of David and David's lord (Mark 12:35-37). What, then, does the inspired Christological statement mean when it calls the Messiah "lord"? It has been argued by some that this verse should be rendered "God said to my God..." They insist that David knew of a duality in the Godhead and under inspiration declared the eternal Sonship and Deity of the one who was to become the man Jesus.

Such a theory involves a misuse of the Hebrew language which can easily be cleared up. The two words for "lord" in the sentence "the 'Lord' said to my 'lord'" are significantly different. The first "Lord" is Yahweh. It is quite true that Old Testament texts containing this word are sometimes in the New Testament transferred to Jesus *when he functions as an agent for Yahweh* (just as the angel of the Lord who exercises the authority of Yahweh is sometimes equated with Yahweh).[15] In Psalm 110:1, however, there is no question that the first Lord mentioned (Yahweh) refers to God, the Father, the One God of Israel (as it does on some 6700 occasions). The second word for "lord" (here, "my lord") is *adoni*,[16] meaning, according to all

---

[15] E.g. Judges 13:3, 6, 9, 13, 15, 16, 17, 18, 20, 21, compared with v. 22.

[16] I.e., *adon* with the personal suffix "*i*" ("my"). It is amazing that a number of commentaries wrongly assert that the second lord is *adonai*. See, for example, *The Bible Knowledge Commentary* (ed. Walvoord and Zuck, representing Dallas Theological Seminary faculty, Victor Books, 1987) which states mistakenly that "my lord" in Ps. 110:1 "translates the Hebrew *adonay*, used only of God" (73). Unfortunately this comment suggests that the Messiah is God Himself. In fact the Hebrew for "my lord" is not *adonai* but *adoni*, which is *never* used of God but often of the king of Israel and other human superiors. This surprising error of fact is symptomatic of the widespread confusion of

standard Hebrew lexicons, "lord," "master," or "owner," and it refers here, by way of prediction, to the Messiah.[17] If David had expected the Messiah to be God, the word used would not have been *adoni,* but *adonai,* a term used exclusively for the One God.[18]

Psalm 110:1 provides a major key to understanding who Jesus is. The Hebrew Bible carefully distinguishes the divine title *adonai,* the Supreme Lord, from *adoni,* the form of address appropriate to human and angelic superiors. *Adoni,* "my lord," "my master" on no occasion refers to the deity. *Adonai,* on the

---

God with the Messiah. 1 Sam. 24:6 is typical of the Hebrew manner of distinguishing "my lord, the king" from the Lord God. No one reading Ps. 110:1 could imagine that the Messiah was the Lord God. The Messiah is the Lord's anointed. See Luke 2:11, 26 for Luke's carefully-worded titles. The "Lord Christ" (Luke 2:11) is the "my lord" of Ps. 110:1. There are thus two Lords: the one Lord God and the one Lord Messiah, Jesus. That is exactly Paul's creed in 1 Cor. 8:4-6. Robert Sumner in his *Jesus Christ Is God* (Biblical Evangelism Press, 1983) bases his major argument for the Trinity on Psalm 110:1: "Jesus' reference was to the oft-quoted Ps. 110:1, readily acknowledged by the Jews of His day to be both Davidic and Messianic, where King David called the Christ 'my Lord' using one of the names of deity, *Adonai*" (321). He then goes on to find the complete Trinity in Jehovah, *Adonai,* Spirit. Accurate reporting of the language facts would make that conclusion impossible. The same error about the word "lord" in Psalm 110:1 appears frequently in evangelical literature. See, for example, Herbert Lockyer, *All the Divine Names and Titles in the Bible* (Zondervan, 1975): "Here, Jehovah speaks to Adonai words that are properly applied to Christ" (15). The Lockman Foundation NASV marginal note on Acts 2:36 likewise reports the Hebrew word as *Adonai.* They happily agreed to correct the mistake in future printings.

[17] Both the Pharisees and Jesus recognized this text as a divine oracle addressed to the coming Messiah, son of David. See Matt. 22:41-45.

[18] The reader should note that this distinction is not clearly described in *Strong's Concordance — Hebrew and Chaldee Dictionary,* word nos. 113, 136.

other hand, is the special form of *adon*, Lord, reserved for address to the One God only.[19]

A reader of the Hebrew Bible is schooled to recognize the vital distinction between God and man. There is an enormous difference between *adoni*, "my master," and *adonai*, the Supreme God. No less than 195 times in the Hebrew canon *adoni* marks the person addressed as the recipient of honor *but never as the Supreme God*. This important fact tells us that the Hebrew Scriptures expected the Messiah to be not God, but the human descendant of David, whom David properly recognized would also be his lord.[20]

In a book devoted entirely to a study of Psalm 110 in early Christianity David Hay notes that there are no less than "thirty-three quotations and allusions to Psalm 110 scattered throughout the New Testament...Many of these references are set in passages of high theological consequence."[21] Psalm 110:1 is surrounded with "a special aura of prophetic revelation."[22] It is

---

[19] The difference is one which depends on the Hebrew vowel points. It is clear that the distinction between *adonai* and *adoni* has been faithfully preserved since ancient times. The translators of the LXX in the 3rd century BC attest to a careful distinction between the forms of *adon* used for divine and human reference by translating *adoni* as *to kurio mou*, "my lord." The NT validates this translation. In Ps. 110:5 the divine title *adonai* appears (here Yahweh supports the Messiah by standing at his right hand, cp. Ps. 109:31; 16:8) and the LXX renders *adonai*, as usually, *kurios*. The Lord (God) of verse 5 is thus sharply distinguished from David's human lord, the Messiah (v. 1).

[20] For an analysis of the occurrences of *adoni*, see Herbert Bateman, "Psalm 110:1 and the New Testament," *Bibliotheca Sacra* 149, (1992): 438-453. The author, as a Trinitarian, argues that the Psalm cannot apply primarily to Jesus because *adoni* describes a human Messiah! Bateman's Trinitarianism causes him to dismiss the obvious direct Messianic reference of this Psalm. Jesus had no doubt that he was that "lord" (Matt. 22:41-45), and he knew that he was not the One God.

[21] *Glory at the Right Hand: Psalm 110 in Early Christianity* (Nashville: Abingdon, 1973), 15.

[22] Ibid., 21.

clear from Jesus' discussion with the Pharisees, as well as from the Jewish Targum reflecting an ancient tradition, that Psalm 110:1 designated the Messiah in his relation to the One God. The former was a Davidic, Messianic figure, "the prince of the world to come." New Testament allusions to Psalm 110:1 suggest that this verse formed part of the earliest Christian creeds and even hymns. Evidently some august person, according to the divine oracle, was to enjoy a unique position at the right hand of the Deity. But who was this? The second member of a Triune Godhead?

Such an idea is absolutely impossible in a biblical context. What the Psalm does provide is an invaluable key to the nature and identity of the Messiah as the appointed agent of God. In a crucial apostolic sermon, laying the foundation of the faith, Peter declared that at his ascension Jesus, "a man whom they had crucified," was now confirmed in his royal status as "Messiah and Lord" (Acts 2:22, 23, 36). It is here that we encounter the supreme truth of Christology. Jesus, however, is not the Lord God, Yahweh, but the Lord Messiah based, as Peter asserts, on the oracle of Psalm 110:1. It is on this bed-rock definition of Jesus' status that all New Testament Christology is built. Jesus is the lord whom David addressed prophetically as "my lord" (*adoni*). Jesus is indeed *kurios* (lord) but certainly not the Lord God. That title, *adoni*, invariably distinguishes a *human* superior from the One God in the Old Testament. It is a distinction which is clear cut and consistent. *Adonai*, by contrast, marks the one and only supreme God of the Bible 449 times.

It is unusual for scholarly writing actually to misstate the facts about a word appearing in the Hebrew or Greek text. Astonishingly, however, a remarkable error crept into statements on high authority regarding the identity of the Messiah in this crucial Christological passage in Psalm 110:1. That verse, often cited by the New Testament, legitimates the title "lord" for Jesus. Yet it has been the subject of extraordinary attack from the theological pen. Neither the Hebrew nor the Greek of the Septuagint and the New Testament will permit that "lord" to be Deity. Both Testaments unite, therefore, in their opposition to the idea of the Trinity. It is to Jesus as "lord" that the Church directs

her worship, service and even petition.[23] Jesus, on the basis of
Psalm 110:1, is David's lord ("my lord") and thus "*our* Lord
Jesus Christ." The Father of Jesus remains uniquely the one Lord
God, who is also "the God of our Lord Jesus Christ" (Eph. 1:17).
"God" and "lord" therefore point to a crucial difference of rank.
The Messiah is not "coequal God."

Notice now the evidence of widespread confusion in the
treatment of this Psalm. The status of Jesus as the human *adoni*
has proved to be an embarrassment to later "orthodoxy." A
Roman Catholic writer, in an effort to support his traditional
doctrine of the eternal Son, states:

> In Psalm 110:1 "Yahweh said to Adonai: Sit thou at my
> right hand." This passage is cited by Christ to prove that
> he is Adonai, seated at the right hand of Yahweh (Matt.
> 22:44). But Adonai "my master," as a proper name, is
> used exclusively of the Deity, either alone or in such a
> phrase as Yahweh Adonai. It is clear, then that in this
> lyric Yahweh addresses the Christ as a different Person
> and yet identical in Godhead.[24]

The information is incorrect. The second lord of the Hebrew
text is specifically not *adonai* but *adoni*. The latter is never a
divine title. The former always designates the Deity. The whole
Trinitarian argument from this Psalm fails because the facts of
the language are wrongly reported.

In an article appearing in the *Evangelical Quarterly*, William
Childs Robinson states with confidence that:

> It has long been held and taught in the Southern
> Presbyterian Church that Christ is Jehovah; that is, that
> He who was worshipped as Jehovah by the Old
> Testament saints did, without ceasing to be God, become
> man "for us men and for our salvation"...But the
> Scottish professor of systematic theology in Union

---

[23] It is granted that in the New Testament prayer is generally offered to
the Father through the Son.

[24] Walter Drum, S.J., "Christology," *Encyclopedia Americana* (1949),
694.

Seminary, New York, has recently challenged this statement, writing in *The Presbyterian of the South* as follows: "The orthodox view is surely not that 'Christ is Jehovah' — such a phrase is new to me."[25]

The author then contends that the proposition "Jesus is Yahweh" is an age-long axiom of the Church and the acme of orthodoxy.

The misgivings of the Union Seminary professor point to a deep-seated uneasiness about the equation of the Messiah with God. Dr. Robinson nevertheless argues that because Jesus is called *kurios* (lord) he must be God. He refers to Luke 2:11 which introduces the Savior as "the Lord Messiah" and concludes that this means "Christ-Jehovah." He then turns to Acts 2:34-36, where Peter quotes Psalm 110:1 to establish Jesus' status as "lord." But he misreads the Hebrew text and claims that Jesus is sitting as "the Lord *Adonai* at the right hand of Jehovah." "This lofty celestial Messiahship — pyramiding the eschatological Son of Man, *Adonai* at the right hand of Jehovah" proves that Jesus is Jehovah.[26] But the facts are against him. The Messiah is not called *adonai* as he asserts, but *adoni*. The Hebrew Bible does not confuse God with a human being as Trinitarianism does.

The famous *Smith's Bible Dictionary* ignored the human title given to the Messiah in Psalm 110:1 and then appealed to this text as evidence for a Trinitarian Jesus:

Accordingly we find that, after the Ascension, the Apostles labored to bring the Jews to acknowledge that Jesus was not only *the Christ*, but was also a *Divine* Person, even the Lord Jehovah. Thus for example, St. Peter, after the outpouring of the Holy Ghost on the Day of Pentecost by Christ, says "Therefore let all the house of Israel know assuredly, that God has made that same Jesus, whom you crucified, both LORD (*Kurion*, Jehovah) *and Christ*" (Acts 2:36).

25 William Childs Robinson, "Jesus Christ Is Jehovah," *Evangelical Quarterly* 5:2 (1933): 144.
26 Ibid., 155.

A subsequent editor, however, was uneasy with this tour de force, which presented Peter as an adherent to the later church councils. He issued a corrective in an editorial footnote:

> In ascribing to St. Peter the remarkable proposition that "God has *made* Jesus Jehovah," the writer of this article appears to have overlooked the fact that *kurion* ("Lord") refers to *ho kurio mou* ("my lord") in verse 34, quoted from Psalm 110:1 where the Hebrew correspondent is not Jehovah but *adon*, the common word for "lord."[27]

The same misinformation about the crucial title "lord" for the Messiah reappears even in the prestigious *International Critical Commentary* on the Gospel of Luke: "In the Hebrew we have two different words for Lord: 'Jehovah says to Adonai.' Psalm 110 was always believed to be Messianic, and to have been written by David."[28] There are two different words certainly, but as reported by Dr. Plummer, God was talking to Himself rather than His human agent the Messiah. Once again Trinitarian dogma was forced back into Scripture at the cost of changing the words of the text.

Numerous examples of the same error of information can be found in older commentaries and surprisingly also in the Scofield Bible notes on Psalm 110:1: "The importance of the 110th Psalm is attested by the remarkable prominence given to it in the N.T. It affirms the Deity of Jesus, thus answering those who deny the full divine meaning of his N.T. title of Lord." But how does it affirm the "Deity of Jesus" when the Hebrew title applied to him designates, in every one of its 195 occurrences, human (and occasionally angelic) superiors? The phrase "to my lord" used in the oracle addressed to the Messiah in Psalm 110:1 appears 24 times. On these occasions men or women address men, especially the king. On every occasion when "my lord" (*adoni*) and Yahweh appear in the same sentence, as in Psalm

---

[27]"Son of God," *Smith's Dictionary of the Bible*, ed. Hackett (Baker Book House, 1971), 4:3090.

[28]Alfred Plummer, *Gospel According to S. Luke, International Critical Commentary* (Edinburgh: T&T Clark, 1913), 472.

110:1, "my lord" invariably contrasts the One God with a human person. Readers of the Hebrew Bible are constantly exposed to the difference between God and His agents. "O LORD (Yahweh), the God of my master (*adoni*) Abraham" (Gen. 24:12). "The LORD (Yahweh) has greatly blessed my master (*adoni*)" (Gen. 24:27). "The LORD (Yahweh) has given my lord (*adoni*) the king vengeance on Saul" (2 Sam 4:8). The title "my lord the king" occurs frequently as an address to Israel's sovereign.

Readers of the English Bible are accustomed to recognizing "LORD," in capitals, as the translation of the original Yahweh. They may also know that the form "Lord" (with capital L) indicates the original divine title *adonai*. In Psalm 110:1, however, the distinction is unfortunately lost — and only in this single case — when the Messiah appears in many versions as Lord (with capital) where the word is not *adonai*, the divine title, but *adoni*, "my lord, the (human) king." The false impression is thus created that the Messiah is the One Divine Lord since in all of its 449 occurrences *adonai* appears in English as Lord (with initial capital). *The Cambridge Bible for Schools and Colleges* points out that the Revised Version "has rightly dropped the capital letter on lord [in Ps. 110:1], as being of the nature of an interpretation. My lord (*adoni*) is the title of respect and reverence used in the Old Testament in addressing or speaking of a person of rank and dignity, especially a king (Gen. 23:6; 1 Sam. 22:12 and frequently)."[29]

The consistent distinction between human and divine references, indicated by a vital difference in the pointing of the Hebrew word Lord, has been ignored or misrepresented in translation, Bible notes and commentary under the pressure of Trinitarian dogma. The correction of "Lord" to "lord" in the Revised Version of Psalm 110:1 was preserved in the RSV and NRSV. It is properly rendered also in the Jewish Publication Society translation, in Moffatt and in the Roman Catholic New

---

[29] A.F. Kirkpatrick, *Psalms* (Cambridge University Press, 1901), 665.

American Bible.[30] Other modern translations continue to give
the impression that the Hebrew Bible's oracle about the Christ,
so precious to apostolic Christianity, places Jesus in the category
of Deity. The long-standing cherished view that Jesus is the Lord
God should give way to the biblical testimony that he is in fact
the Lord Messiah, David's human superior, the unique human
agent of the One God of Israel. The application of Old Testament
Yahweh texts to Jesus means that he acts on behalf of the One
God, his God and Father. It does not mean that he *is* Yahweh.
When, however, Jesus is *called* "lord," "the Lord Jesus," "the
Lord Jesus Christ," "the Lord Christ" and "our Lord," this is
positively not an indication that he is Yahweh. These titles
inform us that he is the Lord *Messiah* as specified by the
foundational Christological text in Psalm 110:1.

Jesus' appointed Apostle followed his master's argument
from Psalm 110:1 when he described the status of the Messiah in
relation to God. With the Hebrew Bible in mind, Paul carefully
distinguishes, in a critical creedal statement, between the "one
God, the Father," and the "one Lord Jesus Christ." Paul has not
split the *Shema* of Israel between two persons. This would be to
abandon his precious Jewish creed. Paul in fact makes a clear
unitarian declaration: "There is no God but One...There is One
God, the Father" (1 Cor. 8:4, 6). He then claims for Jesus a
lordly status based on the central Christological affirmation, by
divine oracle, that he is the promised "my lord, the King
Messiah, the Lord's anointed" (Ps. 110:1; Luke 2:11): "There is
one Lord Jesus *Messiah*" (1 Cor. 8:6). This is his full official
title. Peter had likewise proclaimed in Acts 2:34-36, with
apostolic authority derived from the Messiah, that Jesus was the
appointed Lord Christ, in accordance with Psalm 110:1, as
distinct from, and as the servant of, the Lord God.

Neither the Jews nor Jesus misunderstood their own
language on this critical matter of defining God and His Son.
They never thought that Psalm 110:1 had introduced distinctions

---

[30] *The Companion Bible* of E.W. Bullinger mistakenly informs us in
its notes on Ps. 110:1 that the second lord is *adonai*.

in the Godhead or that God was speaking to Himself. It is only by reading a Trinitarian or Binitarian point of view into this text that the claim that the Messiah was to be fully God can be upheld. The "lord" expected by King David was to be both his descendant or son as well as his superior and master, but emphatically not Yahweh Himself.[31] Psalm 110:1 stands as a barrier against any expansion of the Godhead into two or three persons. The evidence of the Hebrew Scriptures is contradicted by the suggestion that the New Testament sees the Son of God as a member of the Godhead. Traditional orthodoxy has substituted its own definition of Lord, as it applies to Jesus, and advanced the extraordinary and very un-Hebrew idea that God is more than a single person, in opposition to the definitive oracular utterance of Psalm 110:1.

In an article with the title "God or god?: Arianism, Ancient and Modern,"[32] Donald Macleod ends with a cry for orthodox Trinitarianism by insisting, "We cannot call a creature, however glorious, *Lord*!" He appears to have overlooked the fact that David, in his inspired prophetic utterance about the Messiah, a text precious to Jesus and used by him in controversy to silence opposition, did in fact designate the Messiah as his exalted human lord (*adoni*). From ancient times until now this Christological pearl of great price has been thrown away. In Bart Ehrman's fascinating study *The Orthodox Corruption of Scripture*[33] he records extensive evidence of deliberate alteration of the New Testament manuscripts (some such corruptions found their way into our translations) by which Jesus is called God instead of Christ. In the quotation of Psalm 110:1 in Luke 20:42 the text of the Persian harmony of the Gospels has been changed

---

[31] The point may be confirmed by I. Howard Marshall, *Acts, Tyndale New Testament Commentaries* (Grand Rapids: Eerdmans, 1980). Speaking of the quotation of Psalm 110:1 by Peter in Acts 2:34, Marshall says, "the attribute of lordship...is given to Jesus; he is *not equated with Yahweh*" (80, emphasis added).

[32] *Evangelical Quarterly* 68:2 (1996): 121-138.

[33] (Oxford University Press, 1993), 85.

so that it no longer reads "the Lord said to my lord," but "God said to my God." The absence of any such division of the Godhead in the true text of the Bible has not prevented the orthodox from forcing on the inspired records, whether by actual tampering with the documents or in commentary, a startling substitution of a title of Deity for the Messiah.

New Testament Christians would certainly agree that Jesus functioned in the role of Yahweh as His agent. That he was *actually* Yahweh was out of the question. Their confessions on this subject are clear. How then did Jesus' closest followers define the status of their master? Jesus was deeply interested in that question. He deliberately inquired of them, "But who do you say that I am?" (Matt. 16:15). Their answer is crucial to our understanding of the Christian faith.

III. DID JESUS' FOLLOWERS THINK HE WAS GOD?

"Paul never equates Jesus with God."
— Professor W.R. Matthews

If the account of Jesus' life is accurate, his mother's most carefully guarded secret must have been the matter of her son's Deity. Townspeople who had enjoyed a lifetime acquaintanceship with Jesus and his family were astonished at his prowess and wisdom, but offended by the authority with which he taught. Their response to his teaching and miraculous powers was one of skepticism. They questioned: "Is not this the carpenter's son? Is not his mother called Mary, and his brothers, James and Joseph, and Simon and Judas? And his sisters, are they not all with us? Where did this man get all these things? And they took offense at him" (Matt. 13:55-57). They evidently considered him to be a man like themselves, a member of a human family composed of brothers and sisters, the son of a tradesman well known in the local community.

His immediate family obviously never thought that Jesus had made a claim to be God. At one point they invited him to leave his home area because he constituted a personal risk to their safety. John tells the story:

> And after these things Jesus was walking in Galilee; for he was unwilling to walk in Judea, because the Jews were looking for an opportunity to kill him...His brothers therefore said to him, "Depart from here and go into Judea, that your disciples also may see the works which you are doing. For no one does anything in secret, when he himself tries to become known publicly. If you do these things, show yourself to the world." For not even his brothers were believing in him (John 7:1-5).

Even when we allow for the fact that Jesus' family did not accept his claims, nothing in the story leads us to think that they had rejected Jesus because he thought he was God. None of the Gospel reports suggests that the Messiah's family was privy to any information about him being God — information that would put a chasm between them and him.

Luke, presenting an account of the Christian faith to Theophilus, failed to make any point about the Deity of Jesus. He calls him Son of God, but this is because of his virgin birth (Luke 1:35). "Son of God" (not "God the Son") was also a recognized Messianic title. If Luke talked to the mother of Jesus to confirm the story of the virgin birth, either she failed to mention the matter of Christ's Deity or Luke considered it unimportant. Could it be that the idea of Jesus having preexisted as part of the Godhead had never occurred to them? Had Mary thought of herself as mother of God, she certainly would have mentioned that fact.

It is a very natural concept for one reared in a modern Christian environment to accept the idea of a two- or three-person God, though no one has been able to give a logical explanation of how three who are each called "God" can in fact be "one God." It stands as part of our religious heritage. To believe otherwise is to run the risk of being stamped a dangerous heretic. To the first Christians, however, the idea of a second, preexistent person in the Godhead was unthinkable. Raymond Brown, a Roman Catholic theologian and certainly no foe of the Trinitarian concept by training, makes the point that Matthew and Luke "show no knowledge of [Jesus'] preexistence; seemingly for them the conception was the becoming (begetting) of God's Son."[1] If Jesus did not preexist there is no eternal Son. There is no evidence, therefore, that Matthew and Luke believed in the Triune God.

---

[1] *The Birth of the Messiah* (London: Geoffrey Chapman, 1977), 31, fn. 17.

We must review the Trinitarian method of handling this problem — the widely acknowledged sparseness of hard evidence in Scripture for the Trinitarian or Binitarian concept.

Trinitarian exponents such as Warfield are in agreement that "the New Testament writers certainly were not conscious of being setters forth of strange gods. In their own estimation they worshipped and proclaimed just the God of Israel and they laid no less stress than the Old Testament itself upon His unity." But further remarks by Warfield prove puzzling:

> The simplicity and assurance with which the New Testament writers speak of God as a Trinity have, however, a further implication. If they betray no sense of novelty in so speaking of Him, this is undoubtedly in part because it is no longer a novelty so to speak of Him. It is clear, in other words, that as we read the New Testament, we are not witnessing the birth of a new concept of God. What we meet with is a firmly established concept of God. The doctrine of the Trinity does not appear in the New Testament in the making, but as already made.[2]

According to Warfield, the Trinitarian position is this: 1) We believe in a three-person God. 2) The doctrine is not developed in the New Testament. 3) It must already have been an established doctrine by the time the New Testament was written and no longer considered a point of discussion because of its wide acceptance. Even though it is never mentioned by name, the writers wrote with "simplicity and assurance" about this unnamed, unexplained doctrine. Warfield was apparently encouraged by the thought that in the Hebrew Bible "[there are] certain repetitions of the name of God which seem to distinguish between God and God."[3] One such example he found in Psalm 110:1, but he apparently had not examined the Hebrew text

---

[2] "Trinity," in the *International Standard Bible Encyclopedia* (Grand Rapids: Eerdmans, rep. 1983), 4:3014.

[3] Ibid.

which, as we have seen, carefully distinguishes between God and the Messiah who is not God.

In view of the words of Jesus' disciples, his family and acquaintances, the whole premise of Warfield's argument is untenable. Those who knew Jesus intimately certainly regarded him as a man who could not be compared with any other human person. But they did not think he was the God of Israel. How is it that Luke, for example, says not a word about what had to be the most revolutionary religious concept ever to be entertained by the Jewish-Christian community? The idea that at some point in his career a man was suddenly discovered to be the God-man of the Trinity would have been cause for widespread discussion. To omit the record of this extraordinary event would have been akin to the history books of the United States failing to make mention of the founding fathers or the Civil War, or British historians ignoring World Wars I and II and Winston Churchill. The idea is inconceivable. The novel idea that Jesus was God would have caused a major doctrinal upheaval deserving the most comprehensive attention. It could not have crept silently into the minds of the monotheistic Jewish apostolic community. A new concept about the Deity would certainly have provoked furious controversy.

Peter's Confession of Faith

Peter was given a magnificent opportunity to express himself on the subject of Jesus' identity when he was specifically asked by Jesus: "But who do you say that I am?" Peter answered: "You are the Christ [Messiah], the Son of the living God." Jesus' response to this celebrated confession of faith is a key to the understanding of the whole New Testament. Jesus applauded Peter's inspired insight by replying: "Blessed are you...because flesh and blood has not revealed this to you, but my Father who is in heaven" (Matt. 16:15-17). Peter's definition of Jesus' identity is simple and clear. It is a definition repeatedly underlined throughout the New Testament. It is also the refreshingly uncomplicated statement of a disciple of Jesus unaware of any of the complexities of Trinitarianism. Unfortunately, this central Christian confession has been seriously misunderstood. With complete disregard for the biblical meaning of the term "Son of God," it has been contended that Peter meant to say that Jesus was "very God."

It should be recognized that the addition of the term "Son of the living God" to the title "Messiah" (Matt. 16:16) in no way alters the fact that Jesus was a fully human person. The parallel passages in Luke and Mark (Luke 9:20; Mark 8:29) record Peter's recognition of Jesus as the "Christ of God" and simply "the Christ," respectively. These writers did not feel the need to amplify the title further. This proves that Matthew's added phrase "Son of the living God" does not dramatically affect the identity of Jesus. "Son of God" is virtually a synonym for Messiah based on Psalm 2:2, 6, 7: Messiah (anointed one) = King = Son of God. Both titles — Messiah and Son of God — point to the expected Son of David, King of Israel. Son of God is the equivalent in the New Testament of King of Israel (John 1:49). Solomon was also "Son of God" (2 Sam. 7:14), as was collectively the whole nation of Israel (Exod. 4:22). Highly significant also is Hosea 1:10, where Israel at its future restoration will be worthy of the same title given by Peter to Jesus, "sons of the living God."

As a nation the Jews were anxiously awaiting the promised Messiah. The factor in Jesus' Messiahship which caused offense was Jesus' insistence that he must suffer death rather than throw off the Roman yoke. It would be only through resurrection and his eventual return to the earth at the Second Coming that the promised Kingdom of glory would be established. It is true that Peter was slow to grasp that the Messiah had first to suffer death. Nevertheless, he was warmly commended by Jesus because he had understood that his master was indeed the Messianic Son of God. Peter had been privileged to hear the message Jesus gave to Israel. He had witnessed his healing miracles; he had been in attendance when Jesus had confounded the religious leaders by his superior wisdom; he had seen authority exercised over demons, and the dead resurrected. He could consult the Old Testament and observe how Jesus had exactly fulfilled the many prophecies concerning the predicted Savior of the nation. What God revealed to Peter was based on hard verifiable evidence.

And confession of Jesus as Messiah was to be for all time the foundation of the Church's faith (Matt. 16:16, 18).

Without the benefit of previous indoctrination that Jesus was an eternally preexistent being and therefore God, a reader of the New Testament would gather that the expected Messiah was a real human person, a descendant of Abraham and David, supernaturally begotten (Matt. 1:20). Like us, he came into the world a helpless infant; grew in knowledge and wisdom; experienced all the common weaknesses of humanity — hunger, thirst and weariness; had the deep emotions of any person; expressed anger, compassion, and fear of death; had a will of his own and prayed that he might escape the cruel death he knew he faced. He died the death of a mortal man, and before his death, as a loving and compassionate son, provided for the continued welfare of his mother. After his death, Jesus' followers reacted initially as though he were a man who had failed in his task of bringing about the restoration of Israel, as other so-called Messiahs before him had also failed (Luke 24:21). Were our minds not clouded by centuries of indoctrination and an unfortunate misunderstanding about the meaning of the title "Son of God" in the Jewish environment of that time, we would have little difficulty understanding, as Peter did, that Jesus was the Messiah, not God.

Was Israel really supposed to be taken by surprise by the arrival of God Himself? What was the Messiah to be according to the expectations of the prophets of Israel? A man, God-man, higher order of angel? What were Peter and the rest of Israel looking for? History shows that a number of men had posed as the Savior of Israel and gained a following among the Jewish community. The nation correctly expected the liberator to come from the kingly line of David. They anticipated a man who would ascend the restored throne of David, vested with power to extend his rule to encompass all nations. This is what all the prophets had foreseen. Thus the last question the disciples asked Jesus before his final departure was, "Lord, is it at this time you are restoring the Kingdom to Israel?" (Acts 1:6). They had every reason to believe that Jesus, as Messiah, would now bring about the promised restoration. Jesus' answer was merely, "It is not for you to know the times or epochs which the Father has fixed by His own authority" (Acts 1:7). Jesus did not question the fact that the Kingdom would one day be restored to Israel. The *time* of the great event was not to be revealed. That the Messiah would restore the Kingdom was the common thinking of Jesus and his disciples. It was, after all, what all the prophets had constantly predicted.

The disciples expected the Messiah to be born from the seed of David. As it would have appeared to any monotheistic Jew, the term Son of God carried the royal meaning it had acquired in the Old Testament. It designated a human being, a king especially related to God and invested with His spirit. That it implied the Deity of Jesus in a Trinitarian sense would have been the most astounding, revolutionary information ever to invade the mind of Peter or any other religious Jew. Nowhere among the recorded words of the early Apostles, with the possible exception of Thomas, is there even the slightest indication that they were dealing with a God-man. Did Judas know he was betraying his creator and God? And on the occasions when the disciples deserted Jesus, were they aware they were leaving God? Did they believe God was washing their feet at the Last Supper? When Peter took out his sword to cut off a soldier's ear, did he think that the God who had created him was somehow incapable of protecting Himself? At the Mount of Transfiguration, after the disciples saw a vision of Jesus in a future glorified state along with Moses and Elijah, they wanted to build three tabernacles, one for each of these three men (Matt. 17:4).[4] Why was no distinction made between these three, if one of them were God?

---

[4] The event was a preview of the future Kingdom of God and supplied the necessary encouragement for the disciples, following the announcement of Jesus' death (Matt. 16:21). See also 2 Pet. 1:16-18 for the link between the Second Coming (and Kingdom) and the Transfiguration. The preview of the return of Christ in glory provided a glimpse (in vision) of Elijah and Moses who would then be restored to life by resurrection (1 Cor. 15:53). Luke 9:27, 28 expressly links Jesus' saying about the kingdom to the event which happened eight days later.

The human Messiah had appeared in Galilee as bearer of the One God's message of the Kingdom (Luke 4:43; Mark 1:14, 15, etc.). The Gospel of the Kingdom contained such a realistic and vivid expectation of future glory that a rivalry arose among the disciples as to who would be the greatest in that coming Kingdom. The message of the Kingdom had to do with the land promised to Abraham — promises not yet fulfilled. It concerned the reestablishment of the throne of David and the permanent restoration and expansion of the fortunes of the nation of Israel.[5] Its prophets were concerned with Israel's future existence as a witness to the One God within a new society organized under a theocracy. Heaven, as a reward for disembodied souls, was completely outside the disciples' thinking. What they looked forward to was inheritance of the earth (Matt. 5:5; 20:21; cp. Rev. 5:10) and future rulership with the Messiah in a world restored to paradise, as all the prophets had foreseen.[6] The restoration of the world from the chaos of Satan's rule was their dream. They finally gave their lives to advance that message, but they did not live to see the fulfillment of their hopes.

This Jesus looked like the one who could make real the prophets' aspirations. He was empowered to raise the dead, to feed multitudes from virtually nothing and to escape unharmed the attempts of the authorities to kill him. He confounded critics by his wisdom. Since the time was ripe for the Messiah to arrive on the scene, it appeared that Jesus would give substance to the nation's age-long dreams. No wonder others wanted to make him king immediately (John 6:15). How appropriate for the Messiah that they should scatter palm leaves in his path, giving him a reception due to royalty. Yet he refused the offer, and shortly afterwards the excited hopes of his followers lay shattered. Behind the stone door of a guarded tomb lay the lifeless body of

---

The disciples were to experience an extraordinary and exceptional vision of the kingdom during their present life.

[5] Acts 1:6; cp. Matt. 5:5; Acts 3:21; Rom. 4:13; Heb. 11:8.

[6] Matt. 19:28; Rom. 5:17; 1 Cor. 6:2; 2 Tim. 2:12; Rev. 2:26; 3:21; 5:10; 20:1-6; Isa. 32:1.

their Messiah. One man never quite seemed to give up. "A man named Joseph who was a member of the Council, a good and righteous man (he had not consented to their plan of action), a man from Arimathea...who was waiting for the Kingdom of God; this man went to Pilate and asked for the body of Jesus" (Luke 23:50-52).

Where were his closest associates shortly after his death? When crucifixion seemed to end all hope of Israel's restoration and their own promotion to royal position in the Messiah's Kingdom, Peter and a number of them returned to their business venture. One would have thought that human curiosity at least would have caused them to join the women at the tomb to see what was going to happen to their dead "God." Their reaction, however, tells us that they viewed the death of Jesus as that of an extraordinary human being, ending the story of another fallen hero-Messiah.

They seemed temporarily to lose sight of their answer to his question, "Who do you say that I am?" An earlier question, "Who do men say that the Son of Man is?" revealed a sharp division among those outside his immediate circle. Some said he was "John the Baptist; others Elijah; but still others Jeremiah or one of the prophets" (Matt. 16:14). The variety of answers is not unlike the conflicting opinions current today. Some say he never existed; others that he was a great moral teacher — a mere mortal like us but given superhuman rank through the virgin birth story, as part of early Christian mythological embroidery. Some say he was God, preexisting, who became a God-man and then returned to his former position as God through a resurrection. Some have written books to prove his resurrection was a plot faked by his followers, designed to promote a new religion. Others advance the idea that he was a superior preexisting or pre-human angel, [7] the first of God's creation. Most claim some Bible authority for these widely divergent views.

---

[7] The very term "pre-human" suggests that such a Jesus was not really human. If his origin was an angel, that is what, at the core of his being, he really would be.

Some contend that it is irrelevant what we believe, if we follow his moral and social precepts. This might appear a reasonable approach, but a number of important biblical considerations are against it. Jesus defined the whole point of the Christian faith with the words: "This is eternal life, that they *know* You, the only true God, and Jesus Christ whom You have sent" (John 17:3). Obviously, proper identification of God and the Messiah has everything to do with eternal life. If these were matters of minor importance, why did Jesus ask his central question about his own identity and so powerfully commend Peter for his insight that Jesus was the Messiah? (Matt. 16:15-19). The Apostle Paul evidences a great deal of anxiety when he warns the church at Corinth about a deception involving the acceptance of "another Jesus" (2 Cor. 11:1-4). There is also the crucial statement about Jesus in 1 John 4:2: "every spirit that confesses that Jesus has come in the flesh is from God." This, too, makes the matter of proper identification critically important.

It is only from the words of the Savior and his followers that we can determine which is the correct identification of Jesus among all the competing ideas. We know how the disciples viewed their master during his lifetime, and we have briefly traced their reactions immediately after his death. But what of the resurrected Jesus? If these men were trying to enhance this new religion by faking a resurrection, as some allege, they might also have claimed Deity for him, as was the common honor given heroes and rulers of that age. The idea was far from unique. The book of Acts reports that when King Herod took his throne and spoke, the people shouted, "The voice of God and not of a man!" He would have been better served by a less enthusiastic greeting. The result of his refusal to reject the flattery was death. His body was eaten by worms (Acts 12:21-23).

Roman emperors were deified and worshipped as gods. The Apostle Paul avoided King Herod's fate by rejecting the multitude when they claimed for Paul that "the gods have become like men and have come down to us" (Acts 14:11). Paul was quick to put considerable distance between himself and any such idea. Not only is there no evidence that Jesus was held to be God during his lifetime by his closest followers, but the resurrection itself did nothing to change the disciples' perception of Jesus as a man. They did not now think that Jesus was really God. They simply believed that God had resurrected a human being. On the day of Pentecost, Peter gave what is considered by Christianity to be a critically important statement about the faith:

> Men of Israel, listen to these words: Jesus the Nazarene, a *man* attested to you by God with miracles and wonders and signs which God performed through him in your midst, just as you yourselves know — *this man*, delivered up by the predetermined plan and foreknowledge of God, you nailed to a cross...and put to death (Acts 2:22, 23).

What a marvelous opportunity to attest to the death of a second person in the Godhead, to emphasize the enormity of the crime of deicide. Peter continues: "And so, because he [David] was a prophet and knew that God had sworn to him with an oath to seat one of his descendants upon his throne, he looked ahead and spoke of the resurrection of the Messiah" (Acts 2:30, 31). Peter reflects the teaching of his master. From Jesus' birth to his death and after his resurrection, it is impossible to find any definite biblical statement which disturbs the strict unitary monotheism of Jesus and his chief disciple's Jewish (and Christian) belief.

Luke's Understanding of Jesus' Origin

Luke, the physician, was a careful historian and shrewd observer. He was an ardent disciple and evangelist of apostolic Christianity. As he explained in the introduction to his first volume, he deliberately set out to investigate and document the Christian faith as he knew it, by consulting firsthand witnesses who had known Jesus (Luke 1:1-4). In his second volume, the book of Acts, Luke implies that he had spent much time in the company of Paul as they traveled together. It would be quite extraordinary if Paul and Luke were divided over the issue of the origin of Jesus. In his account of the miracle of Jesus' birth

through virginal conception, he makes no mention whatever of
Jesus having previously existed. His record describes the
miraculous conception of a human person who comes into being
in the womb of his mother. Luke wrote two whole volumes of
the Bible (contributing more of the New Testament than any
other writer) without so much as a hint of belief in a preexistent
second member of a Trinity. When the angel Gabriel announced
the arrival of the long-promised Messiah to Mary, he informed
her that she would "bear a son, and name him Jesus. He will be
great...and the Lord will give him the throne of his father David"
(Luke 1:31, 32). Gabriel spoke of a *future* greatness to be gained
through divine appointment to the throne of Jesus' celebrated
ancestor. There was no indication from the angel that Mary was
to carry in her body one who had preexisted as God or a superior
angel. The good news was that she was to conceive and bear a
son, who would thus be the Son of God as well as the Son of
David. The faith of Luke, and of the Christian community for
which he wrote, could hardly be more clearly defined.

Luke recorded the fact that Mary's son was to be conceived
in a miraculous way, by a special divine intervention: "The Holy
Spirit will come upon you, and the power of the Most High will
overshadow you; and for that reason the holy offspring shall be
called the Son of God" (Luke 1:35). There is no word of an
"eternal Sonship" here; simply the promise that her offspring
would be called Son of God *because of the miracle which God
would perform in her* — a miracle which would involve the One
God directly in the birth of a unique human being, Israel's
promised Messiah.

We are presented in these verses, on the authority of God's
emissary, with a plain statement about the origin of Jesus as Son
of God. The miraculous conception in Mary, according to Luke,
was the immediate cause of the divine Sonship of Jesus. It is "*for
that reason*" (Luke 1:35) — the conception by Mary through the
power of God's Holy Spirit — that Jesus was to be called the
Son of God. A French commentator on this passage nicely
renders the Greek, *dio kai*, as "*c'est précisément pourquoi*"

("that is precisely why," "for that reason indeed") he shall be called the Son of God.[8]

It is not difficult to see that Luke's view of Jesus' Sonship is at variance with the traditional idea that one who already existed as God and Son of God had entered the womb of Mary. If this were so, the conception of Jesus would not be the cause of Jesus' divine Sonship. He would have been the Son of God already. Alfred Plummer makes an honest appraisal of Luke's account of Jesus' beginning: "The title 'Son of the Most High' (1:32) expresses some close relationship between Jesus and Jehovah but not the divine Sonship of the Trinity."[9] The author calls our attention to the fact that Christians are also called "sons of the Most High" (Luke 6:35), but this does not make them eternally preexistent beings. It is only under the influence of doctrinaire Trinitarian thinking and a distortion of the Hebrew usage of the title "Son of God" that many read into Luke's account a "God, the Son" unknown to Luke.

Another candid admission that Luke did not think of Jesus preexisting his birth comes from a leading Roman Catholic scholar, Raymond Brown. He emphasizes the fact that Matthew and Luke "show no knowledge of preexistence; seemingly for them the conception was the becoming (begetting) of God's Son."[10] Brown points out that the traditional concept of preexistence means that the conception of Jesus was the breaking off of an existence as God and the beginning of an earthly career, but not the begetting of God's Son. Yet for Luke, Jesus *begins to exist* in the womb of Mary — "conception is causally related to

---

[8] S. Lyonnet, "L'Annonciation et la Mariologie Biblique," in *Maria in Sacra Scriptura* (Acta Congressus Mariologici-Mariani in Republica Dominicana anno 1965 Celebrati, Rome: Pontificia Academia Mariana Internationalis, 1967), 4:59-72. Luke presents us with a Jesus who is fully human, supernaturally conceived, and thus worthy to be called the Son of God.

[9] *Gospel According to S. Luke, International Critical Commentary*, 23.

[10] *The Birth of the Messiah*, 31, fn. 17.

divine sonship."[11] Jesus was begotten as Son of God at his conception. Luke did not think that Jesus had had a pre-human life. Luke, therefore, could not have been a believer in the Triune Godhead.[12]

Referring to the word "therefore" in Luke 1:35, Brown says that "it involves a certain causality."[13] Jesus' Sonship is derived from the miraculous conception. This, he says, "is an embarrassment to many orthodox theologians because in traditional incarnational theology a conception by the holy spirit does not bring about the existence of God's Son."[14] Brown then makes reference to theologians who "try to avoid the causal connection 'therefore...' in Luke 1:35 by arguing that the conception of the child does not bring the Son of God into being."[15] Brown finds himself unable to agree with them. What Brown has disclosed is simply the reluctance of the average Bible student to admit that Scripture, in this critical matter of the origin and nature of Jesus, does not agree with what he or she has accepted as truth without careful examination.

If the conclusions of the Nicene and the later Chalcedonian Councils were complex and confusing, the account of Luke is quite the opposite. According to him, Jesus was a human person deriving existence and personality from his mother, Mary, herself a descendant of David. If he were not a fully human person, how could he be the promised Messiah, the seed (descendant) of Abraham and David? How could a person who has existed from eternity be a descendant of David in any

---

[11] Ibid., 291.

[12] In the absence of any mention of the preexistence of Jesus in Luke-Acts, it would be unwise to find a reference to an ante-natal existence in Luke 10:18. Jesus may well be speaking here of Satan's descent to counterattack in view of Jesus' exorcisms, or alternatively Jesus sees in vision Satan's eschatological fall, "knowing that he has only a short time" (Rev. 12:12), or his final defeat when the kingdom comes.

[13] Ibid.

[14] Ibid.

[15] Ibid.

meaningful sense? Trinitarian views of Jesus seem to eliminate his descent from David, and thus his claim to be the Messiah.

Would the concept of a second person in the Godhead, a preexistent divine being becoming a helpless fetus in the womb of his mother, Mary, while all the time retaining his Godhood, have made any sense to Luke? If some special God-given revelation had been granted to anyone, Paul, Peter or Mary, with whom Luke must have checked thoroughly before composing his story of the foundations of the original faith, would he not have made some slight mention of this momentous event? We must remember that Trinitarian teaching officially maintains that Jesus possessed "impersonal human nature" (the doctrine known technically as "anhypostasia"), but that he was *not a human person*. That denial stems logically from the mistaken premise that Jesus is God, an eternal member of the Triune Godhead. The argument is this: If the ego of Jesus, the single center of his personality, is God, it must follow that the human element in him cannot be another ego or self. Thus it must be said that his humanity is really "impersonal human nature." To say that Jesus had a second human ego would make him two persons.

All of this extraordinary complexity is unknown to any writer of Scripture. It is significant that Gabriel, Luke and Matthew, dealing with the origin of Jesus, take no notice at all of the supposed eternal preexistence of the Son of God who became man, and are unaware of any complexities about the humanity of the Savior. Judged by today's religious standards and the opinions of many theologians, Gabriel, Luke, and Matthew were most unorthodox and might even be accused of being non-Christian.

The Messiah of the Book of Hebrews
A special emphasis is placed on the humanity of Jesus in the book of Hebrews. Jesus is clearly very much part of the human race:

> Heb. 2:17. "Therefore he had to be made like his brothers in all things." (His brothers were all human beings.)

Heb. 7:14. "For it is evident that our Lord was a descendant of Judah." (As the son of David he was part of the human race.)

Heb. 5:8. "Although he was a Son, he learned obedience from the things he suffered." (He suffered like any other human person. God does not learn obedience.)

Heb. 2:18. "He himself was tempted in that which he suffered." ("God cannot be tempted," James 1:13).

Heb. 5:7. "[Jesus] offered up both prayers and supplications with loud crying and tears to the One who was able to save him from death." (If he were God he should have been able to save himself.)

Heb. 4:15. "For we do not have a high priest who cannot sympathize with our weaknesses, but one who was tempted in *all* things as we are." (God cannot be tempted.)

Heb. 4:4. God, not Jesus, rested at creation; i.e., God was the Creator.

Heb. 2:12. Jesus joins Christians in the worship of God.

Dunn acknowledges that the book of Hebrews has often been thought to support the preexistence of Christ: "The special contribution of Hebrews is that it seems to be the first of the New Testament writings to have embraced the specific thought of a preexistent divine Sonship." But note his conclusion:

> *It would certainly go beyond our evidence to conclude that the author has attained to the understanding of God's Son as having had a real personal preexistence.* In short, a concept of preexistent sonship, yes; but the preexistence perhaps more of an idea and purpose in the mind of God than a personal divine being.[16]

---

[16] *Christology in the Making* (Philadelphia: Westminster Press, 1980), 55, 56, emphasis his.

When the book of Hebrews speaks of Jesus (Heb. 2:6-8) it refers to the classic passage in the Psalms having to do with the destiny of man: "What is man, that You remember him? And the Son of Man, that You care for him? Yet You have made him a little lower than God [or the angels], and crowned him with glory and majesty. You make him to rule over the works of Your hands; You have put all things under his feet" (Ps. 8:4-6).

Could this passage speaking originally of mankind be applied to Jesus if he was in fact God? How could he be "lower than God [or the angels]" and at the same time, even as a man, be fully God?

The book of Hebrews has been used to support an eternal past existence for the Messiah. Such proofs rely heavily on inference drawn from single verses. For example, "God...in these last days has spoken to us in a Son, whom He appointed heir of all things, through whom also He made the worlds" (Heb. 1:2). It has been supposed by some that this verse is evidence that Jesus created the world. The verse is more properly translated "*through* [not by] whom also He [God] made the *ages*." There is nothing here which implies that Jesus created the heaven and earth. What is said is that the One God, who on His own testimony, as we have seen, was unaccompanied in the act of creation (Isa. 44:24), established the ages of human history with Jesus at the center of His purpose, prior to speaking through the Son only "in these last days." It is not difficult to conceive that the Messiah's life, death, and rulership of the world would impact all ages, past, present and future. The same picture of Jesus as the cosmic center of God's design for the world is found in Colossians 1:15-18. In Hebrews it is highly significant that God did *not* speak through a Son in Old Testament times but only "at the end of those days" (Heb. 1:2). There is a strong suggestion here that the Son is not eternal but comes into existence as the historical Jesus.

What emerges from the first two verses of the book of Hebrews is that Jesus was not God's agent to Israel in Old Testament times. God spoke through persons other than Jesus in the past. Angels were often agents of God. This does not mean that the "angel of the Lord," who represented the God of Israel, was the preexistent Son of God, as sometimes claimed. Quite specifically, our author argues, God did not address any angel as "Son" (Heb. 1:5). That privilege was reserved for God's unique Son, Jesus. This fact should lay to rest any theory that Jesus preexisted as an angel. The notion that he could have been Michael, the archangel, is positively excluded by the first chapter of Hebrews. The ministry of the Son of God is far superior to that of angels, though they had been instrumental in the giving of the law at Sinai (Gal. 3:19).

The writer of Hebrews calls our attention to a different period of time when he says: "For He did not subject to angels the inhabited earth to come concerning which we are speaking" (Heb. 2:5). He has in mind not past events but a new era coming. The preeminence of the Messiah as head of this new creation of the future is a pervasive New Testament teaching. The author of Hebrews underlines the fact that Jesus came into an inheritance superior to that of the angels. His was the rightful inheritance of a first-born son: "For to which of the angels did He ever say, 'You are My Son, today I have begotten You'?" (Heb. 1:5). Jesus could not have been God. He was a being created by the Father. Begetting or fathering implies beginning, and God has no beginning. Jesus was the first-born of God's *new* creation. His origin was unique, involving a miraculous conception (Luke 1:35), but he was neither God nor literally preexistent. Nor was he the Melchizedek of Genesis 14:18-20. Melchizedek was not the Son of God but *like* him, as Hebrews 7:3 says. Melchizedek did in fact have a genealogy, though it is not recorded in the Scripture. The mysterious priest of whose lineage there is no scriptural record was not the supreme God! (God anyway in the Hebrew Bible is "not a man.") Translations are correct when they designate Melchizedek as "this man" (Heb. 7:4). He is also the person "whose genealogy is not traced from the Levites" (Heb. 7:6), but the point is that it *is* traceable to someone. "Whose genealogy" (v. 6) implies that he had one, as everyone does. Admittedly all this sort of argumentation based on the absence of the recorded ancestry of a priest-king is very remote to us in the twentieth century. This is all the more reason why the Bible should be studied in the light of its own context and often with the help of those whose business it is to be informed about its background.[17] The mentality of those who say, "I just study the Bible, not commentaries" may turn out to be a passport to disaster and ignorance.

What the writer to the Hebrews and Paul tried to make clear was the preeminence of Jesus as "first-born from the dead, so that he might come to have first place in everything" (Col. 1:18). The first-born son by Jewish law received the greatest inheritance. The book of Hebrews describes the elevated position of the Son: "And when He *again* brings the first-born into the world [NASV], He says, 'And let all the angels of God worship him'" (Heb. 1:6). New Testament writers found it necessary to underline the magnitude of Jesus' office as Messiah. Why did the author not state plainly that Jesus was the One God? This would have established his superiority over the angels, Moses, and Joshua beyond any doubt. Since the author knew with Peter and the Apostles that Jesus was the Messiah (Matt. 16:16), he had to demonstrate from Scripture his superiority over all other created authorities. Note also that it was God, not Jesus Messiah, who rested at creation (Heb. 4:4). This makes little sense if the Son had performed the work of the Genesis creation — a fact which he denied in Mark 10:6. In the light of Isaiah 44:24, Jesus could hardly have thought of himself as present with God in Genesis 1.

Without question the humanity of Jesus as High Priest was another special point to be emphasized in the book of Hebrews. Confusion has arisen, however, over verse eight of the first chapter: "But of the Son He says, 'Thy throne, O God, is forever and ever.'" Brown presents the following observations:

> Vincent Taylor admits that in v. 8 the expression "O God" is vocative spoken of Jesus, but he says that the author of Hebrews was merely citing the Psalm and using its terminology without any deliberate intention of suggesting that Jesus is God. It is true that the main point

---

17 Modern commentary is particularly helpful on the Jewish background of the language of Hebrews 7 in regard to Melchizedek.

of citing the Psalm was to contrast the Son with angels and to show that the Son enjoys eternal domination, while the angels were but servants. Therefore in the citation no major point was being made of the fact that the Son can be addressed as God. Yet we cannot presume that the author did not notice that his citation had this effect. We can say at least, that the author saw nothing wrong in this address, and we can call upon a similar situation in Heb. 1:10, where the application to the Son of Psalm 102:25-27 has the effect of addressing Jesus as Lord. Of course, we have no way of knowing what the "O God" of the Psalm meant to the author of Hebrews when he applies it to Jesus. Psalm 45 is a royal Psalm; and on the analogy of the "Mighty God" of Isaiah 9:6, *"God" may have been looked on simply as a royal title and hence applicable to Jesus as the Davidic Messiah.*[18]

Raymond Brown rightly senses the strong Messianic atmosphere of Hebrews 1. The "Mighty God" of Isaiah 9:6 does indeed mean, as defined by the Hebrew Lexicon, "divine hero, reflecting the divine majesty."[19] It is precisely that same Messianic sense of the term "God" which allows the psalmist to address the King as "God," without inviting us to think that there are now two members of the Godhead. The quotation of Psalm 45:6 in Hebrews 1:8 brings that same Messianic use of the word God into the New Testament. We should not misunderstand this

---

[18] *Jesus, God and Man* (New York: Macmillan, 1967), 24, 25, emphasis added.

[19] Brown, Driver and Briggs, *Hebrew and English Lexicon of the Old Testament* (Oxford: Clarendon Press, 1968), 42. Cp. the plural *elim*, "gods," used of persons other than the One God. At Qumran angels are called "*elim*," including Michael. The *New International Dictionary of Old Testament Theology and Exegesis* comments: "the openness to using divine names for principal angels has obvious implications for NT Christology" (ed. Willem A. VanGemeren, Paternoster Press, 1996, 1:402).

very Jewish use of titles. It is a serious mistake to think that the Messiah has now stepped into the space reserved for the One God, the Father. However exalted the position of Jesus and despite his function as God's representative, the strict unipersonal monotheism of Israel's faith is never compromised by any New Testament writer.

The writer to the Hebrews joins the rest of the New Testament in proclaiming Jesus as God's royal Messiah. The promise of the man Messiah's coming Kingdom is, of course, found frequently in Scripture. Paul told the Gentile world in the clearest of terms that God "has fixed a day in which He will judge [or administer] the world in righteousness through *a man* whom He has appointed, having furnished proof to all men by raising him from the dead."[20]

The man Jesus lived and died on this earth and by his obedience qualified to be the first righteous world ruler. Through his resurrection and the power now conferred on him by his Father, he will return at the appointed time to sit on the throne of his father David, ruling and judging the earth. He remains, however, even in his resurrected state "the man, Messiah Jesus" (1 Tim. 2:5), a testimony to the wonderful thing God has done through and for man. One would do a grave injustice to the writer of Hebrews to insist that he was trying to present a preexistent God-man in the first chapter of his epistle.

The often repeated notion that unless Jesus is God we have no Savior, has no scriptural backing. On the contrary, the Bible attests to the astonishing plan God is executing through a chosen human being. We must understand that the source of all Christian hope is found in this man, Jesus, whom God raised from the dead. If Jesus were not a member of the human family, as we are, then we have no assurance that human beings can be resurrected to eternal life. Jesus' resurrection proved to the Church that the man Messiah was indeed worthy of the exalted

---

[20] Acts 17:31, quoting Ps. 96:13, where the psalmist states that God is coming to "rule the world in righteousness," an occasion for the greatest rejoicing (vv. 11, 12). This is Paul's proclamation of the coming Kingdom to the Athenians.

titles ascribed to the Messiah in the Old Testament. His resurrection was the hope that motivated the early Church. If it had happened to one man then it could happen to them.

Jesus the Man

The earliest followers of Jesus seem to make a special point of emphasizing the humanity of Jesus. This is particularly true of the letter to the Hebrews. "Since then the children share in flesh and blood, he himself likewise also partook of the same...Therefore, he had to be made *like his brothers in all things*, that he might become a merciful and faithful high priest" (Heb. 2:14, 17). It is fair to ask: How could he be tempted as we are, share in flesh and blood, and be made like his brothers in all things, unless he was as completely mortal and human as we? A being who is God encased in human flesh or one who is fully God and man is not a human being.

The Roman Catholic writer, Thomas Hart, candidly faces the problem posed by the later doctrine of the Trinity when he observes that:

> The Chalcedonian formula [the council's decision declaring Jesus both God and man] makes genuine humanity impossible. The conciliar definition says that Jesus is true man. But if there are two natures in him, it is clear which will dominate. And Jesus becomes immediately very different from us. He is omniscient, omnipotent, omnipresent. He knows the past, present, and future...He knows exactly what everyone is thinking and going to do. This is far from ordinary human experience. Jesus is tempted but cannot sin because he is God. What kind of temptation is this? It has little in common with the kinds of struggles we are familiar with.[21]

As high priest, "that prophet," and the descendant of Abraham and David, Jesus does not transcend the boundaries of humanity, even though he is uniquely the Son of God. Paul

---

[21] *To Know and Follow Jesus* (Paulist Press, 1984), 46.

contrasts Jesus with the first human being, Adam, to establish Jesus' position as the Messiah. To the Corinthians he wrote: "Since by a man [Adam] came death, by a man [Jesus] also came the resurrection of the dead...The first Adam became a living soul. The last Adam became a life-giving spirit...The first man is from the earth, earthy; the second man is the Lord from heaven" (1 Cor. 15:21, 45, 47). Adam was made out of the dust of the ground. Jesus originated from the power of God's spirit active in Mary and will reappear at his Second Coming as the life-giving being he became at his resurrection.

There is no evidence that any of the Apostles was the innovator of a new view of Jesus as God. Paul knows only of a Messiah who is a man, the final Adam. He makes a categorical distinction between him and his Father in his first letter to Timothy. In a classic statement about the Christian creed, he says, "For there is one God and one mediator also between God and man, the *man* Christ Jesus" (1 Tim. 2:5). This is a fine summary of Christian belief. As if to thwart any possible confusion between God and man, he contrasts the One God with the *man* Messiah. Not only this, he makes belief in the One God and the man Messiah the basis of the knowledge of the truth which leads to salvation (1 Tim. 2:4, 5). Paul's linking of salvation, the knowledge of truth, and a proper understanding of the identity of God and Jesus should not be missed.

After the resurrection Peter likewise knows of no Messiah other than the "man Jesus." He introduces the Savior to his fellow countrymen with the words: "Men of Israel, listen to me. Jesus the Nazarene, a *man* attested to you by God..." (Acts 2:22). Luke quotes Paul's statement to the Greeks that "God has fixed a day in which He will judge the world in righteousness through *a man*" (Acts 17:31). Both Peter and Paul described a resurrected person, the Messiah who was destined to return to judge and rule. Jesus was still defined as a man. It is part of God's infinite wisdom that He commits all judgment to a man who has experienced life in common with mankind.

The New Testament is filled with plain statements about a human Jesus who had to be tested in *all* points even as we are (Heb. 4:15). Someone who was fully God and fully man cannot be totally human. This is the root of the Trinitarian problem. It is a sheer impossibility, in biblical terms, to confuse the One God with a human being. However much God may give His spirit to frail man, and however exalted the resurrected Jesus has become, man, from the biblical point of view, is dust animated by spirit, and not body and separable soul, which is a Greek idea.[22] "Human being" by definition denotes mortality, subjection to frailty and death. "It is appointed unto man once to die..." (Heb. 9:27). Jesus suffered the ultimate fate of all mankind — not that he needed to die, since he committed no sin. Nevertheless, bearing the penalty of mankind's sins, he died. God cannot die. We must emphasize the point: *A Savior who is God cannot die, and therefore did not die for our sins. The fact that Jesus died for our sins is proof in itself that he was not God.* It is obvious sophistry to maintain that the immortal God died! Those who argue that only the body of Jesus died still fall into the trap of saying that Jesus himself did not die. All such arguments based on dualism are anyway quite unbiblical. The major point for the coherence of the whole faith is that Jesus *himself* died.

Jesus' entire life was lived under the limitations of a human being. He became angry and tired (Mark 3:5; John 4:6), though he never sinned. He had to learn obedience by what he suffered (Heb. 5:8). He could not retreat into a divine mental capsule to escape the rigors and battles of daily life. By his own admission, he did not possess all knowledge: he did not know the day of his return (Mark 13:32). As a child, he needed to grow in wisdom (Luke 2:52). He had to ask his disciples on one occasion, "Who touched me?" (Mark 5:30). He wept (John 11:35) and knew discouragement. He evidently did not possess the qualities of

---

[22] Cp. D.R.G. Owen, "Body and Soul in the New Testament," in *Readings in Christian Theology*, ed. M.J. Erickson (Baker Book House, 1967), 86: "In Hebrew thought, as we have seen, the word translated 'soul' regularly stands simply for the personal pronoun and means the self, and the phrase 'body and soul'...stands for the Hebrew idea that man is an 'animated body' and not for the Greek view that he is an 'incarnated soul.'"

omniscience (Mark 13:32), omnipresence (John 11:32) and immortality, which are the indispensable characteristics of Deity.

First-century Jews and Christians were looking for a human Messiah to rule a new order on earth from the promised land. The decision by fourth- and fifth-century theologians that this unique human person called Jesus was "very God of very God" would have been shocking to the first-century Christian community which had a clear idea about the Messiah's lineage: "For it is evident that our Lord was descended from Judah" (Heb. 7:14). Matthew records the expectations of the Jewish nation and the threat they posed to Gentile rulership (Matt. 2:2-6). The Gentile ruler, Herod, was deeply concerned to hear of the eastern magi's search for the one who was to be born King of the Jews. Any new dynasty would challenge his authority. Herod made inquiry of the chief priests and scribes as to where this Messiah was to be born. Matthew records their reply: "In Bethlehem of Judah...And you, Bethlehem, land of Judah, are by no means least among the leaders of Judah, for out of you shall come forth a Ruler" (Matt. 2:5, 6). All this was common knowledge. A biased translation in the King James Version about the Messiah's "everlasting origins" in Micah 5:2 (quoted in Matt. 2:6) should not mislead us. The promise of the Messiah could be traced to "the distant past."[23] It was from the tribe of Judah that the Messiah would arise to inherit the throne of his father David. Jews were looking for a human deliverer, supernaturally endowed with divine wisdom and power (Isa.

---

[23] See NEB and *The New International Commentary* on Micah 5:2 (Grand Rapids: Eerdmans, 1976), 343. The same Hebrew expression is found in Deut. 32:7 (*y'mot olam*). *Y'may olam* appears in Mic. 7:14; Amos 9:11; Isa. 63:9, 11. *The Hastings Bible Dictionary* (Edinburgh: T&T Clark, 1912), extra vol., 696, translates the expression in Micah 5:2 as "remote antiquity," adding that "days of eternity" wrongly suggests the eternal preexistence of the Messiah. See also the *Cambridge Bible for Schools and Colleges*: "More obvious and perfectly suitable to the context, ['origins' refers to] his descent from the ancient Davidic family — cp. Amos 9:11, where 'the days of old' evidently refers to the reign of David."

11:1-5), but certainly not for God to become man. Of this latter idea the Old Testament had nothing to say.

The resurrection of an eternal person undermines the marvel of what God has done in and through a human being and for the whole human race. The fact that God has dealt so wonderfully with human beings, by providing a human being to blaze the trail to salvation, puts immortality within the reach of every person. Christians today trust in the false hope of a vague reward in heaven after death. Apostolic hope rested in the fact that their promised deliverer, a mortal, had conquered death by being restored from the grave. Moreover, he promised to return to the earth to reward the faithful with positions in his Messianic Kingdom[24] and to reestablish the greatness of Israel. The burning question the disciples posed to Jesus before he was taken to the right hand of the Father could not have been more fitting: "Will you at this time restore the Kingdom to Israel?" (Acts 1:6). His reply was that it was not for them to know when this stupendous event would take place. That it was destined to happen, as all the prophets had foreseen, was confirmed by Jesus. The time factor remained uncertain.[25]

The hero known to these earliest Christians was no God-man. He was the finest son of Israel, the scion of the family of David, the most distinguished of the children of Judah, yet uniquely the Son of God from his conception. He had taught in their midst, died and risen again. His career inspired in them the same hope of resurrection. A drastic new portrait of the Savior was to emerge in post-biblical times. The later "Jesus" of the church councils embraced by the fourth- and fifth-century believers was a curious distortion of the real human Jesus of the Gospels. Despite protests to the contrary, the Jesus of the new official creed only *appeared* to be a man. His real "ego," it was claimed, was the Eternal Person of the Triune Godhead. The

---

[24] Rev. 2:26; 3:21; 5:10; 20:1-4; 1 Cor. 6:2; Matt. 19:28; Luke 22:28-30; 2 Tim. 2:12.

[25] The same expectation is found in Acts 3:21.

Jesus of the councils seems to have swallowed up the real, historical, human Messiah of the Christian records.[26]

The humble carpenter from Nazareth would be a better guide to truth than the decisions of the council supervised by a Roman emperor who was ill-equipped to decide the far-reaching issue about Jesus' identity. He paid little attention to the fact that Jesus himself made no claim to be God. The councils failed to inform us that Jesus did nothing to usurp the authority of the One God of Israel and agreed with his fellow Jews that God was one person alone (John 5:44; 17:3; Mark 12:29).

Once true mortality and humanity were stripped from the Messiah, historical reality fell under a cloud. The Oriental concept of reincarnation made its first inroad under the guise of the Incarnation. Greek speculation and mythology entered the faith by the back door with devastating consequences. Canon Goudge's comment bears repetition: "When the Greek and Roman mind instead of the Hebrew mind came to dominate the Church there occurred a disaster in doctrine and practice from which we have never recovered."[27]

This observation merits further examination. Is the loss of the biblical doctrine of God to be traced ultimately to the infiltration of alien Greek philosophy?

Doubting Thomas

But what of doubting Thomas? When this former skeptic exclaimed to the resurrected Jesus, "My Lord and my God" (John 20:28), did he, in a single sentence, and before (as Trinitarians admit) his companions had any idea of the Deity of

---

[26] Cp. Martin Werner's observation that "the dogma of Christ's Deity turned Jesus into a Hellenistic redeemer-god, and thus was a myth propagated behind which the historical Jesus completely disappeared" (*Formation of Christian Dogma: An Historical Study of Its Problems*, A & C Black, 1957, 298).

[27] "The Calling of the Jews," in the collected essays on *Judaism and Christianity* (Shears and Sons, 1939). The departure from biblical truth in the direction of paganism has its roots in the philosophical speculations of second-century Church Fathers. See further p. 137.

Jesus, establish a theology that made Jesus part of a Trinity and therefore "very God of very God," along the lines of the Nicene or the later Chalcedonian formulas? Did he declare Jesus to be part of a two-person Godhead as others assert? In spite of Thomas' clear application of the term "God" to Jesus in John 20:28, the well-known theologian Emil Brunner makes the following pointed observation:

> The history of Christian theology and of dogma teaches us to regard the dogma of the Trinity as the distinctive element in the Christian idea of God...On the other hand we must honestly admit that the doctrine of the Trinity did not form part of the early Christian New Testament...It was never the intent of the original witnesses to Christ in the New Testament to set before us the intellectual problem — that of three divine persons — and then to tell us silently to worship this mystery of three-in-one. There is no trace of such an idea in the New Testament. This "mysterium logicum," the fact that God is three yet one, lies wholly outside the message of the Bible. It is a mystery which the Church places before the faithful in her theology...but which has no connection with the message of Jesus and the Apostles. No Apostle would have dreamt of thinking that here are three divine persons whose mutual relations and paradoxical unity are beyond our understanding. The mystery of the Trinity...is a pseudo-mystery which sprang out of an aberration in logical thought from the lines laid down in the Bible, and not from the biblical doctrine itself.[28]

The meaning of words must be sought within the environment in which they were written. The Bible was not composed in the 20th century, nor did its writers know anything of the subsequent creeds and councils. Context is all-important in determining an author's intent. Within the pages of John's

---

[28] *Christian Doctrine of God, Dogmatics* (Westminster Press, 1950), 1:205, 226, 238.

Gospel Jesus never referred to himself as God. The fact is that the New Testament applies the word God — in its Greek form *ho theos* — to God, the Father alone some 1350 times. The words *ho theos* (i.e., the one God), used absolutely, are nowhere with certainty applied to Jesus. The word Thomas used to describe Jesus in John 20:28 was indeed *theos*. But Jesus himself had recognized that the Old Testament called the judges "gods," when he referred in John 10:34 to Psalm 82:6: "Has it not been written in your law, 'I said, You are gods'?" *Theos* (here in the plural, *theoi*) appeared in the Greek Septuagint version of the Old Testament as a title of men who represented the one true God.

Jesus on no occasion referred to himself as God in the absolute sense. What precedent did Thomas have for calling Jesus "my God"? Without question, early Christians used the word "god" with a broader meaning than is customary today. "God" was a descriptive title applied to a range of authorities, including the Roman emperor. It was not limited to its absolute sense as a personal name for the supreme Deity as we use it today. It is from the early Church that the biblical words come to us, and it is from that New Testament environment that we must discover their meaning.

Martin Luther's idea that "the Scriptures begin very gently, and lead us on to Christ as a man, then to one who is Lord over all creatures, after that to one who is God"[29] finds little support in the New Testament. It reflects the pressure of having to square received tradition with the text of the Bible. The recorded teaching of Jesus is against any departure from the strict unipersonal monotheism of the Torah. Affirming the creed of Israel, Jesus had proclaimed: "Hear, O Israel! The Lord our God is one Lord" (Mark 12:29). He expressed his allegiance to Israel's most emphatic statement of belief. His words were hardly calculated to lead the disciples "very gently" to believe in another who is God. Such a concept is most contradictory. Read

---

[29] Cited by Klaas Runia in *The Present-Day Christological Debate*, 97.

in its clarity, with words retaining their original meaning, Jesus' absolute confirmation of the cardinal tenet of Judaism should be seen as proof positive of his approval of the unitary monotheism of the Old Testament.

Thomas, who could not believe a resurrection had taken place until he had hard, verifiable evidence, finally understood the exalted position which Jesus assumed as the risen Messiah. The longed-for national greatness for Israel now looked to be a real possibility. The claim of Jesus to be the promised Messiah was now confirmed. Jesus finally became Thomas' Lord and the "God" of the Coming Age of the Kingdom. Thomas was well acquainted with the Old Testament predictions about the Kingdom. The promise to Israel was that "a child will be born to us, a son shall be given to us, and the government will be on his shoulders; and his name will be called Wonderful, Counselor, Mighty God, Eternal Father, Prince of Peace" (Isa. 9:6).

This was a clear, unmistakable statement about a coming Messiah. But this "Mighty God" of Isaiah 9:6 is defined by the leading Old Testament Hebrew lexicon as "divine hero, reflecting the divine majesty."[30]

As for the expression "Eternal Father," the title was understood by the Jews to mean "the father of the Coming (Messianic) Age." The Greek (Septuagint) word for "eternal" in this case need not convey the idea of "forever and ever," "for all eternity" past and future, as we normally understand it, but contains the concept "related to the (future) age." Truly Jesus, the Lord Messiah, will be the parent of the Coming Age of the Kingdom of God on earth until "all things are subjected to him. Then the Son himself will be subjected to the one [God, the Father] who subjected all things to him [Jesus], that God may be

---

[30] Brown, Driver and Briggs, *Hebrew and English Lexicon of the Old Testament*, 42. This same authority records that the word "God" (*el*) used by Isaiah is applied elsewhere in Scripture to "men of might and rank, as well as to angels." (See Exod. 15:11, "among the gods"; Ezek. 31:11, "a god of the nations"; 32:21, "mighty gods"; 17:13, "gods of the land"; Job 41:25, "gods," i.e., mighty men.) *El* refers to someone other than the One God in Ezek. 28:2.

all in all" (1 Cor. 15:28). It was widely recognized by the Jewish community that a human political leader could be called father. Isaiah states of a leader in Israel: "I will entrust him with your authority. And he will become a father to the inhabitants of Judah and Jerusalem" (Isa. 22:21).

Thomas, unlike Judas, had come to recognize the one who was to be the "God" of the Coming Age, replacing Satan, the "God" of this present age (2 Cor. 4:4). Thomas had not suddenly arrived at a revolutionary new belief that Jesus was "very God of very God." There was nothing in the Old Testament concerning Jesus' Messiahship which predicted that an eternal immortal being was to become a human person as the promised King of Israel. Nevertheless the human king could on rare occasions be addressed as "God" as in Psalm 45:6, where he is also given the title "lord" (v. 11). Both "Lord" and "God" are Messianic titles, and appropriately used by John who wrote his whole book to convince us to believe that Jesus was the Messiah (John 20:31).

Reality struck home to the skeptic Thomas when he recognized that it was the resurrected Jesus through whom God was going to restore the fortunes of Israel. Thus Jesus became "God" to Thomas in a way parallel to the sense in which Moses had enjoyed the status of "God" in the presence of Pharaoh: "The Lord [had] said to Moses, 'See, I make you God to Pharaoh'" (Exod. 7:1). These titles of high honor bestowed on God's human instruments did not infringe upon the strict monotheism of the Old Testament. Nor should they imply the overthrow of the Bible's first principle: God is one person, not two or three (Mark 12:29). The angel of the Lord in the Old Testament could also be called "God" as representing the One God of Israel (Gen. 16:9, 10, 11, 13). Yahweh's authority was transferred to him because God's "name was in him" (Exod. 23:20, 21). In the contemporary world "God" did not mean what it means to us today. An inscription dated 62 BC calls King Ptolemy XIII "the lord king god." Medieval Jews referred to David as "our Lord David" and "our Lord Messiah," based on Psalm 110:1 (cp. Luke 2:11).

A nineteenth-century Trinitarian theologian has this to say about Thomas' address to Jesus: "Thomas used the word 'God' in the sense in which it is applied to kings and judges (who are considered as representatives of Deity) and preeminently to the Messiah."[31]

But what of the later Apostle Paul? Is there biblical evidence that this former strict Pharisee abandoned his Old Testament Jewish heritage and enlarged his concept of God to include a second and third person, thus building a foundation for the doctrine of the Trinity?

---

[31] C.G. Kuehnoel, cited by W.G. Eliot, *Discourses on the Doctrines of Christianity* (Boston: American Unitarian Society, 1886), 79.

IV. PAUL AND THE TRINITY

"Apparently Paul did not call Jesus God."
— *Professor Sydney Cave*

No more militant foe ever lashed out in anger at early Christians than a man named Saul (Acts 8:1-3). Nor did a more learned theologian enter the early Church than this same Saul who became known as Paul, a prolific writer and a leading spokesman for first-century Christianity. Branded by some modern demythologizers as an impossible visionary and by others as a psychotic drug-user, he has continued to withstand the harsh judgment of his critics and today remains a standard-bearer for Christianity.

Because of the extreme fervency of his belief, Paul had aligned himself with a group about whom Jesus warned that there would be a time coming when "whoever kills you [Christians] will think that he has offered service to God" (John 16:2). Paul's misguided zeal led him to adopt a murderous policy of persecution against the newly-founded Christian sect.

It is not the purpose of this book to assess the whole range of Paul's theology. Specifically, we want to examine his harmony or disharmony with both the Old Testament and the words of Jesus, the Messiah, on the key issue of the nature of the Godhead.

Paul claimed special revelation from the resurrected Jesus. While many may contend that reason and revelation are incompatible, it is our premise that the two are not at odds. Paul serves to illustrate this point. No part of the revelation given to Paul by Jesus assaults reason. Allowing for an element of progressive revelation, Paul's Christianity is not in disagreement with the earlier teaching of the historical Jesus or with the other

New Testament writers. He has not departed from the Messiah's doctrine of God.

Highly placed in Jewish religious circles, Paul states that he was "circumcised the eighth day, of the nation of Israel...a Hebrew of Hebrews; as to the Law, a Pharisee;...a persecutor of the Church; as to the righteousness which is in the Law, found blameless" (Phil. 3:5, 6). Without question this background would have made him uncompromisingly monotheistic — a convinced advocate of belief in the one true God *as a single person*.[1] As we would expect, Paul's rabbinical training had instilled in him the firmest conviction that there was but one God, the creator of all things. It is evident that he agreed completely with the recently crucified Messiah about the law which Jesus had called the greatest of all commandments. To an inquiring scribe the Messiah had said: "The foremost [commandment] is, 'Hear, O Israel! The Lord our God is one Lord; and you shall love the Lord your God with all your heart...'" (Mark 12:29, 30). As a Pharisee, Paul would unquestionably have endorsed the scribe's enthusiasm for Jesus' monotheism: "Right, teacher, you have truly stated that He is one; and there is no one else besides Him" (Mark 12:32). Paul's Jewish heritage had placed the single-person God at the pinnacle of his belief. His devotion to the One God of the Hebrew Bible remained, after his conversion to Christianity, the prime motivating force behind all his activity.

There is no hint anywhere in Paul's writings that he had ever disagreed with the early Church about the person of God. His pre-conversion hostility was directed toward Jesus' claim to be the Messiah, which he thought constituted a threat to the

---

[1] This is clearly demonstrated by his declarations in 1 Cor. 8:4, 6; Eph. 4:6; and 1 Tim. 2:5. In other areas of his theology, such as the relationship of the Law to the new Jew/Gentile community, Paul expressly departs from his Pharisaic point of view. As a Pharisee he could not have written Galatians 3 and 4. Under inspiration from the risen Jesus he there declares the Law of Moses to have been temporary. Paul's indifference to Mosaic legislation about circumcision makes the same point loudly and clearly.

established religion of the nation of Israel. Numerous recognized biblical scholars, after a careful examination of the evidence, do not think that Paul ever disturbed the waters of the Jewish conviction that God was a single person. Sydney Cave states: "Apparently Paul did not call Jesus God."[2] C.J. Cadoux agrees: "Paul habitually differentiates Christ from God."[3] One may search Paul's writings in vain for a plain statement that Jesus is God, meaning a preexistent "eternal Son," second member of a coequal Trinity. Hebrews 1:8 alone (whether or not Paul wrote this book is unclear) may be claimed as a text in which Jesus is, *in some sense*, certainly called "God." A handful of other texts may or may not contain a reference to Jesus as "God." The evidence is disputed by scholars for grammatical and syntactical reasons. These verses certainly, therefore, cannot be relied on as "proof-texts." Since we know that in the Bible the term "God" does not always mean "the Supreme God," it is impossible to substantiate Trinitarianism from isolated verses in which Jesus may or may not be referred to as "God."

The Trinitarian problem must be analyzed from the perspective of Paul's strictly monotheistic Jewish background, Luke's reports of Paul's ministry in Acts and, of course, his recorded epistles. One question is critical: If Paul became a Trinitarian or a Binitarian, when did it happen? Was he taught the Trinity by the other Apostles, by revelation from Jesus, the Messiah, or was it slowly developed over the period of his lifetime, the reality finally bursting upon him, drastically modifying his former belief in God as one person? There is simply no hard evidence to confirm any such development. Given the deep indoctrination of the Jewish mind in regard to monotheism, particularly in the case of this zealously religious Jew, the novelty of such a concept should have consumed pages of the Bible.

---

[2] *The Doctrine of the Person of Christ* (Duckworth, 1925), 48.

[3] *A Pilgrim's Further Progress: Dialogues on Christian Teaching* (Blackwell, 1943), 40-42.

When the very foundation of a religion is changed, some clear explanation is required. Such drastic theological revolutions do not pass unnoticed; witness the volumes written and the sometimes bloody controversy waged by advocates of the Trinity against the protests of the strict unitarians. A divine revelation to introduce belief in a tripersonal God would have been acceptable and reasonable. But where both revelation is lacking and reason assaulted, there is little basis for accepting such an extraordinary idea as the Trinity. In the words of a British clergyman, himself a Trinitarian, "reason is affronted and faith stands half aghast" at the Trinity.[4]

When Paul was in attendance at the conference at Jerusalem, discussion centered around circumcision and other Old Testament laws. How far were these to be imposed upon Gentile Christians? (Acts 15:5ff.). The decision was rendered by James, the leader of the Jerusalem church. It was this same James who stated, when writing to the scattered Church as "the twelve tribes who are dispersed abroad" (James 1:1): *"You believe that God is one.* You do well; the demons also believe, and shudder" (James 2:19). At this point in church history, there is nothing which suggests a radical change of understanding about the nature of God.

The absence of any new revelation defining the Trinity presents a problem to the Trinitarian writer, E. Calvin Beisner, when he defends the orthodox point of view in his book, *God in Three Persons*. We examine his work because he quotes the Apostle Paul in support of his thesis. Early in chapter one he cites the Nicene Creed, as it was promulgated at the Council of Constantinople in 381 AD: "I believe in one God, the Father Almighty, maker of heaven and earth, and of all things visible and invisible. And in one Lord Jesus Christ, the only begotten Son of God, Light from Light, true God from true God...and in the Holy Ghost, the Lord and Giver of Life..."

---

[4] Bishop Hurd, *Sermons Preached at Lincoln's Inn*, 2:287, cited by John Wilson in *Unitarian Principles Confirmed by Trinitarian Testimonies*, 321.

Beisner then asks the question: "Does the New Testament contain such a doctrine [the Trinity] either explicitly or implicitly? And...if so, how does it?"[5] The answers which scholars give to both these questions, Beisner points out, are "to say the least, widely variant."[6] He maintains, nevertheless, that the Trinity is found in the Bible. The gist of his argument runs as follows: There is in the New Testament one and only one true God; there is a person called the Father who is called God; there is a person called the Son who is also called God.[7]

In the section entitled "Monotheism in the New Testament," Beisner makes the excellent point that a monotheistic view "pervades the whole outlook of Jesus,"[8] and he cites John 17:3: "Now this is eternal life: that they know You, the only true God, and Jesus Christ, whom You sent."

Beisner then adds the evidence of Paul, who deliberately sets out to answer the question whether there are more gods than one. Paul's words are as follows: "We know that an idol is nothing at all in the world and that there is no God but one. For even if there are so-called gods, whether in heaven or on earth (as indeed there are many gods and many lords), yet for us there is but one God, the Father...and there is but one Lord, Jesus Christ" (1 Cor. 8:4-6).

Beisner correctly points out that Paul's answer to the monotheistic question was that "there is no God but one." "This monotheistic viewpoint," he adds, "rules the whole New Testament, but is nowhere more strongly stated than here in the writings of Paul."[9]

It is at this critical point in the argument that we must look carefully at what Paul actually says. All will agree about Paul's belief that there is "only one God," but who, according to Paul,

---

[5] *God in Three Persons* (Tyndale House Publishers, 1984), 24.

[6] Ibid.

[7] Ibid., 26.

[8] Ibid.

[9] Ibid., 27.

is that *one God*? Is there "one God — the Father" (unitarianism) or "one God — the Father, Son and Holy Spirit" (Trinitarianism)? Beisner appears to overlook Paul's crucially important definition of monotheism: "To us [Christians] there is but *one God, the Father*" (1 Cor. 8:6). Paul names the one God as the Father, and he adds no other person. He goes on to say, certainly, that there is one Lord, Jesus Christ, but he does not say (here or anywhere else) that Jesus is "the *one God*." The one God of Paul's monotheism, expressly stated and in harmony with everything we have read in the Old Testament and in the teaching of Jesus, is *the Father alone*.

According to the ordinary rules of language, where we have a number of more than one, the prefix "mono-" no longer applies. For instance, if a man has two wives he is no longer monogamous but polygamous. On this basis, with many Jews and Muslims, we question the validity of speaking of Trinitarianism as monotheism, certainly not as monotheism in the Hebraic, Old Testament sense. It is hard for us to avoid the conclusion that three persons, each of whom is called God, amount to three Gods. We are aware that this is denied by Trinitarians; however, we have also noted that a number of theologians complain that ordinary believers *do* think of the Triune God tritheistically, i.e., as three Gods. It is difficult not to sympathize with Hans Küng who expresses "the genuine concern of many Christians and the justified frustration of Jews and Muslims in trying to find in such [Trinitarian] formulas the pure faith in one God."[10]

Had Jesus or Paul anywhere spoken the language of the Trinity that "the three are one" or "the one is three," we would be compelled to consider it a part of revelation and accept it as Christian doctrine. But history knows little of this sort of talk about the Godhead until three hundred years after the ministry of Jesus. By that time theology had passed into the hands of men who had not shared the close association of the Apostles with

---

[10] Cited by Pinchas Lapide, *Jewish Monotheism and Christian Trinitarian Doctrine*, 40.

Jesus, the Messiah, and who were products of a very different theological formation. We deplore, with Hans Küng, "the Hellenization of the Christian primordial message by Greek theology."[11] It is one thing for Christians to maintain that there is only one God spoken of in the Bible. It is quite another thing to convince Christians that there are three persons in that one God. The capacity of theologians to persuade believers that two or three persons are really one God must rank as one of the great marvels of Christian history. We wonder how normally reasonable people can so readily accept what is ultimately declared to be an incomprehensible mystery. This is all the more remarkable when the Bible's own creedal statements never hint at any such terminology. There is no hint of a conundrum in the transparently simple affirmation that "there is one God, the Father" (1 Cor. 8:6).

Paul never relinquished the idea that one, with reference to God, meant numerically one. He obviously had not abandoned his Jewish unitary monotheism when he declared in a letter to Timothy: "For there is one God, and one mediator between God and men, the *man* Christ Jesus" (1 Tim. 2:5). Here, one person only, the Father, is declared to be the *one* God. In the same sentence, another individual is called *the man* Christ Jesus. This imposes a considerable strain on Trinitarianism. Paul upholds the same creed in his letter to the church at Ephesus. He speaks of "the God of our Lord Jesus Christ, the Father of glory" (Eph. 1:17) and goes on to assert in a later chapter that "there is one body and one Spirit...*one Lord*, one faith, one baptism, *one God* and Father of all" (Eph. 4:4-6). We all understand the "one Spirit" and the "one hope" to be numerically one. But God, for Paul, is also one, in the mathematical sense. He is "the Father of our Lord Jesus Messiah." Paul's point of view is no different when he writes to the Galatians: "Now a mediator is not for one party only; *whereas God is only one*" (Gal. 3:20).

There is a remarkable consistency in Paul's writings when he speaks of God as a single being, namely the Father of Jesus. To

---

[11] Ibid.

say that Paul made the transition to belief in a multipersonal being is most problematic. His creedal declarations are distinctly in line with the unrestricted monotheism of Jesus and the whole Jewish heritage which they shared.

When Paul insists "that there is no God but one," he goes on to explain, "however not all men have this knowledge" (1 Cor. 8:4, 7). We are tempted to think that not much has changed since the first century. Condensing Paul's plain statements in 1 Corinthians 8:4, 6, we have the assertion that "there is no God but the Father." Trinitarianism must surely bow before this pure monotheism. Perhaps Thomas Jefferson's polemic against Trinitarian dogma may not be too harsh. He regarded it as a relapse from the "true religion Jesus founded in the unity of God into unintelligible polytheism." Writing to Jared Sparks, a minister friend, he regretted the subsequent growth of the dogma which he called the "hocus-pocus phantasm of a God like another Cerberus [the three-headed dog in Greek mythology who guarded the gates to Hades], with one body and three heads."[12]

It was Paul who expressed to the church at Corinth his fear "lest as the serpent deceived Eve by his craftiness, your minds should be led astray from the *simplicity* and purity of devotion to Christ. For if one comes and preaches *another Jesus* whom we have not preached...you put up with this beautifully!" (2 Cor. 11:3, 4). We contend that the notion of God as one person is simplicity itself. A God who is two or three persons, yet only one being, is complex in the extreme. Not the least of the problems of the Trinity is the fact that Jesus and God are obviously, in the Bible, two distinct persons in the modern sense of that word — as much different individuals as any father and son.

Not without reason, the words of Paul have been vulnerable to the criticism that they sometimes seem contradictory. This has added fuel to the flames of the Trinitarian controversy. Peter warned that there are in Paul's writings "some things hard to understand, which the untaught and unstable distort, as they do also the rest of the Scriptures, to their own destruction" (2 Pet.

---

[12] C.B. Sanford, *The Religious Life of Thomas Jefferson*, 88, 89.

3:16). If this is so, there is all the more reason to base our understanding of Paul's doctrine of God on his explicit creedal declarations. By no means should we allow other, less clear passages in his writings to obscure the transparently simple propositions with which he defines the Godhead.

Philippians 2

Many have viewed Paul's statement in Philippians 2:5-8 as proof that he believed in a Messiah who was both preexistent and God in his own right. The passage reads as follows:

> Have this attitude among yourselves which was also in Christ Jesus, who, although he existed in the form of God, did not regard equality with God a thing to be grasped, but emptied himself, taking the form of a bond-servant and being made in the likeness of men. And being found in appearance as a man, he humbled himself by becoming obedient to the point of death, even to death on a cross.

A number of Paul's primary statements about the One God should be recalled as we approach this passage:

> (1) To the only wise God, through Jesus Christ, be the glory forever (Rom. 16:27).

> (2) For there is one God, and one mediator also between God and men, the man Christ Jesus (1 Tim. 2:5).

> (3) There is one body...one Lord, one faith...one God and Father of all (Eph. 4:4-6).

> (4) There is no God but one...There is one God, the Father...and one Lord, Jesus Christ (1 Cor. 8:4, 6).

> (5) The blessed and only Sovereign, the King of Kings and Lord of Lords, who alone possesses immortality and dwells in unapproachable light, whom no man has seen or can see (1 Tim. 6:15, 16).

If Paul knew Jesus was a coequal, preexistent member of the Godhead, could he have penned the texts quoted above which obviously restrict the One God to one person, the Father? If so, the charge that he had confused his converts about the nature of the Godhead would seem to be in order. It is also remarkable that Luke, who chronicled Paul's ministry in the book of Acts, fails to make the slightest mention of Paul's new-found truth about the Triune Deity. Paul made the claim for himself that "he did not shrink from declaring the whole purpose of God" (Acts 20:27). Surely somewhere this momentous knowledge about the Trinitarian Godhead would have emerged in his writings and sermons if he had considered it an important part of Christian tradition.

Paul made repeated reference to the *one God*, meaning the Father alone, even in contexts where both the Father and the Son are mentioned together. And there is a striking absence of any unambiguous statement showing Jesus to be the preexistent God-man, a member of the eternal Godhead, and fully deserving the title "God" in the absolute sense. Paul does not blur the distinction between the *one God*, the Father, and Jesus, His Son, the Lord Messiah. However much he insists that the two function in complete harmony, he never forgets that the Father is the One God of his monotheistic heritage. It is perplexing to think that, in the midst of all his insistence that God is a unique person, he would, without explanation, ask us to believe that Jesus is also the one God. Such a drastic overthrow of the framework of true religion would have aroused the anger of the Jewish segment of the Church and have been the cause of extended controversy. There is no evidence for any such debate.

We must avoid at all costs reading our own twentieth-century interpretations into the writings of the first-century Church. Words must be permitted to mean what they meant in their own context. Paul's thinking is consistent. He expressed himself elsewhere with complete clarity when he defined who the One God was. With many commentators, ancient and modern, we question whether the early Church really understood this passage in Philippians as a forerunner of the Nicene formula — that Jesus was very God of very God, eternally preexistent and creator?

James Dunn approaches the text attempting to lay aside the tendency to read later Christological developments into Paul's ideas: "Our task has once again been the crucial but difficult one of trying to attune our twentieth-century ears to the concepts and overtones of the 50s and 60s of the first century AD in the eastern Mediterranean."[13] He concludes that "the preexistence-incarnation interpretation of Philippians 2:6-11, etc., owes more to the later Gnostic redeemer myth than it does to Philippians 2:6-11." He warns us of the danger of reading into Paul's words the conclusions of a later generation of theologians, the "Fathers" of the Greek Church in the centuries following the completion of the New Testament writings.[14]

It is widely acknowledged that we tend to find in Scripture exactly what we have conceived as already being there, since none of us can easily face the threatening possibility that our "received" understanding does not coincide with the Bible. (The problem is compounded if we are involved in teaching or preaching the Bible.) A religious doctrine which has been accepted intellectually and emotionally is dislodged with great difficulty.

The context of Paul's remarks in Philippians 2 shows him urging the members of his congregation to be humble. It has been asked whether it is in any way probable that Paul would enforce this simple lesson by asking his readers to adopt the frame of mind of one who, having been eternally God, made the decision to become man? Is that sort of comparison in any way relevant to our human condition? It might also seem strange for Paul to refer to the preexistent Jesus as Jesus, the Messiah, thus reading back into eternity the name and office he received at birth.

Paul elsewhere does not hesitate to call Jesus a man. He often defines the Messiah's role by drawing on parallels between Adam and the man Jesus. This is clearly shown in 1 Corinthians 15:45-47 where Paul writes: "So it is written, 'The first man, Adam, became a living soul.' The last Adam [Jesus] became a life-giving spirit...The first man is from the earth, earthy; the

---

[13] *Christology in the Making*, 125.
[14] Ibid., 128.

second man is from heaven." Paul insists that Jesus is still, even
at his Second Coming, *man*, as was Adam who was made from
the dust of the ground. Paul notes in Romans 5:12-15:

> Through one man [Adam] sin entered into the
> world...Nevertheless death reigned from Adam until
> Moses over those who had not sinned in the likeness of
> the offense of Adam, who is a *type* of him [Jesus] who is
> to come...For if by the transgression of the one the many
> died, much more did the grace of God and the free gift of
> the *one man*, Jesus Christ, abound to many.

In Philippians 2 Paul describes the exalted status of the man
Jesus. As the reflection of God, his Father, he was in the "form
of God" (the text does not say he *was* God), but did not consider
such "equality with God" a privilege to be exploited for his own
glory. Jesus, who as Messiah *was* invested with a functional
equality with God and was destined to sit at the right hand of the
Father, humbled himself by being the servant of mankind, even
to the point of submitting to a criminal's death on the cross.
Jesus did not take advantage of his royal position as God's legal
representative but adopted the character of a slave. The contrast
is between the rank of God — Jesus being God's commissioner
— and the rank of a servant. The contrast is not, as is often
thought, between *being* God in eternity and becoming man.[15]
Giving up his right to rule, and refusing Satan's offer of power
over the world's kingdoms (Matt. 4:8, 9), Jesus obediently
played the role of a servant willing to suffer at the hands of a
hostile world. What Paul has in mind is the career of the *man*
Christ Jesus (1 Tim. 2:5), not the incarnation of a preexistent
member of the Godhead. Jesus' humility is the exact opposite of
the arrogance of Adam. The former did not abuse his God-given
status as reflecting God his Father, nor did he take advantage of
his privilege for selfish ends. Adam, under the Devil's influence,
tried to grasp at an equality with God to which he was not

---

[15] In Phil. 2:7 there is no mention of being born. The word *genomenos*
simply means "becoming." Jesus adopted the status of servant and
appeared as an ordinary man.

entitled. Jesus, by perfect obedience to God, was able to mirror the mind and personality of the One God, his Father.

In describing the exemplary life of the Messiah on earth, Paul intended no reference to a preexistent being. He was appealing to the Philippians to be humble like Jesus. Jesus had been a model of humility and service. Yet he had been born into the royal family of the House of David and had qualified through self-denial for the exalted status of world ruler, as Psalm 2 had predicted centuries before he was born. When asked by Pilate: "So you are a king?" his answer was, "You speak correctly. This is why I was born, and for this I have come into the world" (John 18:37). Jesus overcame a natural ambition to conquer the world (though he will legitimately conquer Antichrist's forces at his *second* coming). His example of patient submission to the will of God had led to his exaltation to the right hand of the Father. The point was not that a preexistent member of the Trinity had regained a position temporarily surrendered, but that a real human being, the Messiah, in whom the character of the Father was perfectly reflected (Col. 1:15), had demonstrated humility and obedience and had been supremely vindicated and exalted by God. Paul elsewhere describes Jesus' career as a demonstration of humility when he observes that "although [the Messiah] was rich, yet for your sake he became poor, so that you through his poverty might become rich" (2 Cor. 8:9). The Messiah, though designated King of Israel and the world, sacrificed himself for others. Without of course making the same claims as Jesus, Paul uses similar language of his own career. He was "poor, though making many rich, having nothing yet possessing all things" (2 Cor. 6:10) and "sought no glory...when we might have been burdensome as the Apostles of Christ" (1 Thess. 2:6). Paul also saw himself and fellow Apostles as Messianic suffering servants when he applied Isaiah's "servant prophecies" to his own mission (Acts 13:47; cp. Isa. 42:6; 49:6).

The traditional Trinitarian reading of Philippians 2 depends almost entirely on understanding Jesus' condition "in the form of God" as a reference to a preexistent life as God in heaven, instead of legal identity with God as a human person on earth. Unfortunately translators have done much to bolster this view.

The verb "was" in the phrase "was in the form of God" occurs frequently in the New Testament and by no means carries the sense of "existing in eternity," though some versions try to force that meaning into it. In 1 Corinthians 11:7, Paul said that a man ought not to cover his head since he is in the image and glory of God. The verb "is" here is a form of the same verb rendered "was" describing Jesus as "in the form of God." Paul's intention was not to introduce the vast subject of an eternally divine, second member of the Trinity who became man, but to teach an important lesson in humility, based on the example of the historical Jesus. There is no clear evidence in this passage that Paul was a Trinitarian who believed in the traditional doctrine of the Incarnation.

We suggest the following rendering of the original of Philippians 2:5-8: "Adopt the same attitude as Messiah Jesus: Who, though having divine status, did not consider his equality with God something to be exploited for his own advantage, but made nothing of his rank by taking the role of a slave and by being like other men. Appearing to be like an ordinary man, he humbled himself by being obedient to the point of death, even death by crucifixion." There is nothing in the text which requires us to think of a preexistent being.

The Messiah's exaltation to the right hand of God is the fulfillment of Psalm 110:1. It has been well argued that the text should read, "*in* the name of Jesus every knee will bow," not "*at* the name of Jesus..." (Phil. 2:10). Thus the supreme exaltation of Jesus to the right hand of the Father does not alter the fact that all that Jesus accomplished is for the glory of God. The lord at God's right hand, it must be remembered, is *adoni* ("lord"), which is never the title of Deity.

Colossians 1:15-17

To emphasize the exalted position of the resurrected Messiah, his authority over all rivals and his supreme position in God's plan, Paul wrote to the people at Colossae:

> And he is the image of the invisible God, the first-born of all creation. For by [literally, "in"] him all things were created, both in the heavens and on the earth, visible and

invisible, whether thrones or dominions or rulers or authorities — all things have been created by [literally, "through"] him and for him. And he is before all things and in him all things hold together (Col. 1:16).

Some have considered this passage sufficient evidence to overthrow all Paul said elsewhere about the Christian creed as belief in "one God, the Father." Several points should be noted. The Trinitarian scholar, James Dunn, speaking of the above passage in Colossians 1:15-20, makes a crucial observation:

We must grasp the fact that Paul was not seeking to win men to belief in a preexistent being. He did not have to establish the viability of speaking of preexistent wisdom. Such language was commonly used, common ground, and was no doubt familiar to most of his readers. Nor was he arguing that Jesus was a particular preexistent being...What he was saying is that wisdom, whatever precisely that term meant for his readers, is now most fully expressed in Jesus — Jesus is the exhaustive embodiment of divine wisdom; all the divine fullness dwelt in him. The mistake which many make (unconsciously) is to turn Paul's argument around and make it point in the wrong direction. Because language which seems to envisage preexistent divine beings is strange to modern ears, it is easy to assume (by an illegitimate transfer of twentieth-century presuppositions to the first century) that this is why the language was used (to promote belief in preexistent divine intermediaries) and that Paul was attempting to identify Christ with or as such a being.[16]

We quote Professor Dunn at length because of his important statement about the danger of reading Paul as though he must have been familiar with the much later decisions of church councils. Paul should be read in his own Hebrew context. Dunn

---

[16] *Christology in the Making*, 195.

does not write as an anti-Trinitarian. But he finds no support for the Trinity in this passage. He continues:

> But Paul's talk was of course conditioned by the culture and cosmological presuppositions of his own day. So he was not arguing for the existence of preexistent divine beings or for the existence of any particular divine being...And the meaning is, given the understanding of this language within Jewish monotheism, that Jesus is to be seen as the wise activity of God, as the wisdom and embodiment of God's wisdom more fully than any previous manifestation of the same wisdom whether in creation or in covenant.[17]

Dunn's analysis is sufficient to show that this passage of Scripture does not establish belief in a Deity of two or three persons. Several further points should be made. Paul specifically calls Jesus the first-born of all creation. Taken in its natural sense, the expression first-born excludes the notion of an uncreated, eternal being. To be born requires a beginning. God's first-born is "the highest of the kings of the earth" (Ps. 89:27). Paul employs a well-known Messianic title. Jesus, in the mind of Paul, is not God, but the Messiah — and there is an enormous difference.

According to many translations, Paul says that "all things were created *by* him [the Messiah]." The prepositions in Colossians 1:16 need to be translated exactly (as seen in the marginal versions of standard Bibles). What Paul actually wrote was that "all things" — in this case "thrones, dominions, rulers and authorities" — were created "in" Jesus, "through" him and "for" him. It was not that Jesus was the creator in the opening verse of Genesis, but that he was the center of God's cosmic hierarchy. All authorities were to be subjected to the Son who would finally hand all back to his Father, the principal to whom he owed allegiance, that "God [the Father] might be all in all" (1

---

[17] Ibid., 195, 196.

Cor. 15:28).[18] It would be strange to say that Jesus created all things for himself (Col. 1:16). The point is rather that God made all things with Jesus in mind, with him as the occasion for creation, and thus for him. As first-born, Jesus is heir to the universe which God brought into existence with His promised Son as the designated heir of the creation. Paul is focusing in this passage on the new creation initiated by the resurrection of Jesus, who is the first-born from the dead (Col. 1:18). The reference to creation of angelic authorities does not imply the existence of Jesus at the time of the original creation. As always context is the important factor in interpretation. Paul's concentration in this passage is on "inheritance," "kingdom," and "authorities" (Col. 1:12, 13, 16). This strongly suggests that he has in mind the Messiah's headship over the entire creation as the new order which God had in mind from the beginning, and of which Jesus as first-born is the appointed head.

Expressions which, as Dunn says, sound remote to twentieth-century ears and therefore need especially careful handling, provide no basis for belief in Jesus' preexistence. Paul believed that God planned that the Messiah should have preeminence over all that has been created, visible or invisible, in heaven or on earth, either thrones, dominions, rulers or authorities. Jesus was the starting point of all God's creative activity — the key to God's entire purpose as well as the embodiment of God's wisdom. The Messiah, however, was not an eternal being but a human person to be revealed at his appointed time, now qualified, as first-born from the dead, to "head up" the new order (Eph. 1:10).

---

[18] We note that according to J.H. Moulton, ed., *Grammar of New Testament Greek* (T&T Clark, 1963), Col. 1:16 should be rendered "for *because of* him [Jesus]..." (3:253). This gives a very different sense from "by him..." Note also the *Expositor's Greek Commentary* (ed. W. Robertson Nicoll, Grand Rapids: Eerdmans, 1967) on this verse: "*en auto*: This does not mean 'by Him'" (504). Translators seem to have paid little attention to these authorities.

1 Corinthians 10:4

Many believers in the personal preexistence of Jesus have appealed to the words of the Apostle in 1 Corinthians 10:4, where he says of the Israelites in the wilderness that they all drank "the same spiritual drink: for they drank of that spiritual rock that followed them; and that rock was Christ." As John Cunningham stated:

> It is argued from this text that Christ personally accompanied the people of Israel as they journeyed through the wilderness to the promised land. To lend support to this theme, Deuteronomy 32:4 and Psalm 18:2 are cited because Yahweh (God) is there described as a rock. It is reasoned that since God is the rock and Christ is also the rock who accompanied Israel, Christ must therefore be Yahweh or the God of the Old Testament.[19]

A text which surveys God's activity over the ages says, "God spoke long ago to the fathers through the prophets in many portions and in many ways, but [in contrast] in these last days has spoken to us in His Son" (Heb. 1:1, 2). This would seem to confirm that until his human birth Jesus was not Son of God nor God's messenger to man. This same book of Hebrews points out that the Word was spoken through angels in Old Testament times (Heb. 2:2). If the message to Israel was through the same preexistent Jesus who became man, the writer of this New Testament book seems to lack any such information. Messages were given through prophets and angels certainly, but never was there a hint that the Old Testament message was transmitted through the one who later came to be identified as the Son.

1 Corinthians 10:4 taken by itself, without considering its context or Paul's use of Hebrew ways of thinking, might suggest that Christ was alive before his birth. There are numerous other Scriptures in which angels were the instruments used to convey God's messages to Israel. Stephen speaks of Moses and the

---

[19] "That Rock Was Christ," Restoration Fellowship, 1981. We are indebted to this writer for the substance of the argument as well as to James Dunn's *Christology in the Making*, 183, 184.

giving of the Law: "This is the one who was in the congregation in the wilderness together with the angel who was speaking to him on Mt. Sinai...He received the oracles to pass on to you" (Acts 7:38). Acts 7:53 states that they had received the Law as ordained by angels and yet did not keep it. Paul also speaks of the role of angels in contrast to a later revealer called the "seed" (the Messiah): "Why the Law then? It was added because of transgressions, having been ordained through angels...until the 'seed' [Jesus] would come, to whom the promise had been made" (Gal. 3:19). Paul goes on to confirm the oneness of God: "Now a mediator is not for one party only, whereas *God is only one*" (Gal. 3:20). It is clear in each of these passages that the giving of the Law through angels forms an important part of the argument. But it should be noted that the common theme is the superiority of the Gospel to the Law. The Law was mediated only by angels but the Good News (Gospel) was brought by the Son of God and is therefore incomparably superior. Certainly Paul did not believe that Jesus was a preexisting angel.

Christ could not have had any part either in giving the Law to Israel or in ministering to the Israelites in the wilderness. Paul's use of the word "seed" or descendant is most pointed. The "seed" — identified as Christ — had not yet arrived and was not yet active in God's service.

It is clear that for Paul the "seed" referred to here and in other places, the seed of Abraham (Gen. 22:18), the seed of Judah (Gen. 49:10), and the seed of David,[20] means specifically Jesus the Christ, the promised descendant of the patriarchs and David. Romans 1:3 contains a direct reference to the origin of Christ as God's Son. The Gospel concerns "His Son, who was born of a descendant [seed] of David according to the flesh." The repeated insistence on a Son who was born of a woman and who was the descendant of a human being is inescapable. The Messiah was to arise from the human race. This is exactly what the Jews of the day and the early Church believed and expected. For Paul to have taught that the Messiah was actually and

---

[20] 2 Sam. 7:12-14 with Isa. 11:1; Rom. 1:3; 2 Tim. 2:8.

personally present with Israel in the wilderness, already the Son of God, would have been a staggering contradiction of the words of the prophets.

We must guard against an over-literal, wooden reading of 1 Corinthians 10:4, bearing in mind the Hebraic use of symbolism and Jewish ways of speaking. It is not uncommon for Scripture to use the verb "to be" in a less than literal sense. Jesus said, "This cup is my blood of the New Covenant" (Luke 22:20). The verb "is" does not imply one-to-one identity; the language is figurative: "The cup represents my blood."

The immediate context of 1 Corinthians 10:4 contains clues to the way Paul is thinking. Paul sees Israel's experiences in the wilderness as examples — "types" or models of present Christian experience. As Paul says, "these things happened to them 'typically'" (1 Cor. 10:11). The passing of the Israelites through the Red Sea was a "figure" of Christian baptism. The "spiritual" food mentioned in verse three is clearly the manna miraculously given daily to Israel over a period of 40 years. They also drank from a "spiritual rock."

To use this single reference to the rock which followed Israel as proof of a pre-human Jesus misses the point of Paul's lesson. It also overlooks the fact that the Jews did not expect the Messiah to be anything other than a human person. A closer look at the Old Testament story Paul has in mind shows that there are two incidents involving a rock recorded during the wilderness wanderings of the Israelites. It is important to notice the difference between them.

The first occurred just after the miraculous giving of the manna. Israel arrived at Rephidim and immediately began to complain about a lack of water, whereupon God commanded Moses to strike the rock. Water gushed out and the people's thirst was satisfied (Exod. 17:1-6). The striking of the rock typified the fact that Christ, our rock, was later to be smitten for the sins of mankind. The water also foreshadowed the miraculous giving of the Holy Spirit, the water of life described by Jesus: "If any man is thirsty, let him come to me and drink" (John 7:37). The rock in the wilderness was a representation of the Messiah who was yet to come as provider of the Holy Spirit.

The second "rock" incident occurred toward the end of the wandering in the wilderness. Again Israel complained of a lack of water and again God provided for their needs. This time He clearly instructed Moses to speak to the rock, but in his anger Moses disobeyed and struck the rock twice (Num. 20:1-12). In smiting the rock instead of speaking to it Moses was guilty of destroying the meaning of the "type." The rock in Exodus typified Christ in the flesh, smitten to give to us the water of life, while the rock in Numbers typified Christ our High Priest not to be smitten twice but only to be addressed, to supply the water of life.

The first incident occurred at the beginning of the wanderings, the second at the end; both incidents form a parable of Christ's continuous presence with his people now during their "wilderness wanderings," the Christian journey towards the "promised" land of the Kingdom of God.

The two incidents we have looked at took place in entirely different locations and there is a different Hebrew word for "rock" used in each place. In Exodus 17 the word is *tsur*, and in Numbers 20 it is *sela*. What then does Paul mean when he states that "they drank of that spiritual rock which *followed* them"? Obviously, a literal rock did not accompany Israel through the wilderness. A better answer is that Paul is using the language of Christian experience and reading it back into the Old Testament type. This is shown clearly by his reference to baptism at the beginning of his discussion. The Israelites were not literally baptized. In fact, we are told that the water did not come near them; they walked dryshod through the Red Sea. But their experience is a close enough parallel for Paul to say they were "baptized into Moses." Likewise, the rock did not literally follow them. It was simply a "model" or "type" of Christ accompanying Christians through life. This, in fact, is exactly what Paul himself asserts: "All these things happened to them *typically*" (1 Cor. 10:11).

The evidence is much too slight to support the idea that Paul was attempting to introduce a new dogma about a preexistent God/man. This would clash with his own statements elsewhere about how the Christ came into being. If he were proposing that the Messiah was really a person coequal with God, such a radical departure from his Jewish heritage would require much more elaboration.

We must guard against the mistake of reading later Trinitarian tradition into first-century Hebraic literature. The truth about Jesus' identity and origin must be based strictly on the information available from the writings of the early Church as recorded in the Scriptures. It is all too easy to fall into the trap of reading Scripture through lenses tinged with doctrines formulated in the second to fifth centuries.

There are distinct prophecies relating to Jesus in the Old Testament, but none takes him outside the limits of the human family. Most will agree that the first prophecy concerning a coming Savior appears in Genesis where God told the serpent, "I will put enmity between you and the woman, and between your seed and her seed; you shall bruise him on the heel and he shall bruise you on the head" (Gen. 3:15). It was clearly the human descendant of Eve who would eventually subdue the serpent or Satan. Both Jews and Christians believe that this prophecy was to be fulfilled in the Messiah; but neither group finds anything in this text about the Messiah already being alive.

When we hear Paul preaching to the Gentile world represented by the men of Athens, his words are reminiscent of an Old Testament prophet. Referring to the One God of Israel he says: "The God who made the world and all things in it, since He is Lord of heaven and earth, does not dwell in temples made with hands" (Acts 17:24). This is similar to Isaiah's statement: "I, the Lord, am the maker of all things, stretching out the heavens by Myself, and spreading out the earth; who was with Me?" (Isa. 44:24). To interfere with this fundamental Jewish monotheism and introduce another uncreated person as an active agent in the Genesis creation is offensive to Paul's evident belief in the basic tenets of Jewish theology, primarily its unbending unitary monotheism.

It was not until the fourth century, over three hundred years after the death of the founder of Christianity, that church officials found it necessary to formulate Trinitarian dogma officially and impose it on believers as a formal condition for membership in the Church and for salvation.

We must ask how and why this happened. Many present-day believers have had little exposure to the story of the development of the Trinitarian creed. If neither Jesus nor Paul ever abandoned belief in the Old Testament concept of God as a single person, just how did belief in a Godhead of two or three persons arise? The story of the emergence of this new, alien and massively influential belief system is remarkable.

V. FROM THE HEBREW WORLD OF THE BIBLE
TO THE TWENTIETH CENTURY
VIA GREEK PHILOSOPHY

"Post-apostolic writings are mixed with ideas foreign to apostolic Christianity. The latter is unintentionally distorted and misrepresented." — G. T. Purves

> To properly study the discipline known as philosophy, it is not enough just to learn what great thinkers believed. You must learn to think for yourself. Accept something only if, after you have thought about it, it seems correct to you. Then you will be doing and not just learning about philosophy; you will be a philosopher.[1]

This excellent advice applies equally to the study of theology. It prompts us to reflect on the critical issue of the changes which came over apostolic Christianity when, beginning in the second century, the faith became accommodated to its Graeco-Roman environment. Biblical Christianity itself, despite differences of emphasis within the New Testament canon, presents a "philosophy." It claims to define what is of ultimate value (e.g., "Seek first the Kingdom of God," Matt. 6:33; "There is one God, the Father...and one Lord Jesus Messiah," 1 Cor. 8:6, etc.); it offers an account of the meaning of existence and of a supreme divine purpose being worked out in history. Our concern, however, is to explore the question as to how far the original "faith once delivered to the saints," which Jude urged his contemporaries not to abandon (Jude 3), may gradually and

---

[1] Rogers and Baird, *Introduction to Philosophy* (Harper & Row, 1981), 21.

often imperceptibly have suffered a radical alteration under the influence of alien philosophies. If such a process has taken place, it would seem to be in keeping with a "truth-seeking" philosophy that we endeavor to recover what has been lost or obscured.

Non-Trinitarians have frequently been identified with the "heretics," who were inclined in return to charge orthodoxy with having switched the labels. However, a number of commentators from the orthodox camp itself have sounded an alarm that all may not be well with a situation in which "Christians adapted to the [Hellenistic] culture in order to survive and in an effort to win converts."[2] Eberhard Griesebach, in an academic lecture on "Christianity and Humanism," delivered in 1938, observed that "in its encounter with Greek philosophy Christianity became theology. That was the fall of Christianity."[3]

The problem thus highlighted stems from the fact that traditional orthodoxy, while it claims to find its origins in Scripture, in fact contains elements drawn from a synthesis of Scripture and neo-Platonism.[4] The mingling of Hebrew and Greek thinking was set in motion first in the second century by an influx of Hellenism through the Church Fathers, whose theology was colored by the Platonists Plotinus and Porphyry.[5] The effects of the Greek influence are widely recognized by theologians, though they go largely unnoticed by many believers.

G.A.T. Knight states that:

> Many people today, even believing people, are far from understanding the basis of their faith...Quite unwittingly they depend upon the philosophy of the Greeks rather than upon the Word of God for an understanding of the world they live in. An instance of this is the prevailing belief amongst Christians in the immortality of the soul.

---

[2] Ibid., 5.

[3] Cited by Robert Friedmann in *The Theology of Anabaptism* (Herald Press, 1973), 50.

[4] Rogers and Baird, *Introduction to Philosophy*, 5.

[5] Ibid.

Many believers despair of this world; they despair of any meaning in a world where suffering and frustration seem to rule. And so they look for a release for their souls from the weight of the flesh, and they hope for an entry into the "world of the spirit," as they call it, a place where their souls will find a blessedness they cannot discover in the flesh. The Old Testament, which was of course the Scriptures of the early Church, has no word at all for the modern (or ancient Greek) idea of "soul." We have no right to read this modern word into St. Paul's word "psyche," for by it he was not expounding what Plato had meant by the word; he was expressing what Isaiah and what Jesus meant by it...There is one thing sure we can say at this point and that is that the popular doctrine of the soul's immortality cannot be traced back to the biblical teaching.[6]

Despite these warnings, however, popular preaching, claiming the name of Christ, continues to promote just such a doctrine of escape to heaven at death as a disembodied soul.

The complaint that Scripture is constantly read through spectacles tinged with neo-Platonism was made also by Neill Hamilton, whose concern was with the effect of Greek thinking on our reading of biblical eschatology (doctrine about the future): "My impression is that the consensus of opinion in the Church is still more controlled by an extra-Christian idea of the immortality of the soul, than by any conception formed after listening faithfully to the New Testament witness."[7]

This evidence warns us that new layers of meaning have been superimposed on the biblical documents. The process must result in a loosening of the bond which ties us to the original intention of the biblical writers. Clearly, if we transfer a given term into a new linguistic context, there is a grave danger that its meaning may be entirely lost. In fact, the Bible "story" might

---

[6] *Law and Grace* (Philadelphia: Westminster Press, 1962), 78, 79.

[7] "The Last Things in the Last Decade," *Interpretation* 71 (April, 1960): 136.

thus be transformed almost beyond recognition. The question arises as to how well we are hearing the voice of the Apostles, especially if we are unaware of the tension which our heavily Greek-influenced heritage imposes on our reading of Scripture.

The translation of the Bible into the language of neo-Platonism seems to have affected some of the primary terms dealing with the biblical view of man. It has also worked to obscure the biblical view of Christ and thus of the Godhead itself. The issue is critical since the creeds defining the Trinity for posterity were formed in a Graeco-Roman milieu.

The Wider Christological Issues

The impetus for this exploration into the biblical portrait of Jesus and his relation to God arises from a prolonged reflection on the troubled history of Christology. The findings of scholars of the pre-Nicene development of the doctrine of Christ frequently suggest that a corrupting influence was at work on the Christian faith as it moved away from the shelter of its original Hebrew environment into the menacing atmosphere of Greek philosophy. The transition may have involved much more than simply a legitimate restatement of Christian truth for Gentile believers. The Christ of the fourth- and fifth-century church councils emerged as a figure essentially different from the Jesus whom the New Testament writers proclaim, with a united testimony, to be the promised Messiah in whom God's purpose for the world is being worked out.

A number of striking quotations will illustrate the point that all was not well with the faith as it succumbed to the temptation to borrow religious concepts from its pagan environment. L.W. Grensted, writing in 1933, observed about the development of Christianity that:

> The heritage from philosophy came in more insidiously. In the second century we find Justin Martyr and others proclaiming Christianity as a philosophy of the schools...The logos of Stoicism is identified with the Logos of John...The growing web of fantasy...still remained a very real danger, and so remains down to this present day...Meanwhile, and most serious of all, a

radical confusion had fallen upon the doctrine of God. The personal God of Judaism was very imperfectly fused with the demigods of popular Greek religion and with the metaphysical abstracts whereby the philosophers had sought to make the concept of God adequate as a basis for thought and for being.[8]

Christology was not left untouched by the reshaping of the doctrine of God; but can the New Testament, with its heritage in the prophets of Israel, be invaded by Greek philosophy without the loss of an essential element? Filson's concern is evident in the following statement:

> The primary kinship of the New Testament is not with this Gentile environment, but rather with the Jewish heritage and environment of which we spoke in the first half of this lecture. We are often led by our traditional creeds and theology to think in terms dictated by Gentile and especially Greek concepts. We know that no later than the second century there began the systematic effort of the Apologists to show that the Christian faith perfected the best in Greek philosophy...The New Testament speaks always with disapproval and usually with blunt denunciation of Gentile cults and philosophies. It agrees essentially with the Jewish indictment of the pagan world.[9]

Misgivings about the way in which Greek philosophy has damaged the faith are common enough. Norman Snaith's warnings are among the most outspoken:

> There have always been Jews who have sought to make terms with the Gentile world, and it has in time meant the death of Judaism for all such. There have been Christians from the beginning who have sought to do this. Often it has been done unconsciously, but whether

---

[8] *The Person of Christ* (London: Nisbet and Co. Ltd., 1933), 122.

[9] F. Filson, *The New Testament Against Its Environment* (London: SCM Press, 1950), 26, 27.

consciously or unconsciously, the question needs to be faced as to whether it is right. Our position is that the reinterpretation of biblical theology in terms of the ideas of the Greek philosophers has been both widespread throughout the centuries and everywhere destructive to the essence of Christian faith...The whole Bible, the New Testament as well as the Old Testament, is based on the Hebrew attitude and approach. We are of the firm opinion that this ought to be recognized on all hands to a greater extent. It is clear to us, and we hope that we have made it clear in these pages to others, that there is often a great difference between Christian theology and biblical theology...*Neither Catholic nor Protestant theology is based on biblical theology.* In each case we have a dominion of Christian theology by Greek thought...We hold that there can be no right answer [to the question, What is Christianity?] until we have come to a clear view of the distinctive ideas of both Old and New Testaments and their difference from the pagan ideas which so largely have dominated Christian thought.[10]

Contemporary writers on Christology may be found in one of two camps. The first stalwartly maintains the so-called orthodox view of the person of Christ despite the enigmas of the figure they describe:

Jesus...could be "the only Son" ("only-begotten" means unique), and man's true representative, "perfect God and perfect man," with two "natures" in one "person," without confusion, change, division or severance (a quotation from the doctrinal decision of the Council of Chalcedon) [451 AD]. Jesus was "man," not "a man"; his ego, personality, was divine, preexistent, clothing itself and operating in a human body; He "came into history, not out of it"; He was God in and working through man, not a man raised to the divine level. His

---

[10] *The Distinctive Ideas of the Old Testament* (London: Epworth Press, 1944), 187, 185, 188, emphasis added.

> manhood was full and complete, he was fully "integrated," even if subject to the limitations of a Jew of his age and place...The foregoing may strike us as dry and academic and abstruse. That is the result of our approach, that of the Greek mind...Not only did Jesus and his first disciples accept Jewish monotheism without question; He expressly reaffirmed it (St. Mark 12:29ff.). Belief in one God the Creator is thus the foundation of the Christian faith, and we must discard at the outset any idea that the doctrine of the Trinity either abandons or modifies it.[11]

On the other hand, many in the course of Christian history have wondered whether such "orthodox" definitions of the person of Christ can be so easily wedded with Jesus' plainly unitarian creed, as cited by Mark (12:29ff.). The contemporary Roman Catholic scholar, Thomas Hart, reviews orthodox Christology with the reminder that:

> Jesus is called man in the generic sense, but not a man. He has a human nature but is not a human person. The person in Him is the second Person of the Blessed Trinity. Jesus does not have a human personal center. This is how the Council [of Chalcedon] gets around the problem of a split personality.

He goes on to examine:

> the shortcomings that many theologians find today in the Chalcedonian model...1. Divine nature and human nature cannot be set side by side and numbered as if they were similar quantities. 2. The Chalcedonian formula makes a genuine humanity impossible. [This difficulty] flows from the divinity overshadowing the humanity and from Jesus not having a human personal center...3. The Chalcedonian formula has a meager basis in Scripture.

---

[11] R.J.W. Bevan, *Steps to Christian Understanding* (Oxford University Press, 1958), 140, 167.

The Council calls Jesus true God. The New Testament shies away from calling Jesus God.[12]

The Problem of Language

A host of problems arises from the traditional proposition that Jesus is "God," in the sense required by orthodox creeds. Does the New Testament really present us with this definition of the Savior, or are we perhaps misunderstanding some of the data, and so distorting the New Testament's Christological message? Is there perhaps a semantic barrier between our customary reading of key New Testament words and the original intention of the authors of Scripture?

An Englishman visiting America and remarking that he is "mad about his flat" should not expect to be understood. The situation will be a good example of Shaw's quip that England and America are two countries separated by a common language. In England, the Englishman will convey the notion that he is "excited about his apartment." Across the Atlantic it will be thought that he is "angry about his flat tire." A similar breakdown in communication occurs if an Englishman announces in America that Tom and Jane have "broken up." Americans will think that the pair has ended a relationship. In England the same words inform us that their school term has ended.

An American was once asked in England: "Do you want a pie?" The question came from a man delivering milk, known in England as a milkman, though the word will have little meaning in America where milk is bought in stores. The American was surprised that the milkman would be selling pies until she realized that what he really intended, veiled by his cockney accent, was, "Do you want to pay?" Again, a serious misunderstanding arose because one party's use of words was foreign to the one he was addressing.

A similar "crossing of lines" occurs when Bible readers are unfamiliar with the "language" of the authors of the New

---

[12] *To Know and Follow Jesus,* 44-48.

Testament. This does not mean that everyone needs to learn Greek. They must, however, appreciate that the New Testament Hebrew Christians do not necessarily use words as we do in the twentieth century. (We all recognize that even since 1611, when the King James or Authorized Version was translated, some words have undergone a complete change of meaning.) In order to read the Bible intelligently, we need to enter into the thought-world of the New Testament. We must "hear" words as they heard them. If we do not, we may seriously misunderstand the faith which the Apostles intended to communicate to us.[13]

---

[13] The point was made in an interesting way by a former clergyman of the Church of England who sensed his inability to cope with the documents which he was charged to interpret. David Watson wrote: "A sympathetic study of traditional Jewish religion can reveal the extent to which the modern English Christian gives a meaning to the words of the New Testament *different from that which was in the minds of the Jewish writers.* Greek was the language they used to convey the universal Christian message, but their mode of thinking was to a large extent Hebraic. For a full understanding it is necessary for the modern Christian not only to study the Greek text, but to sense the Hebraic idea which the Jewish writers sought to convey in Greek words. I cannot claim to have become very skilled in this, but made enough progress to discover *how greatly I had misinterpreted the Bible in the past.* Like all ordained Christian ministers I had spoken dogmatically, authoritatively from the pulpit, which no one may occupy without license from a Bishop; and much of what I had said had been misleading, because my own mind was incapable of giving a correct interpretation of the book I was authorized to expound. For me the realization of this fact made nonsense of the distinction between clergy and laity, and was the main cause of my relinquishment of my orders.

"In describing my own intellectual deficiencies, and the process by which I discovered my inability to grasp the meaning of the Bible across the vast linguistic gulf separating me from its Jewish writers, I can surely claim to write with first-hand knowledge. From what I know of the clergy in general I see no reason for supposing that I was peculiar in suffering from this particular deficiency. In fact, the authority of the Protestant ministry as a whole, the claim to be able to understand the Bible and expound it as the word of God, is in my view a vast confidence trick. I am not accusing the clergy of being

The Term "God" and the Issue of the Trinity in John

What, for example, do the biblical writers mean by the all-important word "God"? Do they mean, as we do, an uncreated divine being who has always existed? Very frequently God is the name for the supreme being.[14] But does the word "God" have another meaning in the Bible?

If we report that we have been introduced to the "president," it may be thought that we have met the President of the United States. On the other hand it is quite possible that the context of our remark will allow our audience to know that we mean, say, the president of the local bank. Fortunately there is not much room for misunderstanding. We all recognize that the term "president" can be used at different levels. It is, so to speak, an "elastic" term capable of referring to persons in different offices. The word itself, however, is ambiguous. Its meaning must be determined by its context. We would not consider someone very

---

fraudulent, or even insincere. The confidence trick is collective; individually those who engage in it are deceived by it, just as when I began to expound the Bible from pulpits, I was fully confident that I was able give a correct interpretation.

"Some may believe that the rite of ordination itself bestows divine grace sufficient to overcome any liability to mislead a congregation through an incorrect interpretation. If this view is held, however, it must be reconciled with the indisputable fact that the Christian ministry as a whole has produced a large number of different, and often irreconcilable versions of the Christian faith, all supposed to have been derived from the same biblical record...Any claim that training and ordination produce the only authentic Christian teaching is fraudulent.

"The thirty-nine Articles of the Church of England state specifically in no uncertain terms that true Christian doctrine is derived not from the Church's councils and traditions, but from the Bible alone. Anglo-catholics believe the very opposite; consequently when one of them after induction to a benefice reads the Articles publicly, and declares his assent to them, he virtually commits perjury. It is, however, legalized perjury" (*Christian Myth and Spiritual Reality*, London: Victor Gollanz, 1967, 28-30).

14 *Ho theos*, i.e. "the [one] God," refers in the New Testament to the Father some 1325 times.

intelligent who insisted that the word "president" always and invariably means "President of the United States."

If we read the Bible with our twentieth-century conviction that "God" invariably means an eternal, uncreated being, we quickly run into trouble at 2 Corinthians 4:4, where Satan is called "God." Our original theory about the term "God" has to be adjusted to allow a secondary meaning for God, not to be confused with the use of God in the absolute sense. In John 10:34 we find the plural, "gods." An examination of the context would reveal that Jesus here spoke of the leaders of Israel as "gods." They were representatives of God to whom God addressed His word and as such were given a divine title (Ps. 82:6). But no one would think that they were "Gods" in the same sense as the One God. A Jewish writer of the first century, Philo, speaks of Moses as "god and king": "Did not Moses also enjoy an even greater partnership with the Father and Maker of the universe, being deemed worthy of the same title? For he was named god and king [*theos kai basileus*] of the whole nation."[15]

The words of Thomas, addressed to Jesus in John 20:28, read: "My Lord and my God." Because many readers of the Bible have been conditioned to believe that Jesus is "God" in the sense in which we use that word in the twentieth century, they jump to the conclusion that this must be what Thomas meant. Jesus must therefore be an eternally preexistent being. But if Jesus is "God" in that absolute sense, why only a few verses earlier does Jesus address his Father as "my God," calling Him at the same time "your God," the God of the disciples? When Jesus addressed the Father as "my God" (John 20:17) he acknowledged that he was inferior to God, the Father. Jesus is not, therefore, God in the absolute sense. For Thomas, too, Jesus is "God" in a qualified sense, as Messiah, the supreme legal agent of the One God. The one whom Thomas calls God is himself inferior to the One God addressed by Jesus as his God. Thus understood, Jesus remains within the category of Messiah, Son of God, a category which John expressly imposes on his

---

15 *Life of Moses*, 1:155-158.

entire book (John 20:31). Fundamental to John's whole Christological outlook there are two primary facts: Jesus is to be believed in as "Messiah, Son of God," while the Father's unique status is preserved as "the only true God" (John 17:3) and "the one who alone is God" (John 5:44).

Most significantly, the promised Messiah was given the title God in Psalm 45:6: "Thy throne, O God, is for ever and ever." In the next verse it is made clear that this "God Messiah" has been blessed by *his* God: "Therefore God, thy God, has anointed you..."[16] The highest honor was given to Jesus by Thomas when he addressed him with the royal Messianic titles "Lord" and "God," derived from Psalm 45:6, 11. New Testament evidence that Jesus is God *in the same sense as God the Father* is scant indeed. If we are sensitive to the proportions of the biblical use of the term God, we will note the fact that it refers to the Father over 1325 times in the New Testament, while "God" is used of Jesus only twice with complete certainty (other possible cases in which Jesus is called God are all doubtful, as is well known, for grammatical and syntactical reasons). These facts suggest that the very occasional use of "God" for Jesus is a special reference. Obviously, then, it might be very misleading to say in the twentieth century that "Jesus is God," unless we first understand in what sense that word is used by John (and Thomas whom he reports). Our use of words must not dictate the Bible's usage. We may not simply rely on the sound of a word without inquiring about its meaning. Above all, we must be willing to let go of a dogmatic insistence on acceptance of doctrine without inquiry. Such inflexible adherence to the way we have always believed blocks the search for truth which is the hallmark of the growing Christian (Acts 17:11).

Scholars Point to the Adverse Effects of Philosophy

Nineteenth-century liberalism raised the issue of the negative effect of Greek philosophy on the original faith. The celebrated

---

[16] Heb. 1:8, quoting Ps. 45:6, applies the title God, used in a qualified sense, directly to Jesus.

Adolf Harnack maintained that the Gospel had been obscured by the acute hellenizing which gave rise to traditional formulations about Christ. The desire to separate Jesus and his teaching from the accretions of Greek philosophy encouraged a healthy freedom to explore new ideas. Unfortunately, liberalism developed its own assumptions. We may suspect that its theology was sometimes more an attempt to reassure itself that its own modern beliefs were reflected in the teaching of Jesus, than a successful return to apostolic faith. It appears that the Hebrew thought world of the Bible remained unpopular.

The Spirit of Truth and the spirit of tolerance should not necessarily be equated. Nevertheless, where tolerance encourages free inquiry and a setting aside of traditional presuppositions, truth is likely to emerge. The "liberal" tendency created an atmosphere in which traditional doctrines could be questioned. The process of reassessing every aspect of belief encouraged a consideration of the way in which post-biblical Greek metaphysics had led to a loss of the biblical Christ. The loosening of the grip exercised by traditional dogma has proved to be a positive result of post-enlightenment theology. Discontent with Nicean/Chalcedonian definitions of Jesus has surfaced repeatedly. The search for the Jesus of history has continued into our own time. It received a new impetus when the *Myth of God Incarnate* was published in 1977.[17]

Harnack had been right to point to the problematic Hellenization of the original Hebrew-oriented faith. It is a failure to distinguish between what is truly of Scripture and what of tradition which leads many contemporary "evangelicals" to equate opposition to the dogma of Christ's coeternal divinity with an attack on Scripture itself. "Evangelicals," while they rally under the banner of *sola scriptura*, are sometimes unable to distinguish Scripture from traditional *interpretations* of Scripture. Lindbeck sounds the alarm when he points out that "most biblical Protestants adhere to post-biblical Trinitarianism,

---

[17] Ed. John Hick (London: SCM Press, 1977).

but they act as if those teachings were self-evidently biblical."[18] F.F. Bruce's shrewd observation deserves the closest attention: "People who adhere to belief in the Bible only (as they believe) often adhere in fact to a traditional school of interpretation of *sola scriptura*. Evangelical Protestants can be as much servants of tradition as Roman Catholics or Greek Orthodox, only they don't realize that it is tradition."[19]

To Michael Servetus, and the Dutch Anabaptists led by Adam Pastor, as well as to the whole community of Polish Anabaptists, the Trinity was a deviation from biblical monotheism, a mistaken attempt to translate apostolic belief in one God, the Father,[20] into the language of Greek metaphysics. Worse still, the creeds and the Councils of Nicea and Chalcedon were used in coercive and destructive ways to force belief in these dogmas. This was all the more regrettable since the terminology of the discussion on Christology was itself a jumble of ambiguous terms — in sharp contrast to the Bible's plainly unitarian creed.

The freedom to explore apart from the "tyranny of dogma" (represented, for example, by the Athanasian Creed which threatens death to deviants from orthodox Trinitarianism) led to the rediscovery of a frequently forgotten element in the Church's presentation of Jesus — his humanity. It was widely admitted that traditional understandings of Jesus had often suffered from a latent "docetism" (belief that Jesus only seemed to be human), which for John, the Apostle, signaled very "antichrist" (1 John 4:2; 2 John 7). Moreover, traditional formulations about Christ seemed to demonstrate a fondness for a particular interpretation of John 1:1, to the exclusion of the very human portraits presented by Matthew, Mark, Luke, and Acts. In fact, the Gospel of John had been allowed a more than proportionate influence in the formation of Christology. Could this have been because the

---

[18] *The Nature of Doctrine and Religion: Theology in a Postliberal Age* (Philadelphia: Westminster Press, 1984), 74.

[19] From correspondence, June 13th, 1981.

[20] 1 Cor. 8:6; 1 Tim. 2:5; John 17:3; Eph. 4:6.

style of John's writing, while actually very Hebraic, appealed to the speculative Greek mind, and could be easily misunderstood and distorted by Gentiles?

We suggest that the tendency to obscure the humanity of Christ arose in opposition to the central and essentially simple New Testament affirmation of Jesus *as Messiah*, the second Adam, supernaturally conceived, yet coming into existence in the womb of his mother. This view of Jesus' origin we may with Raymond Brown usefully call "conception Christology."[21] Brown insists that Matthew and Luke know nothing of a literal preexistence of the Messiah.[22] They could not therefore have been Trinitarians in the traditional sense. Jesus' conception for them is his coming into being. The germ of later Trinitarian theology should be sought elsewhere than in these Gospel accounts. Should it be ascribed to John and Paul? Or to a distortion of their writings caused by the speculative tendency of Greek philosophy? This influence was apparently already at work when John, writing at the end of the first century, pointedly emphasizes, against an incipient Gnostic docetism, the humanity of Jesus (1 John 4:2; 2 John 7). He came *en sarki*, "as a human person," not "into a human body" which is a very different matter. John seems in his first epistle to be correcting an emerging misunderstanding of his "logos" doctrine in the Gospel (John 1:1-3). It was the *impersonal* "eternal life" which was "with the Father" (1 John 1:2) before the birth of Jesus, *not* the Son himself preexisting. In other words, John intended us to understand that when the Word became flesh (John 1:14), the transition was *not that of a divine person becoming a human person, but of an impersonal personification (cp. Wisdom in Proverbs 8:22, 30) — the "word" of God — becoming embodied as a human being.*

The subsequent development of Trinitarian thinking was encouraged by a misunderstanding of the Hebrew notion of "word" by Justin Martyr. For John, "logos" signified not a

---

[21] *The Birth of the Messiah*, 150, fn. 52.

[22] Ibid., 31, fn. 17.

second person in the Godhead, but the self-expressive activity of God. Justin, who as Platonist had been accustomed to thinking of the "logos" as an intermediary between God and man, not unnaturally reads Jesus back into the "logos" and thinks of him as the *preexisting Son*, a person numerically different from and subordinate to the One God. Justin then proceeds to find Jesus in the Old Testament, even identifying him with the angel of the Lord, before his incarnation. Yet even in Justin we are a long way from the final creedal formulation of the Council of Chalcedon. The important point to be noted is that developed Trinitarianism cannot be traced back to the New Testament, through the earliest Church Fathers. These Fathers always thought of Christ as subordinate to the One God. Some believed the Son had a beginning.

The point at which Greek philosophy was able to interfere with biblical teaching was the Gospel of John and particularly his prologue. A misunderstanding of John's Gospel led to the projection of Jesus back onto the preexisting "logos." Thus the simple Messianic Christology of the Synoptics and also of John (provided he is not read from a speculative Greek perspective) was obscured. It has been the task of the Cambridge *Myth of God Incarnate* theologians to raise the question as to whether "talk of Jesus' preexistence ought probably in most, perhaps in all cases, to be understood on the analogy of the preexistence of the Torah, to indicate the eternal divine purpose being achieved through him [cp. 1 Pet. 1:20], rather than preexistence of a fully personal kind."[23]

If this is the right reading, then John Robinson's observation about the Fathers' treatment of John is correct:

> Patristic theology of whatever school abused these [Johannine] texts by taking them out of context and *giving them a meaning which John never intended.* Functional language about the Son and the Spirit being

---

[23] Maurice Wiles, *The Remaking of Christian Doctrine* (London: SCM Press, 1974), 53. Cp. Wiles' observation in *The Myth of God Incarnate,* 3: "Incarnation, in its full and proper sense, is not something directly presented in Scripture."

> sent into the world by the Father was transposed into that
> of eternal and internal relationships between Persons in
> the Godhead and words like "generation" and
> "procession" made into technical terms which New
> Testament usage simply will not substantiate.[24]

Complaints about mistreatment of John's concept of the "word" have frequently been steam-rollered into obscurity. It is time for some significant voices to be heard. In 1907 the Professor of Systematic Theology at Jena in Germany produced his *System der Christlichen Lehre*, the culmination of a lifetime's reflection on the nature of the Christian faith. In company with many later distinguished commentators the professor put his finger on the Trinitarian problem which arises when the "Word" of John 1 is treated as a preexisting second *Person or Being* rather than a synonym for the wisdom and creative purpose of the One God. No Trinitarianism is found in John's prologue if the "Word" is given a lower-case "w" and if it is thought of as a way of describing the intention or Plan of God, not (at that stage) the *Son* of God.

Hans Wendt of Jena subjects the problem to a penetrating analysis. He shows that when the "word" is understood in a Hebrew sense as God's creative activity — based on its consistent appearance in that sense in the Old Testament — there is no warrant whatsoever for thinking that John meant to say: "In the beginning was the coeternal Son of God and the Son was with the Father and the Son was God." Such an interpretation merely confuses the great central principle of all revelation that God is a single person. If the Word is the Son in a pre-human condition, then both Father and Son are equally entitled to be thought of as the supreme Deity. This development, however, dealt a fatal blow to the monotheism of the Hebrew Bible, that monotheism which Jesus had publicly confirmed (Mark 12:28, 29) in the presence of both an inquiring theologian and his own

---

[24] "The Fourth Gospel and the Church's Doctrine of the Trinity," *Twelve More New Testament Studies* (London: SCM Press, 1984), 172, emphasis added.

circle of disciples. If the "word" in John 1 is taken to mean "the word of God," it is clear that John has in mind the creative word of Genesis 1:1-3, Psalm 33:6, 9; 119:103-105. A fatal step was taken, says Professor Wendt, when the "word" of John's prologue was understood, not in terms of its Hebrew background, but in the Alexandrian and Philonic sense as an intermediary between God and man.

> The opening sentences of John's Gospel, which might sound like the philosophy of Philo, could be understood by an educated Jew or Christian without any reference to Philo. Therefore we should not argue from Philo's meaning of "word" as a hypostasis that John also meant by "word" a preexisting *personality*. In the remainder of the Gospel and in 1 John, "word" is never to be understood in a personal sense...It means rather the "revelation" of God which had earlier been given to Israel (10:35), had come to the Jews in Holy Scripture (5:38) and which had been entrusted to Jesus and committed by him to his disciples (8:55; 12:48; 17:6, 8, 14, 17; 1 John 1:1) and which would now be preserved by them (1 John 1:10; 2:5, 14). The slightly personifying way in which the word is spoken of as coming into the world (1:9-14) is typical of the personifying style of the Old Testament references to the word (Isa. 55:11; Ps. 107:20; 147:15; cp. 2 Thess. 3:1). It cannot be proved that the author of the prologue thought of the word as a real person. Only the historical Jesus and not the original word is said to be the Son (John 1:14, 18). But in this Son there dwelt and worked the eternal revelation of God.[25]

Professor Wendt goes on to point out that John's apparent connection with Philo is not to be explained by his adoption of Philo's philosophical idea of the word. The fact is that the Apostle is trying to refute the intrusion of Philo's philosophy by

---

[25] *System der Christlichen Lehre* (Göttingen: Vandenhoeck und Ruprecht, 1907), Pt. 2, ch. 4, 353, 354. The translation from the German is mine.

representatives of the Alexandrian school who early on opposed the Truth with their speculation (cp. Acts 18:24-28). John aimed his prologue at them. The irony of history is that orthodoxy eventually fell for the very same philosophical speculation, proposed a preexisting "second God," and used John to support this departure from monotheism! Modern translations of the prologue with their capitalized Word and the use of masculine pronouns for *logos* are an abiding testimony to the Philonic Greek philosophy which has confused the Hebrew faith of the New Testament. John has been twisted and misunderstood and the casualty was the unitary monotheism of Jesus and his followers (John 5:44; 17:3).

Professor Wendt's perceptive analysis deserves the widest hearing:

> From the time of Justin the *logos* Christology became dominant in Christian theology...This *logos* teaching created a contact and an agreement with the philosophy of Late Antiquity. The main problem for the latter was how to determine the relationship of the lower, material world to the transcendental world of God and the spirit. To solve this problem the existence of "middle beings" was posited. These beings were emanations of the deity and represented a gradual means by which the gap between God and man could be bridged. Christian speculation about the *logos* as the intermediary in creation was directly related to this hellenistic, philosophical speculation, since it offered a similar solution to the same cosmological problem...But the combining of the cosmological, philosophical with religious and soteriological interests contained an inner self-contradiction. If the *logos* teaching were to offer an adequate solution to the cosmological problem, the *logos* had to be presented as a real, mediating person, proceeding indeed from God but less than God, so that as mediator the *logos* could link God with man. If on the other hand the mediator were to bring salvation then his being must be of equal value with the salvation he is to bring to mankind... He must be thought of "as of a God"

(2 Clem. 1:1). As either the cosmological view or the soteriological view prevailed, so correspondingly the distance of the *logos* from God or his similarity with God was emphasized.[26]

The contradiction involved in the *logos* speculation is represented by the opposing arguments of the followers of Arius and Athanasius. Both camps believed in the *logos* as a preexisting *person.* But, as Professor Wendt observes, this conception of the *logos* as a personal being led to a disturbing consequence. "When not only a personal, heavenly preexistence but an eternal, co-essential existence with the Father was attributed to the Son, *the idea of the unity of God was lost.* This was the important complaint of all Monarchians [supporters of the strict unity of God]."[27]

Wendt concludes in his section on "Difficulties with the Early Christological Dogmas": "Monotheism, which for the Christian view of God is not an insignificant matter but of fundamental importance, was impaired...If the *logos* which belongs to the eternal God is a person and as such to be distinguished from the person of the Father, there inevitably arises a plurality in God and pure monotheism is destroyed."[28] Such is the problem presented by orthodox Trinitarianism.

The close association of Jesus with the One God of Israel does not lead to the Christological conclusions of the creeds. The development which culminated at Nicea and Chalcedon may be traced in three major stages. Firstly the "logos" of Greek philosophy was identified by the Alexandrian theologians with the preexistent Christ. Secondly Origen postulated the unbiblical doctrine of the eternal generation of the Son. Thirdly the so-called Athanasian Creed, reflecting the Trinitarianism of Augustine, abolished all subordination of the Son to the Father and reduced the distinctions within the Godhead to a point where

---

26 Ibid., 357, 358.

27 Ibid., 359.

28 Ibid., 368.

it is all but impossible to say how "the Three" are to be described.

It appears that the complex post-biblical controversies about how to define the Son in relation to the Father could have been avoided if the Hebrew terminology of the Bible had been retained. Geoffrey Lampe, in his perceptive analysis of patristic Christology, complains that:

> the Christological concept of the preexisting Son reduces the real, socially and culturally conditioned personality of Jesus to the metaphysical abstraction "human nature." It is universal humanity which the Son assumed and made his own...But universal humanity is an abstract notion...According to this Christology, the eternal Son assumes a timeless human nature or makes it timeless by making it his own; it is a human nature which owes nothing essential to geographical circumstances; it corresponds to nothing in the actual concrete world. Jesus Christ has not after all "come in the flesh."[29]

Mosheim remarked that "controversies relating to the Trinity took their rise in the second century from the introduction of Grecian philosophy into the Church."[30] The study of biblical theology has brought to light evidence which compels us to consider seriously this distortion of the faith which occurred when Greek philosophy was added to the simpler Hebraic framework of the Bible. We end with three further quotations. These invite us to renew our investigation of the history of doctrine in the ongoing search for truth. Canon H. Constable wrote in 1893:

> Christian men are now inquiring whether accepted views of human nature and future punishment are derived from philosophy and tradition, or from Scripture. They are beginning to suspect that a vast amount of current theology has human philosophy for its source. Figures in the field of religious thought, which they used to think

---

[29] *God as Spirit* (London: SCM Press, 1977), 144.

[30] *Institutes of Ecclesiastical History* (New York: Harper, 1839).

were figures of Christ, his prophets and his Apostles, they are beginning to suspect are figures of the evil spirit, figures of Plato, and of the various Fathers who derived their theology in great measure from him.[31]

Alfred Vaucher summons us to return to biblical faith:
Across the pages of the Old and New Testament the clear waters of revealed truth flow like a majestic river. It is God who only has immortality, offering to men and communicating to men His divine imperishable life. But paralleling this stream flows the muddy river of pagan philosophy, which is that of human soul, of divine essence, eternal, preexisting the body and surviving it. After the death of the Apostles the two streams merged to make unity of the troubled waters. Little by little the speculation of human philosophy mixed with divine teaching. Now the task of evangelical theology is to disengage the two incompatible elements, to dissociate them, to eliminate the pagan element which has installed itself as a usurper in the center of traditional theology; to restore in value the biblical element, which only is true, and which alone conforms to the nature of God and of man, His creature.[32]

Emerging from that early confusion over the nature of God and man will be the pristine biblical monotheism of the prophets, Jesus and the Apostles. God will be perceived again as one Person, the Father of Jesus, His uniquely conceived Son, the Messiah. The full humanity of Jesus, eclipsed by the speculative and abstract theology of the Church Fathers, must be reinstated as the basis of the New Testament creed that Jesus is the Messiah,[33] herald of the coming Kingdom of God on earth.

Scholars of various backgrounds unite in their testimony to the corruption of the Christian faith from the second century

---

[31] *Hades or the Intermediate State* (n.p., 1893), 278.

[32] *Le Problème de l'Immortalité* (n.p., 1957), 6.

[33] Matt. 16:16; John 9:22; 20:31; Acts 5:42; 9:22, etc.

onwards. Messianic hopes were gradually forgotten. The notion of the Kingdom of God on earth disappeared. Immortality at death took the place of the resurrection:

> Like all concepts the meaning of religious terms is changed with a changing experience and a changing worldview. Transplanted into the Greek worldview, inevitably *the Christian teaching was modified — indeed transformed.* Questions which had never been asked came into the foreground and the Jewish presuppositions tended to disappear. Especially were *the Messianic hopes forgotten* or *transferred to a transcendent sphere beyond death.* When the empire became Christian in the fourth century, *the notion of a Kingdom of Christ on earth* to be introduced by a great struggle all but disappeared, remaining only as the faith of obscure groups. Immortality — the philosophical conception — took the place of the resurrection of the body. Nevertheless, the latter continues because of its presence in the primary sources, but it is no longer a determining factor, since its presupposition — *the Messianic Kingdom on earth — has been obscured.* As thus the background is changed from Jewish to Greek, so are the fundamental religious conceptions...We have thus a peculiar combination — *the religious doctrines of the Bible run through the forms of an alien philosophy.*[34]

1 John 4:2

Early attempts by various factions to cast doubt on the real humanity of Jesus were met by John's strong warning to his disciples that "many deceivers have gone out into the world, those who do not acknowledge Jesus Christ as coming in the

---

[34] G.W. Knox, D.D., LL.D, professor of philosophy and the history of religion, Union Theological Seminary, New York, *Encyclopedia Britannica*, 11th ed., Vol. 6, 284.

flesh. This is the deceiver and the antichrist" (2 John 7; cp. 1 John 4:2).

The *Translator's New Testament*[35] renders this verse in a way which clears up uncertainty about the phrase come in the flesh: "Many deceivers have gone out into the world who do not accept the fact that Jesus came as a human being. Here is the deceiver and the antichrist." John's clear stand in favor of the humanity of Jesus is meant to expose as antichristian any system which calls in question the fact that Jesus was a real human being. We have seen in an earlier chapter that the official Trinitarian position is that the Savior possessed impersonal human nature, *but was not a human person.*

A being who is or was both God and man could hardly be truly human, tempted in all points even as we are. As so many critics of the Trinity have complained, the traditional teaching that Jesus was God is incompatible with belief that he was really human. The God-Man of the post-biblical councils appears to be dangerously like "another Jesus" of whom Paul warned in his second letter to the Corinthians (2 Cor. 11:4).

The irony of all this bitter, age-old controversy is that all factions, unitarians, Binitarians, and Trinitarians, claim to be worshipping only one God. Those who insist that Jesus is God argue that he is worthy of worship, an act offered only to God. If that point of view were sustained, we would have to conclude that two persons are worthy of worship as God. To propose a Godhead of two or three persons contradicts the many plain biblical statements that God is a single person. It is futile to escape this conclusion by holding that the creeds do not mean by person what we today mean by person. In the Bible the Father and Jesus are obviously persons in the modern sense — two different individuals.

The solution to the puzzle is that "worship" in Scripture is offered not only to God but to human persons who hold positions of dignity. The Greek verb *proskuneo* is used both of worship to God and doing obeisance to human persons. Thus, for example,

---

[35] British and Foreign Bible Society, 1973.

the king of Israel is worshipped in association with God (1 Chron. 29:20, KJV; the word is *proskuneo* in the LXX). Daniel was worshipped (Dan. 2:46). The saints are worshipped (Rev. 3:9, KJV). Jesus is worshipped as Messiah, but only one person, the Father, is worthy of worship as God. It is highly significant that another Greek word, *latreuo*, which is used of religious service only, is applied in all of its 21 occurrences exclusively to the Father in the New Testament.

Readers of the King James Version are given the false impression that Jesus is God because he is "worshipped." The same argument would prove that David and the saints are also God! It is the modern usage of our word "worship" which leads readers to suppose that Jesus was worshipped as God.

God and His human servants are frequently in close association. "And the people feared the Lord and believed the Lord and His servant Moses" (Exod. 14:31). "And all the people greatly feared the Lord and Samuel" (1 Sam. 12:18). "And all the congregation blessed the Lord God of their Fathers, and worshipped the Lord and the king" (1 Chron. 29:20). "Hezekiah and the princes blessed the Lord and His people Israel" (2 Chron. 31:8).

Modern translations have helped to clarify the issue of "worshipping Jesus." In Matthew 8:2, for example, we read of a leper who came and "prostrated himself before him" (Translators' New Testament).

All this is not to deny that Jesus is the one of whom it is said, "Worthy is the Lamb that was slain to receive power and riches and wisdom and might and honor and glory and blessing." As Messiah, Jesus, the accredited representative of the Creator, is honored in association with the One God, his Father (Rev. 5:12, 13). But he also joins the saints in the Lamb's song of praise to the Father (Rev. 15:3; cp. Heb. 2:12, where the Messiah praises God). He is the beginning and end of God's great plan of salvation (Rev. 1:17). Yet he died (Rev. 1:18), a fact which plainly means that he cannot be God since God cannot die. Only the Almighty is the Supreme God. In Revelation 1:8 (cp. 1:4) the Father is both the Alpha and Omega and the Lord God Almighty "who is coming." The latter title, *pantokrator*, is nowhere given to Jesus, despite the attempts of some red-letter Bibles to apply this verse to the Son, perpetuating the long-standing confusion of the Messiah with God. The risen Jesus actually receives a revelation from the Father (Rev. 1:1), demonstrating once again that the Son is not the omniscient God!

In Revelation 22:12, 13 it may well be that the angel (the "he" of verse 10) speaks, as in the Old Testament, as God, representing Him. The Alpha and Omega of verse 13 probably refers, as does Revelation 1:8 and 21:6, to the Father for whom the angel is speaking. The Almighty God is the one "who comes" in Revelation 1:8, and His coming may be described also in Revelation 22:12, followed by the divine title in verse 13. *Jesus* is the speaker again from verse 16.

It is a fascinating paradox that John, who is so anxious to maintain that Jesus was a real human being, who tired and was hungry, has been misunderstood to teach that Jesus was fully God in a Trinitarian sense. John's Gospel repeatedly refers to "God" as the Father. Yet from John's later epistle we detect that some even in his time were trying to force a definition of Jesus into his writings which he never intended. The evidence is this: In John's Gospel the *logos* (word), being a somewhat ambiguous term, might be liable to misunderstanding. It might be thought that John meant that a second eternal person existed alongside the Father. But this was not at all what John had in mind, and he takes the opportunity at the beginning of his first epistle to make himself clear. It was, he says, "eternal life" which had been "with the Father" (1 John 1:2).[36] It was that impersonal "word of life" or "life" (1 John 1:1, 2) which had now been manifested in a real human person, Jesus. What preexisted was not the Son of God, but the word or message or promise of life. That promise of life was expressed in a human individual, the Messiah of Israel. Incarnation in the Bible does not mean that the second member of a Trinity became man, but the purpose of God to grant

---

[36] Cp. "the word was with God" (John 1:1).

immortality to His creatures was revealed, demonstrated, and embodied in a unique human being.

VI. THE TRINITY AND POLITICS

"Know then, my friend, that the Trinity was born above three hundred years after the ancient Gospel was declared; it was conceived in ignorance, brought forth and maintained by cruelty." — William Penn

A historian has correctly stated:

> Christianity, by identifying truth with faith, must teach — and properly understood, does teach — that any interference with truth is immoral. A Christian with faith has nothing to fear from the facts; a Christian historian who draws the line limiting the field of inquiry at any point whatsoever, is admitting the limits of his faith.[1]

The fearful believer obstructs the whole point of the Christian venture which is to seek progressive understanding of truth.

History, unfortunately, is often seen through the eye of the beholder, particularly if a historical matter is viewed from a narrow secular or religious perspective. Examine the lives of the founders of any religious group; read the account in books, magazines, and newspapers written by secular writers. Then study the same life from an autobiography or the works of faithful devotees. There is little agreement beyond a few matters of fact and minor unerasable statistical data. Given time and distance a huge gap develops between historical reality and a canonized version of the facts. It has taken skill to hide the dark side of the lives of the founding fathers of religious groups such as, for example, the Church of Jesus Christ of Latter-Day Saints (Joseph Smith) and Presbyterians (John Calvin).

---

[1] Paul Johnson, *A History of Christianity* (New York: Atheneum, 1976), viii.

By contrast, frank disclosures about the lives of Bible heroes
appear in the sacred record — right down to the details of
drunkenness and loose sexuality. Yet we seem to find it
necessary to sanitize the lives of later religious leaders.
Unpalatable and harsh as it may seem to some, we could
speculate that this tendency relates to the biblical statement made
by Jesus: "A corrupt tree cannot produce good fruit" (Matt.
7:18). Could it be that candid disclosure might reveal the
upsetting seeds of corruption? Stupendous efforts are made to
present the lives of famous religious leaders in as saintly a mode
as possible. It is hoped that this lends credence to their doctrines
and the belief systems they passed on to posterity.

Similarly, when we read the various accounts of the origin of
the Trinity, we are astonished at the way different sources color
the same subject. Some Christian writers hold that the Trinity
was already completely at home in Christian circles by the time
the New Testament was composed. New Testament authors
therefore saw no need to make other than indirect reference to
the Trinity. It was supposedly so much an accepted part of
church tradition that they scarcely bothered to record what would
have been the most dramatic change ever to invade the religious
community of the first century. Other writers, recording the same
theological event, are in complete disagreement. They point to a
bloody centuries-long battle among Christians, in which
thousands paid with their lives, before the Trinity was finally
canonized as Christian dogma, more than three centuries after
the death of Christianity's founder.

The Church has been ready to support great political leaders
when they further the Christian cause and back its ecclesiastical
control. At the Edict of Milan in 313 AD the Emperor
Constantine secured age-lasting honor from the Christian Church
by granting complete toleration to all Christians and other cults.
A few years later he charted the rough course which led to the
settlement of disputes over doctrine between rival factions. The
result was the first major step toward the formal incorporation of
Trinitarian belief into Christianity.

Most Christians would be surprised at the implications of the
observation of the Roman Catholic scholar, W.E. Addis.

Commenting on the religious turmoil caused by the attempt to introduce the idea that God was more than one person, he said:

> The bulk of Christians, had they been let alone, would have been satisfied with the old belief in one God, the Father, and would have distrusted the "dispensation," as it has been called, by which the sole Deity of the Father expanded into the Deity of the Father and the Son..."All simple people," Tertullian wrote, "not to call them ignorant and uneducated...take fright at the 'dispensation'...They will have it that we are proclaiming two or three gods."[2]

Those Trinitarians who believe that the concept of a Triune God was such an established fact that it was not considered important enough to mention by the time the New Testament was written should be challenged by the remarks of another writer, Harold Brown:

> It is a simple fact and an undeniable historical fact that several major doctrines that now seem central to the Christian faith — such as the doctrine of the Trinity and the doctrine of the nature of Christ — were not present in a full and self-defined generally accepted form until the fourth and fifth centuries. If they are essential today — as all of the orthodox creeds and confessions assert — it must be because they are true. If they are true, then they must always have been true; they cannot have become true in the fourth and fifth century. But if they are both true and essential, how can it be that the early Church took centuries to formulate them?[3]

Elsewhere he says: "Heresy appears in the historical record earlier, and is better documented, than what the Church came to call orthodoxy."[4] This startling admission that the religious

---

[2] *Christianity and the Roman Empire* (New York: W.W. Norton, 1967), 174.

[3] *Heresies* (Doubleday, 1984), 20.

[4] Ibid., 4.

world replaced original teaching with a new and different orthodoxy has not gone unnoticed by other observers of the Christian scene. The Jewish writer, Pinchas Lapide, in his dialogue with the Protestant scholar, Jurgen Moltmann, on the Trinitarian doctrine, observes that:

> Whoever knows the development of the history of dogma knows that the image of God in the primitive Church was unitary, and only in the second century did it gradually, against the doctrine of subordinationism, become binary. For the Church Fathers such as Justin Martyr, Irenaeus, and Tertullian, Jesus is subordinate to the Father in everything, and Origen hesitated to direct his prayer to Christ, for as he wrote, that should properly be to the Father alone.[5]

The total picture which arises from history is almost like an arithmetic progression: "In the first century God is still monotheistic in good Jewish fashion. In the second century God becomes two-in-one; from the third century the one God gradually becomes threefold."[6]

Lapide speaks of the "bloody intra-Christian religious wars of the fourth and fifth centuries, when thousands upon thousands of Christians slaughtered other Christians for the sake of the Trinity."[7]

How was this tragic dispute resolved? One man, the Emperor Constantine, changed the course of Christian history. He was the first to bring about a merging of Christianity, paganism and the State under the umbrella of the Roman Empire. As Johnson points out, Constantine no doubt shared the prevailing view that all religious cults should be respected in appeasement of their various national deities. He also notes that Constantine:

---

[5] *Jewish Monotheism and Christian Trinitarian Doctrine*, 39.

[6] Ibid.

[7] Ibid., 40.

appears to have been a sun-worshipper, one of a number of late pagan cults which had observances in common with Christians. Worship of such gods was not a novel idea. Every Greek or Roman expected that political success followed from religious piety. Christianity was the religion of Constantine's father. Although Constantine claimed that he was the thirteenth Apostle, his was no sudden Damascus conversion. Indeed it is highly doubtful that he ever truly abandoned sun-worship. After his professed acceptance of Christianity, he built a triumphal arch to the sun god and in Constantinople set up a statue of the same sun god bearing his own features. He was finally deified after his death by official edict in the Empire, as were many Roman rulers.[8]

In Constantine, the professional soldier, Christianity has embraced an unusual champion. He was the most powerful secular ruler of any age ever to be counted among the Church's heroes. It might be well to ask how closely his life paralleled that of Christianity's founder, who bears the title "Prince of Peace." It was Constantine who by official edict brought Christianity to belief in the formal division of the Godhead into two — God the Father and God the Son. It remained the task of a later generation to bring Christianity to belief in the Triune God.

It was this same Constantine who, with the head of his decapitated rival (his own brother-in-law) dripping blood from his lance, marched in triumph into Rome. He gave credit for his victory to a supposed vision in which he saw the Greek letters Chi-Rho, the first two letters of the name Christ. The story varies with the teller but before this historic slaughter, he ordered that these same letters be painted on his soldiers' shields. Only six years before his triumphant march into Rome, he ordered that hundreds of Frankish rebel prisoners be torn to pieces in an arena. He also stood by while the anti-Christian policies of Diocletian brought about the burning of sacred Christian texts

---

[8] *A History of Christianity*, 67.

followed by the mutilation of believers who refused to worship pagan gods.

Eleven years after winning this heaven-inspired triumph, history divulges that the alleged follower of Jesus murdered an already vanquished rival, killed his wife by having her boiled alive in her own bath — and murdered an innocent son. "His private life became monstrous as he aged. He grew fat, and was known as 'the bull neck...' His abilities had always lain in management...; [he was] a master of...the smoothly-worded compromise."[9] Yet he was "overbearing, egotistical, self-righteous and ruthless."[10] In later years "he showed an increasing regard for flattery, fancy uniforms, personal display and elaborate titles. His nephew, Julian, said he made himself ridiculous by his appearance — [wearing] weird, stiff eastern garments, jewels on his arms, a tiara on his head, perched crazily on top of a tinted wig."[11] His chief apologist, Eusebius of Caesarea, said that this Christian emperor dressed solely to impress the masses; privately he laughed at himself. "But this contradicts much other evidence, including Eusebius' own. Vain and superstitious, he may have embraced Christianity because it suited his personal interests, and his growing megalomania."[12]

The cynic might ask how well Constantine's life reflected the humble carpenter of Nazareth. Despite his baptism just before his death, it has been speculated that Constantine's deeper interest, apart from the normal superstitions of the warriors of that age, may have been largely political. His desire to bring harmony to a divided empire required political astuteness. Constantine's skill would be the envy of latter-day politicians who must curry favor with large blocks of politically active, competing religious groups. In some cases this has entailed

---

9 Ibid., 68.

10 Ibid.

11 Ibid.

12 Ibid.

claiming a "born again" experience at the height of campaigning activities.

Christological Controversy

In the Roman Empire a deep theological difference arose between the Christians in Alexandria and Antioch. These opposing groups constituted a threat to the unity of the Empire. Because of the political potential of the rival factions, these differences had to be resolved. Christians in Alexandria believed that Jesus had preexisted eternally as a divine being and that he had become human by appearing as a man. The Jesus of this theology ran the risk of only "seeming" to be a real human being. In the technical language of Christology the Jesus of the Alexandrian Christians was "docetic" (from a Greek verb meaning "to seem"). The point was that his Deity so dominated his humanity that the latter was only a pretense. The Savior himself was truly God dwelling in a human body, and possessing (so the jargon ran in its developed form following the later Council of Chalcedon in 451 AD) "impersonal human nature." Jesus himself, it was held by the orthodox, was "man," but not "a man."

For those who had grown up around Antioch, the region which included the area of the homeland of Jesus, a different view of Christ prevailed. Here the original monotheism of the Jews, stressing the oneness of God, resulted in a belief in a created Son. The distinctive tenet of this "Arian" Christology was that Jesus, as Son of God, must have had a beginning and, though preexistent, could not have been coeternal and coequal with the Father. At the center of the controversy which developed between the two parties was a priest named Arius, who attracted a sizable following in the Alexandrian Bishop Alexander's domain. Arius' efforts to promote his Christology in Egypt promptly brought about his excommunication.

The marked ideological differences between Rome, Alexandria, and Antioch were matters of concern to the Roman Emperor. The power of religion played so great a role in the stability of the fourth-century Roman Empire that religious turmoil had to be brought under control by the State, lest it disrupt political unity. Constantine determined to resolve the dispute by means of the following identical conciliatory letters sent to each faction, urging reconciliation of differences:

> Constantine the Victor, Supreme Augustus, to Alexander and Arius...How deep a wound has not only my ears but my heart received from the report that divisions exist among yourselves...Having inquired carefully into the origin and foundation of these differences, I find their cause to be of a truly insignificant nature, quite unworthy of such bitter contention.[13]

Constantine was evidently oblivious to the profound theological issues involved in the controversy. When his initial effort failed to resolve the dispute, he called what may have been the single most influential ecumenical council ever convened in the history of the Christian Church. A fateful and far-reaching decision was made on this divisive issue of the nature of Christ and of the Godhead. "The appointed date was early summer 325 AD, the venue the pleasant lakeside town of Nicea...in north-western Turkey, where Constantine had a suitably commodious palace."[14]

> With Christianity having spread as far as Britain in the West and India in the East, for some of the delegates the journey took several weeks, if not months...The hermit Jacob of Nisibis arrived in goatskins accompanied by a persistent horde of gnats. Another delegate was the saintly Nicholas...who was the prototype of the Christmas Santa Claus...Before this bizarre and unprecedented assembly Constantine, dazzlingly robed and dripping with gold and jewels of a decadence earlier Emperors would have abhorred, took his place on a low, wrought-gold chair.[15]

---

[13] Cited by Ian Wilson, *Jesus: The Evidence* (Harper & Row, 1984), 165.

[14] Ibid.

[15] Ibid., 165, 166.

The church historian Schaff, quoting Eusebius of Caesarea, further describes the scene: "The moment the approach of the emperor was announced by a given signal, they all rose from their seats, and the emperor appeared like a heavenly messenger of God, covered with gold and gems, a glorious presence, very tall and slender, full of beauty, strength and majesty."[16]

"It was at this point in history, and before this assembly, that a decision was to be made that would have the most profound consequences for believers in Christ to this day."[17] For reasons best known to himself, this largely biblically illiterate emperor, who did not fully understand the theological issues at hand, presided over one of the most significant debates ever to be conducted by the Church. The resolution adopted by the council was to have dramatically important long-term effects on the entire body of believers. Constantine's judgment favored the minority opinion at the council. The decision taken is accepted by the vast majority of Christians to this day — that Jesus was coequal and coeternal with God, "very God of very God." Thus the second leg of the triangle of the Trinity became dogma. It was to be completed in the next century by the declaration that the Holy Spirit was the third Person of the Godhead.

The Greek philosophically-minded Alexandrian theologians, led by Athanasius, won the day. Those more under the earlier influence of Jewish monotheism were defeated. Dissenters who refused to sign the agreement were immediately banished. The Church was now taken over and dictated to by theologians strongly influenced by the Greek mind. Thus the course of its doctrines was set for the next seventeen centuries. H.L. Goudge's observation is appropriate: "When the Greek mind and the Roman mind, instead of the Hebrew mind, came to dominate the Church, there occurred a disaster from which the Church has

---

16 *History of the Christian Church* (Grand Rapids: Eerdmans, 1907-1910), 3:625.

17 Ian Wilson, *Jesus: The Evidence*, 168.

never recovered, either in doctrine or practice."[18] This control has continued unabated since the fourth century. The political cohesion Constantine sought to bring to the Empire he certainly achieved. These are the facts of history, but at what cost to the cause of truth? The Christian Church to this day unwittingly prostrates itself before the low, wrought-gold throne of Constantine.

Too late some of the Antiochene signatories to the parchment protested in writing to Constantine that they had "committed an impious act, Oh Prince, by subscribing to a blasphemy from fear of you."[19] So wrote Eusebius of Nicomedia. Nevertheless the deed was done. A whole new theology was formally canonized into the Church. Since that time numberless devoted Christians who have disagreed with the emperor's enforced edict have faced torture and death at the hands of the State and often other Christians.

One should not express surprise at the acceptance by Constantine and the Greek theologians of a Deity consisting of two persons. It was in character with a widespread acceptance of multiple deities. The Roman and Greek world was saturated with many gods. The idea of a God becoming man was hardly an innovation (cp. Acts 14:11), nor was the notion of a man being declared God. Constantine had ordered the deification of his father and would be granted the same honor upon his own demise. At his burial he was recognized as the thirteenth apostle.

Today Constantine's monumental decision casts its imposing shadow over the fragmented body of 20th-century Christianity without serious opposition. Constantine's influence seems to continue unchallenged. As is the case with Napoleon, who became the bloody butcher of European manhood; Luther; Calvin; or a modern religious leader such as Joseph Smith, faithful followers do not permit their leaders' halos to tarnish, but continue to burnish their reputations to a bright glow.

---

[18] "The Calling of the Jews," in the collected essays on *Judaism and Christianity*.

[19] Ian Wilson, *Jesus: The Evidence*, 168.

The truth of history may judge them more harshly, but their spiritual descendants seldom tolerate any who would dare to find fault. For two centuries after Constantine, slaughter followed slaughter as professing Christian vied with Christian in a bloody struggle in defense of what became a hardened religious orthodoxy. It was required that one accept belief in the Godhead of two persons (later expanded to a Deity of three persons) or face banishment, exile, torture and death — largely in the interests of political expediency and the preservation of what was dogmatically declared to be unquestionable truth.[20]

Following Constantine, violence became an accepted Christian method of solving disputes. In the early part of the 11th century AD, Christian Crusaders warmed to the prospect of liberating the Holy Land by force of arms. After slaughtering European Jews, they proceeded to wreak havoc on the monotheistic, "infidel" Muslim who controlled the Holy City of Jerusalem. This carnage was instigated under the bloody banner of a Triune God. Some have suggested that Islam might never have found a place in the world if the single-person Deity of the Jew had remained the Christian God.

In all these developments it is hard to find anything remotely harmonious with the life of the founder of Christianity who said, "resist not evil," "turn the other cheek" (Matt. 5:39), "blessed are the peacemakers" (Matt. 5:9), and who promised that the meek would inherit the earth (Matt. 5:5). The same Messiah had protested: "My Kingdom is not of this world [i.e., does not derive its origin from present evil world-systems, though it will be on the earth in the age to come]; if it were then my servants would fight" (John 18:36).[21] Once Christianity had committed

---

[20] A well-researched account of the strong political influence in the formation of Christian dogma is provided by R.E. Rubenstein's *When Jesus Became God: The Struggle to Define Christianity during the Last Days of Rome* (Harcourt, 1999).

[21] Many biblical passages tell us that the Kingdom of God will be established on the earth (Matt. 5:5; 19:28; 25:31; Rev. 5:10; Isa. 2:1-4, etc.) when Jesus returns.

itself to the theological verdict of the secular, conquering arm of the State, acceptance of violence in the Church became established. The Church had made a fatal compromise with the world, a decision which leaves it floundering in uncertainty and doctrinal confusion, prepared also in time of war to kill both its enemies and its own members in enemy lands.

The Catholic Church, when threatened by false doctrine, later considered it the God-given responsibility of the faithful to destroy all opposition through the Inquisition. She saw her protesting children in the Protestant world employ similar means. Dissidents to the Protestant Reformation received equally harsh treatment from powerful Protestant leaders in league with secular government.

Calvin Against Servetus

A remarkable example of how Christian leadership sometimes responds when its age-old doctrine of the Trinity is threatened by the idea that God is a single person, is shown by the reaction of one highly regarded leader of the Protestant Reformation, John Calvin. The unfortunate victim of Calvin's cruelty was the anti-Trinitarian, Michael Servetus.

Servetus, educated in the Catholic religion, trained in civil law and subsequently in medicine, was appalled at the pomp and adoration given to the Pontiff in Rome. After coming under the influence of the early Reformation, Servetus continued his energetic study of the Bible and became the first Protestant to attack the doctrine of the Trinity. His writings leave little doubt that he was exceptionally well-educated, schooled in both Hebrew and Greek. He declared in a somewhat emotive, even abrasive manner that the Catholic dogma of the three divine Persons in the Godhead was a construct of the imagination, a monster compounded of incongruous parts, metaphysical gods, and philosophical abstracts.[22] The accusation attracted the notice

---

22 *General Repository and Review,* ed. Andrews Norton (Cambridge, MA: William Hilliard, Oct., 1813), 4:37.

of Calvin who responded that Servetus "deserved to have his bowels ript out, and to be torn to pieces."[23]

Ironically, although Servetus was largely sympathetic to the Protestant cause, he soon found Protestant Germany and Switzerland off-limits for him. He was, however, able to find a home in the palace of a Roman Catholic Archbishop in France who was an admirer of learned men. By then Servetus had become a skilled physician and the first one to publish an account of the passage of the blood from the right ventricle to the left auricle of the heart. The diversity of his accomplishments showed him to be intellectually the equal of other reformers. His continued correspondence with Calvin on the Trinitarian issue did not, however, ingratiate him with the constituted authority of Geneva, where Calvin had come virtually to control a powerful theocratic system. He told Calvin, "Your Gospel is without the one God, without true faith, without good works. Instead of the one God you have a three-headed Cerberus"[24] (the mythological Greek three-headed dog who guarded the gates to Hell). He further stated to Calvin, "instead of true faith you have a fatal delusion; and good works you say are empty show."[25] These words would certainly not qualify Servetus for the diplomatic corps. But we should not doubt his integrity or the courage of his convictions.

Calvin, true to the spirit of Constantine, vowed to kill him when it was in his power to do so. Servetus determined, however, to publish one more work, designed to restore Christianity to its original purity and to free it from the errors which had polluted the faith. Calvin obtained a copy of Servetus' finished work attacking the Trinitarian doctrine. He then proceeded through an intermediary to have the Catholic Church arrest Servetus. During his incarceration he was treated with respect and after three days was given a key by the jailer for a

---

[23] Ibid.

[24] Ibid., 47.

[25] Ibid.

walk in the gardens. He escaped and walked to freedom; but it turned out to be a death walk.

His freedom was short-lived. Determined to go to Naples in Italy to continue his practice as a physician, he made the unfortunate decision to travel via Geneva. This was Calvin's territory. Ruling with almost absolute power, he had established an ecclesiastical theocracy. Servetus could no doubt reason that if caught, his treatment from fellow Protestants might be more merciful than if he fell into the hands of the Catholic authorities. After his escape, the Catholic Church had tried him in absentia and sentenced him "to be drawn in a dung cart to the place of punishment and there to be burned alive (*tout vif*) by a slow fire, with his books."[26] Tragically, Servetus did not reckon with the character of his Protestant enemy who had said, "if he comes and if any regard be had to my authority I shall not suffer him to escape with life."[27] Calvin later admitted: "I do not conceal that through my exertions, and by my council he was thrown into prison."[28] Calvin would have better served his modern apologists had he not written an account of his dealings with Servetus. But it is not uncommon for followers of any leader to turn a blind eye and remove from public view the most objectionable aspects of their hero's conduct, without strict regard for the facts.

Servetus experienced the full force of the ruthless Calvin. After suffering cruel privation and humiliation, he was bound to the stake with an iron chain, his last book fastened to his thigh. After he had begged

> his executioner not to torment long, the fire was applied to a scanty pile of green oak branches. He lingered a long time in torment, crying out with a piercing voice, "Jesus, Son of the eternal God, have mercy upon me!" At last some of the spectators, out of compassion, threw

---

26 Ibid., 56.
27 Ibid., 48.
28 Ibid., 58.

faggots [burning sticks] upon him to put an end to his misery.[29]

Thus ended the life of a brilliant man whose studies of the Bible put him in opposition to a powerful 16th-century Protestant reformer. Despite any historical disagreement over the strengths and weaknesses of the two antagonists in this tragic drama, the plain fact remains that Servetus was burned at the stake for his opposition to a religious doctrine — the Trinity. He suffered a cruel death for daring to publish his honest, well-studied disagreement with hallowed tradition whose supporter felt threatened. Time has not succeeded in erasing this fearful blot from established Christianity's record.

It would be wrong to believe that religious or secular opposition to belief in a single-person Deity is confined to an ancient past. Through one means or another, covert or overt, the biblical concept of a Deity of one person, the "one God, the Father," of Paul's creed (1 Cor. 8:6), has been hidden under a blanket of contradictory words, phrases and suppressed discussion.

The violence with which the doctrine of the Trinity has been defended casts a pall of suspicion over it. Something seems desperately wrong with a teaching that has precipitated such tragic and bloody episodes in church history. The dogma which even its proponents say cannot be explained and one which makes little sense to the rational mind was the product of Greek thinking. It was at odds with the Hebraic theology in which Jesus and the Apostles were nurtured. The God of Moses, Isaiah, Jesus, and the Apostles was one person, *the Father*. One cannot be made equal to two or three. All that can be done with one is to fractionalize it. Divide it into smaller segments and it is no longer one. Expand it, and in spite of prodigious mental gymnastics on the part of Trinitarians, it cannot be made into two or three and still remain one. (This is not to say, of course, that God may not appoint agents to extend His influence and exercise His authority. But this is not an ontological but a fiduciary

---

[29] Ibid., 72.

relationship.) God will not submit to fractionalization or division. When Christianity took its formal initial step forcing a division of God into two (Father and Son), it fragmented itself, not God. So the Christian world remains to this day; not unified as Christ prayed, but segmented into conflicting denominations. This fact should cause us to ponder the question: If Christ prayed that his Church would be one (John 17:20, 21), was that prayer not answered? Is it possible that today's divided and confused religious community is in fact Christian in name only? Could its primary creed be a deviation from the Bible it loudly claims as its standard?

If we lay aside the imaginative speculations of Greek philosophers and theologians; if we omit argument from inference in our search for the true God and the real Jesus, and rely on Scripture's plain creedal declarations, the Bible reveals that Jesus was the Messiah, Son of God. This is the New Testament's central "dogma." This is the creed of the earliest Christians, and there is no need to alter their perception of the Savior by presenting him as a preexistent super-angel or as the eternal God who became man.

It is reasonable to account for the shift in thinking which now makes it hard for Bible readers to distinguish the legacy of tradition from the original teaching of Jesus and the Apostles. A Christian in search of truth will have nothing to fear from the facts.

VII. THE NATURE OF PREEXISTENCE IN THE NEW TESTAMENT

"Holy Spirit will come upon you...For that reason the holy one to be born will be called the Son of God." — Gabriel

Within the Christian tradition, the New Testament has long been read through the prism of the later conciliar creeds...Speaking of Jesus as the Son of God had a very different connotation in the first century from that which it has had ever since the Council of Nicea (325 AD). Talk of his preexistence ought probably in most, perhaps in all, cases to be understood, on the analogy of the preexistence of the Torah, to indicate the eternal divine purpose being achieved through him, rather than preexistence of a fully personal kind.[1]

The mainstream churches are committed to a certain doctrine about Jesus, but specialists in early Christian thought are questioning the arguments by which that doctrine was reached. New Testament scholars ask if the New Testament teaches it at all, and historians wonder at the gulf between Jesus himself and fully-developed Christianity. These questions are very unsettling, for they imply that Christianity may be in worse condition than was thought. It is perhaps not a basically sound structure that needs only to be modernized, but may be in need of radical reconstruction...The New Testament

---

[1] Maurice Wiles, *The Remaking of Christian Doctrine.*

> never suggests that the phrase "Son of God" just means
> "God."[2]

Yet evangelicalism insists on that equation if one is to be considered a Christian!

"When the Jew wished to designate something as predestined, he spoke of it as already 'existing' in heaven."[3] Thus "preexistence" statements in the New Testament really have to do with foreordination and predestination. It was the Greeks who misunderstood Jewish ways of thinking and turned Jesus into a cosmic figure who entered the earth from outer space. But is such a Jesus a human being? Is he the true Messiah of Israel?

Many dedicated Christians are currently exercised about the Gnostic and mystical tendencies affecting the Church. But many are unaware that philosophical, mystical ideas invaded the Church from the second century onwards via the "Church Fathers," who were steeped in pagan philosophy and laid the foundation of the creeds now called "orthodox." The seed of Trinitarian doctrine was planted in the thinking of Justin Martyr, the second-century Christian apologist who "found in Platonism the nearest approach to Christianity and felt that no break was required with its spirit and principles to pass into the greater light of Christian revelation." "The forces which operated to change apostolic doctrine were derived from paganism…The habits of thought which the Gentiles brought into the Church are sufficient to explain the corruptions of apostolic doctrine which began in the post-apostolic age."[4]

Intelligent Christians need to be informed of these corruptions and how they are currently "canonized" as Scripture by many. Discernment means learning the difference between

---

[2] Don Cupitt, *The Debate About Christ* (London: SCM Press, 1979), vii, 4.

[3] E.G. Selwyn, *First Epistle of St. Peter* (Baker Book House, 1983), 124.

[4] G.T. Purves, *The Testimony of Justin Martyr to Early Christianity* (New York: Randolph and Co., 1889), 167.

revealed truth and pagan, philosophical teachings which originated outside the Bible yet affected what is now called "orthodoxy."

We would ask the reader to consider the disastrous effects of not paying attention to the Jewish ways of thinking found in the Bible, which was written (with the exception of Luke) by Jews. Clearly if Jews do not mean what we mean by "preexistence" we are liable to misunderstand them on basic issues about who Jesus is. There is a huge difference between being predestined or foreordained and actually preexisting. Greek philosophy believed in a "second God," a non-human intermediary between the creator and the world. The true Jesus, however, is the "man Messiah," the one Mediator between God and Man (1 Tim. 2:5). "To us Christians there is one God, the Father...and one Lord Messiah" (1 Cor. 8:6). Note carefully Paul's definition of the One God.

The New Testament is a thoroughly Jewish book. Its writers were all Jews except probably Luke (who, however, is as Jewish as any of the writers in terms of his obvious delight in the Jewish salvation [John 4:22] offered in Jesus to both Jew and Gentile). Modern Bible readers approach basic biblical issues with an entrenched Greek outlook on life. This they have inherited from the churches and early post-biblical creeds which overlooked the fact that Jesus was a Jew who thought and taught in Jewish categories.

There is an anti-Semitic tendency in traditional, creedal Christianity which must be recognized and forsaken. It has dramatically affected Christian doctrine. It has affected the way we define the person of Jesus, the Messiah.

The idea that the soul separates from the body and survives consciously apart from the body is a thoroughly un-Jewish idea (this is well established in the Old Testament perspective — and the New Testament teaching about the nature of man is based on the Old). Modern readers of the Bible are shocked to discover that in the Bible *the whole man dies* and goes into unconsciousness ("sleep") and is returned to life only by the future resurrection of the whole person. Traditional Christianity persists with the mistaken notion that man has an "immortal

soul" which lives on after death. Many Bible readers have not
paid attention to the statement of the *Interpreter's Dictionary of
the Bible:* "No biblical text authorizes the statement that the
'soul' is separated from the body at the moment of death."[5]

The notion that Jesus was really alive and conscious before
his birth in Bethlehem is also a very un-Jewish idea. Human
beings in Hebrew thought do not exist consciously before they
are born. The preexistence of souls belongs to the world of
Greek philosophy and was held by some Church Fathers
(notably the philosophically- and mystically-minded Origen).
But they did not derive this idea from the Bible.

Part of Christian growth is the willingness to admit we have
been deceived, that we have not had sufficient information to
make good decisions on Bible issues.

One most important fact we need to know before we attempt
to understand who Jesus was is this:

> When the Jew said something was "predestined," he
> thought of it as already "existing" in a higher sphere of
> life. The world's history is thus predestined because it is
> already, *in a sense,* preexisting and consequently fixed.
> This typically Jewish conception of predestination may
> be distinguished from the Greek idea of preexistence by
> the predominance of *the thought of "preexistence" in the
> Divine purpose.*[6]

Our scholar goes on to tell us that this typical mode of
Jewish thought is clearly illustrated in 1 Peter. This reminds us
immediately that Peter did not abandon his Jewish ways of
thinking (based on the Hebrew Bible) when he became a
Christian. Peter's letter is addressed to "the elect according to the
foreknowledge [*prognosis*] of God the Father" (1 Pet. 1:2). Peter

---

[5] Ed. G.A. Buttrick (Nashville: Abingdon Press, 1962), 1:802. See
further our article, "Do Souls Go to Heaven?"

[6] E.C. Dewick, *Primitive Christian Eschatology, The Hulsean Prize
Essay for 1908* (Cambridge University Press, 1912), 253, 254,
emphasis added.

believed that all Christians were foreknown, but that did not mean that we all preexisted!

Peter's doctrine of future things is permeated by the same thought that all is foreordained in God's great Plan. God sees everything laid out before Him. Those who have the gift of the spirit will share God's outlook and in faith recognize that the realities of God's plan will in the future become realities on earth. According to Peter the Messiah himself was *foreknown, not just his death for our sins but the person Messiah himself* (1 Pet. 1:20). Peter uses the same word to describe the "existence" of the Son of God in God's plan as he did to describe the "existence" of the Christian Church (v. 2).

Though the Messiah was foreknown (not known, but *fore*known, as was Jeremiah before his birth, Jer. 1:5), he was manifested by being brought into actual existence at his birth (Luke 1:35). This is a typically Jewish way of understanding God's purpose for mankind. He executes the Plan at the appropriate time.

The sort of "preexistence" Peter has in mind is the sort that fits the Jewish environment, not the Greek atmosphere of later, post-biblical Christianity.

> We are not entitled to say that Peter was familiar with the idea of Christ's preexistence with the Father before the incarnation [we are therefore not entitled to claim that Peter was a Trinitarian!]. For this idea is not necessarily implied in his description of Christ as "foreknown before the foundation of the world," since Christians are also the objects of God's foreknowledge. All that we can say is that the phrase *pro kataboles kosmou* [before the foundation of the world] affirms for Christ's office and work a supramundane range and importance...Peter has not extended his belief in Christ's divinity to an affirmation of his preexistence:

his Christology is more like that of the early chapters of
Acts than of John and Paul.[7]

Peter, as the leading Apostle (Matt. 10:2), would have had no
sympathy with either a Trinitarian or Arian (cp. modern
Jehovah's Witnesses) view of Jesus.

We note also that for Peter the future salvation of the
Christians, the Kingdom they are to inherit at the return of
Christ, is likewise waiting in heaven "ready to be revealed in the
last time" (1 Pet. 1:5). The Second Coming is thus to be an
"apocalypse" or unveiling of what is now "existing" but hidden
from our sight. So it is said of Jesus that he was "foreknown,"
and waiting to be *revealed* in God's good time (1 Pet. 1:20).
Neither the Kingdom nor Jesus actually existed in advance. They
were planned from before the foundation of the world.

Paul uses the same concept and language about the future
resurrection and immortality of the saints. He says that we
already "*have* a building from God, a house fit for the coming
age" (2 Cor. 5:1).[8] Our future resurrection body already "exists"
in God's intention and may be thought of as real because it is
certain to be manifested in the future. In that sense we "have" it,
though we obviously do not yet have it literally. The same is true
of the treasure we have in heaven. It is promised for our future.
We will receive the reward of the inheritance (Col. 3:24) when
Christ brings it from heaven to the earth at his future coming.

Foreordination Rather than Literal Preexistence

Having grasped this elementary fact of Jewish (and biblical)
theology and thinking, it will not be difficult to adjust our

---

[7] E.G. Selwyn, *First Epistle of St. Peter,* 248, 250. We disagree that
Peter's idea of Jesus is different from that of Paul and John. It is highly
improbable that the Apostles differed in their view of who Jesus was.

[8] This is the proper translation of *aionios,* i.e., belonging to the coming
age of the Kingdom, not "eternal." This does not of course mean that
the body of the future is temporary. It confers immortality and thus
lasts forever. The acquisition of that body is nevertheless the great
event of the coming age introduced by the resurrection.

understanding of other passages where the same principle of "existence" followed by actual manifestation is found. Thus Jesus says in John 17:5: "Glorify me [now] with the glory which *I had with you* before the foundation of the world." On the basis of 2 Corinthians 5:1 a Christian in the future, after the resurrection at Christ's return, will be able to say that he has now received what he already "had," i.e. laid up for him in God's plan. Christians are said to *have* treasure in heaven (Mark 10:21), that is, a reward stored up with God now and destined to be conferred in the future. This is only to say that they will one day *in the future* "inherit the Kingdom *prepared for [them]* from the foundation of the world" (Matt. 25:34).

When Jesus says that he "had" the glory for which he now prays (John 17:5), he is merely asking for the glory which he knew was prepared for him by God from the beginning.[9] That glory existed in God's plan, and in that sense Jesus already "had" it. We note that Jesus did not say, "Give me back" or "restore to me the glory which I had when I was alive with you before my birth." This notion would have been completely foreign to Judaism. It is quite unnecessary and indeed wrong to read Gentile ideas into the texts of Scripture when we can make good sense of them as they stand in their Jewish environment. The onus is on those who believe in literal preexistence to demonstrate that the texts *cannot* be explained within their own Jewish context. And it should be remembered that the Hebrew Bible, which has much to say in anticipation of the coming Son of God, makes no statement to imply that the Messiah was God destined to arrive from a personal pre-birth existence in heaven. The idea that God can be born as a man is alien to the Jewish environment in which Jesus taught. A revolution would have been required for the introduction of such a novel concept.

The so-called "preexistence" of Jesus in John refers to his "existence" in the Plan of God. The Church has been plagued by the introduction of non-biblical language. There is a perfectly

---

[9] The Synoptic way of expressing the same idea is to talk of the Kingdom "prepared before the foundation of the world" (Matt. 25:34).

good word for "real" preexistence in the Greek language (*pro-uparchon*). It is very significant that it appears nowhere in Scripture with reference to Jesus, but it does in the writings of Greek Church Fathers of the second century. These Greek commentators on Scripture failed to understand the Hebrew categories of thought in which the New Testament is written.

The biblical view of Jesus before his birth has to do with his "existence" *in God's Plan and vision*. Preexistence in the Bible does not mean what it meant in later creeds: the actual conscious existence of the Son of God before his birth at which time he entered the earth and the human condition by passing through the womb of his mother. In Scripture Jesus is produced *from* Mary (Matt. 1:16). Strangely, in the second century, Justin Martyr begins to speak of Jesus coming *through* his mother.

A Jewish and biblical conception of preexistence is most significant for Jesus' understanding of himself as the Son of Man. The Son of Man is found in the book of Daniel. He "preexists" only in the sense that God grants us a vision of *him* — the Human Being — in His Plan for the future. The Son of Man is *a human being* — that is what the words mean. Thus what John wants us to understand is that the *human* Messiah was in heaven before his birth (in God's Plan) and was seen *in Daniel's vision of the future* (Dan. 7; John 6:62). Jesus at his ascension went up to the position which had been previously prepared for him in God's Plan. No text says that Jesus went *back* (*upostrepho*) to God, though this idea has been wrongly imported into some modern English translations to support "orthodoxy." Such mistranslation of the Greek "go to the Father" as "go *back* to the Father" tells its own story.[10] Translations of the Bible are biased in favor of traditional, post-biblical ideas of who Jesus is.

The Son of Man is not an angel. No angel was ever called a "Son of Man" (= member of the human race — with good reason Jesus' favorite self-title). To call the Messiah an angel would be a muddling of categories. Hence scholars rightly report that the

---

[10] See NIV at John 16:28 and 20:17.

idea of preexistence for the Messiah "*antecedent to his birth in Bethlehem* is unknown in Judaism." The Messiah, according to all that is predicted of him in the Old Testament, belongs in his origin to the human race: "'Judaism has never known anything of a preexistence peculiar to the Messiah antecedent to his birth as a human being' (Dalman, *Words of Jesus*, pp. 128-32, 248, 252). The dominance of the idea in any Jewish circle whatever cannot seriously be upheld. Judaism knew nothing of the [literally] *preexistent* ideal man."[11]

To claim to "be before Abraham" (John 8:58) does not mean that you remember being alive before your birth. That is to think like a Greek who believes in the preexistence of souls. In the Hebrew thought of the New Testament one can "exist" as part of God's Plan as did also the tabernacle, the temple, repentance and other major elements of the Divine purpose. Even Moses preexisted in that sense, according to a quotation we introduce later. John the Apostle could also say that Christ was "crucified before the foundation of the world" (Rev. 13:8). This gives us an enormously valuable clue as to the way the New Testament writers understood "preexistence."

There are multiple examples of past tenses in the Hebrew Bible which actually refer to future events. They are "past" because they describe events fixed in God's counsels and therefore certain to be realized. Bible readers disregard this very Jewish way of thinking when they leap to the conclusion that when Jesus said he "had" glory with the father from the foundation of the world (John 17:5), he meant that he was alive at that time. Certainly in a Western frame of reference the traditional understanding is reasonable. But can we not do the Messiah the honor of trying to understand his words in their own Hebrew environment? Should not the Bible be interpreted in the light of its own context and not our later creeds?

---

[11] Charles Gore, *Belief in Christ* (London: John Murray, 1923), 31.

No Preexistence for Jesus in Matthew, Mark and Luke

There is a deafening silence about any real preexistence of Christ in Matthew, Mark, Luke, Acts and Peter, and the whole of the Old Testament. Not only do they not hint at a pre-human Son of God, they contradict the idea by talking of the *origin* (*genesis*) of Jesus (Matt. 1:18) and his *begetting as Son* (Matt. 1:20) *in Mary's womb.*[12] Note that for Arians and Trinitarians, who think that Jesus was begotten in eternity long before his conception/begetting in Mary, this would be a *second* begetting.[13] Luke knows nothing of such an idea. Unprejudiced readers will see (as acknowledged by a host of biblical experts) that the Jesus of Matthew, Mark, Luke Acts and Peter is a human being originating at his conception and birth as do all other human persons. He has not preexisted. Matthew even speaks of the "genesis" of Jesus in Matthew 1:18.

It is a serious imposition on the Gospel of John to understand him to teach a different sort of Jesus than Matthew, Mark and Luke — one who is really an angel or God appearing as a man. Such a non-human Messiah is foreign not only to the rest of the New Testament, but to the whole revelation of God in the Old

---

[12] Note the mistranslation in our versions: The text does not refer to conception, but to "begetting" by the Father through the Holy Spirit. It is the action of the Father which brings the Son into existence. The Son of God, the Messiah, is a supernaturally created person, the Second Adam. Note also in Acts 13:33 the reference to the "raising up" of Jesus, which refers to God's bringing him into being. Verse 34 mentions his subsequent resurrection. The KJV obscures this important distinction.

[13] Justin Martyr is perhaps the first Church Father to speak of a begetting of the Son *prior to* Genesis (i.e. prior to Creation). But he provides no scriptural support for such an ante-mundane begetting of the Son. According to the Bible the Son of God was begotten, as are all human persons, at the time of his conception in his mother's womb. Justin differs from Matthew by saying that the Son came "through" Mary. Matthew holds that he came *from* Mary. This points to the shift of thinking that has taken place by 150 AD, a shift which provided the seed of the later Trinitarian formulation.

Testament in regard to his definition of the coming Messiah. Deuteronomy 18:15-18 expressly says that the Messiah is to arise from a family in Israel. The Messiah is expressly said in this important Christological text *not to be God but God's agent born to the family of Israel.* All Jews who looked forward to the Messiah expected a human person, not an angel, much less God Himself! Though the Jews had not understood that the Messiah was to be born supernaturally, even this miraculous begetting was in fact predicted (Isa. 7:14; Matt. 1:23). A "pre-human" Messiah, however, is nowhere suggested.

According to Isaiah 44:24 God was unaccompanied at the original creation. Jesus in the Gospels attributes the creation to the Father and has no memory of being the agent in the Genesis creation (Mark 10:6; Matt. 6:30; 19:4; Luke 12:28). If Jesus had really been the creator of the Genesis heaven and earth, why does he have no memory of this? Why does he expressly say that God was the creator? The answer is that Jesus worked within the Jewish and biblical framework of the scriptural heritage he had received and which he "came not to destroy."

The spirit of God is available to believers. As they learn to think as God does, they will share the concept that "God speaks of things which do not exist *as though they did*" (Rom. 4:17). It is a mistake to confuse "existence" in the Plan of God with actual preexistence, thus creating a non-fully human Jesus. The Christ of biblical expectation is a human person, supernaturally conceived. The supreme glory of his achievement for us lies in the fact that he really was a human being. He was tempted. But God cannot be tempted (James 1:13).

The "Rock" Apostle whom Jesus appointed to "feed my sheep" has given us a marvelous lesson in how to understand the meaning of preexistence as foreknowledge and predestination. It was Peter whose recognition of Jesus as *the Messiah* was greeted by the excited approval of Jesus (Matt. 16:16-18). Peter and John understood that the glory which Jesus already "had" is the same glory believers subsequent to the time of Jesus (and therefore not yet born when Jesus spoke) also had been given (John 17:22). This means only that things which are fixed in God's counsels "exist" in a sense other than actual existence. We must choose whether to understand the language of the New Testament as Americans or Europeans or as sympathetic to Jesus and his Jewish culture. A verse in Revelation speaks of things "being" before they were created. "They *were* and were created" (Rev. 4:11).[14] Their creation followed from God's original Plan to bring them into being.

A knowledge of the background to the New Testament reveals that Jews believed that even Moses "preexisted" in the counsels of God, but not actually as a conscious person:

> For this is what the Lord of the world has decreed: He created the world on behalf of his people, but he did not make this purpose of creation known from the beginning of the world so that the nations might be found guilty...But He did design and devise me [Moses], who was prepared from the beginning of the world to be the mediator of the covenant (Testament of Moses, 1:13, 14).

If Moses was decreed in the Plan of God, it makes perfect sense that the Messiah himself was the purpose for which God created everything. All things may then be said to have been created on behalf of the Christ. Out of respect for God's revealed Plan and in honor of the human Savior, we should seek to understand his identity in the context of his own Hebrew setting.

A fine statement of the Jewish understanding of "preexistence" is given by the Norwegian scholar, Mowinckel, in his famous *He That Cometh:*

> That any expression or vehicle of God's will for the world, His saving counsel and purpose, was present in

---

[14]The use of the verb "were" is interesting in the light of an alternative reading in John 17:5 which speaks of "the glory which *was* with you." This would be a statement about the preexisting glory (not the pre-human Jesus) which Jesus prayed to have bestowed on him (John 17:5), and also on his followers (John 17:22). See Raymond Brown, *The Gospel According to John, Anchor Bible* (New York: Doubleday, 1966), 743. Note also that Augustine, and many other commentators, find no evidence for literal preexistence in John 17:5.

His mind, or His "Word," from the beginning is a natural way of saying that it is not fortuitous, but the due unfolding and expression of God's own being [cp. John: "the Word was with God and was God"]. This attribution of preexistence indicates religious importance of the highest order. Rabbinic theology speaks of the Law, of God's throne of glory, of Israel and of other important objects of faith as things which had been created by God, and were already present with Him before the creation of the world. The same is also true of the Messiah. It is said that his name was present with God in heaven beforehand, that it was created before the world, and that it is eternal.

But the reference here is not to genuine preexistence in the strict and literal sense. This is clear from the fact that Israel is included among these preexistent entities. This does not mean that either the nation Israel or its ancestor existed long ago in heaven, but that the community Israel, the people of God, had been from all eternity *in the mind of God*, as a factor in His purpose...This is true of references to the preexistence of the Messiah. It is his "name," not the Messiah himself, that is said to have been present with God before creation. In *Pesikta Rabbati* 152b it is said that "from the beginning of the creation of the world the King Messiah was born, for he came up *in the thought of God* before the world was created." This means that from all eternity it was *the will of God that the Messiah should come into existence*, and should do his work in the world to fulfill God's eternal saving purpose.[15]

The proposition introduced by Gentile, philosophically-minded "Church Fathers" that Jesus was either a second "member" of the Godhead (later orthodoxy) or a created angel

---

[15] Transl. G.W. Anderson (Nashville: Abingdon, 1954), 334, emphasis added.

(Arians and in modern times, Jehovah's Witnesses) launched the whole vexed problem of the nature of Christ in relation to the Godhead and put under a fog the true Messiahship of Jesus and his Messianic Gospel about the Kingdom. Jesus of Nazareth is what the Word (God's Wisdom) of John 1:1 *became* (John 1:14).[16] He is the unique expression, as a human being, of the Wisdom of God. It was the Wisdom of God which existed from the beginning, and that Wisdom became a person at the conception of Jesus. This explanation leaves intact the great cardinal doctrine that the One God is the Father and that Jesus is the Lord Messiah, not the Lord God.[17] It was the early Greek Church Fathers who confused the issue of Jewish/Christian monotheism by introducing the idea of a "numerically second God."[18]

It is most significant that Paul often speaks of the gospel as having been hidden in the counsels of God from "ages past."[19] He also says that the Son of God *"came into existence"* from a woman and from the seed of David (Gal. 4:4; Rom. 1:3). It is unimaginable that Paul could have believed in the preexistence of the Son. It would be untrue to say that the Son came into existence at his birth, if in fact he had always existed. It is far more reasonable to suppose that Paul agreed with Peter that the Messiah was hidden in the divine counsels and then revealed in the fullness of time.[20] Paul believed that in Jesus "all things have

[16] Jesus embodies the wisdom of God just as he also embodies the "salvation" of God (Luke 2:30).

[17] Deut. 6:4; Mark. 12:29ff.; 1 Cor. 8:4-6; 1 Tim. 2:5; John 17:3; 5:44.

[18] Justin Martyr, *Dialogue,* 56, 62, 128, 129. Justin believed that the Son was begotten before the Genesis creation, but not that he had always been the Son. Justin, therefore, was not a Trinitarian.

[19] Eph. 3:9; Col. 1:26; 2 Tim. 1:9; Tit. 1:2; cp. 1 Pet. 1:20; Rev. 13:8.

[20] We note James Dunn's justifiable protest against Cranfield's comment on Rom. 1:3. "Unconcerned by his use of anachronistic categories, Cranfield continues to argue that Paul 'intended to limit the application of "who came into existence" to the *human nature* which the One (God's Son, v. 3) *assumed'"* *(Romans 1-8, Word Biblical*

been created" (Col. 1:16). He did not say they had been created "by him."

Finally, it is most unreasonable to claim that "Wisdom" in Proverbs (i.e., "Lady Wisdom") was in fact Jesus, the Son, preexisting. It should not be difficult to discern that "Wisdom" here is a personification of a divine quality, not a person. The proof of this is found not only in all major commentaries but very clearly in the text itself. "I, Wisdom, dwell with Prudence" (Prov. 8:12). If Wisdom is really a (male) Son of God, then who is Prudence?

Preexisting purposes and personifications are all part of the literature of Judaism. A preexistent, non-human Messiah is not. A Messiah who is not a human being approximates much more closely to the pagan idea of preexisting souls and Gnostic "aions." It was that early invasion of paganism which unfortunately began to corrupt the faith, just as Peter and Paul warned (2 Pet. 2; Acts 20:29-31).

That intrusion of paganism resulted in some very strange language about Jesus. His "pre-human existence" signals the fact that he is really not a human being. He has existed as an angel before being born. This is close to the idea of "the gods coming down in the likeness of men" (Acts 14:11). Such a Jesus sounds like a pagan savior figure. There were many such cosmic saviors in the Graeco-Roman world. But there was only one Messiah, whose identity was given long in advance of his birth. He was foreknown (1 Pet. 1:20) and would arise from the House of Israel as an Israelite of the tribe of Judah (Deut. 18:15-18; Acts 3:22; 7:37). That important text in Deuteronomy actually states that the promised agent of God would not be the Lord God, but His spokesman. Christians should be careful to claim allegiance to that Savior. To worship a Savior with wrong ideas about him runs the risk of worshipping another Savior. *The creed of Jesus is the right creed for Christians* (Mark 12:29). As so many scholars know, that creed is not a Trinitarian creed. The One

---

Commentary, Dallas: Word Books, 1988, 15). Cranfield struggles to justify "orthodoxy" from Paul's words. But Paul was neither an "orthodox" Trinitarian nor an "unorthodox" Arian.

God of Israel and of Jesus was and is the Father,[21] "the One and only God" (John 5:44), "the only true God" (John 17:3).

John 1:1

Christology, the study of who Jesus is, has to do with a reasoned statement about the relation of Jesus to the One God of Israel. There is no doubt that for the early Christians Jesus had the value and reality of God. This, however, does not mean that they thought Jesus "was God." It has been held by some that John presents Jesus in metaphysical terms which would appeal to people in the Greek world who thought in terms of abstract ideas familiar to Hellenistic thought. "Orthodoxy" claims John as its bridge to the world of Greek metaphysics — the metaphysics which helped to mold the Jesus of the church councils.

We suggest that we should first see if John can be readily understood in terms of his otherwise very Jewish approach. Why should we attempt to read John as though he were a student of the Jew Philo or of Gentile mystery religion? Why should John be claimed as a supporter of the dogmatic conclusions of the much later church councils? Should we not make sense of him from the Old Testament world of ideas? "What we do know," says a leading Bible scholar, "is that John was steeped in the Old Testament Scriptures. If we wish to understand the historical ancestry of John's Logos [word] concept as he himself understood it, we have to go back to those Scriptures."[22]

It is a considerable mistake to read John 1:1 as though it means "In the beginning was the Son of God and the Son was with the Father and the Son was God."[23] This is not what John

---

[21] John 17:3; John 5:44; 1 Tim. 2:5; 1 Cor. 8:4-6.

[22] C.J. Wright, *Jesus: The Revelation of God*, Book 3 of *The Mission and Message of Jesus: An Exposition of the Gospels in the Light of Modern Research* (New York: E.P. Dutton and Co., 1938), 677.

[23] Cp. the very misleading paraphrase of the Living Bible: "Before anything else existed, there was Christ, with God. He has always been alive and is Himself God. He created everything there is — nothing exists that He did not make" (John 1:1-2).

wrote. The German poet Goethe wrestled to find a correct translation: "In the beginning was the Word, the Thought, the Power or the Deed." He decided on "deed." He comes very close to John's intention. What the evangelist wanted to say was: "The Creative Thought of God has been operating from all eternity."

As a leading British Bible scholar wrote:

> When John presents the eternal Word he was not thinking of a Being in any way separate from God, or some *"Hypostasis."* The later dogmatic Trinitarian distinctions should not be read *into* John's mind...in the light of a philosophy which was not his...We must not read John in the light of the dogmatic history of the three centuries subsequent to the Evangelist's writing.[24]

To understand John (and the rest of the New Testament) we must pay close attention to John's cultural heritage which was not the world of Greek philosophy in which the dogmatic creeds were formed some three hundred years later. When John is read in the light of his Hebrew background he provides no support for the doctrine of a Jesus who is "God the Son," an eternal uncreated Person in a triune Godhead:

> An author's language will confuse us, unless we have some *rapport* with his mind...The evangelist John takes a well-known term *logos,* does not define it, but unfolds what he himself means by it...The idea belonged to the Old Testament, and is involved in the whole religious belief and experience of the Hebrew Scriptures. It is the most fitting term to express his message. For a man's "word" is the expression of his "mind"; and his mind is his essential personality. Every mind must express itself, for activity is the very nature of mind...Thus John speaks of the "Word" that was *with* God, and was *Divine,* to express his conviction that God has ever been Active and Revealing Mind. God, by His very nature, cannot sit in heaven and do nothing. When later in the Gospel Jesus says, "My Father works up till now" he is

---

[24] C.J. Wright, *Jesus: The Revelation of God,* 707.

saying what the Evangelist says in the first verse of the Prologue.

> John's language is not the language of philosophical definition. John has a "concrete" and "pictorial" mind. The failure to understand John [in his prologue] has led many to the conclusion that he is "father of metaphysical [i.e., Trinitarian] Christology," and therefore responsible for the later ecclesiastical obscuration of the ethical and spiritual emphasis of Jesus…The evangelist did not think in terms of the category of "substance" — a category which was so congenial to the Greek mind.[25]

In an illuminating article in the *Bible Review* J. Harold Ellens points out that titles such as Son of God, as used at the time when the New Testament was written:

> were never meant to designate the figures to whom they were applied as divine beings. They meant rather that these figures were imbued with divine spirit, or the Logos. The titles referred to their function and character as men of God, not to their *being God*. Thinking of a human as being God was strictly a Greek or Hellenistic notion. Thus the early theological debates from the middle of the second century on were largely between Antioch, a center of Jewish Christianity, on the one hand, and Alexandrian Christianity, *heavily colored by neo-Platonic speculation*, on the other. For the most part, the Jewish Christians' argument tended to be that they had known Jesus and his family and that he was a human being, a great teacher, one filled with the divine Logos…but that he was not divine in the ontological sense, as the Alexandrians insisted. The arguments persisted in one form or another until Cyril of Alexandria's faction finally won the day for a highly mythologized Jesus of divine ontological being. *Cyril*

---

25 Ibid., 707, 711.

was capable of murdering his fellow bishops to get his way.

By the time of the Council of Nicea in 325 CE, this Alexandrian perspective of high Christology was dominant but not uncontested by the Antiochian perspective of low Christology. From Nicea to Chalcedon the speculative and *neo-Platonist perspective* gained increasing ground and became orthodox Christian dogma in 451 CE. Unfortunately, what the theologians of the great ecumenical councils meant by such creedal titles as Son of God *was remote from what those same titles meant in the Gospels.* The creeds were speaking in Greek philosophical terms: the gospels were speaking in Second Temple Judaism terms…The Bishops of the councils should have realized that they had shifted ground from Hebrew metaphor to Greek ontology and in effect *betrayed the real Jesus Christ.*[26]

It is not difficult to understand that the Bible is abandoned when fundamental terms like Son of God are given new and unbiblical meanings. The church councils under the influence of Greek speculative neo-Platonism replaced the New Testament Son of God with a God the Son fashioned by philosophy. When a different meaning for a title is substituted for the original a new faith is created. That new faith became "orthodoxy." It insisted on its dogmas, on pain of excommunication and damnation (the Athanasian Creed). Nicean dogmatic "orthodoxy" lifted Jesus out of his Hebrew environment and twisted John's Gospel in an effort to make John fit into "orthodoxy's" philosophical mold. And so it has remained to this day.

A revolution is needed to reverse this tragic process. It will come when Christians take personal responsibility for getting in touch with the Bible and investigating it with all the tools now at our disposal. A key to proper biblical understanding is to

---

[26] See "The Ancient Library of Alexandria," *Bible Review* (Feb. 1997), 19-29 and further comments in "From Logos to Christ" ("Readers Reply"), *BR* (June 1997), 4-7, emphasis added.

recognize that the Bible is a Jewish library of books and that Jesus was a Jew steeped in the Hebrew Bible (the Old Testament).

The hidden paganism in Christianity needs to be exposed. The history of orthodoxy shows signs of a spirit which is far removed from the spirit of Jesus. Those who have questioned "orthodoxy" have often been roughly handled.[27] One commentator asks:

> How is that the religion of love has been responsible for some of the worst cruelties and injustices that have ever disgraced humanity?...The Church has persecuted more cruelly than any other religion...Our religious beliefs are propped up on the traditional scaffolding, and many of us are intensely annoyed if the stability of this scaffolding is called in question. The average Catholic [and the same applies to many Protestants] relies on the infallibility of his Church, which he has usually accepted without investigation. To own that his Church has been wrong, and has sanctioned heinous crimes, is almost impossible for him.[28]

Monotheism

Neither Paul nor any other writer of the Bible ever stated that "there is One God: Father, Son and Holy Spirit." No example out of thousands of occurrences of Yahweh and God can be shown to mean "God in three Persons." The Triune God is foreign to the Bible. The words of Paul need careful consideration: "There is no God but one...To us there is *One God, the Father*" (1 Cor.

---

[27]For an illuminating example of misguided religious zeal and cruelty, see the account of Calvin's savage persecution and execution of the Spanish doctor and scholar who questioned the doctrine of the Trinity, in Marian Hillar, *The Case of Michael Servetus (1511-1553) — The Turning Point in the Struggle for Freedom of Conscience* (Edwin Mellen Press, 1997).

[28] Dean W.R. Inge, *A Pacifist in Trouble* (London: Putnam, 1939), 180, 181.

8:4, 6). There is also one Lord Messiah, Jesus (1 Cor. 8:6), but he is the Lord *Christ* (Luke 2:11; Ps. 110:1), the *Son* of the One God, his Father.

The two major players in the Bible are described in a precious divine oracle quoted in the New Testament more than any other verse from the Hebrew Bible: Psalm 110:1. There the One God "Yahweh" speaks to David's lord, who is addressed as *adoni* ("my lord"). *Adoni* in its 195 occurrences never means, as we have seen, the One God. It refers always to a human or (occasionally) angelic superior, *other than* God. Jesus is the lord of David of whom Psalm 110:1 speaks. He was *appointed* Lord and Messiah — appointed by God, his Father (Acts 2:34-36).

Out of respect and honor for Jesus the Messiah, Christians should adopt his Jewish creed in Mark 12:29: "Hear, O Israel, the Lord our God is *one Lord*." God is *one* Lord. Jesus is another Lord. That makes *two* Lords, but the creed knows of only one Lord who is God (Deut. 6:4; Mark 12:29). That is the creed of Jesus and therefore the original and authentic Christian creed. It is also the creed of Paul. May we all joyfully embrace that creed and align ourselves with the Jesus Messiah of history.

VIII. JOHN, PREEXISTENCE AND THE TRINITY

"The clear evidence of John is that Jesus refused the claim to be God." — Professor J.A.T. Robinson

Someone has calculated that singular pronouns describe the God of the Hebrew Bible tens of thousands of times.[1] Each one of these references is a testimony to God as a single individual, not a plurality of persons. It is a standard fact of language, with which no one will argue, that the personal pronoun of the singular number denotes a single person.

The process by which the God of Israel became a Trinity speaks of Gentile failure to penetrate the depths of Jewish monotheism and a tendency to mix a strain of paganism with Scripture. Prodigious efforts have been made to turn the God of Israel into more than one person. "Clues" pointing to the Trinity have been found in the most unlikely places, as for example, the "holy, holy, holy" of Isaiah's vision (Isa. 6:3). Many Trinitarians have now abandoned the struggle to find their creed in the Hebrew Bible. Much unnecessary labor could have been spared if Jesus' and Paul's simple creedal statements had been heeded. It remains an undeniable fact that Jesus agreed with the unitarian creed of Israel (Mark 12:29) and Paul defined the One God as one person. In a passage deliberately contrasting Christianity with paganism, Paul describes the One God as numerically one, as distinct from the many gods of the heathen. Condensing the information provided by Paul in the fourth and sixth verses of 1 Corinthians 8, we find the following creed: "There is no God

---

[1] James Yates, *Vindication of Unitarianism* (Boston: Wells and Lilly, 1816), 66, 153.

except the one God, the Father." Such is the Pauline non-Trinitarian view of God.

The comment of John Milton, the distinguished British poet, theologian and vigorous anti-Trinitarian, confirms our point: "Here [1 Cor. 8:4, 6] 'there is no other God but one,' excludes not only all other essences, but all other persons whatever; for it is expressly said in the sixth verse, 'that the Father is that one God'; therefore there is no other person but one."[2]

It is amazing that Trinitarianism is not satisfied with these transparently simple definitions of the Godhead. It seems bent on leaving behind the creed which belonged not only to the authors of the Old Testament but to Jesus himself. A shift in thinking is unmistakable. Noted names in theology have sensed that a foreign influence has obscured the original faith. C.H. Dodd remarked that "the Jews have preserved in living tradition, elements of the prophetic ideal which belonged to Christianity at the first but were overlaid by Greek metaphysics and Roman law."[3]

The same problem was alluded to by Albert Schweitzer: "The great and still undischarged task which confronts those engaged in the historical study of primitive Christianity is to explain how the teaching of Jesus developed into early Greek theology."[4]

Interference with the Gospel of John

Our translations of John 1:1-4 seem to complicate the simple majesty of the One God of Israel's creed, erecting an unwanted barrier between Christianity, Judaism and Islam. The renowned translator of the English Bible, William Tyndale, was not so sure that John's "word" was one-to-one the equivalent of Christ preexisting. He renders the famous verses: "In the beginning was

---

[2] *Treatise on Christian Doctrine* (republished by the British and Foreign Unitarian Association, 1908), 16, 17.

[3] *Epistle of Paul to the Romans*, cited by Hugh Schonfield, *The Politics of God* (London: Hutchinson, 1970), 105.

[4] *Paul and His Interpreters* (London, 1912), v.

the word [with lower case], and the word was with God, and the word was God...All things were made by *it*...In *it* was life."[5] It seems strange that John 1:1-4, a handful of verses in John, and a few other New Testament passages should be allowed to overthrow the constant and massive biblical evidence for unitary monotheism. The oneness of God was strenuously defended by priest and prophet and by Jesus, who was as ardent an exponent of this part of his Jewish heritage as any of his compatriots.

This chapter is devoted to a discussion of the questions posed by John's account of the person of Jesus. John's rich portrait of Jesus does not include the notion that the Son of God is a preexistent divine person and member of a Trinity. The cherished view of Jesus as uncreated and coequal with the Father is not derived from Scripture; rather, it has been handed down through post-biblical tradition. Attempts to root the idea of preexistence in the Gospel of John involve a distortion of John's intention. Properly exegeted, the writings of the beloved Apostle harmonize with the Synoptic presentation of Jesus as a unique human being deriving his origin from his supernatural conception.

John does not present Jesus as an eternal member of a Triune Godhead but as the fulfillment of God's eternal plan to bring into being the Messiah. Thus for John, as well as for Paul, Jesus preexisted in the mind and purpose of God, rather than literally as a timeless being. Though largely lost in the shuffle of doctrinal change which overcame the Church from the second century, this unorthodox portrait of Jesus had its exponents in the centuries following the writing of the New Testament. It reappears at important junctures throughout church history, notably among the Polish Anabaptists of the 16th century. The modern discussion of Christology has centered around this same issue of the nature of preexistence. The traditional notion of preexistence is destructive to the true humanity of Jesus and diminishes some of the wonder of his achievement on our behalf.

---

5 *Tyndale's New Testament: A Translation from the Greek by William Tyndale in 1534*, ed. David Daniell (New Haven: Yale University Press, 1989), emphasis added.

It also creates the whole problem of the Trinity which many believe only because they are expected to do so. A return to biblical Christology will mean the recovery of Jesus' Messiahship, obscured and disparaged for so long by the post-biblical Christological development.

Problems with the Notion of Literal Preexistence

The very commonly held idea that Jesus was alive before his conception raises a number of questions about his nature. Is it possible to be a human being in any meaningful sense if one does not originate in the womb of one's mother? A number of leading scholars have recently thought not. "We can have the humanity [of Christ] without the preexistence and we can have the preexistence without the humanity. There is absolutely no way of having both."[6] Angels belong in a category different from human beings precisely because of their origin outside the system of human procreation. If the Son of God was really a being who changed himself (or was changed by God) in order to enter the human race through Mary, he clearly belongs to a category of being vastly different from the rest of humanity.

There are other considerations. The Messiah, according to the Scriptures, was to be a descendant of David,[7] of Abraham (Gal. 3:16), and the seed of the woman (Gen. 3:15). Paul constantly thinks of Christ as the last Adam (man). If he existed as a person before his conception, in what sense is he — the real person — a human being and a descendant of David and Abraham? Does Scripture really place Jesus in a class of being whose origin is outside the human womb? Our suggestion is that the evidence often cited from the Bible, mainly from John's Gospel, for belief in a literal preexistence for the Messiah does not stand up under close examination. We maintain that the idea has to be held *prior to* an investigation of the scriptural evidence and then read into the Bible. There is also a significant bias in

---

[6] John Knox, *The Humanity and Divinity of Jesus* (Cambridge University Press, 1967), 106.

[7] Ps. 132:11; Acts 2:30; 2 Sam. 7:14-16; Matt. 1:1.

our standard translations, due to the preconceptions of orthodoxy, which encourages us to read the New Testament through spectacles colored by later dogma. The same bias causes theologians to represent the Apostles, even after Pentecost, as "primitive" believers struggling towards the Trinitarian creed of the post-biblical church councils.

Did John Differ with Matthew, Mark and Luke over the Issue of Preexistence?

By way of background to an examination of John's Gospel, it is vitally important to keep in mind the facts about Jesus' origin presented by the Synoptic Gospels (Matthew, Mark, Luke). Luke set out to put before Theophilus the great Christian truths which the latter had learned as a believer: "the exact truth about the things you have been taught" (Luke 1:4). Few have ever tried to argue that Luke included in his portrait of Jesus a single word suggesting that Jesus was other than a human being, supernaturally conceived, and coming into existence for the first time at his conception. The same may be said of Matthew's and Mark's accounts and of the presentation of Jesus in the book of Acts. Both theologians and historians are agreed that this is so: "In the Synoptics there is no direct statement of the preexistence of Christ...They do not anywhere declare his preexistence."[8]

> First we have the Christology of the Synoptic Gospels, and here it cannot be contended on any sufficient ground that they give us the slightest justification for advancing beyond the idea of a purely human Messiah. The idea of preexistence lies completely outside the Synoptic sphere of view. Nothing can show this more clearly than the narrative of the supernatural birth of Jesus. All that raises him above humanity — though it does not take away the pure humanity of his person — is to be referred only to the *pneuma hagion* [Holy Spirit], which brought about his conception...The Synoptic Christology has for

---

[8] B.F. Westcott, *The Gospel of John* (Grand Rapids: Eerdmans, 1981), lxxxiv, lxxxvii.

its substantial foundation the notion of the Messiah, designated and conceived as the *huios theou* [Son of God]; and all the points of the working out of the notion rest on the same supposition of a nature essentially human.[9]

Preexistence does not belong to the primary data of the Christian faith in the Historic and Exalted Jesus but it is a necessary implicate of that faith [more solid evidence is needed than implication]. It forms no element in the primitive doctrine recorded in the opening chapters of Acts. [In Acts] there is no emergence of the thought that his origin must be transcendent as his destiny — no hint of preexistence. *Christ's place in eternity is in the foreknowledge and the counsel of the Father.*[10]

Most significantly, the view that Jesus existed prior to his birth only in the counsels of God is the one expressed by Peter in his first epistle. At the end of his career he has not changed the view expressed in his early speeches in Acts: "[Jesus] was foreknown before the foundation of the world but manifested in the last days for you" (1 Pet. 1:20). E.G. Selwyn notes correctly: "Nor are we entitled to say that [Peter] was familiar with the idea of Christ's preexistence...For this idea is not necessarily implied in his description of Christ as 'foreknown before the foundation of the world,' since Christians also are objects of God's foreknowledge."[11]

All the faithful were similarly "foreknown" (1 Pet. 1:2), but this obviously does not mean that they preexisted. If Peter did not think that Jesus preexisted his birth, this leading Apostle could not have believed in the Trinity.

---

[9] F.C. Baur, *Church History of the First Three Centuries* (London: Williams and Norgate's, 1878), 65.

[10] *Dictionary of the Apostolic Church* (T & T Clark, 1916), 2:264, emphasis added.

[11] *First Epistle of St. Peter*, 248.

A professor of ecclesiastical history who examined the issue carefully found no evidence for belief in Jesus' preexistence in Matthew, Mark and Luke:

> That Jesus, whose mind was steeped in the prophets, derived his Messianic conception from the common Hebrew source is patent...Whilst his Messianic mission is thus rooted in prophecy, to which Jesus himself appeals in attestation of it, it does not appear that he assumed or ascribed to himself a pre-temporal existence...According to what Matthew and Luke relate of his origin, he is divinely generated. *But he has not preexisted.* He is represented as coming into being in the womb of the Virgin by the generation of the Holy Spirit...No one can reasonably maintain that, according to the versions of his supernatural generation given by Matthew and Luke, Jesus existed before this creative divine act...Nor is there any explicit indication in his own utterance that he himself was conscious of personal preexistence...It is thus not with a preexistent, ethereal being, incarnate in human form, that we have to do in the Synoptic Gospels, but with one who, albeit divinely invested with an exalted vocation and destiny, enters on both in time, and is wholly subject to the conditions of human existence from birth to death.[12]

No one will doubt the thoroughness of Raymond Brown's examination of the birth narratives of the Messiah. He, too, finds that neither Matthew nor Luke believed that Jesus preexisted his conception:

> The fact that Matthew can speak of Jesus as "begotten" (passive of *gennan*) in 1:16, 20 suggests that for him the conception through the agency of the Holy Spirit is the *becoming* of God's Son...Clearly here divine sonship is not adoptive sonship, but *there is no suggestion of an*

---

12 James MacKinnon, *The Historic Jesus* (Longmans, Green and Co., 1931), 375-379, emphasis added.

> *incarnation whereby a figure who was previously with God takes on flesh.*[13]

In the same work he says: "In the commentary I shall stress that Matthew and Luke show no knowledge of preexistence; seemingly for them the conception was the becoming or begetting of the Son of God."[14]

This startling admission from a respected biblical scholar confirms the fact that the doctrine of the Incarnation is not found in Matthew or Luke. The same is true of Mark's Gospel. Brown notes that these are awkward facts for theologians schooled in traditional belief in an eternally preexisting Son:

> Lyonnet, *L'Annonciation*,[15] points out that this [Luke's omission of any reference to preexistence] has embarrassed many orthodox theologians, since in preexistence Christology a conception by the Holy Spirit in Mary's womb does not bring about the existence of God's Son. Luke is seemingly unaware of such a Christology; *conception is causally related to divine sonship for him.*[16]

Traditional Christianity, remarkably, has insisted nevertheless that Jesus did exist before his conception, and as the *Son of God* and the second member of a divine Trinity. This concept, however, cannot possibly be traced to Matthew or Luke. Both present us with a Jesus who began to exist when Mary conceived him under the power of the Holy Spirit. Luke's message is clear: It was the supernatural act of God affecting

---

[13] *The Birth of the Messiah*, 140, 141, emphasis added. Cp. Aaron Milavec, "Matthew's Integration of Sexual and Divine Begetting," in *Biblical Theology Bulletin* 8 (1978): 108: "The Christian doctrine of preexistence would be entirely incompatible with Matthew's depictions of Jesus' origins."

[14] Ibid., 31, fn. 7.

[15] "L'Annonciation et la Mariologie Biblique," in *Maria in Sacra Scriptura*, 4:61.

[16] Brown, *The Birth of the Messiah*, 291.

Mary which *brought into being* the Son of God. No one reading Luke's words could imagine that this person had been the Son of God prior to the miracle which God wrought in Mary. Luke's Jesus begins, like every other human being, in the womb of his mother: "you will conceive in your womb and bear a son...The Holy Spirit will come upon you and the power of the Most High will overshadow you, and *for that reason* the holy offspring shall be called the Son of God" (Luke 1:31, 35).

This key text provides no evidence for thinking that Jesus had an existence prior to conception. For Luke, the Son of God is generated around 3 BC, not in eternity. Matthew is in full agreement with Luke. He declares Jesus to be "the son of David and the son of Abraham" (Matt. 1:1), miraculously conceived by Mary under the influence of the Holy Spirit (Matt. 1:18, 20).

Traditional orthodoxy relies heavily on a number of texts in John's Gospel (John 17:5; 8:58). These are supposed to demonstrate that Jesus' origin is not in the womb of Mary but in eternity, so that he is actually conscious of his pre-mundane existence with the Father. Can these verses really bear the weight of such a stupendous proposition, one which appears to place John's Jesus in a class of being quite different from that of the Synoptics? Or is there another way to read John which brings his testimony into harmony with the other Gospels? The question is one that has surfaced throughout the course of Christian history, notably in the work (among many others) of Paul of Samosata (c. 200-275), Photinus (c. 300-376), the Anabaptist Adam Pastor (c. 1500-1570), Michael Servetus (1511-1553), the Polish Anabaptists, the Englishman John Biddle (1615-1662), and nineteenth-century anti-Trinitarian scholars in America, Britain and Germany, and recently at Cambridge. The remark of Maurice Wiles pointedly restates what has long been the conviction among a minority group of believers:

> Within the Christian tradition the New Testament has long been read through the prism of the later conciliar creeds...Speaking of Jesus as the Son of God had a very different connotation in the first century from that which it has had ever since Nicea. Talk of Jesus' preexistence [in Scripture] ought probably in most, perhaps in all

cases, to be understood, on the analogy of the
preexistence of the Torah, to indicate the eternal divine
purpose being achieved through him rather than
preexistence of a fully personal kind.[17]

The problem for Trinitarians is that they must seek their
main support from John at the risk of contradicting Matthew and
Luke.[18] There is another way, however, to read the Gospel of
John — a way which harmonizes him with his fellow Gospel
writers. That Matthew and John agreed about who Jesus was is
strongly indicated by a simple fact: Matthew 16:16, 18 records
Jesus as making belief that he is *the Messiah* the basis of the
Christian faith. John 20:31 announces John's object in writing
his Gospel. It was to demonstrate exactly the same truth, namely
that Jesus is the Christ, the son of God.

The Word in John's Prologue
Recent commentaries on John admit that despite the long-
standing tradition to the contrary, the term "word" in the famous
prologue of John need not refer to the Son of God before he was
born. Our translations imply belief in the traditional doctrine of
incarnation by capitalizing "Word." But what was it that became
flesh in John 1:14? Was it a preexisting *person*? Or was it the
self-expressive activity of God, the Father, His eternal plan? A
plan may take flesh, for example, when the design in the
architect's mind finally takes shape as a house. What preexisted
the visible bricks and mortar was the intention in the mind of the
architect. Thus it is quite in order to read John 1:1-3a: "In the

---

[17] *The Remaking of Christian Doctrine*, 52, 53.

[18] According to many MSS, Matthew records the genesis or "origin,"
"beginning" of Jesus in Matt. 1:18. It was not just his birth. Mark and
Luke know nothing of a Jesus who preexisted his birth. Luke's birth
narrative expressly excludes an "eternal generation" for the Son, who
becomes God's Son at his conception. A reasonable possibility is that
John's view of Christ is, in fact, in harmony with the other Gospel
writers.

beginning was the creative purpose of God";[19] "it was with God and was fully expressive of God [*theos*]"[20] (just as wisdom was with God before creation, Prov. 8:30). "All things came into being through it." This rendering suits the Old Testament use of "word" admirably: "So shall My word be that goes forth out of My mouth; it shall not return to Me empty, without accomplishing what I desire and without succeeding in the matter for which I sent it" (Isa. 55:11).[21] Jesus is that word expressed as a human being — God's last word to the world, the Son in whom God has spoken at the end of these days (Heb. 1:1, 2). It is significant that the writer to the Hebrews places the Son "in these last days," as the divine agent who follows the prophets. He does not place him in eternity, but thinks of the Son as the historical Christ.

The ambiguity in the Greek (*dia autou*, "through it" or "through him," John 1:3) allows for an *impersonal* word before Jesus is born. The impersonality of the word is suggested by John's own commentary on John 1:1 in 1 John 1:2. It was impersonal "eternal life" which was "with the Father" (*pros ton theon*, 1 John 1:2; cp. the "word" which was *pros ton theon*), i.e., the promise of eternal life to be provided through Jesus. Peter seems to echo the same idea exactly when he describes Jesus as the lamb of God who was "foreknown before the foundation of the world, but manifested in these last days" (1 Pet. 1:20). Only a few verses earlier he uses the same concept of foreknowledge in speaking of God's plan to call Christians to salvation (1 Pet. 1:2). God took note of those whom He later called, but they did

---

[19] Gabriel Fackré in *The Christian Story* (Eerdmans, 1978), 103, refers with approval to Theophilus of Antioch's understanding of the "logos" as God's plan, purpose, reason, and vision and suggests as the translation of John 1:1, "The Vision was with God and the Vision was God."

[20] The NEB attempts to convey the meaning with "What the word was, God was."

[21] For the Old Testament use of the term "word" see Ps. 33:6-12 and James Dunn, *Christology in the Making*, 217, 218.

not preexist literally. Peter's application of this concept to Jesus in verse 20 points to an "ideal preexistence" in the eternal counsels of God, not to an actual existence in an another dimension before birth as a human being. An interesting parallel occurs in the book of Revelation, where all things "were, and were created" (Rev. 4:11). Mounce comments that "this unusual phrase suggests that all things which are, existed first in the eternal will of God and through His will came into actual being at His appointed time."[22]

Trinitarian commentators recognize that there is no compelling reason to believe that the original readers of John's prologue would have thought of the "word" as the Son literally preexisting as a *person*: Until John 1:14 ("the word became flesh"), "it would have been quite possible for the reader to have taken the Word to refer to some supreme cosmic principle or the like."[23] It is a little-known fact that English translations of John 1:2 before the King James Version described the word as "it," not "him." The point is brought into focus by James Dunn. In his exhaustive examination of the traditional doctrine of incarnation, he argues that outside John's Gospel, there is no doctrine of a literal preexistence. Dunn, however, makes the important point that before John 1:14, there is no need to think of the "word" as a second personal being with the Father. Of John 1:1 he says:

> The conclusion which seems to emerge from our analysis [of John 1:1-14] thus far is that it is only with verse 14 ["the word became flesh"] that we can begin to speak of the personal Logos. The poem uses rather impersonal language (became flesh), but no Christian would fail to recognize here a reference to Jesus — the word became not flesh in general but Jesus Christ. *Prior to verse 14* we are in the same realm as pre-Christian

---

22 R.H. Mounce, *The Book of Revelation* (Marshall, Morgan and Scott, 1977), 140 (on Rev. 4:11).

23 Leon Morris, *The Gospel According to John, New International Commentary on the New Testament* (Grand Rapids: Eerdmans, 1971), 102.

talk of Wisdom and Logos, the same language and ideas that we find in Philo, where as we have seen, we are dealing with *personifications rather than persons*, personified actions of God rather than an individual divine being as such. The point is obscured by the fact that we have to translate the masculine Logos as "he" throughout the poem. But if we translated Logos as "God's utterance" instead, it would become clearer that the poem *did not necessarily intend the Logos of vv. 1-13 to be thought of as a personal divine being*. In other words, the revolutionary significance of v. 14 may well be that it marks not only the transition in the thought of the poem from preexistence to incarnation, but also the transition from *impersonal personification to actual person*.[24]

But why do we "have to translate" the masculine *logos* as "he"? Only to support a traditional interpretation of John's prologue. If *logos* is taken as "God's plan," not the Son alive before his birth, a major support is removed from the structure of the traditional view of preexistence and the Trinity in John's Gospel.

A Further Look at John 1:1

Is the current translation of John 1:1 really a translation at all, if by translation we mean the conveying of the original into an intelligible equivalent in the target language? Does the phrase "the Word was with God" mean anything in English? When was your word last "with you"? We suspect that our present standard renderings, though they may be literally correct, simply allow the reader to feel good about his received orthodox Christology of the eternal Son assuming human nature. The capital on "Word" immediately suggests a *person* preexisting. And many readers (11 million copies around the world in many languages) are offered a paraphrase such as the Good News Bible: "Before anything else existed, there was Christ, with God. He has always

---

[24] *Christology in the Making*, 243, emphasis added.

been alive and is himself God. He created everything there is. Nothing exists that he did not make."[25] The reader's orthodoxy is all the more confirmed. But the Roman Catholic scholar Karl-Josef Kuschel in his recent massive treatment of the question of Christ's origin asks: "Why do we instinctively read: 'In the beginning was the Son and the Son was with God'?"[26]

It seems to us that the Hebrew Bible should provide our first line of investigation, if we are to get at John's intention in the prologue. As a professor told me in seminary, "If you misunderstand the Old Testament you will misunderstand the New Testament." Amazingly no occurrence of the Hebrew word *davar* (word) corresponding to John's Greek word *logos* provides any evidence that the "word from the beginning" means a *person*, much less an uncreated second divine person, the Son of God, alongside the One God of Israel's creed. *Davar* in the Old Testament means "word," "matter," often "promise" or "intention," but never a person. The ubiquitous presence of a capital "W" on word in our English versions is unwarranted. John did not say that the preexistent word was a second and distinct person before it became embodied in the Messiah.

Why shouldn't John therefore be saying that God's creative and expressive activity, His word or wisdom, the index of His mind, was "with Him," just as wisdom was "with [*para*] Him" in Proverbs 8:30 (LXX)? Proverbs 8, in fact, has remarkable parallels with what John later says about Jesus. Life is found in the words of Jesus (John 6:63), as it is found in Wisdom. Wisdom cries out just as Jesus does (John 12:44), as he urges people to heed his teaching. What is predicated of Wisdom in Proverbs is elsewhere attributed to God (Job 12:13-16).

Significantly, John always uses the preposition *para* (with) to express the proximity of one *person* to another (1:39; 4:40; 8:38, etc.). Yet in his prologue he chooses *pros* (with), suggesting that "the word" is not meant to designate a *person*

[25] Cp. GNB on 1 John 1:1: "Christ was alive when the world began."
[26] *Born Before All Time? The Debate About the Origin of Christ* (New York: Crossroads, 1992), 381.

alongside God. The first verse of John is reminiscent too of what Wisdom says in Ecclesiasticus 24:9: "God created me from the beginning before the world." There is good evidence that the Hebrew prepositions *im* or *et* meaning "with" can describe the relationship between *a person and what is in his heart or mind.* Here are some interesting examples of the use of the Hebrew prepositions *im* and *et* from the Hebrew Bible:

"*Im* (with), alone = in one's consciousness, whether of knowledge, memory or purpose":[27]

Num. 14:24: "He had another spirit with him" (operating in his mind)

1 Kings 11:11: "This is with thee [Solomon]" (what you want)

1 Chron. 28:12: "The pattern of all that was in the spirit with him" (in his mind)

Job 10:13: "I know that this was with you" (parallel to "hidden in your heart"; "in your mind," NIV; "I know that these things are your purpose," NASV)

Job 15:9: "which is not with us" (we don't understand it)

Job 23:10: "He knows the way which is with me" (the way of which I am conscious)

Job 23:14: "He performs the things which are appointed for me and many such things are with Him" (He has many such purposes); LXX: "He has willed a thing and done it."

Job 27:11: "That which is with the Almighty I will not conceal" (His purposes)

Ps. 50:11: "Wild beasts of the field are with Me" (known to Me, in My thought and care)

---

[27] Brown, Driver and Briggs, *Hebrew and English Lexicon of the Old Testament,* 768.

Ps. 73:23: "I am continually with thee" (in your thoughts)

Et: "a dream or word of Yahweh is said to be *with* the prophet."[28]

Gen. 40:14: "Keep me in mind when it goes well with you" (lit. "Remember me with yourself"). (The Word was what God had in mind.)

2 Kings 3:12: "There is with him the word of the Lord" (cp. 2 John 2: "truth is with us"; Gal. 2:5: "truth remains with you")

Isa. 59:12: "Transgressions are with us" (in our knowledge, present to our mind). (Cp. John 17:5, the glory which Jesus had with God — present to God's mind, as His purpose.)

Jer. 12:3: "You examine my heart's attitude with you" (lit. "You have tried my heart with you")

Jer. 23:28: "The prophet with whom there is a dream" (the prophet who has a dream)

Jer. 27:18: "If the word of the Lord is with them"

Job 14:5: "His days are determined. The number of his months is with you" (known to you)

Prov. 2:1: "Treasure my commandments within you" (= with you)

Prov. 11:2: "Wisdom is with the humble."

In view of this Hebrew background we suggest a translation of John 1:1, 14 as follows: "In the beginning God had a Plan and the Plan was fixed as God's Decree and the Plan was fully expressive of God's mind, and the Plan became embodied in the Man Messiah Jesus."

---

[28] Ibid., 86.

John's Purpose

John in his prologue is counteracting the Gnostic tendency towards a dualistic or pluralistic idea of God. A Gnostic Christian believed that the ineffable, unapproachable God, who was remote and distant from His creation, was mediated to His world by lesser divine figures — "aions," or a single lesser divine figure (the various Gnostic systems differed on this point). Justin Martyr, who certainly did not claim any Gnostic affiliation, nevertheless has no qualms about speaking of the preexisting Son who is "an arithmetically second God," not however uncreated and eternal as the Son in the developed Trinitarian sense, but preexisting as the Son and coming forth at a moment of time just before the Genesis creation. Justin strikes out on a path which is alien to the New Testament when he sees the Son of God active in Old Testament times as the angel of the Lord.

> In the middle of the second century Justin composed his *Apology* and *Dialogue* and in these the influence of philosophy on Christianity appears in full force...He discloses the nexus between pagan forms of philosophy, the bridge by which the former passed over into the latter's territory...[Christianity] found in the Hellenic Judaism of Alexandria the means by which, while preserving its hold on Christian and Hebrew revelation, it could yet adopt the philosophical thoughts and retain the philosophical conceptions of the day.[29]

Tertullian, known as founder of Latin Christianity, like Justin knows of a second divine being who was generated in

---

[29] G.T. Purves, "The Influence of Paganism on Post-Apostolic Christianity," *Presbyterian Review* 36 (Oct., 1888). The disastrous impact of Alexandrian philosophy is well recognized by modern scholars. In the *Bible Review* of June 1997, Professor J. Harold Ellens observed that "from Nicea to Chalcedon the speculative and Neoplatonist perspective of Alexandrian Christology gained increasing ground and became orthodox Christian dogma in 451 C.E."

time by the Father.[30] This Christology, which has ominous affinities with Gnostic dualism, could not have thrived unless it were first supposed that John meant that the Son as distinct from God's word of wisdom had existed from the beginning. The public continues to rely heavily on John 1:1 for the doctrine of the coequal deity of Christ. But what if they had been schooled on any one of the eight English translations which preceded the publication of the King James Version in 1611?[31]

Another line of investigation of John's meaning is the extra-biblical literature of Judaism. In the Qumran *Manual of Discipline* we learn that "By God's knowledge everything comes to pass; and everything that is he establishes by his purpose; and without him [or it?] it is not done." Surely this is an echo of John's "by it [the word] all things came to be and without it nothing came to be" (1:3). In I QS iii 15 we read: "From the God of knowledge is all that is and that is to be," and in the Apocrypha, "O God who hast made all things by Thy word" (Wisdom 9:1) and again, in Sirach 42:15: "I will now remember the works of the Lord, and declare the things that I have seen: In the words of the Lord are His works." In the Odes of Solomon, we learn that "the worlds were made by God's word," and by the "thought of His heart" (16:19).

We are surely in the atmosphere of the God who spoke and it was done in Genesis 1, and in John 1:1 we learn more of the self-expressive and creative activity of the word which (not "who") became Jesus. Jesus is therefore what the word became. I believe that many scholars would come to this sort of interpretation if they were not under the constraints of orthodoxy. How interesting, for example, that the great F.F. Bruce, amazingly,

---

[30] "There was a time when the Son did not exist; God was not always a Father" (*Against Hermogenes*, ch. 3).

[31] With the one exception noted, the following translations rendered John 1:3, "By it all things were made. Without it nothing was made": Tyndale Bible (1535), Coverdale (1550; this version has "the same," rather than "it"), Matthew (1535), Taverner (1539), The Great (Cranmer's) Bible (1539), Whittingham (1557), Geneva (1560), Bishops' Bible (1568).

wrote of John 1:1 and the problem of the preexistence of Christ: "On the preexistence question, one can at least accept the preexistence of the eternal word or wisdom of God which (who?) became incarnate in Jesus. But whether any New Testament writer believed in his separate conscious existence as a 'second Divine Person' is not so clear...I am not so sure that Paul so believed."[32] Is this after all anything different from the plain definition offered us by the standard lexicon of Arndt and Gingrich? They say of the "word" in John 1:1: "Our literature shows traces of a way of thinking that was widespread in contemporary syncretism, as well as in Jewish wisdom literature and Philo, the most prominent feature of which is the concept of the Logos, the independent, personified 'Word' (of God)...this divine 'Word' took on human form in a historical person."[33] It is most reassuring to have this definition offered us by such a prestigious authority. You notice that Arndt and Gingrich said nothing about the word meaning the Son before the birth of Jesus. The "word" in John 1:1, they think, is a personification, not a person.

And yet without belief in that second preexisting Son it is not possible, in many church circles, to qualify as a genuine believer! What an amazing paradox. The situation is different at the level of academic biblical studies.

How much, then, is at stake in the word "word"? Is it a person preexisting or a purpose? Trinitarians sometimes argue as follows: 1) The Word was God; 2) Jesus was the Word; 3) Therefore Jesus was God. These premises must be examined. The Word is not identical with God.[34] It is distinguished from God in some sense by being "with Him." The Word was not a second God. If, then, the Word is neither identical with God (how can it be if it is also "with God"?) nor an independent God,

---

[32] From correspondence, June 13th, 1981.

[33] William F. Arndt and F. Wilbur Gingrich, *A Greek-English Lexicon of the New Testament and Other Early Christian Literature* (Chicago: University of Chicago Press, 1957), 480.

[34] Identity would be expressed by "*o theos*," not "*theos*."

the phrase "the Word was with God" can only mean, as A.E Harvey points out, "that the word was an expression or reflection of God (cf. Wisdom 7:25-6), that it was in some sense divine, i.e. of God."[35]

The second premise, "Jesus was the word," does not have to mean that the word is identical with Jesus from eternity. Jesus is what the word became. He is an expression of the word from his birth as Son of God (John 1:14). To say that Jesus was an expression of God's revealing activity in no way proves that the Son of God was an uncreated member of a Trinity.

Thinking Like Jews

The whole issue of preexistence is profoundly affected by the way we read biblical statements. What does it mean for something to "be" before it exists on earth? Are we dealing with foreordination or literal preexistence? The fact is that "when the Jew wished to designate something as predestined, *he spoke of it as already existing in heaven*."[36] Thus in Colossians 1:5 Paul speaks of the hope of the Christian inheritance of the coming Kingdom being "laid up for you in heaven." The inheritance promised for our future has been in existence in God's plan from eternity. What is future for us is, in this special sense, past for God. Similarly, the mystery of the future Kingdom has been hidden with God in His eternal purposes (Rom. 16:25). So also the wisdom now given to us was ordained before the world for our glory (1 Cor. 2:7-9). According to this manner of describing God's predetermined purposes, the Bible can even say that Jesus was "*crucified* before the foundation of the world" (Rev. 13:8, KJV, RV). What is decreed may thus be said to have taken place in God's intention, though actually the event has not occurred. This important biblical principle appears also in Paul's thought: "God calls things that are not *as though they were*" (Rom. 4:17, KJV). In this context the reference is to Isaac who was "*real in*

---

[35] *Jesus and the Constraints of History* (Philadelphia: Westminster Press, 1982), app. III, 176, 177.

[36] E.G. Selwyn, *First Epistle of St. Peter*, 124, emphasis added.

the thought and purpose of God before he was begotten.[37] "The Almighty addresses...non-existent things...as if existing, because soon to exist according to His purpose."[38] In the same epistle Paul can say that God *"has glorified"* the believers, meaning that their future glory is assured because God has decreed it (Rom. 8:30). Scripture announces 700 years before the birth of Jesus that "a son *has been given* to us" (Isa. 9:6). Modern versions properly translate these past tense verbs into the future — "a son *will be given to us*" — because this is what they imply.[39] It is fair to ask whether this "past tense of prophecy" or "intention" may not appear also in John's Gospel.

We have no difficulty recognizing that God's promise to give Abraham the land referred to the future. Yet it was expressed by a past tense: "To your seed *I have given* this land" (Gen. 15:18). The *Soncino Commentary* observes appropriately: "God's promise is worded as if it were already fulfilled."[40] The past tense must not be taken literally here, for the land had not (and still has not[41]) become Abraham's. Stephen says plainly: "God did not give him a square foot of this land to call his own, yet He promised to give it to him" (Acts 7:5). The apparent contradiction between Genesis 15:18 ("I have given") and Acts

---

[37] Harrison, *Romans, Expositor's Bible Commentary* (Zondervan, 1976), 52, emphasis added.

[38] Moule, *Romans, Cambridge Bible for Schools and Colleges* (Cambridge UP, 1918), 95.

[39] The following "past tenses of prophecy" in the prophets are typical of the Hebrew way of thinking: "My people *have gone* into captivity" (Isa. 5:13); "unto us a son *has been given*" (9:6); "The people who walked in darkness *have seen* a great light" (9:2); "They *have devoured* Israel" (9:12); "He *has come* to Aiath" (10:28); "I *have laid* in Zion..." (28:16); "He *has utterly destroyed* them" (34:2).

[40] Morris Simon, *The Soncino Chumash* (London: Soncino Press, 1947), 34.

[41] Despite a former inheritance of the land under Joshua (Josh. 21:43-45), the prophets expect the ancient promise to Abraham to receive a final, future fulfillment (Jer. 3:18; 30:3).

7:5 ("God did not give") is easily resolved by recognizing the "prophetic past tense" which points to the certainty of *future* fulfillment because of a past decree in God's great purpose. Similarly, God gave the land to Abraham and Isaac (Gen. 35:12), though they did not receive it.[42] We shall suggest the application of this principle to the preexistence language in John when we come to consider John 17:5 (below). But first an examination of John's other "preexistence" texts is in order.

What Does John Mean by Jesus Coming and Being Sent?

Relying on the preconception that Jesus in John's Gospel came from a pre-human existence in heaven, readers of the fourth Gospel claim that Jesus' "coming from the Father," "coming forth from the Father" or being "sent from God" are clear proof of the doctrine of the Incarnation — that the Son preexisted his birth and became man. However, the same language is used of persons for whom no preexistence is claimed. John the Baptist was also "sent from God" (John 1:6). Nicodemus thought that Jesus was a teacher "come" from God, not meaning that Jesus had preexisted, but only that God had commissioned him (John 3:2). Jesus was "from God" (*ek theou*), but disciples are also to be from God (*ek theou*) (John 8:47). In John's language, false prophets have "come forth" (*exerchesthai*) into the world (1 John 4:1), i.e., to preach. Jesus similarly claimed that he had "come forth" to preach the Gospel of the Kingdom (Mark 1:38). Mark has no reference to preexistence anywhere in his Gospel, and Luke's version of the same saying is that Jesus was "sent" by God (Luke 4:43). "Coming" and "being sent" are synonymous ways of expressing the notion that Jesus was commissioned by God as His agent, in the typically Jewish sense of the *shaliach*, or ambassador, who is empowered

---

[42] The writer to the Hebrews expects that Abraham will yet inherit the land in which he once dwelt as a stranger (Heb. 11:9).

with full authority from the one who "sends" him out with a message.[43]

Dunn points out that Moses and the prophets and others are sent by God: "It is evident...that send forth [*exapostellein*] when used of God does not tell us anything about the origin or point of departure of the one sent; it underlines the heavenly origin of his commissioning, but not of the one commissioned."[44]

The point is further established by the remarks of Rengstorf. His comment reveals a persistent tendency of expositors to weave the idea of preexistence into otherwise "innocent" biblical terms: "Linguistically there is no support for the thesis of Zn (Zn Gl. 199 ad Galatians 4:4, 6, as also many older and more recent commentators) that in Galatians 4:4 the *ex* in *exapostellein* indicates that prior to his sending, the one sent was in the presence of the one who sent him."[45]

The same caution should be applied to the use of *exapostellein* (send out) in John. It does not by itself imply that the Son preexisted with the Father before being sent.

To be "sent from God" means to be commissioned to perform a special task for God; and to "come forth into the world" is to appear before the public with a mission. It has nothing to do with existing before one's birth. John is commonly read, however, with the assumption that Jesus was literally sent from a pre-mundane existence in another sphere. Similarly, "coming down from heaven" need not imply a previous existence in heaven in a literal sense. In New Testament language "every good gift comes down from above" (James 1:17; cp. 3:15), not that every gift descends through the sky. The holy city will also come down from heaven (Rev. 21:2). But this

---

[43] Cp. P. Borgen, "God's Agent in the Fourth Gospel," in *Religions in Antiquity: Essays in Memory of E.R. Goodenough*, ed. J. Neusner (Leiden, 1968), 137-148.

[44] *Christology in the Making*, 39.

[45] *Theological Dictionary of the New Testament*, ed. Gerhard Kittel, Gerhard Friedrich and Geoffrey W. Bromiley, trans. Geoffrey W. Bromiley, 10 vols. (Grand Rapids: Eerdmans, 1964-1976), 1:406.

does not prove that it literally floats down out of the sky. This
"descent" language reflects the well-known characteristic of
Hebrew thinking that many of the prominent persons or objects
in God's plan have "existed" in heaven before they are seen on
earth.[46]

When Jesus drew the parallel between his "coming down"
from heaven (John 6:33, 38, 50, 51, 58) and the descent of the
manna from heaven (Exod. 16:4, 15; Num. 11:9, LXX), he gave
no indication that he literally descended. The manna itself did
not literally pass through the skies from God's throne to the
wilderness. It appeared miraculously on earth. Jesus' "coming
down from heaven" means, therefore, that he is God's
miraculous gift to mankind, planned in His eternal counsels.
Jesus also "came into the world," but in Johannine language
every human being equally "comes into the world" (John 1:9)
and the expression simply means to be born: "I am a king. To
this end was I born, and for this cause I came into the world"
(John 18:37). The Synoptic version of this saying conveys the
same sense, though the language is different: "I must proclaim
the Good News of the Kingdom of God...That is the reason for
which I was sent" (Luke 4:43; cp. Mark 1:38).[47]

Jesus Before John

John the Baptist says of Jesus that "he was before me" (John
1:15). Many readers naturally find in these words a confirmation
of their belief that the Son was alive in heaven before his birth.
Morris, however, shows that the ambiguous phrase "before me"
may refer to superiority of rank, rather than priority in time. The
verse may be translated, "A follower of mine has taken
precedence of me, for he (always) was before me, my superior."

---

[46] Cp. Emil Schurer's statement that in Jewish thinking "everything
truly valuable preexisted in heaven" (*The History of the Jewish People
in the Age of Jesus Christ,* T&T Clark, 1979, 2:522).

[47] Cp. John A.T. Robinson, *The Human Face of God* (London: SCM
Press, 1973), 172-179, for an examination of John's use of the same
language for Jesus and believers.

Though the commentary supports the idea that Jesus was before John in time, it admits that "some take 'first' to mean not 'first in time,' 'before,' but 'first in importance,' which will give such a meaning as 'he was my Chief.'"[48] This is how Murray and Abbot understand this verse.[49] John 1:15, 30 cannot be claimed as proof that Jesus existed before his birth.

John 3:13 and 6:62

There has been much discussion about Jesus' enigmatic statement that "no one has ascended to heaven except he who descended from heaven, the Son of Man." If the words are taken as Jesus' own words, rather than a later comment by John, Jesus appears to be saying that he alone has ascended to heaven. Commentators are struck by the surprising use of the perfect tense. "The perfect tense 'has ascended' is unexpected."[50] "The use of the perfect tense is a difficulty, for it seems to imply that the Son of Man has already ascended into heaven."[51] "The difficulty of the verse lies in the tense of 'has ascended.' It seems to imply that the Son of Man had already at the moment of speaking ascended into heaven."[52]

In what sense can Jesus have claimed already to have ascended to heaven? The statement has been taken by some to mean that sometime during his historical ministry Jesus had been literally transported into the presence of his Father. But the Gospels nowhere record such an event. Others have argued for a predictive sense of the past tense, i.e., that the Son of Man was

---

[48] Leon Morris, *The Gospel According to John*, 108, 109.

[49] J.O.F. Murray, *Jesus According to St. John* (London: Longmans, Green, 1936); E.A. Abbot, *Johannine Grammar* (London: A. and C. Black, 1906) cited by Leon Morris in *The Gospel According to John*, 109.

[50] Morris, *The Gospel According to John,* 223.

[51] Raymond Brown, *The Gospel According to John,* 1:132.

[52] C.K. Barrett, *The Gospel According to St. John* (London: SPCK, 1972), 177.

destined to ascend, a prophecy of his ascension after the resurrection.

There is an easier explanation of Jesus' ascent into heaven, based on biblical precedent and Jewish ways of speaking. "No one has ascended to heaven except he who descended from heaven, the Son of Man, who is in heaven" is a figurative description of Jesus' unique perception of God's saving plan. Jesus possesses a unique understanding of the secrets of the universe which he now reveals to all who will listen. The phrase "who is in heaven," which appears in some Greek as well as Latin and Syriac manuscripts, indicates that Jesus, while living on earth, was at the same time also "in heaven" in constant communion with his Father on whom he depended for everything. As the bridge between heaven and earth he claimed to have unique access to divine information. A similar status applies later to all believers whom Paul describes as "seated in heavenly places" (Eph. 2:6).

Jesus' "ascent to heaven" during his ministry points then to his intimate fellowship with his Father. As Son he resides "in the bosom of the Father" (John 1:18). The context of John 3:13 shows Jesus in conversation with Nicodemus about the secrets of immortality. Jesus is "talking about what we *know*" (John 3:11). In contrast to Nicodemus' unfamiliarity with the keys to entering the Kingdom and the necessity of being born again, Jesus says, "Truly I tell you, we are testifying to what we have seen, but you people do not accept our testimony" (John 3:11). Jesus doubts Nicodemus' capacity to receive "heavenly things." It is these heavenly secrets which Jesus is able to reveal because he "has ascended to heaven" and "is in heaven." In Proverbs 30:3, 4 the words of Agur contain a similar reference to ascension to heaven. The object of such an "ascent" is to gain understanding and divine revelation. "Surely I am more stupid than any man. I do not have the understanding of a man. Neither have I learned wisdom. Nor do I have the knowledge of the Holy One. Who has ascended to heaven and come down?" Similarly, Baruch 3:29

asks: "Who has gone up to heaven and obtained her [Wisdom] and brought her down from the clouds?" (cp. Deut. 30:12).[53]

In the case of Jesus, the supreme and final revealer of God's purposes, a bridge from heaven to earth has been built. The Son has "exegeted" the Father (John 1:18). No one but the Son of Man has received such a measure of divine wisdom. At the same time the Son of Man — the Human Being — has descended from heaven, a Jewish expression meaning not that Jesus was alive before his birth, but that he is God's gift to the world (cp. James 1:17; 3:15).

Adam Clarke commented on our passage:

> This seems to be a figurative expression for "no one has known the mysteries of the Kingdom," as in Deuteronomy 30:12 and Romans 10:6; and the expression is found in the generally received maxim that to be perfectly acquainted with the concerns of a place, it is necessary for a person to be on the spot.[54]

A German expositor, Christian Schoettgen, in his *Horae Hebraicae* observed of John 3:13: "It was an expression common among the Jews who often say of Moses that he ascended to heaven and there received a revelation on the institution of divine worship." He quotes the rabbis as saying, "It is not in heaven, that you should say, 'Oh that we had one like Moses the prophet of the Lord to ascend into heaven and bring it [the Law] down to us'" (*Jerusalem Targum* on Deut. 30:12).

In John 6:62 Jesus made a challenging statement about his destiny as the predicted Son of Man. After referring to his own "difficult statements" about being "the bread which came down from heaven" (John 6:58-60), Jesus asked whether this teaching might also cause his audience to stumble: "What if you should see the Son of Man ascending where he was before?"

Jesus spoke of himself in this passage as the Son of Man. As is well known, the title originates in Daniel 7:13 where, 550

---

[53] See Brown, *The Gospel According to John*, 1:128-146.

[54] Cited by John Wilson, *Concessions of Trinitarians* (Boston: Munroe & Co, 1845), 324.

years before the birth of Jesus, Daniel saw a vision of the Son of
Man in heaven receiving authority to rule with the saints in the
future Messianic Kingdom:

> Jesus used [the title Son of Man] of himself with the
> implication that in him was the fulfillment of the vision
> of Daniel...It is the title which he specially employed,
> when he was foretelling to his disciples the Passion as
> the inevitable and predestined issue of his public
> ministry.[55]

The following texts from the Synoptic Gospels illustrate the
point. In each case Jesus speaks of himself as the Son of Man —
a title meaning "member of the human race" — who is destined
to suffer, die, and rise again: "The Son of Man is to go just as it
is written about him" (Matt. 26:24). Mark speaks of the Passion
of the Son of Man as the subject of Old Testament prophecy:
"How is it *written of the Son of Man* that he should suffer many
things and be treated with contempt?" (Mark 9:12).

In John's Gospel also, the title "Son of Man" is associated
with prediction, with what is destined to happen to Jesus in
fulfillment of Old Testament prophecy or typology: "And as
Moses lifted up the serpent...so must the Son of Man be lifted
up" (John 3:14).

The subject of the enigmatic statement in John 6:62 is the
Son of Man, the title which designates Jesus as *the* Human
Being. If we ask where *the Son of Man* was before, the biblical
answer is found in Daniel 7:13. The *man* Messiah was seen in
heaven in a vision of the future which became reality at the
ascension (Acts 2:33), when Jesus had been exalted to the right
hand of God. David had not ascended to heaven (Acts 2:34).
Contrary to much cherished tradition, the patriarchs have not
"gone to heaven." They are sleeping in their graves awaiting the
resurrection of all the faithful (Dan. 12:2; John 5:28, 29). Only
the Messiah was destined for that position. In John 6:62 he
anticipates his future ascension in order to fulfill what was

---

[55] J.H. Bernard, *St. John, International Critical Commentary*
(Edinburgh: T&T Clark, 1948), 1:cxxx, cxxxi.

predetermined for him according to the divine plan revealed in Daniel's vision.

These verses give no support to the doctrine that a second member of the Godhead, the "eternal Son of God," was in heaven before his birth. It is the "Son of Man," a *human person*, who preexists in heaven. There is no "eternal Son" in heaven before the birth of Jesus. Son of Man does not refer to an uncreated second divine being, as required by Trinitarian theology. The texts relate to the activity of the Son of Man. Trinitarians do not claim that the Son of Man, the human Jesus, existed prior to his conception.

Underlying the apparent complexity of John 6:62 is a very simple concept, to which readers of John must become accustomed. Jesus saw himself as fulfilling the foreordained "program" laid out in advance by the Scriptures. What has been promised for him may be said to have actually happened in vision or other prediction before it happens in reality. The Son of Man was in heaven, seen, so to speak, in a "heavenly preview" before he actually arrived there (John 6:62). A similar phenomenon reported by the Synoptics is the appearance *in vision*, not actually, of Elijah and Moses (Matt. 17:1-9). In John 3:13 the Son of Man has already gained access to heavenly wisdom. But later in John 20:17 Jesus states that he has "*not yet ascended* to the Father." The first statement (John 3:13) is to be taken figuratively, while the latter refers to Jesus' actual departure to the Father.

We must reckon with this special mode of thought in John's Gospel, remembering that John was a profound thinker and theologian who delighted to report Jesus' Jewish, and sometimes enigmatic, interchanges with his audience. This should caution us against reading John in a way which sets his Christology in opposition to Matthew, Mark, Luke and the book of Acts. It is significant that the traditional Christology which supports a Trinitarian creed is derived almost exclusively from John without much concern for the Synoptic portrait of Jesus, nor that of Peter in his sermons in the book of Acts and his letters. It is upon Peter's confession of Jesus as the Messiah that the Church is to be founded (Matt. 16:16, 18). Peter gives us no reason to believe that he thought that Jesus literally preexisted his birth. And John wrote with the sole purpose of convincing us that "Jesus is the Christ, the Son of God," certainly not God Himself (John 20:31).

Glory Before the World Was

If one approaches the text with the firm belief that Jesus existed before his birth, no doubt John 17:5 will appear to lend strength to that conviction. "And now, Father, glorify me with Your own self with the glory which I had with You before the world was." In the light of John's conceptual framework, it is questionable whether this verse can be adduced as proof that Jesus was alive from eternity past. In biblical ways of speaking and thinking one may "have" something which is promised in God's plan before one actually has it. Abraham had been given the land by divine contract (covenant) even though he did not yet own any of it. The promise reads: "To your seed *I have given* this land" (Gen. 15:18). At that point his seed did not yet exist. Yet the land had been given to them. God's promise is worded as though it were already fulfilled.

So in John 17:5 the glory which Jesus "had" with the Father was the glory laid up for him in God's purpose for His Son. A striking illustration of this curious use of the past tense is found in verse 22. Here the same glory promised to the Son had been given to disciples who were not yet even living. They were the disciples who would later be converted (verse 20). Speaking of them, Jesus said, "The glory which You gave me, *I have given to them*." The meaning is obviously that Jesus had *promised* to give it to them. They already possessed it, though not actually. Like God, Jesus spoke of "things which are not as though they existed" (Rom. 4:17). When praying for the glory which he knew God had promised him, he similarly speaks of it as glory which he "had" with the Father, meaning that he had it "laid up with the Father," as a deposit potentially his in God's plan. Elsewhere he encouraged the disciples with the promise that their "reward is great in heaven" (Matt. 5:12). The reward was already there waiting to be given to them in the future at the return of Christ (Matt. 16:27). So also the glory to be given to Jesus had been decreed as his possession from the beginning. Now he prayed to receive it.

Commenting on this special use of language, H.H. Wendt, professor of theology at Heidelberg, wrote:

> It rests on a misconception of the New Testament mode of speech and conception if we immediately infer that the declaration of Jesus [in John 17:5], that he had a glory with the Father before the world was created is simply and necessarily identical in meaning with the thought that he himself preexisted...According to the mode of speech and conception prevalent in the New Testament, a heavenly good, and so also a heavenly glory, can be conceived and spoken of as existing with God and belonging to a person, *not because this person already exists and is invested with glory, but because the glory of God is in some way deposited and preserved for this person in heaven.* We remember how, according to the report of Matthew, Jesus also speaks of the treasure (Matt. 6:20) or the reward (Matt. 5:12, 46; 6:1) which his disciples have in heaven with God...; and further, how, in the description of the final judgment of the nations, the kingdom which those blessed of the Father shall inherit is described as one prepared for them from the creation of the world (Matt. 25:34); and how also (Col. 1:5 and 1 Pet. 1:4) the hope of salvation of the Christians is represented as a blessing laid up in heaven for them...Jesus asks for himself not something arbitrary, but what was to be given him according to God's decree and what had always ideally belonged to him...; the presupposition for this declaration, however, is certainly the thought, which finds decided expression at the close of the prayer in verse 24, *that Jesus himself, as the Messiah, did not indeed really exist from the*

> *beginning with God, but was the object of the love of*
> *God, of His loving thoughts, plans and purposes.*[56]

It is crucial to seek biblical meanings for biblical expressions. If we read John within the strictly monotheistic framework which he establishes (John 17:3; 5:44), we should be cautious about attributing to the Messiah a pre-birth existence as an uncreated second member of the Godhead. The pitfall of compromising biblical monotheism can be avoided if we insist, with John and Jesus, that the Father "alone is God" (John 5:44) and that He is "the only true God" (John 17:3). It would be unwise to read into the text our own post-biblical ideas derived from the creeds, when a better solution to the puzzle of John's Christology lies ready at hand within the limits of his own self-imposed Jewish-Christian monotheism.

The view for which we are contending was presented in a number of books written at the turn of the century by the professor of New Testament literature and language at Chicago Theological Seminary, G.H. Gilbert. He first notes that:

> it does not follow from [Jesus' acceptance of "worship"]
> that the blind man regarded Jesus as of the same *nature*
> with God. The term which is translated *worship* is used
> of the homage which subjects pay to their sovereign and
> simply implies that the one who receives it is of a *dignity*
> superior to the one who renders it (cp. Rev. 22:8).

Of Thomas' address to Jesus as "God," he says, "Jesus accepted the homage of Thomas as homage rendered to his Messiahship...There is no suggestion that he regarded the homage as implying that he was of the same substance with the Father."[57]

---

[56] *The Teaching of Jesus* (Edinburgh: T & T Clark, 1892), 2:169-172, emphasis added.

[57] *The Revelation of Jesus, A Study of the Primary Sources of Christianity* (New York: Macmillan Co., 1899), 225, 226. Gilbert was also author of *The Student's Life of Jesus* and *The Student's Life of Paul.*

The point is an important one against the popular notion that because Jesus was worshipped he must be God. "Worship," however, may be offered to kings as representing God, and even to glorified saints (1 Chron. 29:20; Rev. 3:9). It is fallacious, therefore, to argue that because Jesus is "worshipped," he must be God. Jesus can be "worshipped" as Messiah. Only the Father is worshipped as God. The same Greek verb does service for both senses of "worship."

Gilbert addressed the issue of preexistence in John, observing that the Synoptic Gospels do not touch on this subject. Speaking of the glory for which Jesus prayed in John 17:5, Gilbert sees it as a reward for the work which Jesus had now accomplished:

> Jesus possessed this glory before the foundation of the world in the sense that it was divinely purposed for him. He knew that his Messianic work had been planned by God from eternity, and that the glorious outcome of it had been fixed, and was kept in store for him...We conclude, then, that these three passages in John [6:62; 8:58; 17:5], in which Jesus alludes to his preexistence, do not involve the claim that this preexistence was personal and real. They are to be classed with the other phenomena of the Messianic consciousness of Jesus, none of which, either in the Synoptists or in the fourth Gospel, have to do with metaphysical relationships with the Father.[58]

Does a close exegesis of this chapter confirm that this is the right way to understand John's preexistence language? The use of the past tense in John 17 needs to be examined carefully. There are clear indications in this chapter that past tenses may indeed describe not what has actually happened but what is *destined to happen*, because God has already decreed it. We should note first the caution offered by Brown: "In the Johannine references to Jesus there is a strange timelessness or indifference

---

[58] Ibid., 221, 222.

to time sequence that must be reckoned with."[59] Bernard observes that "the predestined end is seen from the beginning."[60]

In his analysis of John 17, Morris notes that "common to all these sections [of John 17] is the desire that the Father's purpose be set forward."[61] In John 17:2 "we have the thought of divine predestination."[62] Brown notices that "the power to grant life would not become fully effective until Jesus' exaltation," though Jesus states that this power "has been given."[63] We can compare John 5:27: "God gave him authority to execute judgment." The authority has been granted, though its implementation must await the resurrection as the next verse says. In John 17:4 Jesus speaks "as if the action were completed."[64] In John 3:35, also, the Father has given all things into Jesus' hand. Hebrews 2:8 agrees: "You *have put* all things in subjection under his feet...Nevertheless, we do *not yet* see all things subjected to him" (Heb. 2:8). Clearly, divinely planned future events may be described in the past tense.

The common principle underlying many of Jesus' statements in his final prayer is that God has decreed to give him power and authority, much of which has not yet been implemented. This pattern of past tenses with future meanings continues: Of John 17:4 Meyer held that Jesus "already includes in this account...the fact of his death as already accomplished,"[65] but Jesus had not yet died. Alford notices that "our Lord stands by anticipation at the end of his accomplished course and looks

---

[59] *The Gospel According to John*, 1:132.

[60] *St. John, International Critical Commentary*, 1:76.

[61] *Gospel According to John*, 716.

[62] Ibid., 719.

[63] *Gospel According to John*, 2:740.

[64] Ibid., 2:741.

[65] *Commentary on the New Testament: Gospel of John* (New York: Funk and Wagnalls, 1884), 462.

back on it as past."[66] Even in John 17:9, since "the historical disciples are a model for all Christians…, the Christians of a future time are envisaged."[67] But Jesus spoke as though his activity on behalf of the Church had already been completed.

When Jesus says "I have been glorified in them," the perfect tense is "more likely proleptic [anticipating the future], pointing forward to *the glory which was yet to come*, but which was certain."[68] "What is already begun, and is certainly to be further accomplished in the near future, Jesus views, speaking in the *perfect* with prophetic anticipation, as completed and actually existing" (verse 10).[69]

Jesus' prayer continues: "I am no longer in the world" (John 17:11). He speaks as if he had already departed. "His departure is so near he can use the present tense of it."[70] Even in verse 12, strictly speaking, Judas had not yet finally perished. Yet it is implied that he has perished, in fulfillment of Scripture as a "divine destiny."[71]

The past tenses with future meanings continue: "I have sent them…" (John 17:18). Morris notes that "when we come to the Apostles we should have expected a present or future in the place of 'I have sent…' It is perhaps more probable that the word is used proleptically. It adds a touch of certainty to the future sending out of the disciples."[72] Meyer makes the same point: "The mission was indeed not yet objectively a fact (John 20:21; Matt. 28:19), but already conceived in its idea in the appointment and instruction for the apostolic office."[73]

---

66 *Greek New Testament*, 823.

67 Brown, *The Gospel According to John*, 758.

68 Morris, *Gospel According to John*, 726, emphasis added.

69 Meyer, *Commentary on the New Testament: Gospel of John*, 465.

70 Morris, *Gospel According to John*, 726.

71 Meyer, *Commentary on the New Testament: Gospel of John*, 466.

72 Morris, *Gospel According to John*, 731.

73 Meyer, *Commentary on the New Testament: Gospel of John*, 468.

Finally, Jesus prays for the disciples who are not yet converted but who will become Christians as a result of the apostolic preaching. Jesus says that the glory which God "has given" him "has been given" to the disciples of all ages (John 17:22). The glory in question:

> the Father has *given* to him, not yet indeed *objectively*, but as a secure possession of the *immediate future*; he has *obtained* it from God, *assigned* as a property, and the actual taking possession is now for him close at hand. In like manner has *he given* this glory…to his *believing ones*, who will enter on the real possession at the Parousia, where they will be glorified together (Rom. 8:17) after they, up to that time, *had been saved in hope* (Rom. 8:24). They are in Christ already his joint-heirs and the spirit which they are to receive will be the down payment (Eph. 1:14; 2 Cor. 1:22; 5:5); but the actual entrance on the inheritance is accomplished at the Parousia.[74]

Here again the past tense vividly describes things which are certainties for the future in God's plan.

Jesus speaks again of the glory which "You have given me" (John 17:24). Morris senses that "Jesus may be referring to the majesty and splendor that will be his in the life to come."[75] This glory had already been "bestowed on [the disciples], but as yet as a possession of hope."[76]

Throughout John 17 Jesus constantly speaks of things awaiting fulfillment in the future as having already happened. He uses the past tense of prophecy which is not uncommon in Scripture. In John 17:5 he prays for the glory which he "had with [the Father] before the foundation of the world." In view of the context in this chapter, it is clear that the glory he "had" is the

---

[74] Meyer, *Commentary on the New Testament: Gospel of John,* 470.

[75] Morris, *Gospel According to John,* 736.

[76] Meyer, *Commentary on the New Testament: Gospel of John,* 471, 472.

glory prepared for him in God's plan. It is the same glory which all the disciples "had" (i.e., "had been given," John 17:22) though they did *not yet have it*. It is the glory destined for Jesus in God's predetermined purpose. He "had" it laid up for him from eternity, just as Christians now "have" their yet future inheritance of the Kingdom of God. It will be manifested on earth at the Second Coming (1 Pet. 1:4, 5). Jesus in John 17 prayed to receive what God had appointed for him. John 17:5, read in the light of its context, provides no basis for the literal preexistence of Jesus.[77] Taken out of that context and in view of subsequent post-biblical teaching about the Trinity, it will appear to bolster the idea that the Son existed, literally rather than notionally, from eternity.

John 17:5 was understood in the way we propose by Polish Anabaptists of the seventeenth century who wrote in the *Racovian Catechism*:

> That a person may have had something, and consequently may have had glory, with the Father before the world was, without its being concluded that he actually existed is evident from 2 Timothy 1:9, where the Apostle says of believers that grace was given to them before the world began. Besides it is here [in John 17] stated that Christ prayed for this glory. Christ beseeches God to give him, in actual possession, with Himself, the glory which he had with Him, in purpose and decrees, before the world was. For it is often said that a person has something with any one, when it is promised, or is destined for him. On this account believers are frequently said by the evangelist to have eternal life. Hence it happens that Christ does not say absolutely that he had had that glory, but that he had had it with the Father; as if he had said that he now prayed to have actually conferred upon him that glory which had

---

77 Brown, *The Gospel According to John*, refers to a textual variant at John 17:5: "Among the Latin Fathers and some Ethiopian MSS, there is support for the reading, 'that glory which was with You,' reading *een* = 'was,' instead of 'I had'" (743).

been laid up for him with the Father of old and before the creation of the world.[78]

Jesus Before Abraham

In John 8:58 Jesus claimed superiority over Abraham. His supreme position, however, depends on the Father who glorifies His Son (John 8:54). He stated that Abraham rejoiced to "see my day" (John 8:56) — that is, Abraham by faith saw Messiah's coming in advance of its actual arrival. The day of Messiah "preexisted," so to speak, in Abraham's mind.[79] The Jews misunderstood what Jesus had said, believing that he had made a claim to be actually a contemporary of Abraham (John 8:57). Jesus reaffirmed his absolute preeminence in God's plan with the astonishing claim, "Before Abraham was, I am [he]" (John 8:58).

To grasp the meaning of the phrase "I am" in this text, it is essential to compare it with John's frequent use of the same phrase, which is in several places connected with the *Messiahship* of Jesus:

John 18:5: "Jesus said to them, 'I am [he]'" (identifying himself as the one they were looking for).

John 6:20: "Jesus [walking on the water] said to them: 'It is I'" (literally, "I am").

John 9:9: "[The man healed of blindness] kept saying, 'I am [he]'" (i.e., "I am the one.")

---

[78] *The Racovian Catechism* (London: Longman, Hurst, Rees, Orme and Brown, translated from the Latin by T. Rees, 1818), 144, 145. The writer of the original text (1609), B. Wissowatius, observes in a note: "that this is the true sense of the passage is directly shown by Augustine and Beda...It also ought to be observed here, that it has been the unanimous opinion of the Jews down to the present day, that the Messiah had no existence before the creation of the world, except in the divine decrees." All existing copies of the catechism in England were ordered by Parliament to be burned in April, 1652.

[79] Rabbinic traditions state that Abraham saw a vision of the whole history of his descendants (*Midrash Rabbah*, XLIV, on Gen.15:18). IV Ezra 3:14 says that God granted Abraham a vision of the end times.

John 4:26: "Jesus said to [the woman at the well], 'I who speak to you am [he]'" (i.e., *the Messiah*, verse 25).

John 8:24: "Unless you believe that I am [he], you shall die in your sins."

John 8:28: "When you lift up the Son of Man, then you shall know that I am [he]."

John 13:19: "I am telling you before it comes to pass so that when it does occur you may believe that I am [he]."

John 9:35-37: "Do you believe in the *Son of Man*?...The one talking to you is [he]."

Cp. John 10:24, 25: "'If you are *the Christ*, tell us plainly.' Jesus answered them, 'I told you, and you do not believe me.'"

John 8:58: "Before Abraham came to be, I am [he]."

At this point John's expressly stated purpose for writing the whole of his Gospel must be kept in mind. His aim was that we should "believe that Jesus is the Christ, the Son of God" (John 20:31). The fact that in the Old Testament God speaks of Himself as "I am [He]" does not lead us, as often thought, to the conclusion that on Jesus' lips "I am [he]" means "I am God" in the Trinitarian sense. Jesus' "I am he" declarations in John can be satisfactorily explained as a claim to be *the Messiah*. As such Jesus presents himself as the unique agent of the One God and empowered by the latter to act on His behalf.

Even if one were to connect Jesus' *ego eimi* ("I am") statements with the words of God in the Old Testament, there would still be no justification for identifying Jesus with God in the Trinitarian sense. Jesus, as Messiah, may bear a divine title without being God. Once the Jewish principle of "agency" is taken into account, it will be readily understood that Jesus perfectly represents his Father. As agent he acts for and speaks for his principal, so that the acts of God are manifested in Jesus. None of this, however, makes Jesus literally God. He remains the human Messiah promised by the Scriptures. Trinitarian theology often displays its anti-Messianic bias, and "overreads" the evidence of John, failing to reckon with his simple monotheistic statements defining the Father as "the only true God," distinct from His Son (John 17:3; 5:44). This procedure sets John against Matthew, Mark, and Luke/Acts. It also blurs the New Testament's central point which is to proclaim the identity of Jesus as the Messiah.

The evidence before us (cited above) shows that the famous phrase *ego eimi* means "I am the promised one," "the one in question." The blind man identifies himself by saying "I am the person you are looking for"; "I am the one." In contexts where the Son of Man or the Christ are being discussed Jesus claims to be "the one," i.e., Son of Man, Christ. In each case it is proper (as translators recognize) to add the word "he" to the "I am." There is every reason to be consistent and to supply "he" in John 8:58 also. Thus in John 4:26, "I am" = "I am [he, the Messiah]." In John 8:58 likewise Jesus declares: "Before Abraham was, I am [he, the appointed Messiah]."

It is important to notice that Jesus did not use the phrase revealing God's name to Moses. At the burning bush the One God had declared His name as "I am who I am" or "I am the self-existent one" (Ex. 3:14). The phrase in the Greek version of the Old Testament reads *ego eimi ho hown*, which is quite different from the "I am he" used by Jesus. If Jesus had indeed claimed to be God, it is quite extraordinary that in a subsequent encounter with hostile Jews he claims *not* to be God, but the unique agent of God bearing the title "Son of God" (John 10:34-36).

It is fair to ask how someone can "be" before he actually is. Is the traditional doctrine of the Incarnation of a second divine being the only possible way of dealing with the Johannine preexistence statements? The pattern of foreordination language found in John's Gospel does not require a literal preexistence of the Son. Abraham rejoiced as he looked forward to the coming of the Messiah. Messiah's day was a reality to Abraham through the eyes of faith. So also the Messiah "existed" as the supreme subject of God's plan long before the birth of Abraham. "Before Abraham came to be, I am [the one]" is a profound statement about God's original plan for the world centered in Jesus, whom John can also describe as "crucified before the foundation of the world" (Rev. 13:8). We have no difficulty grasping how this is to be understood: Jesus was the one appointed — and appointed to die — long before Abraham, as the supreme agent of God's plan. If Jesus was "crucified before Abraham," he himself may be said to have "existed" in the eternal counsels of God. In that sense he was indeed appointed as Savior of the world before the birth of Abraham.

In support of this interpretation we cite again the comments of Gilbert. Of John 8:58 he says:

> Jesus has been emphasizing his *Messianic* claim. He does not say that before Abraham was born the *logos* existed; he says "I am." It is Jesus the Messiah, Jesus the man whom the Father had consecrated to the Messianic work who speaks. Just before this he had spoken of "my day," which Abraham saw (John 8:56), by which we must understand the historical appearance of Jesus as Messiah. Abraham had seen this, virtually seen it in God's promise of a seed (Gen. 12:3; 15:4, 5) and had greeted it from afar (Heb. 11:13). And now it is this one who consciously realizes the distant vision of Abraham who says, "Before Abraham was born, I am." Jesus, therefore, seems to affirm that his *historic* Messianic personality existed before Abraham was born. If that be the case, then its existence before Abraham must be thought of as ideal.[80]

---

[80] *The Revelation of Jesus, A Study of the Primary Sources of Christianity*, 214, 215. The point that the *ego eimi* statements of Jesus have to do with his Messiahship is made also by Edwin Freed in *"Ego Eimi* in John 8:24 in the Light of Its Context and Jewish Messianic Belief," *Journal of Theological Studies* 33 (1982): 163-167. Cp. also Barrett, *Essays on John* (London: SPCK, 1982), 71: "Jesus' *ego eimi* is not a claim to divinity; John has other ways, both more explicit and more guarded, of making this claim."

The Ambiguity of John 8:58

Commentators on the book of John frequently note a certain ambiguity in the sayings of Jesus, especially in connection with the failure of the hostile Jewish audience to grasp what Jesus meant. Orthodoxy is often keen to side with the opinions of the Jews against Jesus. The Jews, it is argued, thought that Jesus was claiming to be God. Therefore he is. But Jesus' hostile audience is not a safe guide to the intentions of Christ. We have already seen that Jesus had to correct the Jewish misunderstanding that he was claiming to *be* God. His claim was that he was the *Son of God*, which is the rank of a human being, not God. In John 8:58 there is an interesting grammatical ambiguity which makes a different translation possible. The standard rendering: "Before Abraham came to be, I am" is not the only way to render the Greek.

It is an elementary fact of language that a Greek aorist infinitive takes its meaning from the context. It may refer to events future or past. Thus Matthew writes, "Before the cock will have crowed" (Matt. 26:34; *prin*, "before," + aorist infinitive). But earlier in the same Gospel we have "before they came together" (Matt. 1:18; *prin* + aorist infinitive). In John's Gospel we have, "Sir, come down before my child dies" (John 4:49; *prin* + aorist infinitive); "I have told you before it comes to pass" (John 14:29; *prin* + aorist infinitive). The question arises, What is the proper rendering of John 8:58? Did Jesus say: "Before Abraham comes to be [i.e., returns to life in the resurrection], I am," or "Before Abraham came to be [i.e., was born], I am [he]"?

It may be that orthodoxy misreads this verse as a proof of a preexistent Christ. Only a few verses earlier Jesus had spoken of resurrection as conferring endless life on those who follow him (John 8:51). The Jews objected that this made Jesus superior to Abraham who was then dead. Jesus justifies his claim by pointing out that Abraham had in fact looked forward to the Messiah's day. The Jews misunderstood Jesus to mean that he and Abraham were contemporaries ("Have you seen Abraham?"; John 8:53, 56, 57). It is possible that Jesus counters with the stupendous claim that he will precede Abraham in the resurrection. Before Abraham gains immortality in the resurrection, Jesus will already be alive and immortal. This would fully justify the claim to be superior to Abraham. "Coming to be" (the aorist infinitive of *ginomai*) is in fact used of resurrection in the Septuagint of Job 14:14: "I will wait until I come to be again."

If the text is read as standard translations render it Jesus will have claimed to be the Messiah appointed from eternity. Or he may be stating his superiority to Abraham in another sense. Abraham anticipated the Messiah's triumph. Jesus will indeed be enjoying endless life as the resurrected Savior long before Abraham reappears in the future resurrection.

Ideal Preexistence

Preexistence in the counsels of God, rather than actual preexistence, fits well in the Jewish environment in which the Gospels were written. In Jewish writings, which provide an essential background for understanding the New Testament: "Preexistence is attributed to the expected Messiah, *but only in common with other venerable things and persons, such as the tabernacle, the law, the city of Jerusalem, the lawgiver Moses himself, the people of Israel.*"[81]

The picture of the Messiah which the Jews had built up from the Old Testament did not include the idea that the Messiah actually existed prior to his birth:

> The apocalyptic picture [of Messiah] is for the most part that of a human prince, majestic, richly endowed — whose advent will inaugurate a glorious future for Israel. The Messiah is to be the instrument of judgment on human oppressors, the victorious avenger of the righteous [as Jesus will be at his Second Coming]. He is human, as Son of Man, though possessed of transcendent gifts of wisdom and power. According to one view, he will appear in days when the tribulation of the righteous

---

[81] C. Ottley, *The Doctrine of the Incarnation* (Methuen and Co., 1896), 59, emphasis added.

has reached its height, and his reign will begin with a wholesale destruction of his foes, after which he will rule in tranquility and peace, the Holy Land being the seat of his dominion...Allusions to his being revealed and to his eternal preexistence, cannot fairly be said to imply more than predestination in the divine purpose and foreknowledge.[82]

Another scholar likewise finds in the background of the New Testament preexistence for the Messiah only in God's plan: "Dalman, than whom I suppose there is no greater authority on Jewish matters, [says]: 'Judaism has never known anything of a preexistence peculiar to the Messiah, *antecedent to his birth as a human being.*'"[83]

---

[82] Ibid., 59, 60.

[83] Charles Gore, *Belief in Christ,* 31.

IX. THE HOLY SPIRIT: A THIRD PERSON OR GOD IN ACTION?

"The conventional conception of the Holy Spirit as a separate and distinct Divine Person is a growth. It was not a belief of early Christianity." — Basil Wilberforce, D.D.

According to orthodox Trinitarianism the Holy Spirit is a third member of the eternal Godhead, coequal and coeternal with the Father and Son. This "Person" or "distinction" in the Godhead, however, has no personal name. The question raised by non-Trinitarians is, Does the Bible really support belief in a third "subsistence" (to use the language of Trinitarians), who is as distinct from the Father as the Son obviously is?

It is hard for us to believe that Scripture, read without the benefit of later creeds, clearly presents the Holy Spirit as a "Person" (whatever that means — Trinitarians seem unable to define the word with any confidence), distinct from the Father and Son. The customary but arbitrary use of the pronoun "He" for the Spirit has conditioned us to think of a third person. A very different impression is created if we render spirit as "it."[1]

Our difficulty in accepting the Spirit as a third person of the Triune God is reflected in an amazing admission of the prominent orthodox Greek church leader, Gregory of Nazianzen, who in 381 AD stated: "Of the wise among us, some hold the Holy Spirit to be a power [*energeia*], others a creature, others for God, and still others are unwilling to decide, out of reverence (as

---

[1]As for example in the KJV in Rom. 8:16 where "the Spirit *itself* beareth witness with our spirit that we are the children of God." But the KJV elsewhere makes the spirit a person as "he."

they say) for the Scriptures, which do not speak plainly on the matter."[2]

Where then had the Trinity been for the three hundred years separating this Greek tradition from the death of the Apostles? Our theologian seems to have been remarkably slow to catch on to what is supposed always to have been apostolic orthodoxy. Does a cover-to-cover reading of the Bible yield a Trinitarian view of the Spirit? If one combs through standard Bible dictionaries, it is obvious that ninety-eight percent of the biblical data is satisfied if we define the Spirit as God in effective action, God in communication, His power and personality extending their influence to touch the creation in a variety of ways. The remaining evidence might be pushed in the direction of later Trinitarianism, but is this justified? Is the Spirit really anything other than God's energy, inspiring human beings to perform extraordinary feats of valor, endowing them with special artistic skill or miraculous powers, and especially communicating divine truth? Granted the new thing that has occurred since Pentecost — the focusing of the Spirit in the risen Christ — there is no need to alter the original revealed meaning of "spirit" as God's vitalizing, inspiring energy and His holy intelligence revealed and transmitted through Christ, heart-to-heart, to those who seek Him and His Truth.

The word "spirit" in the Bible has several different meanings, all related, however, to the basic idea of invisible power and mind. In both Testaments "Holy Spirit" describes the energy of God directed to creation and inspiration. It is God in action and an extension of His personality. Wherever the Spirit is at work, we recognize the operational presence of God: "Renew a steadfast spirit within me. Do not cast me away from Your *presence* and do not take *Your Holy Spirit* from me" (Ps. 51:10, 11). A few verses earlier David desires to have "truth in [his]

---

2 Cited in "Macedonius," *The New Schaff-Herzog Encyclopedia of Religious Knowledge* (Grand Rapids: Baker Book House, 1963), 7:112.

innermost being" and the capacity to know wisdom (Ps. 51:6).[3]
The working of God's Spirit in David would produce this
desirable effect. In another passage "spirit" and the presence of
God are equated: "Where can I go from Your Spirit? Or where
can I flee from Your presence?" (Ps. 139:7). There is a close
connection in Psalm 33:6 between God's Spirit and His creative
activity: "By the word of the Lord the heavens were made, and
all the host of them by the breath [Heb. *ruach*; LXX *pneuma*] of
His mouth." The fact that "spirit" and "breath" are translations of
the same Hebrew and Greek words points to the root meaning of
spirit as God's creative power, the energy behind His utterance.

The Spirit of God is certainly not just an abstract power.
Since it is God in action, it is most personal. It is God's outreach.
God's Spirit is His personality extended to His creation. It can be
resisted by sinful human beings. Thus Israel's rebellion was a
grieving of God's spirit (Isa. 63:10). In the same context we
learn that the "angel of His presence" was actively engaged in
the salvation of God's people (Isa. 63:9). There is evidence here
that angels are involved in the mediation of God's spiritual
activity in human affairs. Luke observed that "an angel spoke to
Philip" (Acts 8:26). Three verses later he says that "the Spirit
spoke to Philip" (verse 29). An "angel of the Spirit" is found in
Jewish literature outside the Bible and might explain Luke's
indirect reference to a divine messenger mediating the spirit of
God.[4]

It is going beyond the evidence of Scripture to equate the
Spirit of God with a person distinct from the One God, *in the
same sense as the Son is distinct from the Father*. There are clear
differences between what the Bible says about the Father and the
Son and what it says about the Spirit. God and Christ are
obviously separate individuals worthy of receiving worship, the

---

[3] Cp. "The spirit in the inner man" (Eph. 3:16), showing the close
connection between truth and spirit, as also in John 6:63.

[4] *Ascension of Isaiah* 4:21; 7:23; 9:36, 39; 10:4; 11:35. The angel is
perhaps identified with Gabriel (*Ascension* 3:16; 11:4). Cp. an
association of Gabriel with the activity of the spirit in Luke 1:26, 35.

Father in His capacity as creator, the Son Jesus as instrument and agent in the salvation of mankind. Yet the Holy Spirit has no personal name. Why is it that in no text of Scripture is the Holy Spirit worshipped or prayed to? Not once does the Holy Spirit send greetings to the churches. When the Apostles write to their churches, greetings are always sent from two persons, the Father and the Son. It is quite extraordinary that Paul would constantly omit mention of the third person of the Trinity, if he believed him to exist. When he charges Timothy to keep the faith, he speaks in the invisible presence of "God and of Christ and of His chosen angels" (1 Tim. 5:21).

A leading biblical theologian of this century, and prominent member of the Church of England, appears to reject the idea that the Bible presents the Spirit as a third person:

> To ask whether in the New Testament the spirit is a person in the modern sense of the word would be like asking whether the spirit of Elijah is a person. The Spirit of God is of course personal; it is God's *dunamis* [power] in action. But the Holy Spirit is not a person, existing independently of God; it is a way of speaking about God's personally acting in history, or of the Risen Christ's personally acting in the life and witness of the Church. The New Testament (and indeed patristic thought generally) nowhere represents the Spirit, any more than the wisdom of God, as having independent personality.[5]

Luke's careful choice of words in three important passages shows how spirit and power are interchangeable terms: John the Baptist will go as a forerunner before the Messiah "in the spirit and power of Elijah" (Luke 1:17). At the conception of the Son of God Mary is told that "*holy spirit* [there is no article in the Greek] will come upon you and the *power of the Most High* will overshadow you" (Luke 1:35). When Jesus announces the coming of the Holy Spirit at Pentecost he states his intention to

---

5 Alan Richardson, *Introduction to the Theology of the New Testament* (London: SCM Press, 1958), 120.

"send forth the promise of my Father upon you; but you are to stay in the city until you are clothed with *power* from on high" (Luke 24:49). The term "Spirit of God" in one passage is replaced by "the finger of God" in the parallel text (Matt. 12:28; Luke 11:20). The "finger of God" hardly describes a person.

The spirit which operated in the early Church was recognized as the "Spirit of Jesus," his very personality extended to empower and inspire the believers. Luke writes: "And they passed through the Phrygian and Galatian region, having been forbidden by the Holy Spirit to speak the word in Asia; and when they had come to Mysia, they were trying to go into Bithynia, and the Spirit of Jesus did not permit them" (Acts 16:6, 7). There is apparently no essential difference between the Spirit of God and the Spirit of Jesus: "You are not in the flesh but in the Spirit if indeed the Spirit of God dwells in you. But if anyone does not have the Spirit of Christ, he does not belong to him" (Rom. 8:9). In the same passage Paul speaks of the Spirit interceding for the saints. Since he does not elsewhere recognize the Spirit as a third person it is reasonable to think that he sees no difference between the intercession of the Spirit and the intercession of Christ mentioned in the same context (Rom. 8:27, 34). While Christ himself is with the Father, his Spirit is active in the hearts of believers.

Some have argued that there must be a third person associated with God and Christ since intelligence and goodness are ascribed to the Holy Spirit. For example, Nehemiah writes of God giving His "good Spirit to instruct them" (Neh. 9:20). It is obvious, however, that the Spirit of God possesses all the qualities of God. But there is no need to think of the Spirit as a distinct person. A simpler explanation is given by Paul when he compares the Spirit of God with the spirit of man. He begins by speaking of God's Spirit: "The Spirit searches all things, even the depths of God." He then compares the activity of this "spirit" with the inner self-consciousness of man. "Who among men knows the thoughts of a man except the spirit of a man which is in him? Even so the thoughts of God no one knows except the Spirit of God" (1 Cor. 2:10, 11). The spirit of a man is to his own thoughts as the Spirit of God is to His own thoughts. Holy Spirit is therefore "holy intelligence," a revelation of the very mind of God. Spirit and heart are often closely connected, even interchanged, in the Hebrew Bible. What could be more reassuring than that God opens up His innermost plans and purposes to us, speaking heart-to-heart with man, His creature, and effecting this liaison by means of His own creative intelligence and spirit.

Prominent Trinitarian writers seem to have gone far beyond the evidence of Scripture when they assert that the third person of the Trinity was involved in a conversation when God said, "Let us make man in our own image" (Gen. 1:26). Torrey wrote:

> There are many who say that the doctrine of the Trinity is not in the Old Testament, that while it is in the New Testament it is not in the Old Testament. But the doctrine of the Trinity is in the Old Testament in the very first chapter of the Bible. In Genesis 1:26 we read, "And God said, '*Let us* make man in our image, after *our likeness.*'"[6]

It seems imaginative to say that God here spoke to the Holy Spirit. God does not speak to His own Spirit. He would be talking to Himself (unless by "spirit" an angel-messenger of God is meant). Is there anywhere in Scripture a hint of God speaking to His Holy Spirit? Such an idea is as foreign to the Bible as the notion that the Holy Spirit is to be worshipped or thanked, as Torrey recommends.[7] The hymn which encourages us to "praise Father, Son and Holy Ghost" originates in a milieu which has lost track of the biblical doctrine of the Spirit. Torrey even tells us that the *Shema* of Israel (Deut. 6:4) is really a Trinitarian creed.[8] The plural form of *elohim* is the basis of his argument, which has been rejected by a mass of Trinitarian scholars. Why is it that popular literature makes such an appeal while the much

---

[6] R.A. Torrey, *The Holy Spirit* (Fleming Revell Co., 1977), 20.

[7] Ibid., 13, 19.

[8] Ibid., 21, 22.

more thorough investigations of recognized authorities on the Hebrew language go unnoticed?

In Jesus' last discourses to his disciples he speaks of the "comforter" who will come to encourage the faithful after Jesus has been taken to the Father. Since "comforter" (*parakletos*) is a masculine word in Greek, translators who believed in the "third Person of the Trinity" rendered the following pronouns as "he" and "him." The same "comforter" is, however, also "the spirit of the truth." This title hardly suggests a person. If we do not assume the Holy Spirit to be a person distinct from the Father and Son, the texts will be rendered as follows:

> If you love me you will keep my commandments, and I will ask the Father and He will give you another comforter to remain with you until the [coming] age, the spirit of the truth, which the world cannot receive, because it does not see it or know it [*auto*, neuter agreeing with spirit]. But you know it [*auto*] because it remains with you and will be in you. I will not leave you as orphans; I will come to you...But the comforter, the holy spirit, which the Father will send in my name, it [*ekeinos*, masculine in Greek to agree with *parakletos*, but translated as "he" only if it is assumed a person is meant] will teach you all things and remind you of all the things I spoke to you (John 14:15-18, 26).

The comments of the Trinitarian James Denny are instructive:

> What strikes us here is the new name given to the Spirit—"another Comforter." It is indeed only the name which is new. In idea it answers closely to the only promise of the Spirit which we find in the Synoptic Gospels. The expression "another Comforter" implies that the disciples have already had experience of one, namely Jesus Himself. As long as He was with them their strength was reinforced from Him and when He goes, His place is taken by the Spirit. There is another power with them now which does for them what Jesus did before. Yet is it really another? In 1 John 2:1 it is Jesus who is the Paraclete [Comforter], even after

Pentecost, and even here (John 14:18), He says, "I come
to you." *The presence of the Spirit is Jesus' own
presence in Spirit.*[9]

The equation of God's or Jesus' Spirit with their vitalizing
power and personality is most obvious in the rest of Scripture.
Jesus says to the disciples, "When they deliver you up, do not be
anxious beforehand about what you will say. Whatever will be
given you at that time, speak, for it is not you who speak but the
Holy Spirit" (Mark 13:11). Luke's version makes it clear that the
Spirit speaking in the disciples is Christ himself: "Settle it
therefore in your hearts not to meditate beforehand how to
answer, for *I* will give you speech and wisdom which your
adversaries shall not be able to resist or refute" (Luke 21:14, 15).
A fulfillment of this promise occurred when the enemies of
Stephen were not able "to resist the wisdom and Spirit by which
he spoke" (Acts 6:10). It is illuminating to find that "the Holy
Spirit" of Mark 13:11 is simply, in the parallel passage in
Matthew 10:20, "the spirit of your Father." Both passages are
further clarified by Luke who sees the spirit of God as God
acting to communicate his utterance and wisdom to the
beleaguered disciple (Luke 21:15). This view of the Spirit is
entirely in line with the Hebrew Bible. But it would be
impossible to insert a definition of the Spirit as a person distinct
from the Father and Son in these passages.

Should the plain evidence of almost every part of Scripture
be disturbed by a handful of verses in John's Gospel? Alan
Richardson concludes that for John "Christ Himself comes in the
coming of the Spirit...The Spirit who interprets the Scriptures is
none other than the Lord Himself."[10] John actually calls Christ
the Comforter in his first epistle (1 John 2:1). This is the only
other occurrence of *parakletos*. Paul's view is exactly the same.
He says "The Lord is the Spirit and where the Spirit of the Lord
is, there is freedom" (2 Cor. 3:17).

---

[9] "Holy Spirit," *Dictionary of Christ and the Gospels* (Edinburgh: T &
T Clark, 1917), 742.

[10] *Introduction to the Theology of the New Testament*, 121.

A Trinitarian scholar and commentator on the Gospel of John summed up his findings: "We are not to infer that John regarded the Spirit as a personality in the sense of the later Church doctrine. The discourses of John dwell on the relation of the Father to the Son *without any thought of a third person coordinated with them in one Godhead*."[11]

Another biblical scholar of the last century defined the comforter: "The divine power, *personified* as an assistant, is compared here as in John 15:26 to the ambassador of a prince, who speaks only in accordance with the charge entrusted to him by the sender, and agreeably to his will and pleasure."[12]

There is insufficient evidence to show that Paul believed in "three persons in one God." We have seen that Paul understood the Spirit as the self-awareness and mind of God. When he speaks of the Spirit as a heavenly power distinct from the Father and helping Christians with prayer, he refers in the same passage to Christ himself "pleading for us" (Rom. 8:26, 34). The Spirit is Christ himself extending his influence to the believers.

In summary we may say that the Holy Spirit in the Hebrew Bible (the Old Testament) was never thought of as a person distinct from the Father. The following statement was made by an eminent professor of biblical languages:

> It cannot be proved, out of the whole number of passages in the Old Testament in which the Holy Spirit is mentioned, that this is a person in the Godhead; and it is now [c. 1775] the almost universally received opinion of learned commentators, that, in the language of the Jews, the "Holy Spirit" means nothing more than divine inspiration, without any reference to a person.[13]

---

[11] E.F. Scott, *The Fourth Gospel* (T & T Clark, 1926), 342, emphasis added.

[12] C.T. Kuinoel, cited by Wilson, *Concessions*, 372, emphasis added.

[13] J.D. Michaelis, *Remarks* on John 16:13-15, cited by Wilson, *Unitarian Principles Confirmed by Trinitarian Testimonies*, 477.

What of the New Testament? In our own time Karl Rahner says plainly: "*Ho theos* [God] is never used in the New Testament to speak of the *pneuma hagion* [Holy Spirit]."[14] Acts 5:3, 4 is no exception. Some Trinitarians offer these verses as proof of a third person in the Trinity — God, the Holy Spirit. The texts equate lying to the Holy Spirit with lying to God. The Holy Spirit here means the power and authority invested by God in Peter. Those who lie to Apostles speaking in the name of God and by His Spirit are rightly said to lie to the Spirit and to God. The point is confirmed by a comment from Paul: "He who despises us despises not men but God, who has given us His Spirit" (1 Thess. 4:8). There is a striking parallel in the Old Testament when the Israelites rebelled against Moses and Aaron. Moses told them that their rebellion was "not against us, but against God whose messengers we are." The "equation" of Moses and Aaron with God does not, of course, make the former part of the Godhead (Exod. 16:2, 8). The Spirit of God did, however, reside in Moses and it may be that the Israelite rebellion mentioned in the Psalms was directed against "Moses' spirit" (Ps. 106:33, AV, RV, RSV), or possibly against the angel of God's presence who was invested with the authority and power of Yahweh (Isa. 63:9-11).[15]

Our impression is that distinguished Trinitarians are sometimes tied to the official creed despite their own reservations about the way in which it is expressed. Luther disliked the term Trinity: "The word Trinity is never found in the Divine Records, but is only of human invention, and therefore sounds altogether cold."[16] Calvin sensed that prayer to a Triune God is unscriptural: "I dislike this vulgar prayer, 'Holy Trinity, one God! Have mercy on us!' as altogether savoring of

---

[14] *Theological Investigations* (Baltimore: Helicon Press, 1963), 1:143.

[15] Cp. Exod. 23:21 where the angel bears God's name.

[16] *Concessions*, 331.

barbarism. We repudiate such expressions as being not only insipid, but profane."[17]

But why, if God really is a Trinity, should one object? What indeed is wrong with the expression "Mother of God" (which Protestants reject) if indeed Jesus was God and Mary was his mother? And if the Holy Spirit is really a distinct personality, was he the Father of Jesus, rather than God, the Father? It was the Spirit which caused Mary's conception (Luke 1:35).

When the mature John the Apostle wrote his first epistle, he confined his use of "spirit" to an activity of God and an endowment given to Christians: "By this we know that we abide in Him and He in us, because He has given us [a portion] of His Spirit [*ek tou pneumatos autou*]" (1 John 4:13). God does not give a portion of a person, but a measure of His mind and power. John is thinking of something which can be quantified, as does Peter when quoting a passage referring to a pouring out "from My spirit" (Acts 2:17). Persons, surely, are not poured out. But God can grant the provision of His limitless energy. The language is quite inappropriate for the Spirit as a third person. In another passage John speaks of the Spirit as "that which witnesses," because it is itself the truth in our minds (1 John 5:6). As is well known a famous spurious verse follows this text. It speaks of the three witnesses "in heaven, the Father, the Word and the Holy Spirit; and these three are one." These words "have no right to stand in the New Testament."[18] They are omitted from modern translations of the Bible. Their first appearance in Greek is in 1215 and only as a translation of the Latin *Acts of the Lateran Council*. Not until the sixteenth century are the words found in any Greek manuscript, and then only as a translation of a Latin version of the Bible.[19]

Jesus' command to baptize "into the name of the Father, the Son and the Holy Spirit" (Matt. 28:19) is of no weight in proving

---

[17] *Concessions*, 40.

[18] B.M. Metzger, *A Textual Commentary on the Greek New Testament* (United Bible Society, 1971), 715.

[19] Ibid.

that Jesus believed in a Trinity of three coequal persons, since he recognized the Father as "the only true God" (John 17:3) and subscribed to the non-Trinitarian creed of Israel (Mark 12:29). As the Trinitarian Michaelis said: "It is impossible to understand from this passage, whether the Holy Spirit is a person. The meaning of Jesus may have been this: Those who were baptized should, upon their baptism, confess that they believed in the Father and the Son, and in all the doctrines inculcated by the Holy Spirit."[20]

Paul's benediction which spoke of "the grace of the Lord Jesus Christ, the love of God and the fellowship of the Holy Spirit" (2 Cor. 13:14) is also not a Trinitarian formula, though it will sound Trinitarian if one approaches the text with the preconception that Paul believed in three eternal persons. Paul elsewhere spoke of "the fellowship of the Spirit" and "comfort in Christ" (Phil. 2:1). These passages can be explained as the influence of Jesus through his Spirit working in the believers. It is unnecessary to postulate the existence of the third member of a Trinity. An unusual use of *pneuma hagion* (holy spirit) by Paul's companion Luke strongly suggests that for him the Spirit was always the divine influence, not a third person. He speaks of "Holy Spirit of the mouth of David" (Acts 4:25). The expression recalls David's own consciousness that "the spirit of the Lord spoke by me; His word was in my tongue" (2 Sam. 23:2). In Jewish literature of the New Testament period we find the same picture of inspiration: "The spirit of righteousness descended into Jacob's mouth" (Book of Jubilees 25:14). All such language does not fit the idea of a distinct person. The same difficulty faces Trinitarianism when the Spirit is quantified, as when Malachi speaks of God having "the residue of the Spirit" (Mal. 2:15). John also thinks of the Spirit as given in different quantities. Jesus received it in full "measure" (John 3:34). Paul likewise speaks of "the supply of the Spirit of Jesus Christ" (Phil. 1:19). The language suggests a reservoir of power rather

---

20 *The Burial and Resurrection of Jesus Christ*, 325-327, cited in *Concessions*, 281.

than a person. It is significant that Paul depends on the prayers of the church for continuous help from the Holy Spirit.

A serious difficulty for Trinitarianism is the fact that nothing is said in the earliest post-biblical times of the Spirit as the third person in the Godhead. No formal Trinitarian definition of the Holy Spirit appears until 381 AD at the Council of Constantinople. Only then was it declared that there are "three Persons in one God." More than three hundred years after the ministry of Jesus, the leaders of the Church were uncertain about the nature of the Holy Spirit. Even then many of them did not think of the Holy Spirit as a person.[21] There is, therefore, no unbroken Trinitarian tradition linking us with the writings of the Apostles.

The biblical data is adequately explained by thinking of the Spirit as the mind, heart and personality of God and Christ extended to the creation. The Spirit has personality because it reflects the persons of the Father and the Son. Holy Spirit is another way of speaking of the Father and Son in action, teaching, guiding and inspiring the Church. We see no need to posit the existence of a third person, separate and distinct from God and His Son. There is in fact biblical support for a "trinity" of Father, Son and believers who are united and bonded by the Holy Spirit. Thus John reports Jesus as praying "that they may be one, as You, Father are in me and I in You, that they may also be one in us...I in them, Thou in me, that they may be perfect in one" (John 17:21, 23). The Holy Spirit, the Spirit of the truth, is the mind of the creator graciously made available to suffering humanity. Access to the Holy Spirit is found in the words of Jesus, which are "spirit and are life" (John 6:63). Christians possess the anointing which teaches them true doctrine, guards them against the destructive lies of the devil, and enables them to remain in union with Christ (1 John 2:27). We cannot help thinking that the real function of Holy Spirit is obscured when attention is diverted to the question about the Spirit as a third member of the Godhead. The enormous significance of the Spirit

---

[21] Philip Schaff, *History of the Christian Church*, 3:664.

lies in its being God Himself in His creative and communicating function, opening His very heart to His creatures. "The Spirit speaks" is not different from "God speaks." Word, wisdom and spirit are closely connected. These are divine attributes of the One God, not persons distinct from Him. Defining the Spirit as a third person is unnecessary. It raises a speculative problem (with catastrophic results). The problem arose when a divine attribute (which may sometimes in the Bible be personified) was turned into a person.

There is no good reason for abandoning the obvious analogy between the expression "spirit of Elijah" (Luke 1:17) and "spirit of God." The spirit of Elijah is not a different person from Elijah, nor is God's spirit a different person from God. The spirit of God provides us with insight into the innermost being of the Deity. We encounter God as He extends Himself through His spirit, predominantly in the words of Scripture which are "inspirited" (2 Tim. 3:16). When we read that "the Lord was sorry that He had made man on the earth and He was grieved in His heart" (Gen. 6:6), it was the spirit of God which was grieved (cp. Eph. 4:30). When God's eyes and heart resided in the Temple (1 Kings 9:3), one could equally say that His spirit was present there. The close association of spirit, mind, heart and word(s) appears in the revealing words of Proverbs 1:23: "Turn at my reproof, I will 'bubble forth' My spirit on you. I will make My words known to you." Moffatt catches another facet of meaning with "I will make my mind known to you." The Revised Standard Version exposes the intellectual aspect of the spirit: "I will pour out my thoughts on you," while the Jerusalem Bible allows us to see yet another layer of meaning: "I will open my heart to you."

God's spirit is His holy intelligence, character and disposition, the index of the plans and purposes of His heart. Through the Spirit we are invited to participate in that range of divine activity, becoming "holy as God is holy," and being privy to the secret counsel which He longs to share with us: "The intimacy of the Lord is for those who fear Him, and He will make them know His covenant" (Ps. 25:14).

Knowing nothing of later dogma, Paul freely interchanges "spirit" and "mind," thus giving us an apostolic definition of the Holy Spirit. "Who has known the mind [*nous*] of the Lord, or who became His counselor?" (Rom. 11:34). The Hebrew text Paul is quoting reads "Who has directed the *spirit* of the Lord?" (Isa. 40:13). By receiving the Spirit, which is equivalent to "receiving the knowledge of the truth" (Heb. 10:26), we gain access to the divine personality extended to us in the Spirit.

X. THE CONFLICT OVER THE TRINITY
IN CHURCH HISTORY AND THE CURRENT DEBATE

"In the fifth century Christianity had conquered paganism and paganism had infected Christianity." — Macaulay

Historical Anticipations of the Present-Day Debate about Preexistence

The problem of preexistence (and therefore of the Trinity), and its effect on the nature of the Savior, has had a long history in the Church. In recent years it has been exercising the minds of a number of prominent biblical scholars who have wondered whether our legacy from the Church Fathers does less than justice to the unitary monotheism professed by the Apostles.[1] The question has also persisted as to how far the Jesus of the creeds may be considered a genuinely human person.[2] A historical sketch will help to set the scene for the contemporary debate.

We note first that Justin Martyr (c. 114-165) was one of the first of the post-biblical writers to develop the doctrine of the preexistence of Christ, though he acknowledged that not all of his fellow believers shared this view. He confessed to the Jew, Trypho, that:

> Jesus may still be the Christ of God, though I should not be able to prove his preexistence as the Son of God who made all things...For though I should not prove that he

---

[1] Mark 12:29-34; John 5:44; 17:3; 1 Cor. 8:4-6; Eph. 4:6; 1 Tim. 2:5, etc.

[2] Cp. Thomas Hart, *To Know and Follow Jesus* and the well-known *God Was in Christ* by Donald Baillie (London: Faber, 1961).

had preexisted, it would be right to say that in this respect only I have been deceived, and not to deny that he is the Christ..., though it should appear that he was born man of men...For there are some...of our race who admit that he is Christ, while holding him to be man of men; with whom I do not agree.[3]

Trypho, speaking as one familiar with Jewish expectations about the Messiah, adds his voice to those who "think that Jesus was a man, and being chosen of God was anointed Christ." He considers this a more probable opinion than Justin's. Though Trypho may here be referring to an adoptionist Christology (i.e., Jesus became Son of God only at his baptism), as distinct from Luke's conception Christology (Jesus is the Son of God by virtue of his miraculous conception; Luke 1:35), it seems clear from his debate with Justin that belief in preexistence is not at this stage the universally held tenet of "orthodoxy" which it later became. It is also remarkable that "Justin nowhere asserts that the Father, Son and Spirit constitute one God, as became the custom in later ages. Strictly speaking he was a unitarian, as were the orthodox Fathers generally of his time: that is they believed the Son to be a being really distinct from the Father, and inferior to Him."[4]

A further indication of dispute over John's Gospel and preexistence is found in the writings of the Greek Church Father Epiphanius (c. 310-403), who was interested in identifying "heresy." He refers to a group of Gentile believers, the Alogi (c. 180), who had been accused of rejecting the Gospel of John.

---

[3] *Dialogue with Trypho*, chs. 48, 49.

[4] Alvan Lamson, D.D., *The Church of the First Three Centuries* (Boston: Houghton, Osgood & Co., 1880), 80. Justin, however, set the direction for later development towards Trinitarianism by asserting the literal preexistence of Jesus. Trinitarianism was not the belief of the post-apostolic period at least for 80 years, as is shown by the admission of *The New Schaff-Herzog Encyclopedia* of *Religious Knowledge* that in the period 100-180 "there is nothing to show that at that time Christ was regarded as the actual Godhead" (Harnack, "Monarchianism," 7:453).

Joseph Priestley ventures the opinion that the Alogi were criticized by Epiphanius because "they explained the 'logos' in the introduction to John's Gospel in a manner different from him."[5] Thus the crucial matter of the meaning of "logos" in John's prologue was already the cause of uncertainty. The resolution of the question about the nature of preexistence in John in favor of belief in a preexistent *Son* was to have a profound and lasting effect on what became the orthodox Christology of the creeds. The doctrine of the Trinity cannot be sustained unless it can be shown that Jesus existed as the *eternal Son of God* before his birth. Protests against a particular reading of John, which set up tension between him and the Synoptic view of Christ, emerge again.

Dynamic Monarchianism

Before long a reaction set in against the evident threat to monotheism posed by the introduction of a "second God" in the form of the preexisting Christ. Justin and other early writers were steeped in philosophy before becoming Christians. It was all too easy for them to indulge their capacity for speculation and to read John's prologue as if it agreed with a Greek view of the universe:

> The Apologists of the second century were more familiar with Platonic cosmology than they were with biblical soteriology, and hence stretched the Christian doctrine to fit a philosophical procrustean mold. They conceived God as above and beyond all essence, ineffable, incommunicable, impassible, exalted beyond any commerce with matter, time or space. This Platonic God put forth the Word...by an act of His will to be His intermediary for creation, revelation and redemption. *The doctrine construes the Son as preexistent.*[6]

---

[5] *History of the Corruptions of Christianity* (J. & J.W. Prentiss, 1838), 21.

[6] William Childs Robinson, "Jesus Christ Is Jehovah" (Part 2), *Evangelical Quarterly* 5:3 (1933): 275, emphasis added. For the

The reaction came when a group of believers protested that the Godhead was strictly one — a "monarchy." Theodotus the tanner raised the issue of the humanity of Jesus in Rome around 190-200. Appealing to the strictly monotheistic statement of Paul in 1 Timothy 2:5, he maintained that Jesus was not entitled to be called God. His successor, another Theodotus, continued to champion a view of Jesus as a man supernaturally conceived. Some thirty years later Artemas, holding the same "dynamic monarchian" understanding of the Godhead, contended against the Roman bishop that the ancient Christology which monarchians were defending was being distorted by the official Church.

Paul of Samosata

The issue of the nature of preexistence surfaces next in the theology of Paul of Samosata, bishop of Antioch, in the middle of the third century. Though Paul was officially condemned for heresy in 268 AD, modern writers have appreciated the force of his protest against "orthodoxy." "Our theology has been cast in a scholastic mold," wrote Archbishop Temple. "We are in need of and we are being gradually forced into a theology based on psychology. The transition, I fear, will not be without much pain; but nothing can prevent it." Temple went on to say that "we must not forget that there was a very early attempt made by Paul of Samosata. He saw serious difficulty in the formulation of the Church's belief concerning Christ so long as this was expressed in terms of substance, and tried to express it in terms of will."[7]

Another party to the dialogue, Professor Bethune-Baker, expressed his conviction that "Paul of Samosata had behind him a genuine historical tradition, to which, in our reconstruction of

---

development of Trinitarianism in the post-biblical period, see M.M. Mattison, *The Making of a Tradition* (Ministry School Publications, 1991).

[7] *Foundations* (London: Macmillan & Co., 1913), 226.

doctrine, we must return."[8] Loofs, the historian of Christology, came to the conclusion that Paul of Samosata "is one of the most interesting theologians of the pre-Nicene period, because he stands in the line of a tradition which had its roots in a period before the deluge of Hellenism swept over the Church."[9]

Paul of Samosata's understanding of the "logos" was that it had no independent existence apart from God; in other words that there was no Son until the *conception* of Jesus. A widespread familiarity with this same tradition is remarkably confirmed by a casual observation of Origen in his commentary on John. He stated that there were "numerous Christians who employed only the *name* of the 'logos' for the preexistent Christ (without its philosophical connotation and only in the sense of an *utterance* of the Father) which came to expression in a Son when Jesus was conceived" (cp. Heb. 1:1, 2). They did not ascribe to the "logos" a separate hypostasis or individuality.[10] It is interesting that Tertullian (c.155-230) translates "logos" by *sermo*, "speech." He then notes that "it is the simple use of our people to say [of John 1:1] that the word of *revelation* was with God." He himself urged that "logos" should be understood as "whatever you think" and "speech" as "whatever you understand." Referring to a time before creation, he adds that "although God had not yet sent forth His Word, He had it both with and in reason within Himself."[11] It is clear that the "word" was not yet understood as the Son preexisting eternally, as in later orthodoxy.

---

[8] Cited by F.W. Green, "The Later Development of the Doctrine of the Trinity," in *Essays on the Trinity and the Incarnation* (Longmans, Green & Co., 1928), 259.

[9] Ibid. Cp. the remark of Canon Goudge that "when the Greek and Roman mind instead of the Hebrew mind came to dominate the Church, there occurred a disaster in doctrine and practice from which we have never recovered" ("The Calling of the Jews," in the collected essays on *Judaism and Christianity*).

[10] F.W. Green, *Essays on the Trinity and the Incarnation*, 262.

[11] Tertullian, *Ad Praxeus*, 5.

Green concedes that Paul of Samosata's doctrine of the Trinity (not the Trinity as later formulated) was "at least as scriptural as that of Origen, and it was based upon a sound and widespread tradition in the Church."[12] He then goes on to make the remarkable assertion that:

> It cannot be too strongly emphasized that the Antiochene tradition knew nothing of the term Son as applied to the preexistent Logos, in whatever sense used. By the word "Son" they always meant the historical Christ...Loofs remarks that the transference of the conception of Son to the preexistent Logos by the Alexandrian theologians was the most important factor in the establishment of the pluralistic character of Christian doctrine.[13]

Speaking of Jesus as the preexistent Son was the fatal shift which removed the Savior from the category of human being and launched the series of fearful disputes about Christ. Once the beginning of Jesus ceased to be at his conception, speculation ran wild, the unity of the Godhead was threatened and Jesus was no longer the "man Messiah" predicted by the Hebrew Bible. A reconstruction which confines the term "Son" to Jesus as the human Christ would seem to have a firm basis in early church history, as well as in the Bible itself. It is heartening to find William Temple supporting a more authentic understanding of the nature of preexistence in John: "The Johannine identification of Christ with 'logos' had originally meant, in the writings of the evangelist, 'You believe in a single world-principle, but you do not know its character; we do; it was made flesh in the person of Jesus of Nazareth.'"[14]

The late distinguished scholar of the Bible, F.F. Bruce, seems to hold a view of preexistence which leaves open the question as to whether in John 1:1 *the Son* preexisted. He says: "On the preexistence question, one can at least accept the

---

12 F.W. Green, *Essays on the Trinity and the Incarnation*, 64.

13 Ibid.

14 *Foundations*, 227.

preexistence of the eternal word or wisdom of God, which (who?) became incarnate in Jesus. But whether any New Testament writer believed in his separate conscious existence as a 'second Divine Person' before his incarnation is not so clear."[15]

Bruce's frank question is most revealing. If no New Testament writer did in fact believe that the Son of God was a preexistent second divine person, it must follow that no New Testament writer believed in the Trinity.

Photinus and the Photinians

Objection to the preexistence of Jesus emerges again in the fourth-century Bishop Photinus of Sirmium. His understanding of Jesus was probably identical with that of Paul of Samosata. Photinus maintained that the Sonship of Jesus began at his supernatural conception. Several councils condemned him for saying that the Son existed before Mary only in the foreknowledge and purpose of God. The church historian Sozomen described Photinus as acknowledging that "there was One God Almighty, by whose own word all things were created." Yet Photinus would not admit that "the generation and existence of the Son was before all ages; on the contrary he alleged that Christ derived his existence from Mary." The tradition which denied the literal preexistence of the Son survived in Spain and southern Gaul until at least the seventh century. Photinians, along with certain followers of a Bishop Bonosus who denied the preexistence of Christ, were condemned as heretics by the Synod of Toledo in 675.[16]

---

[15] From correspondence, June 13th, 1981.

[16] See M.M. Mattison, "Biblical Unitarianism from the Early Church Through the Middle Ages," *A Journal from the Radical Reformation: A Testimony to Biblical Unitarianism* 1 (winter 1992): 4-13. A wealth of information in regard to all aspects of the Trinitarian controversy can be found in this journal, published from 1991-2000. Back issues may be obtained from 800-347-4261. Further resources may be found at www.restorationfellowship.org.

Michael Servetus and Adam Pastor

The Spaniard Michael Servetus (1511-1553) was one of the most articulate exponents of anti-Nicene Christology. His underlying thesis was that the fall of the Church dated from the disastrous intervention by Constantine into the affairs of Christian doctrine at Nicea. He argued that acceptance of Jesus Christ as the Messianic Son of God should be the basis of a reconstructed Christology. The Son, he claimed, came into being at his conception in Mary. He then dismissed as philosophical Greek speculation all talk of a premundane "eternal generation" of the Son. He saw the Holy Spirit as the power and personality of God extended to creation, not a distinct person of the Godhead. Servetus emphasizes that the Son may be thought of as eternal only with respect to God's *intention* to generate him at a later moment in history.[17] As is well known, Servetus paid for his "heretical" Christology with his life. He was burned at the stake in Geneva, at the instigation of the Roman Catholic Church and the Protestant reformer, John Calvin, on October 27th, 1553. This tragic episode is a grim reminder of the terrible violence and misguided zeal that has marked some "magisterial" forms of professing Christianity.[18]

The issue of preexistence was a critical concern among Dutch Anabaptists of the 16th century in the dispute between Menno Simons and a fellow Anabaptist, Adam Pastor (c. 1500-1570). A former monk, originally named Rodolf Martens, Pastor was unquestionably "the most brilliant man and scholar in the entire Dutch Anabaptist community of his day."[19] Pastor's Christology anticipates contemporary questioning of the nature of preexistence, and a similar Christology has emerged in the

---

[17]   G.H. Williams, *The Radical Reformation* (Philadelphia: Westminster Press, 1962), 271, 322, 333.

[18] For details of Calvin's treatment of Servetus, see R.H. Bainton, *Hunted Heretic: The Life and Death of Michael Servetus* (Beacon Press, 1953), and Stefan Zweig, *The Right to Heresy* (Beacon Press, 1951).

[19] H.E. Dosker, *The Dutch Anabaptists* (Judson Press, 1921), 58.

work of the twentieth-century Dutch theologians Hendrikus Berkhof and Ellen Flesseman.[20] Pastor disavowed orthodox Trinitarianism in 1547 at Emden and was immediately excommunicated by Simons and Obbe Philips. As we see from Pastor's *Difference Between True Doctrine and False Doctrine*,[21] he denied the preexistence of Christ. Not surprisingly, Sandius and other Polish anti-Trinitarian writers refer to Pastor as "the man in our fatherland who had been the first and able writer in that direction," i.e., the view that the "word" of John 1:1 was not a person, but God's creative word or will personified.[22] H.E. Dosker remarks that "When we read Adam Pastor we have to rub our eyes to see whether we are awake or dreaming. What he has to say is so startlingly modern that it bewilders the reader. And we wake up to see that not all modernity...is modern."[23]

Pastor is critical of Menno's and Melchior Hoffman's doctrine that the word only passed through Mary without coming at all in touch with her body. This would make Mary a kind of surrogate mother who did not really conceive Jesus as Scripture states. Such a Christology could hardly escape a charge of docetism and Gnosticism. Pastor insists that Christ is truly human and the descendant of David, supernaturally conceived. His view would seem to coincide well with what Raymond Brown describes as that of Luke and Matthew. It is certain that the Polish Anabaptists a century later claimed Pastor as the first man who had clearly articulated their views about preexistence. Without doubt, Adam Pastor anticipates the modern discussion about the humanity of Jesus when he defines the "logos" not as a

---

[20] See Hendrikus Berkhof, *Christian Faith* (Grand Rapids: Eerdmans, 1979), and Ellen Flesseman, *A Faith for Today*, trans. J.E. Steely, (Association of Baptist Professors of Religion, Box A, Mercer University, 1980).

[21] *Underscheit tusschen rechte und falsche leer* (Bibliotheca Reformatoria Nederlandica), 5:315-581.

[22] Dosker, *The Dutch Anabaptists*, 163.

[23] Ibid., 93.

preexisting person, but as the self-expressive activity of God putting forth His energy in creation, in revealing truth and in generating the Messiah.[24]

John Biddle, Father of English Anti-Trinitarians

John Biddle (1615-1662), educated in classics and philosophy at Oxford, embarked on an "impartial search of the Scriptures" after he began to question received church doctrine. From 1641 to 1645 Biddle was headmaster of Crypt School, Gloucester. It was during this period that his close study of the New Testament caused him to become disaffected with the doctrine of the Trinity. The matter was of such a serious nature that the magistrates issued an order for his arrest and imprisonment. Following a debate with Archbishop Ussher (of chronology fame), Biddle summed up the result of his study of early Christianity: "The Fathers of the first two centuries, or thereabouts, when the judgments of Christians were yet free, and not enslaved with the determinations of Councils, asserted the Father only to be the one God."

Biddle complained that the Greek philosophical language of the creeds was "first hatched by the subtlety of Satan in the heads of Platonists, to pervert the worship of the true God." Parliament lost no time in ordering that Biddle's work be burned. In 1648 the British government passed what has been called the "Draconian Ordinance" for the punishment by death of "Blasphemies and Heresies," aimed at Biddle's claim that Trinitarian doctrine introduces "three Gods, and so subverts the Unity of God, so frequently inculcated in Scripture." The Athanasian Creed is no answer to the problem: "for who is there (if at least he dare make use of reason in his religion) who seeth not that this is as ridiculous as if one should say, Peter is an

---

24 For a fuller account of Adam Pastor, see A.H. Newman, "Adam Pastor, Anti-trinitarian, Anti-paedobaptist" in *Papers of the American Society of Church History* (G. Putnam's Sons, 1917), 2nd series, 5:98. See also Anthony Buzzard, "Adam Pastor: Anti-Trinitarian Anabaptist," *A Journal from the Radical Reformation* 3:3 (spring 1994): 23-30.

Apostle, James an Apostle, John an Apostle; yet there are not three Apostles but one Apostle?"

In 1655 Biddle was committed to Newgate Prison for "publicly denying that Jesus Christ was the Almighty or the Most High God."

Supporters of Biddle were quick to point out that all Christians must be considered guilty of death by Parliament's latest attempt to suppress anti-Trinitarianism, for "he that saith that Christ died, saith that Christ was not God, for God could not die. But every Christian saith that Christ died, therefore every Christian saith that Christ was not God."

A petition for the release of Biddle described him as "a man, though differing from most of us in many great matters of faith, yet by reason of his diligent study of the Holy Scripture, sober and peaceable conversation, which some of us have intimate and good knowledge of, we cannot but judge every way capable of the liberty promised in the Government."

Though only forty-seven years old, Biddle had spent nearly ten years of his life in prison for his insistence that God was a single person. He died in prison in 1662, "a victim of *odium theologicum* and the filthy conditions of the place in which he was lodged." A sympathetic biographer wrote of Biddle's "great zeal for promoting holiness of life and manners; for this was always his end and design in what he taught. He valued not his doctrines for speculation but for practice."[25]

John Milton, Sir Isaac Newton, John Locke

The celebrated British poet, John Milton (1608-1674), is less well known for his *Treatise on Christian Doctrine*, the contents of which were lost to the public for 150 years after his death. Rediscovered in 1823, the treatise demonstrated Milton's biblical arguments against orthodox Trinitarianism. Milton desired only:

> to communicate the result of my inquiries to the world at
> large; if, as God is my witness, it be with a friendly and

---

[25] Information for this section is taken from H.J. McLachlan's *Socinianism in Seventeenth-Century England* (Oxford University Press, 1951), 163-217.

> benignant feeling towards mankind, that I readily give as
> wide a circulation as possible to what I esteem my best
> and richest possession, I hope to meet with a candid
> reception from all parties..., even though many things
> should be brought to light which will at once be seen to
> differ from certain received opinions.

He continues with a plea to "all lovers of truth" that they
"prove all things" in the light of Scripture. His only desire is to
defend the Bible against tradition:

> For my own part, I adhere to the Holy Scriptures alone
> — I follow no other heresy or sect. I had not even read
> of the works of the heretics, so called, when the mistakes
> of those who are reckoned for orthodox, and their
> incautious handling of Scripture, first taught me to agree
> with their opponents whenever these opponents agreed
> with Scripture.[26]

Milton builds his anti-Trinitarian case on the explicitly
unitarian creedal statements of the New Testament. His
argument is characterized by a tight logic, detailed knowledge of
the biblical languages, and some frustration at traditional
attempts to avoid Paul's unitarian statement that "there is no God
but the Father": "It is wonderful with what futile subtleties, or
rather with what juggling artifices, certain individuals have
endeavored to elude or obscure the plain meaning of these
passages."[27]

Milton is familiar with the full range of Trinitarian argument
and his reply makes an invaluable contribution to the modern
discussion.

Sir Isaac Newton (1642-1727) and John Locke (1632-1704)
are reckoned to be among the finest minds of the seventeenth
century. With Milton they protested the creation of
mystifications which are not found in the Bible. Their arguments

---

[26] John Milton, *Treatise on Christian Doctrine* (London: British and
Foreign Unitarian Association, 1908), x, xi.

[27] Ibid., 20.

are "ultimately logical and commonsensical."[28] Both maintained that the essence of Christianity is to acknowledge Jesus as the Messiah, not God.[29]

The Contemporary Debate about Preexistence

The issue of preexistence was the focus of John Knox's illuminating essay on the *Humanity and Divinity of Christ*. His major point is that "the assertion of Christ's preexistence, placed a strain, so to speak, upon the humanity of Jesus which it was unable to bear."[30] He then goes on to maintain that in the Gospel of John the humanity of Christ is "in the formal sense, unambiguously and strongly affirmed, but in actual fact, has been so transformed by the divinity surrounding it on all sides, as it were, as no longer to be manhood in any ordinary sense." With these words he reflects his objection to John's portrait of Jesus. But does John really contradict himself? Only, we submit, when interpreted by the later creeds. Knox sets the terms of the debate which has continued with particular interest in the Christology of John and the nature of preexistence. If, indeed, John thought of Jesus as personally preexisting as *Son*, does not this automatically negate his real humanity? Knox is convinced that it does: "We can have the humanity without the preexistence and we can have the preexistence without the humanity. There is absolutely no way of having both."[31] Knox believes that "It is simply incredible that a divine person should have become a fully and normally human person — that is, if he was also to continue to be, in his essential identity, the same person."[32]

---

[28] Christopher Hill, *Milton and the English Revolution* (New York: Viking Press, 1977), 286, 296.

[29] See Locke's *The Reasonableness of Christianity as Delivered in the Scriptures* (1695).

[30] John Knox, *The Humanity and Divinity of Christ* (Cambridge University Press, 1987), 53.

[31] Ibid., 106.

[32] Ibid., 98.

The traditional picture of Jesus as the Incarnation of a preexisting Son is an acute problem for Knox. He views orthodox Christology as "half story and half dogma, a compound of mythology and philosophy, of poetry and logic, as difficult to define as to defend...This is true of the patristic Christology generally (and therefore of the formal Christology we have inherited)."[33]

These concerns have recently been tackled by a number of distinguished theologians, showing that the ancient problem of the nature of the divine and human in Jesus is as alive as ever.

Knox considers the development towards a preexistent Christ to be a distortion, involving, whether we like it or not, a denial of the full reality of Jesus' humanity. He points out that the protestations of the Church Fathers that their Jesus was fully human are less than convincing, because "There are, in the case of words no less than with other things, ways of taking back with one hand what one has just given with the other. One may affirm the humanity as a formal fact and then proceed so to define or portray it as to deny its reality in any ordinarily accepted sense."[34]

In this opinion he is fully supported by Norman Pittenger who makes the following important judgment about patristic Christology, which drew its inspiration largely from its reading of John:

> In my judgment a fundamental difficulty with the Christology of the patristic age is that while in word it asserted the reality of the humanity of Jesus Christ, *in fact* it did not take that humanity with sufficient seriousness...[Interestingly, he excepts Paul of Samosata from this criticism.] The tendency of Christological thinking in the mainstream of what was believed to be "orthodox" was far more heavily weighted on the side of the divinity than the humanity in Jesus.[35] Orthodox

---

[33] Ibid., 98, 99.

[34] Ibid., 62.

[35] Cp. Thomas Hart, *To Know and Follow Jesus*, especially 44-48.

Christology, even when the excesses of Alexandrine teaching were somewhat restrained at Chalcedon in AD 451, has tended toward an impersonal humanity which is, I believe, no genuine humanity at all.[36]

This seems to be precisely the problem. But Knox is wrong to blame John for introducing this distortion. John was not guilty of any such dissembling over the humanity of Jesus. Rather, the problem lies with the misunderstanding by the Nicene Church Fathers, and some of their predecessors, of John's "logos" and thus of the meaning of preexistence. The later official formula that Jesus was "man" but not "a man" (which remains on the books of traditional Trinitarianism to this day) does not reflect John's intention at all, for there is no conceivable way of being "man" except by being "a man."[37]

---

[36] *The Word Incarnate* (Nisbet, 1959), 89.

[37] Cp. the bewilderment of A.T. Hanson when he reflected on what he had been taught in seminary about the orthodox definition of Jesus: "During my theological formation I was well instructed in the traditional account of the Incarnation of God in Jesus Christ. I distinctly remember being told that the Word of God, when he assumed human nature, assumed impersonal humanity; that Jesus Christ did not possess a human personality; that God became man in Christ Jesus, but that he did not become a man...Two considerations have persuaded me that this traditional Christology is incredible" (*Grace and Truth: A Study in the Doctrine of the Incarnation*, London: SPCK,1975, 1).

The same perplexity is expressed by Oliver Quick, *Doctrines of the Creed* (Nisbet, 1938): "If we affirm that Jesus was a human person, we are driven either into an impossible conception of a double personality in the incarnate Son of God, or else into the Christology of liberal Protestantism which we have found to be inadequate. If we deny that Jesus was a human person, we deny by implication the completeness of his manhood and stand convicted of Apollinarianism. Dr. Raven urges (see his book, *Apollinarianism*) that most of those whom the Catholic tradition has honored as doctors of orthodoxy were in fact Apollinarian, though they condemned Apollinarius" (178). Cp. Norman Pittenger's observation that "Chalcedon failed to prevent a modified Apollinarianism from becoming the orthodoxy of the Middle Ages" (*The Word Incarnate*, 102).

In the light of these considerations, it is not difficult to see that the charge of docetism may well be leveled at the orthodox definition of Christ. If being human means being a man, and orthodoxy has to shy away from saying that Jesus was "a man," perhaps this criticism should be accepted. But does John demand that we believe in a preexistent "God, the Son"? Many have thought so, and have clung to the orthodox belief in preexistence, despite whatever dangerous approximation to "Apollinarianism" (i.e., a heresy which denies the humanity of Christ) may be involved. The recent work of three leading scholars shows not only the acute nature of the problem but suggests the way to a solution — a solution which is not new, though credit is not always given by modern writers to those who in earlier church history had already pointed in the right direction. The solution follows the exegesis of John which we proposed earlier.

James Dunn and James Mackey

James Dunn, in an extensive study, set out to examine the question of the Incarnation (and thus the Trinity) in the New Testament.[38] He rescues the traditional view only in John's Gospel, arguing that Paul and the other New Testament writers think only of a notional or ideal preexistence of Christ, and therefore not of a preexistent Son. An important contribution to the debate was made by James Mackey in 1983.[39] In a chapter entitled "The Problem of the Preexistence of the Son," he starts by wondering how something can preexist itself, "what exactly, according to this term [preexist] preexists what else, and in what sense it does so." He notes that it is exactly these questions which lead to the difficulties involved in traditional incarnational and Trinitarian theology. He notices that exegetes are "often the unconscious victims in the course of their most professional work of quite dogmatic (that is, uncritical) assumptions."[40]

---

[38] *Christology in the Making.*

[39] *The Christian Experience of God as Trinity* (London: SCM Press, 1983).

[40] Ibid., 51.

Mackey attempts to track down the real origin of the term "preexistence" in relation to Christ, noting that scholars often read it into passages which are traditionally supposed to contain it. In the Synoptics, he argues, the term Son of God certainly will not bear the meaning "preexistent Son," but properly fits the Old Testament designation of the King of Israel as Son of God. "The logical path to alleged preexistence," he maintains, "is a tortuous one."[41] Firstly, the surviving Jewish sources point only to "a kind of notional preexistence of the Messiah in so far as his name, i.e., his essence and nature, preceded the formation of light by God on the first day of creation...In Jewish thought the celestial preexistence of the Messiah does not affect his humanity."[42]

Furthermore, this sort of preexistence is:

> part and parcel of the revelation model in human imagining by which God, who is not bound by our time, had in mind in eternity or before anything else was created, the one who was the key to all existence, who would bring all to consummation, and for whom (in whom, through whom) all could therefore be said to be created.[43]

Mackey goes on to make the important point that John's description of Jesus as *monogenes* (unique) does not imply the *unigenitus* (only-begotten) of the Vulgate, as though Jesus was the only Son. It means rather that he was unique among others of that genre. He quotes Schillebeeckx, who says that John's adjective gives us "no basis in Johannine theology for the later scholastic theology of procession of the Son from the Father within the Trinity, *per modum generationis* (by birth)."[44] On this evidence, confirmation is secured for the thesis that John does not go beyond the "conception Christology" of Luke, since

---

[41] Ibid., 56.

[42] Ibid., 56, 57.

[43] Ibid., 57.

[44] Ibid., 59.

Sonship in John nowhere implies, despite the patristic view, a Sonship in eternity.

Furthermore, Mackey argues that it is unnecessary to read John's "Word" other than in the sense in which Jewish "wisdom" had already been thought of, as God's plan preexisting. "This Word, like wisdom [Proverbs 8:30] was with God in the beginning and through it [not him] all things were made."[45] Once again Schillebeeckx supports him. "The Gospel of John speaks of Jesus of Nazareth when he appeared on earth."[46] Mackey adds that the "descent" (i.e., Jesus "came down from heaven") language in John does not involve belief in literal preexistence. Rather, John means to say that Jesus is the definitive revelation of God's nature. Even the most impressive claim of Jesus that "before Abraham was, I am" points not to a conscious pre-human life, but to his absolute significance in the divine plan, particularly his Messianic office as foreseen by Abraham. Mackey concludes with a strong statement:

> If we have any remaining respect for what we too often and too glibly profess to be the normative role of Scripture, we simply may not pretend that Scripture gives us any substantial information about a second divine "Person" or hypostasis distinct from both God the Father and the historical Jesus before Jesus was born, or "before the world was made."[47]

The warning is a strong one that the traditional Trinitarian doctrine is not found in the Bible.

John A.T. Robinson

The age-old issue of preexistence, and in particular the question whether John intends us to understand that Jesus was a personally preexisting divine being, was vigorously debated in

---

[45] Ibid.

[46] Ibid.

[47] Ibid., 64.

the magazine *Theology*.[48] The discussion began with an exchange of letters between James Dunn and Maurice Wiles. The critical issues arising from this dialogue were discussed in the subsequent comments of Robinson.[49]

Robinson begins by observing that Wiles and Dunn agree that within the New Testament, only John presents Jesus as having a pre-human existence. Wiles regards this as a disastrous Christological development, undermining the humanity of Jesus and thus encouraging a charge of docetism. Robinson, however, points out that in his epistles John reacts violently to any suggestion that his Jesus is other than fully human — "come in the flesh." This leads Robinson to disagree with Wiles and Dunn that in his Gospel John means us to understand that Jesus was a preexistent divine being. The discussion thus recalls the problem raised by Paul of Samosata and later by some of the Anabaptists, especially in Poland.

Robinson raises the question whether we are reading John as he intended. Are we not perhaps approaching John with spectacles tinged with the later patristic developments in Christology? Using Dunn's own caveat, Robinson urges us to understand John's words as his original readers would have understood them. Robinson reminds Dunn that the latter admits that for Paul Jesus was the expression of God's wisdom, "the man wisdom became."[50] Dunn had conceded that even John 1:14 provides no solid basis for the traditional doctrine of Incarnation. In fact, it marks "the transition from impersonal personification to actual person."[51] With this Robinson agrees. Further, Dunn and Robinson share the view that John's "word" is the utterance of God personified, not a divine person, distinct

---

[48] 85 (Mar. and Sep. 1982). For a most useful summary of the modern discussion, see Klaas Runia, *The Present-Day Christological Debate*.

[49] "Dunn on John," *Theology* 85 (Sept 1982): 332-338.

[50] *Christology in the Making*, 212.

[51] Ibid., 243.

from God. Only when Jesus is conceived does the "word" become personalized as distinct from personified.

Robinson was unable to agree with Dunn, however, that "the Word's preexistence as a person with God is asserted throughout [the Gospel]."[52] Robinson urges us to confine our understanding of the preexisting word, even in John, to "God's utterance," His "power and purpose." The point is simply this: We should see the shift from the understanding of John's "word" as God's self-expression to the notion that it means a preexistent divine person, *outside the range of the New Testament*. John should not be held responsible for the shift. The shift happened *to* John when he was misinterpreted by an early Gnostic tendency, which left its mark on patristic theology. It does not happen *in* John. Robinson believes that the "word," which was *theos* ("God," John 1:1), was fully expressive of God's plan, purpose and character. That "word" became fully embodied in a human person when it became flesh (John 1:14). Jesus is therefore what the word *became*. He is not to be identified one-to-one with the preexisting word, as though he himself preexisted. The difference is a subtle one but has devastating implications for the whole development of Christology. Thus it was not that the word was a person, a hypostasis, who then assumed human nature as well as his own, but that the word was "anhypostatic," impersonal, though fully expressive of God, until it became an individual historical person in Jesus. Jesus, therefore, is a fully human person "exegeting" the One God for humanity (John 1:18).

This reading of John has the enormous advantage of avoiding the dangers of a docetic presentation of Christ, as well as a polarization between John and the Synoptics, who know nothing of a preexistent Christ. It further allows the term "word" to bear its Old Testament, Jewish meaning of "purpose" or "plan," or even "promise." Jesus can then be seen as the fulfillment of the ancient promise to Abraham which is so important for Matthew and Luke. Jesus is God's creative

---

[52] Ibid., 250.

salvation plan expressed in a human person. The "divinity" of Jesus is not diminished since "he who has seen him has seen the Father" (John 14:9). But it is "divinity" in a sense other than that expressed by Trinitarian orthodoxy. For the divinity is God's activity working in and through a perfectly surrendered human person. Jesus, on this reading, is not God in the Trinitarian sense, but a human person fully expressing God, His agent for the reconciliation of the world. The wonderful thing that God has done will then be seen in terms of the glorification of a perfectly obedient human person who was genuinely tempted as we are. This portrait will harmonize with the Synoptic view of Jesus. Above all, it avoids a presentation of Jesus as a rather less than fully human being who from eternity was himself God. The truth will then emerge that Jesus was "*in the form of* God" (Phil. 2:6), not that he *was* God. "God was *in* Christ" (2 Cor. 5:19), but Christ was not God.

With his intense examination of Scripture Robinson points the way back to the biblical picture of Jesus as the perfect mirror image of his Father, the Christ whose perfect obedience and sacrifice qualify him to be truly "Son of God." It is to be regretted that Robinson did not confirm belief in the supernatural conception of Jesus which for Matthew and Luke constitutes the miracle by which the One God brought into being the head of the new creation, the sinless Messiah, Son of God.

Frances Young

It is easy to sympathize with those biblically-minded scholars who responded to the *Myth of God Incarnate*.[53] It seemed as though the very pillars of Christianity were being shaken. Some of the proponents of the new view of Jesus apparently believed very little of the Bible. John Stott, representing evangelicalism, repeats the orthodox reasons for believing in the full Deity of Jesus. He insists that Jesus was a real man, but does not tell us how exactly that can be in view of Leo's Tome (approved by the second Anglican Article, 1563)

---

[53] Ed. John Hick (London: SCM Press, 1977).

that the eternal Son "took man's nature." Many have felt that a being who is "man" without being "a man" is far less human than "the man Messiah Jesus" of Paul's creed (1 Tim. 2:5). Stott grants that Jesus did not go about declaring unambiguously that he was God. Nevertheless the "transfer of God-titles and God-texts from Yahweh to Jesus has an unavoidable implication. It identifies Jesus as God."[54] Furthermore Jesus is worshipped which proves he is God.

Frances Young was among the contributors to the *Myth of God Incarnate*. It is appropriate to include in this chapter a summary of her remarkable essay, "A Cloud of Witnesses," because it represents the feeling of many who have fought for the biblical Jesus without subscribing to orthodox Christology. Professor Young exposes the weaknesses of traditional views of Jesus. She complains that the richness of the New Testament's Christological insights has been obscured by the confession of him as incarnate Son of God. There is a refreshingly new way of reading the New Testament witness to Christ: "If we avoid reading the New Testament with spectacles colored by later dogma, we find emerging a Christological picture — or rather pictures — quite different from later orthodoxy."[55] "[Jesus] was the embodiment of all God's promises brought to fruition. Such a Christology, I suggest, represents New Testament Christology better than the idea of incarnation, and it was in fact the germ of more and more Christological ideas as the whole of the Old Testament was seen as fulfilled in Christ."[56]

Frances Young restores the biblical picture of Jesus functioning for God without being God: "Paul neither calls [Jesus] God, nor identifies him anywhere with God. It is true he does God's work; he is certainly God's supernatural agent, who acts because of God's initiative."[57]

---

54 *The Authentic Jesus* (Marshall, Morgan and Scott, 1985), 33.

55 *The Myth of God Incarnate*, 14.

56 Ibid., 19.

57 Ibid., 21.

The author's clear view of the Bible's distinction between God and Jesus enables her to see through the errors of the Fathers. She is not persuaded that in the development of Christology "the questions were asked in the right way, or the right solutions were found."[58] The orthodoxy which finally emerged was supported by "inadequate argument and distorting exegesis."[59] Understanding Jesus as God incarnate was dictated by the prevailing philosophical environment. Indeed there are striking similarities between neo-Platonism's triadic cosmology and the Trinity.

Most helpful is Frances Young's criticism of the entrenched idea that only God Himself can secure salvation for us and that therefore Jesus must be God. The problem with the orthodox view is that the immutable God is incapable of suffering, temptation, or death. Athanasius' treatment of Jesus' temptation falls into docetism and leads to his apparently nonsensical conclusion that Jesus "suffered without suffering": "the suggestion that while the 'body' or the 'man Jesus' suffered on the cross, the Logos somehow suffered in sympathy because it was 'his body' or 'his man,' even though by his very nature he could not possibly suffer."[60]

This essay provides a compelling refutation of the comfortable view that the Fathers faithfully transmitted the New Testament portrait of Christ. Rather, their philosophizing led to the "blind alleys of paradox, illogicality and docetism."[61]

George Carey
George Carey, who subsequently became Archbishop of Canterbury, rose to the defense of the traditional doctrine of the Incarnation in *God Incarnate: Meeting the Contemporary Challenges to a Classic Christian Doctrine*. The strength of his

---

[58] Ibid., 23.

[59] Ibid.

[60] Ibid., 27.

[61] Ibid., 29.

essay lies in his justifiable protest against the tendency amongst some of the *Myth of God Incarnate* writers to redefine Jesus in the interests of making him more acceptable to modern scientific man. Carey is rightly disturbed by the denial of Christ's virginal conception, his sinlessness, and his resurrection as an objective fact of history. The *Myth* contributors thus undermined the force of their own biblical objections to the orthodox Incarnation. Their unfortunate ambivalence about the supernatural, especially the resurrection, inevitably detracted from their well-argued objections to Trinitarianism. "Liberals" thus often wave a red flag at conservatives. Nevertheless, a "liberal" may be more objective in his investigation of the Bible, since he is less intent than a conservative on defending a traditional system.

It is possible to believe firmly in what Carey calls Jesus' "special, unique bond with God,"[62] without subscribing to the belief that he was God. Even Carey hesitates to call him God outright. He prefers a less direct description of him as "in some form God."[63] The way is thus opened for an understanding of Jesus between the extremes of some of the *Myth* exponents and full-blown Trinitarianism. If the new Christology would affirm the supernatural elements of the biblical picture of Jesus, and if Carey could reconsider the weaknesses of "sending" language as a proof of preexistence, a more scriptural Christology could emerge. Jesus must certainly be proclaimed, following apostolic precedent, as the exclusive way to salvation. But the potential of Christians to be "filled with all the fullness of God" (Eph. 3:19) should balance orthodoxy's stress on "the fullness of Deity" (Col. 1:19; 2:9) in Jesus as a proof of his being God.

Carey's defense is vulnerable at several points. Where is the biblical support for the creed's claim that he was "begotten before all ages," which Carey seems to affirm without the backing of New Testament evidence? And why is it clear that God's "sending His Son" means that the Son was alive before

---

[62] *God Incarnate: Meeting the Contemporary Challenges to a Classic Christian Doctrine* (InterVarsity Press, 1977), 7.

[63] Ibid., 18.

his conception? Peter has no thought of preexistence in mind when he says that God "having raised up Jesus, *sent* him" to preach to Israel (Acts 3:26). Jesus was commissioned to preach, not sent from a previous life. It appears that standard lexical authorities recognize the weakness of the argument from the word "send," while the pressures of maintaining the status quo in Christology may cause expositors to overlook them.

Karl-Josef Kuschel

In 1990 there appeared in Germany, from the camp of Roman Catholic scholarship at its most sophisticated, a full-length study of the issue of the preexistence and the Trinity: *Born Before All Time? The Dispute over Christ's Origin.* Karl-Josef Kuschel examined the competing Christologies of Harnack, Barth and Bultmann and then embarked on his own analysis of the New Testament data. He asks the right questions: "Is the Jesus of history taken seriously?" and "Did not the concrete meaning of 'flesh' become a mere abstraction in Barth and Bultmann?"[64] He wonders whether either theologian, whose influence has been massive, "really understood the New Testament rightly"[65] in their portrait of Jesus Christ. Shockingly, as another German theologian, Wolfgang Pannenberg, had said, "Barth does not primarily develop his doctrine of the Trinity on the basis of exegetical evidence," echoing the telling remark of Ernst Fuchs that "if there were no biblical texts, Barth's outline would be preferable."[66]

Professor Kuschel then examines the role of wisdom in the Hebrew Bible, finding it to be identical to God's creative word and to the Torah as the blueprint which guided God at creation. He argues that the man Jesus is the embodiment of this preexisting wisdom and not the eternal Son who predated his birth in Bethlehem. Kuschel maintains that in Philippians 2 there is no statement about Christ being equal to God. Rather Christ is

---

[64] *Born Before All Time? The Dispute over Christ's Origin,* 174.

[65] Ibid.

[66] Ibid., 179.

"the great contrasting figure to Adam."[67] Kuschel agrees with James Dunn that there is no preexistent Son in Paul. As for John's Gospel, "God is essentially never other than the Father of Jesus Christ."[68] He asks why the prologue of John does not begin (as so many instinctively read it), "In the beginning was the Son and the Son was with God and the Son was God."[69]

This monumental critique of orthodox Trinitarianism supports our conviction that "the history of the Christology of Jewish Christianity...needs urgent investigation...not only for the cause of historical justice but also for the cause of ecumenical understanding."[70] The dominating theology of the Council of Chalcedon "hardly touches on the earthly life and earthly history of Jesus."[71] Indeed the relationship between the Father and Son proposed by the council "would not have been understood by a Jewish Christian like Paul any more than it would have been by John."[72]

Professor Kuschel's brilliant study, with enthusiastic approval of Hans Küng who writes the foreword, alerts us to Trinitarianism's threat to monotheism as well as to its power to erect unnecessary barriers against dialogue with Jews and Muslims. *Born Before All Time?* echoes in our time the long-standing tradition of protest against "orthodox" views of Jesus which seem to suppress his humanity and thus obscure his Messiahship.

Karl-Heinz Ohlig

In 1999 a brilliant history of the Trinitarian problem was published, also in Germany. Karl-Heinz Ohlig's *Ein Gott in drei Personen? Vom Vater Jesu zum "Mysterium" der Trinität (One*

---

[67] Ibid., 251.

[68] Ibid., 276.

[69] Ibid., 381.

[70] Ibid., 394, 395.

[71] Ibid., 425.

[72] Ibid., 409.

God in Three Persons? From the Father of Jesus to the "Mystery" of the Trinity) exposes the tenuous connection of the Bible with Trinitarianism. The author makes the excellent point that Trinitarian dogma has long kept Jews and Muslims at arm's length from Christianity. Ohlig breaks a long-standing taboo. He does not resort to vague talk of "mystery" as an explanation for the Trinity. He gives us a wonderfully succinct and information-packed account of the development of Trinitarianism. He attributes this development to cultural pressures upon the Church, beginning in the early second century. He laments the loss of original Jewish monotheism and makes the excellent point that since Jesus was not a Trinitarian, why should his followers be? Furthermore, since Trinitarianism did not emerge in its final form until the fifth century, and was certainly not present in the second century as a dogma about three eternal Persons, which stage in its evolution should be binding on Christians? Ohlig maintains that it is illegitimate historically and theologically to make the doctrine of the Trinity normative for believers:

> Theologically considered, the Trinity grew out of a syncretism of Judaism and Christianity with Hellenism and a resulting combination of Jewish and Christian monotheism with Hellenistic monism [belief in one God]...What the theologian thus discovers poses a question to theology about the legitimacy of such a construct. When it is clear — and there is no way around this — that Jesus himself knew only the God of Israel, whom he called Father, and knew nothing about his own later "being made God," what right have we to call the doctrine of the Trinity normative and binding on Christians?...However we interpret the various stages of the development of the Trinity, it is clear that this doctrine, which became "dogma" in the East and West, has no biblical basis and cannot be traced continuously

back to the New Testament...Gradually, theology must face the facts. [73]

Ohlig's observations strongly confirm the findings of an earlier celebrated professor of the history of doctrine, who wrote:

> The Apologists laid the foundation for the perversion/corruption (*Verkehrung*) of Christianity into a revealed [philosophical] teaching. Specifically, their Christology affected the later development disastrously. By taking for granted the transfer of the concept of Son of God onto the preexisting Christ, they were the cause of the Christological problem of the fourth century. They caused a shift in the point of departure of Christological thinking — away from the historical Christ and onto the issue of preexistence. They thus shifted attention away from the historical life of Jesus, putting it into the shadow and promoting instead the Incarnation. They tied Christology to cosmology and could not tie it to soteriology. The Logos teaching is not a "higher" Christology than the customary one. It lags in fact far behind the genuine appreciation of Christ. According to their teaching it is no longer God who reveals Himself in Christ, but the Logos, the inferior God, a God who as God is subordinated to the Highest God (inferiorism or subordinationism).

---

[73] *Ein Gott in drei Personen?* Mainz: Matthias Grünewald-Verlag, 1999, 123-125, translation ours.

In addition the suppression of economic-trinitarian ideas by metaphysical-pluralistic concepts of the divine triad (*trias*) can be traced to the Apologists.[74]

---

[74] Friedrich Loofs, *Leitfaden zum Studium der Dogmengeschichte* (*Manual for the Study of the History of Dogma,* 1890), Halle-Saale: Max Niemeyer Verlag, 1951, part 1, sec. 18: "Christianity as a Revealed Philosophy. The Greek Apologists," 97, translation ours.

XI. THE CHALLENGE FACING TRINITARIANISM TODAY

"The developed concept of three coequal partners in the Godhead found in later creedal formulations cannot be clearly detected within the confines of the canon."
— Oxford Companion to the Bible

Contemporary Trinitarianism faces a formidable battery of arguments which have undermined some of its cherished biblical "proofs." Unknown to most churchgoers there is a corpus of non-Trinitarian (in fact, if not in name) rather than anti-Trinitarian literature which in various ways abandons some of the main props of Trinitarianism. Anti-Trinitarianism has long presented its case by showing that various orthodox Trinitarians have explained key Trinitarian verses in a unitarian way. A remarkable compendium of *Concessions of Trinitarians* was produced by John Wilson in 1845.[1] The work has relevance for the ongoing discussion of the Trinity. Surveying a vast amount of scholarly writing, it documents non-Trinitarian explanations by Trinitarians of verses popularly thought to support the Trinity. Contemporary as well as nineteenth-century theological literature provides evidence of similar concessions. This chapter examines some of the points presented as Trinitarian "proofs" in more popular literature on the Bible. It appears that a large number of Trinitarians no longer rely on these arguments to support an orthodox view of the Godhead.

---

[1] Boston: Munroe & Co.

The Plural Form of *Elohim*

The organization Jews for Jesus and other evangelical groups continue to find the Triune God in the Hebrew Scriptures. The plural form of the Hebrew word for God, *elohim*, however, does not provide clues pointing to the Trinity. It is as misleading to talk of *elohim* as a "uniplural" word as it is to say that *echad*, "one," hints at a plural Godhead. One cannot successfully argue the Trinity from the fact that *echad* can modify a noun like "cluster" or "herd" and therefore might lead us to think that God is compound. *Echad* is simply the numeral "one" in Hebrew. "Yahweh is one Lord," so the creed of Israel states (Deut. 6:4). *Echad* appears as a modifier for "Abraham" (Ezek. 33:24; Isa. 51:2), and it may sometimes be properly rendered as "unique" (Ezek. 7:5). Its normal meaning is "one and not two" (Ecc. 4:8). There is nothing at all in the word "Yahweh" which suggests a plurality, especially since the word occurs with singular verbs and pronouns in all of its multiple thousands (about 5,500) of occurrences. If singular pronouns, constantly designating the One God, cannot persuade the reader that God is a single individual there is little else in language that can. *Elohim* has singular verbs in nearly all of its 2500 references to the One God. An occasional anomaly proves as little as the fact that Joseph's master is described by a plural noun several times (Gen. 39:2, 3, 7, 8, 19, 20). Will anyone contend that "Joseph's master [plural in Hebrew] took [singular verb] him" is incorrectly translated? Abraham is the "masters" (plural in Hebrew) of his servant (Gen. 24:9, 10). Is there plurality in Abraham? No one would want to alter the translation of another passage in Genesis: "The man who is lord of the land spoke harshly to us." But though the verb is singular the noun has a plural form, "the lords of the land" (Gen. 42:30).[2] We have in these examples the same plurality in Abraham, Potiphar and Joseph as is supposedly found in *elohim* when it refers to the Supreme God. These facts warrant the observation of the writer in the *Encyclopedia of Religion and Ethics*: "It is exegesis of a mischievous if pious sort

---

2 See also Gen. 42:33: "The man who is 'lords' of the land."

that would find the doctrine of the Trinity in the plural form *elohim*."[3]

The article on God in the same work concludes: "There is in the Old Testament no indication of distinctions in the Godhead; it is an anachronism to find either the doctrine of the Incarnation or that of the Trinity in its pages."[4]

The definition of *elohim* ("God") supplied by the *Illustrated Bible Dictionary* contradicts the notion that God is "three Persons": "Though a plural form, *elohim* can be treated as a singular, in which case it means the one supreme Deity...There is only one supreme God and He is *a Person*."[5]

God Is One

A consideration of the use of the numeral "one" in connection with God is enlightening. No one has any difficulty with the following statements. According to Ezekiel, "Abraham was one [Heb. *echad*, Gk. *heis*]" (Ezek. 33:24). The NIV translates this fact into plain English: "Abraham was only one man." Jesus used the word "one" in the same way to mean a single individual: "Do not be called Rabbi; for one [*heis*] is your Teacher, and you are all brothers. And do not call anyone on earth your father; for one [*heis*] is your Father, who is in heaven. And do not be called leaders; for one [*heis*] is your Leader, that is, Christ" (Matt. 23:8-10). In each case "one" means one person. For Paul Christ is "one person" *(heis)*: "[God] does not say, 'and to seeds,' as of many, but rather to *one*, 'and to your seed,' that is Christ" (Gal. 3:16). A few verses later exactly the same language applies to God. Paul says: "Now a mediator is not for one party only [literally 'not of one,' *heis*]. But God is one [*heis*]" (Gal. 3:20). The meaning is that God is "one party" or "one person." All this is consistent with the uniform testimony of Scripture that the One God is the Father of Jesus. It is true that *heis* can

---

[3] W. Fulton, "Trinity," in *Encyclopedia of Religion and Ethics*, 12:458.

[4] W.T. Davison, "God (Biblical and Christian)," in *Encyclopedia of Religion and Ethics,* 6:252-269.

[5] (InterVarsity Press, 1980), 571, emphasis added.

designate a collective unity: "you are all one in Christ" (Gal. 3:28). This meaning is quite inappropriate in the case of God who is constantly described by singular pronouns and equated with the Father, who is obviously one person.

These facts present an acute problem for Trinitarianism. Some have been driven to the extreme of maintaining that the word "Father" in the New Testament may describe not one person of the Trinity but all three, "Father, Son and Holy Spirit":

> Sometimes "Father" is used not of One who is distinct from the Son and the Holy Spirit — a distinct Person of the Godhead — but of the Godhead Himself. Let us give some examples of this...[Paul says that] there is only one God who has real existence, and it is the One that Christians worship. So he writes, "But to us there is but one God, the Father" (1 Cor. 8:6). Here the word "Father" equals the words "one God." Paul is saying that there is but one God, and is not thinking of the Persons of the Godhead at all. It is in this sense that he uses the word "Father," just as he does in Ephesians 4:6, where he writes of "one God and Father of all."[6]

The writer struggles with Paul's plainly unitarian definition of God as "One God, the Father." The strength of Olyott's own conviction that God is really three forces him to imagine that "the Father" actually means three persons. The theory is imaginary. The writer cannot allow himself to think that Paul might not have been a Trinitarian.

Is Jesus "Mad, Bad or God"?

Trinitarians are trapped by the well-worn slogan that Jesus must be either a liar, a lunatic or the Supreme God. They have not been able to conceptualize another category — that of the Messiah. When Anderson Scott described the view of Jesus presented by the book of Revelation, he gave us the clue to the biblical picture of Jesus: "[John] carries the equating of Christ

---

[6] Stuart Olyott, *The Three Are One* (Evangelical Press, 1979), 28, 29.

with God to the furthest point *short of making Them eternally equal.*"[7]

Assessing Paul's Christology he says: "St. Paul never gives to Christ the name or description of God...Reviewing the whole of Paul's utterances regarding Christ, the total impression is that of a monotheistic conviction consistently resisting the impulse to do this very thing — to call Jesus God."[8]

The correctness of this evaluation is confirmed by the startling fact that there is no text in the New Testament in which the term *ho theos* ("God") means "Father, Son and Holy Spirit." The reason appears to be that no writer thought that God was "three-in-one." It ought to be a matter of concern to Trinitarians that when they say "God," they mean the Triune God, but when the New Testament (or indeed the whole Bible) says "God," a Triune God is never meant. It would be hard to find more conclusive evidence that the Triune God is not the God of Scripture. Our point is confirmed by Karl Rahner: "Nowhere in the New Testament is there to be found a text with *ho theos* [literally, 'the God'] which has unquestionably to be referred to the Trinitarian God as a whole existing in three Persons. In by far the greater number of texts *ho theos* refers to the Father as a Person of the Trinity."[9]

We disagree that the Father is part of a Trinity, but Rahner's observation is correct: God in the New Testament almost invariably means the Father of Jesus and never three persons or "Persons."

Incarnation in the Synoptic Gospels

An important question about Trinitarianism is raised by the complete lack of evidence for the doctrine of the Incarnation in the Gospel of Luke (the same may be said of Matthew). Raymond Brown observes: "There is no evidence that Luke had

---

[7] "Christology," *Dictionary of the Apostolic Church*, 1:185, emphasis added.

[8] Ibid., 194.

[9] *Theological Investigations*, 143.

a theology of Incarnation and preexistence: rather for Luke (1:35) divine Sonship seems to have been brought about through the virginal conception...Jesus was conceived and born, and that is solidarity enough with the human race."[10]

Luke defined who Jesus was with complete precision when he first called him "the Lord Messiah," i.e., "the Lord Christ," and a few verses later designated him "the *Lord's* Christ [Messiah]" (Luke 2:11, 26). The title "Lord Messiah" is found also in Jewish literature contemporary with Luke (Ps. Sol. 17:32; 18:7). It describes the promised deliverer of Israel, the age-old hope of the nation. The same Messianic description is given to a historical sovereign of Israel in the Septuagint rendering of Lamentations 4:10. In no case does this royal title imply that the Messiah is God. It is derived from Psalm 110:1 where the Messiah is to be David's "lord," i.e., his king.

Luke selects a second title for Jesus, "the Lord's Messiah," because it is exactly equivalent to the Old Testament expression "the Lord's Anointed," the king of Israel. David speaks of King Saul as "my lord, the Lord's anointed [Messiah]" (1 Sam. 24:6; cp. v. 10). Abner should have guarded Saul, "the lord, your king," "your lord, the Lord's anointed [Messiah]" (1 Sam. 26:15, 16). Jesus is the ultimate Anointed One, the promised king of Israel. Luke's descriptions of him are in complete harmony with John who introduces Jesus as "Son of God" and "king of Israel" (John 1:49). Paul recognizes that Christians serve "the Lord Messiah" (Col. 3:24), and Peter, who had declared in an early sermon that God had appointed Jesus "Lord and Messiah" (Acts 2:36), towards the end of his life urges believers to sanctify "the Lord Christ in your hearts" (1 Pet. 3:15). In the last book of the Bible the glorified Jesus is still "the Lord's Anointed [Messiah]" (Rev. 11:15; 12:10). The much overlooked title of Jesus as "the Lord Messiah" is constantly brought before us in the New Testament's favorite name for him, "the Lord Jesus Messiah."

Trinitarianism confuses the Lord God with the anointed or *appointed* lord, the king. The category of Messiah is entirely

---

10 *The Birth of the Messiah,* 432.

adequate to account for the New Testament understanding of Jesus. The Bible does not need the "help" of further developments in Christology which go beyond the confession that Jesus is the Christ, the Son of God. As Christ, Jesus is the perfect image of the One God. The character and work of Jesus demonstrate the character and work of his Father, as an agent represents his sender.

Eternal Sonship

It is an uphill battle for Trinitarians to support the notion of "eternal Sonship" from Scripture. A contemporary Trinitarian informs us that Jesus proceeded "by eternal generation as the Son of God from the Father *in a birth that never took place because it always was.*"[11] We wonder whether such mystifying language helps to promote the truth of the Christian faith. In Scripture the begetting of the Son *did* take place and it took place in time. The classic prediction of the Messiah's appointment to kingship appears in Psalm 2:7. The One God declares: "You are My Son; today I have begotten you." Luke knew that the Son of God was miraculously begotten in the womb of Mary (Luke 1:35). In a sermon at Pisidian Antioch Paul preached about the birth of the Messiah, showing that God had "raised up Jesus," i.e., brought him on the scene fulfilling the "begettal" prediction of Psalm 2.[12] Luke had already used the same expression — "raise up" — of the birth of the promised prophet.[13] There is no such thing in Scripture as a begetting or generation of the Son in eternity, other than in the decrees of God.

---

[11] Kenneth Wuest, *Great Truths to Live By* (Grand Rapids: Eerdmans, 1952), 30, emphasis added.

[12] See Acts 13:33, quoting Ps. 2:7. "Raising up" here refers more naturally to the birth of Jesus, not his resurrection. Paul goes on to refer to the raising of Jesus *from the dead* in the next verse. The KJV seems to have confused the issue by inserting the word "again" after "raised up" in v. 33.

[13] Acts 2:30 (Rec. Text); Acts 3:22; 3:26; 7:37.

A distinguished Trinitarian of the last century expressed his bewilderment at the idea of a sonship which has no beginning and thus of the whole doctrine of an "eternal Son." Speaking of Luke 1:35 Adam Clarke noted:

> We may plainly perceive here that the angel does *not* give the appellation of *Son of God* to the *divine nature* of Christ, but to the *holy person or thing, to hagion,* which was to be born of the Virgin, by the energy of the holy spirit...Here I trust that I may be permitted to say, with all due respect to those who differ from me, that the doctrine of the *eternal Sonship* of Christ is, in my opinion, anti-scriptural and highly dangerous. This doctrine I reject for the following reasons. 1. I have not been able to find any express declaration in the Scriptures concerning it. 2. If Christ is the Son of God as to his divine nature, then he cannot be eternal: for son implies father, and father implies the idea of generation, and generation implies a time in which it was effected and time also antecedent to such generation. 3. If Christ is the Son of God as to his divine nature, then the Father is of necessity prior, consequently superior to him. 4. Again, if this divine nature were begotten of the Father, then it must be in time, i.e., there was a period in which it did not exist and a period when it began to exist. This destroys the eternity of our blessed Lord and robs him at once of his Godhead. 5. To say that he was begotten from all eternity is in my opinion absurd, and the phrase eternal son is a positive self-contradiction. Eternity is that which has no beginning, nor stands in any reference to time. Son supposes time, generation and Father: and time also antecedent to such generation. Therefore the conjunction of these two terms Son and eternity is absolutely impossible, as they imply essentially different and opposite ideas.[14]

---

[14] *Clarke's Commentary* (New York: T. Mason and G. Lane, 1837) on Luke 1:35.

An eminent biblical scholar, known as "the father of American biblical literature," Moses Stuart, had the following to say on this subject. He spoke as a Trinitarian. "The generation of the Son *as divine, as God,* seems to be out of the question — unless it be an express doctrine of revelation, which is so far from being the case, that I conceive that the *contrary is plainly taught.*"[15]

But can the doctrine of the Trinity stand if there is no scriptural support for "eternal generation"?

DISPUTED TEXTS

Discussion of the Trinity often centers around a handful of New Testament verses which are meant to prove that Jesus is the Supreme Deity rather than the perfect reflection of Deity, the authorized human ambassador of the One God. Some modern proponents of Trinitarianism produce these verses as though it were self-evident that their testimony favors Trinitarianism. There is a strong tradition among Trinitarians of the highest repute, however, that these texts do not establish the Deity of Jesus.

Does the New Testament Call Jesus God?
Titus 2:13; 2 Peter 1:1

A number of contemporary discussions advance the so-called "Granville Sharp's rule" to support their claim that Jesus is called "the great God and Savior" in Titus 2:13. Sharp contended that when the Greek word *kai* (and) joins two nouns of the same case, and the first noun has the definite article and the second does not, the two nouns refer to one subject. Hence the disputed verse should read "...our great God and Savior Jesus Christ," and not as the King James Version has it, "...the great God and our Savior Jesus Christ." The rule about the omission of the article, however, cannot be relied on to settle the matter. As Nigel Turner (who writes as a Trinitarian) says:

---

[15] Moses Stuart, *Answer to Channing*, cited by Wilson, *Concessions*, 315 (emphasis is Stuart's).

Unfortunately, at this period of Greek we cannot be sure that such a rule is really decisive. Sometimes the definite article is not repeated even where there is clearly a separation in idea. "The repetition of the article was not strictly necessary to ensure that the items be considered separately" (Moulton-Howard-Turner, *Grammar*, Vol. III, p. 181. The reference is to Titus 2:13).[16]

Since the absence of a second article is not decisive, it is natural to see here the appearing of God's glory as it is displayed in His Son at the Second Coming. There is an obvious parallel with Matthew's description of the arrival of Jesus in power: "For the Son of Man is going to come in the glory of his Father with his holy angels" (Matt. 16:27). Since the Father confers His glory upon the Son (as He will also share it with the saints), it is most appropriate that Father and Son should be closely linked. Paul had only a few verses earlier spoken of "God the Father and Christ Jesus our Savior" (Titus 1:4).

A wide range of grammarians and biblical scholars have recognized that the absence of the definite article before "our Savior Jesus Christ" is quite inadequate to establish the Trinitarian claim that Jesus is here called "the great God." At best, the argument is "dubious."[17] It is unfortunate, as Brown says, "that no certainty can be reached here, for it seems that this passage is the one which shaped the confession of the World Council of Churches in 'Jesus Christ as God and Savior.'"[18] It should also be noted that the Roman emperor could be called

---

[16] *Grammatical Insights into the New Testament* (Edinburgh: T & T Clark, 1965), 16. An unfortunate misprint occurs in Nigel Turner's statement. The word "not" is omitted before "repeated," reversing Turner's intention to point out that the article does not have to be repeated to separate two distinct subjects. We had ample opportunity to discuss this matter with the late Dr. Turner.

[17] See Raymond Brown, *Jesus, God and Man,* 15-18.

[18] Ibid., 18. Cp. Nels Ferré's objection that this title implies a docetic Jesus ("Is the Basis of the World Council Heretical?" *Expository Times* 73:12 (Dec., 1962): 67).

"God and Savior," without the implication that he was the Supreme Deity. Even if the title "God and Savior" were most exceptionally used of Jesus, it would not establish his position as coequal and coeternal with the Father. It would rather designate him as the One God's supreme agent, which is the view of the whole Bible.

The same grammatical problem faces expositors in 2 Peter 1:1. Henry Alford is one of many Trinitarians who argue that Jesus is not called "God" in this verse. For him the absence of the article is outweighed here, as in Titus 2:13, by the much more significant fact that both Peter and Paul normally distinguish clearly between God and Jesus Christ. The writer of the *Cambridge Bible for Schools and Colleges* agreed that "the rule that the one article indicates the one subject... [cannot] be too strongly relied upon as decisive."[19] A Trinitarian writer of the last century was much less generous to those who sought proof of the Deity of Christ in the omission of the article: "Some eminently pious and learned scholars...have so far overstretched the argument founded on the presence or absence of the article, as to have run it into a fallacious sophistry, and, in the intensity of their zeal to maintain the 'honor of the Son,' were not aware that they were rather engaged in 'dishonoring the Father.'"[20]

The last statement may in fact be true of the whole effort of orthodoxy to make Jesus equal in every sense to the Father.

Romans 9:5

Some Trinitarians offer Romans 9:5 as conclusive proof that Jesus is "God over all" and therefore part of the Godhead. It depends which translation one reads, because there are some seven different ways of punctuating the verse in which either

---

[19] A.E. Humphreys, *The Epistles to Timothy & Titus* (Cambridge University Press, 1895), 225.

[20] Granville Penn, *Supplemental Annotations to the New Covenant*, 146, cited in Wilson, *Unitarian Principles Confirmed by Trinitarian Testimonies*, 431.

Christ or the Father is called "God blessed forever."[21] The issue
is: Should we read "of whom, according to the flesh, is Christ,
who is over all. God be blessed forever," or "of whom, according
to the flesh is Christ, who being God over all, is blessed
forever"? Among older commentators Erasmus, though a
Trinitarian, was cautious about using this verse as a proof text:

> Those who contend that in this text Christ is clearly
> termed *God*, either place little confidence in other
> passages of Scripture, deny all understanding to the
> Arians, or pay scarcely any attention to the style of the
> Apostle. A similar passage occurs in Second Corinthians
> 11:31: "The God and Father of our Lord Jesus Christ,
> who is blessed forever"; the latter clause being
> undeniably restricted to the Father.[22]

Using the principle of comparison of text with text, it is most
likely that Paul describes the Father as "God over all." Paul
uniformly makes a distinction between God and the Lord Jesus.
In the same book Paul blesses the Creator and there is no reason
to doubt that the Father is meant (Rom. 1:25). In another passage
he speaks of "God our Father, to whom be the glory
forevermore. Amen" (Gal. 1:4, 5). Romans 9:5 is an obvious
parallel. It should not be forgotten that the word *theos*, God,
occurs more than 500 times in Paul's letters and there is not a
single unambiguous instance in which it applies to Christ. A
number of well-known textual critics (Lachmann, Tischendorf)
place a period after the word "flesh," allowing the rest of the
sentence to be a doxology of the Father. Ancient Greek
manuscripts do not generally contain punctuation, but the *Codex
Ephraemi* of the fifth century has a period after "flesh." More
remarkable is the fact that during the whole Arian controversy,
this verse was not used by Trinitarians against the unitarians. It
clearly did not attest to Jesus as the second member of the
Godhead.

---

[21] For a full examination of the various possibilities, see the essays in
the *Journal of the Society of Biblical Literature and Exegesis,* 1883.

[22] *Works,* ed. Jean Leclerc, 10 vols. (Leiden, 1703-1706), 6:610, 611.

In modern times Raymond Brown finds that "at most one may claim a certain probability that this passage refers to Jesus as God."[23] In the conservative *Tyndale Commentary* on Romans, F.F. Bruce warns against charging those who treat the words as applicable to the Father with "Christological unorthodoxy."[24] It is proper to add that even if Jesus is exceptionally called "God," the title may be used in its secondary, Messianic sense of one who reflects the divine majesty of the One God, his Father.

When the detail of grammatical nuance has been fully explored, balances of probability will be weighed in different ways. It is incredible to imagine that the Christian creed should depend on fine points of language about which many could not reasonably be asked to make a judgment and experts disagree. The plain language of Paul's and Jesus' creed is open to every student of the Bible: "There is no God except one...There is for us [Christians] one God, the Father" (1 Cor. 8:4, 6).

That "one God" is as distinguished in Paul's mind from the "one Lord Jesus Messiah" as He is from the many gods of paganism. The category of "one God" belongs exclusively to the Father, that of "Lord *Messiah*" exclusively to Jesus. Jesus himself had provided the basis of Paul's simple understanding of the phrase "one God." Both master and disciple shared the creed of Israel who believed in God as one, unique person.

The Technicalities of John 1:1

John 1:1 has been subjected to a minute analysis by commentators of every shade of opinion. It is obvious that some modern translations are blatantly Trinitarian *interpretations*. *The Living Gospels*[25] reads: "Before anything else existed there was Christ, with God. He has always been alive and is Himself God." But that is to raise the whole Trinitarian problem. Suddenly God is two persons. A little-known fact is that the "word" was not

---

[23] *Jesus, God and Man*, 22.

[24] *Romans, Tyndale New Testament Commentaries* (Grand Rapids: Eerdmans, 1985), 176.

[25] Tyndale House, 1966.

assumed to be a second *person* in translations prior to the King James Version. The Bishops' Bible of 1568, replaced by the King James Bible in 1611, understands the word to be impersonal, and uses the pronoun "it," as does the Geneva Bible of 1560.

It is an assumption that by "word" John meant a second uncreated personal being alongside the One God. John elsewhere recognizes that the Father is the "only true God" (John 17:3) and "the one who alone is God" (John 5:44). Many have recognized an obvious connection between the "word" and what is said of Wisdom in the Hebrew Bible. In Proverbs "Wisdom" is personified and is said to be "with" God (Prov. 8:30). John says that the "word" was "with [*pros*] God." In the Old Testament a vision, word or purpose is said to be "with" the person who receives it or possesses it. The word has a quasi-existence of its own: "The word of the Lord is with him"; "the prophet...has a dream with him." It was in the heart of David (literally, "with his heart") to build a temple. Wisdom is "with God."[26] The latter is a striking parallel to John's opening sentence. In the New Testament something impersonal can be "with" a person, as, for example, where Paul hopes that "the truth of the Gospel might remain with [*pros*] you," present to the mind (Gal. 2:5). At the opening of John's first epistle, which may provide just the commentary we need on John 1:1, he writes that "eternal life was with [*pros*] the Father" (1 John 1:2). On the basis of these parallels it is impossible to say with certainty that the "word" in John 1:1-2 must mean a second member of the Trinity, that is, the Son of God preexisting.

John goes on to say that "the word was God" (John 1:1). Intense discussion of the exact meaning of "God" (which has no definite article) has made the whole passage seem complex. According to some a rule established by Colwell demands that the absence of the article does not weaken John's intention to say that the word was fully God and identified with Him. Others

---

[26] 2 Kings 3:12; Jer. 23:28 (Heb.); 1 Kings 8:17; 2 Chron. 6:7; Job 12:13, 16; Job 10:13: "with you" is parallel to "concealed in your heart," i.e., "fixed in your decree." See also Job 23:10, 14.

have insisted that "God" without the article is John's way of telling us that the word had the *character* of God and was fully expressive of His mind. The Trinitarian Bishop Westcott's opinion is much respected and has the tentative approval of Professor Moule:

> Bishop Westcott's note [on John 1:1], although it may require the addition of some reference to idiom, does still, perhaps, represent [John's] intention: "[God] is necessarily without the article (*theos,* not *ho theos*) inasmuch as it describes the nature of the Word and does not identify His Person. It would be pure Sabellianism to say that 'the Word was *ho theos.*'"[27]

The bishop's point was that the "word" cannot be distinct from God (with God) and at the same time identified with Him. This would blur all distinctions in the Godhead. Rather, John describes the nature of the "word," and the absence of the article before God "places stress upon the qualitative aspect of the noun rather than its mere identity. An object of thought may be conceived of from two points of view: as to *identity* or *quality.* To convey the first point of view the Greek uses the article; for the second the anarthrous construction is used."[28]

After a close analysis Philip Harner suggests: "Perhaps the clause should be translated, 'the Word had the same nature as God.'"[29] He adds that "there is no basis for regarding the predicate *theos* as definite."[30] "Thus," says another scholar,

---

[27] C.F.D. Moule, *An Idiom Book of New Testament Greek* (Cambridge University Press, 1953), 116.

[28] Dana and Mantey, *A Manual Grammar of the Greek New Testament* (New York: Macmillan, 1955), sec. 149.

[29] "Qualitative Anarthrous Predicate Nouns: Mark 15:39 and John 1:1," *Journal of Biblical Literature* 92 (1973): 87.

[30] Ibid., 85.

"John 1:1b denotes, not the identity, but rather the character of the Logos."[31]

The difficulty facing translators is how to convey these subtle nuances in English. James Denny insisted that the New Testament does not say what our English translations suggest: "The Word was God." He meant that in Greek "God" (*theos*) without the article really means "having the quality of God," not being one-to-one identified with God.[32] One attempt to convey the right shade of meaning is found in the translation: "The word was god."[33] Unfortunately standard English translations convey the wrong sense. As Harner says, "The problem with all these translations [RSV, Jerusalem Bible, New English Bible, Good News for Modern Man] is that they could represent [the idea that word and God are interchangeable]."[34]

The prologue to John's Gospel does not require belief in a Godhead of more than one person. It is most likely that John is correcting a contemporary Gnostic tendency to distinguish God from lesser divine figures. John's intention is to bind the "Wisdom" or "word" of God as closely as possible to God Himself. The word is God's own creative activity. Thus John says that from the beginning God's wisdom, which the One God had with Him as an architect has his plan, was fully expressive of God. It was God Himself in His self-manifestation. All things were made through this plan. The same "word" was finally

---

[31] D.A. Fennema, "John 1:18: 'God the Only Son,'" *New Testament Studies* 31 (1985): 130.

[32] *Letters of Principal James Denny to W. Robertson Nicoll* (London: Hodder and Stoughton, 1920), 121-126.

[33] C.C. Torrey, *The Four Gospels — A New Translation* (New York: Harper, 1947, second edition).

[34] Harner, "Qualitative Anarthrous Predicate Nouns: Mark 15:39 and John 1:1," 87. The equivalence of "word" and "God" he lists as "clause A," *ho theos en ho logos*, and it is described on p. 84 of his article. The translation "the Word was God" misleads readers into thinking that John is promoting the Trinitarian idea that the word (and therefore Jesus) is equivalent to the Supreme God.

embodied in a human being, the Messiah, when Jesus was born, when the "word became flesh" (John 1:14). Jesus is therefore what the word became. He is the perfect expression of the mind of God in human form. Jesus is not to be identified one-to-one with the word of John 1:1, as though *the Son* existed from the beginning. Jesus is the divinely authorized messenger of God and, like the word, has the character of God.

James Dunn's conclusion about John's intention confirms a non-Trinitarian reading of John 1:1-3, 14:

> The conclusion which seems to emerge from our analysis [of John 1:1-14] thus far is that it is only with verse 14 ["the word became flesh"] that we can begin to speak of the personal Logos. The poem uses rather impersonal language (became flesh), but no Christian would fail to recognize here a reference to Jesus — the word became not flesh in general but Jesus Christ. *Prior to verse 14* we are in the same realm as pre-Christian talk of Wisdom and Logos, the same language and ideas that we find in Philo, where as we have seen, we are dealing with *personifications rather than persons*, personified actions of God rather than an individual divine being as such. The point is obscured by the fact that we have to translate the masculine Logos as "he" throughout the poem. But if we translated Logos as "God's utterance" instead, it would become clearer that the poem *did not necessarily intend the Logos of vv. 1-13 to be thought of as a personal divine being*. In other words, the revolutionary significance of v. 14 may well be that it marks *not only the transition in the thought of the poem from preexistence to incarnation, but also the transition from impersonal personification to actual person*.[35]

This reading of John has the enormous advantage of harmonizing him with the testimony of Matthew, Mark and Luke

---

[35] *Christology in the Making*, 243.

and allowing the undivided unity of the One God, the Father to remain undisturbed.

Mark 13:32

This verse reports Jesus' statement that he did not know the day of his return. It seems plainly contradictory to assert that omniscient Deity can be ignorant in any respect. Some Trinitarians appeal to the doctrine of the divine and human natures in Jesus to solve the problem. The Son did in fact know, but as a human being he did not. This seems little different from saying that one is poor because one has no money in one pocket, though in the other pocket one has a million dollars. In this text it is *the Son* as distinct from *the Father* who did not know. It is therefore quite impossible to plead that only the human nature in Jesus was ignorant. The Bible anyway does not distinguish "natures" in Jesus as Son of God and Son of Man. Both are Messianic titles for the one person. If a witness in a court of law were to be asked whether he had seen the defendant on a certain day and he replies in the negative, meaning that he had not seen him with his defective eye, though he did with his sound eye, we would consider him dishonest. When Jesus referred to himself as the Son, he could not have meant a part of himself. The theory by which Jesus did and did not know the day of his future coming would render all of his sayings unintelligible. The plain fact is that a confession of ignorance is incompatible with the theory of the absolute Deity of Jesus.

A comparable difficulty faces Trinitarians when they assert that only the human part of Jesus died. If Jesus were God, and God is immortal, Jesus could not have died. We wonder how it is possible to maintain that "Jesus" does not represent the whole person. Nothing in the Bible suggests that Jesus is the name of his human nature only. If Jesus is the whole person and Jesus died, he cannot be immortal Deity. It appears that Trinitarians argue that only Deity is sufficient to provide the necessary atonement. But if the divine nature did not die, how on the Trinitarian theory is the atonement secured?

It is hard to understand why God, if He so chooses, may not appoint a uniquely conceived, sinless human being as a sufficient offering for the sins of the world. It is unconvincing to insist that only the death of an eternal person can atone for sin. Scripture does not say so. It does, however, say that Jesus died and that God is immortal. The inference as to the nature of Jesus seems inescapable.

Matthew 1:23 (Isaiah 7:14)
It is sometimes asserted that the name Immanuel — "God is with us" — given to Jesus proves that he is God. If that were so, then the child born soon after the prediction was given by Isaiah in the days of Ahaz would also have been God. The name, however, does not tell us that Jesus is God, but that in his life God has intervened to save His people. The parents who in Old Testament times called their son Ithiel (Prov. 30:1) — "God is with me" — did not believe their offspring to be Deity. Names of this type indicate the divine event associated with the life of the individual so named. God, the Father of Jesus, was certainly with Israel as He worked through His unique Son. In the life of Jesus, the Son of God, God had visited His people. A Trinitarian scholar of the last century wrote: "To maintain that the name Immanuel proves the doctrine [of the Deity of Jesus] is a fallacious argument, although many Trinitarians have urged it. Jerusalem is called 'Jehovah our Righteousness.' Is Jerusalem also divine?"[36]

John 10:30
In this verse Jesus claimed to be "one" with his Father. The word "one" in this much discussed text is the Greek term *hen*. It is not the masculine numeral *heis* which describes the Godhead in the Christian creed announced by Jesus (Mark 12:29). It is unfair that the Jehovah's Witnesses are sometimes attacked in popular presentations of the Trinity for saying only what even conservative evangelical commentators admit: "The expression ['I and the Father are one'] seems...mainly to imply that the Father and Son are united in will and purpose. Jesus prays in

---

[36] Moses Stuart, *Answer to Channing*, cited in *Concessions*, 236.

John 17:11 that his followers may all be one (*hen*), i.e., united in purpose, as he and his Father are united."[37]

This is what unitarians (and numerous Trinitarians) have maintained for many centuries. The Trinitarian Erasmus saw the danger of pushing this verse beyond its natural meaning: "I do not see how this text is of any value in confirming the opinion of the orthodox, or in restraining the pertinacity of the heretic."[38]

The meaning of the statement is quite clear in its context. Jesus has been talking about the Father preserving the sheep. Since Jesus' power is derived from his Father, that power is able to keep the sheep safe. Jesus and the Father are one in respect of the preservation of the sheep. John Calvin was at this point wiser than some of his modern exponents. He remarked that "the ancients improperly used this passage to prove that Christ is of the same substance as the Father. For [Jesus] does not argue concerning unity of substance, but speaks of his agreement with the Father; so that whatever is done by Christ will be confirmed by the Father's power."[39]

Another Trinitarian authority observes that "if the doctrine of the Trinity, and the unity of essence, be immediately inferred, this is a faulty application of the dogmatic system, because the context of the passage is neglected."[40]

It is customary for Trinitarians to assume that the hostile Jewish impression of Jesus' words must be the correct one. Since they accused him of blasphemy and "making himself equal with God" (John 5:18), it is maintained that Jesus must have been making a Trinitarian claim. It is unfair to assume that the Jews had properly evaluated Jesus' words. If they had, there would have been no need for Jesus to justify himself further. He need only have repeated that he was in fact the Supreme God. In his

---

[37] R.V.G. Tasker, *John, Tyndale Commentaries* (Grand Rapids: Eerdmans, 1983), 136.

[38] Cited by Wilson, *Concessions*, 353.

[39] Cited by Wilson, *Concessions*, 354.

[40] C.F. Ammon, cited by Wilson, *Concessions*, 355.

much neglected response to the angry Jews (John 10:34-36) Jesus argues: "Since magistrates and judges are in Scripture expressly called 'gods,' it is unjust to charge me with blasphemy because I, whom the Father has appointed as the Messiah and therefore one greater than all kings, superior to all prophets, announce myself to be the Son of God, that is the Messiah, perfectly reflecting the will of my Father." Jesus links his own authority with that of the human "gods," whom God so designated (Ps. 82:1, 6). Granting that he was far superior to any previous "divine authority," a correct idea of his status is to be gained, so Jesus maintained, by considering that even Israelite leaders were entitled to be called "gods." Jesus is the highest human authority, fully and uniquely authorized by the Father.

Trinitarian conviction about unity of substance causes them to misread John's "sender/agent" description of Jesus. In seeing Jesus men were seeing God; in believing in him they were believing in God; in honoring him they were honoring God and in hating him they were hating God.[41] None of this requires a Trinitarian explanation. John gives us a beautiful picture of a miraculous human individual in whom God has invested His Spirit and to whom God has extended His authority and character — and all this in a way never seen before or since. Jesus is the unique ambassador for the One God. It is not that God has become man, but that God has provided in the promised descendant of David the man who is the *raison d'être* of His cosmic plan.

John 20:28

The well-known words of Thomas to Jesus, "My Lord and my God," are supposed to be decisive for the full Deity of Christ. Jesus, however, had already denied being God (see above on John 10:34-36). John distinguishes Jesus from the one and only God, his Father (John 17:3). Readers of the New Testament often do not realize that the word "God" can be applied to a representative of God. There is good evidence that John

---

[41] John 14:9; 12:44; 5:23; 15:23.

incorporates into his portrait of Jesus as Messiah, ideas drawn from the Messianic Psalm 45. In answer to Pilate, Jesus declared that he was a king whose task was to bear witness to the truth (John 18:37). There is an Old Testament background to this theme. Psalm 45 is written in praise of the Messiah (Heb. 1:8), who is addressed as "most mighty," and urged to "ride prosperously in the cause of Truth" (vv. 3, 4). The psalmist foresees that the king's enemies "will fall under you" (v. 5). The royal status of this leader is emphasized when the writer addresses him with the words "O God" (Ps. 45:6). The career of the Messiah outlined in Psalm 45 is reflected in John's observation that Jesus' enemies recoiled at his claim to be the Messiah and "fell to the ground" (John 18:6).[42] Thomas' recognition of Jesus as "God" is a beautiful fulfillment of the Psalm's highest address to the King of Israel. In that Psalm the Messiah is acclaimed as the Church's Lord and "God." But the "God" Messiah has been appointed by his God, the One and only Infinite God (Ps. 45:7).

Jesus himself was interested in the use of the word "God" for human rulers (John 10:34; Ps. 82:6). The Messiah is supremely entitled to be called "God" in this special sense, particularly because he embodies the "word" which is itself *theos* (John 1:1). It is possible that John adds one further statement about Jesus as "God." He declares him to be (if this is the correct manuscript reading — the point is disputed) "unique son, 'God' [*theos*]" (John 1:18). This is the ultimate Messianic description, expressing the fact that Jesus is the image of the One God. As Son of God, however, he is to be distinguished from the one who is underived, namely his Father. It remains a fact that John wrote his entire book to prove that Jesus was the Christ (John 20:31), and that the God of Jesus is also the God of the disciples (John 20:17). An unusual occurrence of *theos* in reference to Jesus should not overturn John's and Jesus' uniform insistence on the creed of Israel. It is an unwarranted advance (2 John 9 should be

---

[42] See Reim, "Jesus as God in the Fourth Gospel: The Old Testament Background," *New Testament Studies* 30 (1984):158-160.

noted) beyond the intention of John to make him the innovator of the equation "Christ" = "the Supreme God." It is sufficient to believe in Jesus as the Messiah, Son of God (John 20:31).

1 John 5:20

Some writers who promote the idea that the New Testament calls Jesus God in the same sense as his Father tell us that 1 John 5:20 definitely says that Jesus is the true God. The text reads: "And we know that the Son of God has come, and has given us an understanding so that we might know the true one; and we are in the true one, in His Son Jesus Christ. This is the true God and life eternal."

Many Trinitarians do not think that Jesus is here described as the true God. Henry Alford, the distinguished British expositor and author of the famous commentary on the *Greek Testament*, refers to a tendency which has played a major role historically in the interpretation of the Bible. He remarks that the Fathers interpreted 1 John 5:20 doctrinally rather than exegetically. In plain words they were influenced more by a desire to defend their already established theological position than a determination to give the actual meaning of the text.

Alford compares John's statement about the one God in 1 John 5:20 with the structure of similar sentences in the epistles of John. He also notes the obvious parallel in John 17:3, where Jesus is carefully distinguished from the one God. He concludes that expositors seeking the plain sense of this passage will not see the phrase "true God" as a reference to Jesus but to the Father. This (*houtos*) in the last sentence of 1 John 5:20 does not have to refer to the nearest noun (Jesus Christ in this case).

Henry Alford cites two passages from John's epistles to make his point: "Who is the liar but he who denies that Jesus is the Christ? This is the antichrist" (1 John 2:22). "For many deceivers went forth into the world, namely they who do not confess Jesus Christ coming in the flesh. This is the deceiver and the antichrist" (2 John 7). From these two passages it is clear that "this" does not necessarily refer back to the immediately preceding noun. If it did, it would make Jesus the deceiver and the antichrist. The pronoun "this" in 1 John 5:20 refers rather to the preceding phrase "Him who is true," describing the Father, not Jesus. If we compare John 17:3 we shall see 1 John 5:20 as an echo of that verse: "This is eternal life, that they should believe in You [the Father], the only true God, and in Jesus Christ whom You have sent."

In his book *The Trinity in the New Testament*, the Trinitarian Arthur Wainwright comes to the same conclusion.[43] He does not think that Jesus is called true God in 1 John 5:20. Henry Alford, who had the highest regard for the Scriptures, concludes: "I own I cannot see, after this saying of our Lord, 'You are the only true God' (John 17:3), how anyone can imagine that the same Apostle can have had in these words (John 17:3) any other reference than that which is given in those (1 John 5:20)."[44]

If we carefully weigh the evidence, it seems beyond question that John never departed from belief in the unipersonal God of his Old Testament heritage. This brings him in line with his beloved Master who likewise never veered from devotion to the One God of Israel.

The Argument from History

Since Scripture is the final arbiter in matters of Christian belief, many may not feel a need to examine Trinitarianism from a historical point of view. To others it will be of interest to learn that the doctrine of the Trinity as it was solidified at Nicea (325 AD) and Chalcedon (451 AD) was the end product of a process of development. It is quite impossible to demonstrate belief in three coequal, coeternal persons from the Christian writings before the end of the second century. This fact is widely recognized by Trinitarian scholars. Roman Catholics frankly admit that their doctrine of the Trinity came to them not from the Bible but from post-biblical tradition. Cardinal Hosier's remark from the 16th century deserves to be heard: "We believe the

---

[43] (London: SPCK, 1962), 71, 72.

[44] *Greek Testament,* ad loc. cit.

doctrine of a Triune God because we have received it by tradition, though it is not mentioned at all in Scripture."[45]

The remarks of another Roman Catholic scholar present Trinitarians with a similar challenge:

> That the Son is of the same essence as the Father or consubstantial with Him is not manifest in any part of Sacred Scripture, either by express words or by certain and immutable deduction. These and other opinions of the Protestants no one can prove from the sacred writings, the traditional word of God being laid aside...Scripture itself would, in many places, have seemed to exhibit the opposite, unless the Church had taught us otherwise.[46]

Some Protestant theologians, while remaining Trinitarians, have admitted the difficulty of basing the Trinity on the Bible:

> It must be owned that the doctrine of the Trinity, as it is proposed in our [Church of England] Articles, our Liturgy, our Creeds, is not in so many words taught us in the Holy Scriptures. What we profess in our prayers we nowhere read in Scripture — that the One God, the one Lord, is not only one person but three persons in one substance. There is no such text in the Scripture as this, that "the Unity in Trinity and the Trinity in Unity is to be worshipped." None of the inspired writers has expressly affirmed that in the Trinity none is before or after the other, none is greater or less than the other, but the whole three persons are coeternal together and coequal.[47]

---

[45] *Confessio Fidei Christiana* (1553), ch. 27.

[46] James Masenius, *Apud Sandium*, 9-11, cited by Wilson, *Concessions*, 54.

[47] Bishop George Smalridge, *Sixty Sermons Preach'd on Several Occasions*, no. 33, 348, cited by Wilson, *Unitarian Principles Confirmed by Trinitarian Testimonies*, 367.

If the Trinity had its origin in the Bible we would expect to be able to trace it back in an unbroken tradition through the earliest post-biblical writers. But can this be done? There are many in the Trinitarian camp who confess the difficulty in finding Trinitarianism in the writings of leading exponents of the faith before the Council of Nicea. The facts have been documented in an informative article by Mark Mattison.[48] Quoting original sources as well as standard authorities, Mattison demonstrates that the "Trinitarianism" of Justin Martyr and Theophilus involves a clear element of subordination in the Son. Irenaeus, also of the second century, speaks of the Father as *autotheos*, God in Himself. The divinity of the Son is derived from that of the Father. This is not true of developed Trinitarianism, in which all three persons are coequal. Tertullian (c. 160-225) believed in the preexistence of the Son but expressly denied his eternity: "God has not always been Father and Judge, merely on the ground of His having always been God. For He could not have been the Father previous to the Son, nor a judge previous to sin. There was, however, a time when neither sin existed *nor the Son*."[49]

Another influential Church Father, Origen (c. 185-254), clearly did not think of Christ as coequal with the Father. In his commentaries on John he maintains that "God, the Logos," i.e., the Son, is "surpassed by the God of the universe."[50] "The Son is in no respect to be compared with the Father; for he is the image of his goodness, and the effulgence not of God, but of his glory and of his eternal light."[51] Although Origen was the first to develop the idea of the "Eternal Son," he insists on the

---

[48] "The Development of Trinitarianism in the Patristic Period," *A Journal from the Radical Reformation* 1 (summer 1992): 4-14. See also M.M. Mattison, *The Making of a Tradition*. Reprinted non-Trinitarian works mainly from the 19th and 20th centuries are now available from C.E.S., P.O. Box 30336, Indianapolis, IN 46230.

[49] *Against Hermogenes*, ch. 3.

[50] *Commentary on John,* ii, 3.

[51] Ibid., xiii, 35.

subordinate position of Christ. "The Father who sent Jesus is alone good and greater than he who was sent."[52] Origen actually denied that prayer should be offered to Jesus and taught that he is not the object of supreme worship.[53] *The Oxford Dictionary of the Christian Church* points out that Origen considered the Son to be "divine only in a lesser sense than the Father. The Son is *theos* (god), but only the Father is *autotheos* (absolute God, God in himself)."[54]

The earliest "Apologists" and Church Fathers were not Trinitarian in the same sense as the later creed of Nicea. This fact may be verified by reading the original writings of these exponents of the faith or by consulting standard authorities on church history. A 19th-century German scholar wrote, "The doctrinal system of the ante-Nicene church is irreconcilable with the letter and authority of the formularies of the Constantinian, and, in general of the Byzantine councils, and with the Medieval systems built upon them."[55] This fact is just as obvious in the twentieth century. *The Westminster Dictionary of Christian Theology* states that subordinationism "was in fact characteristic of pre-Nicene Christology. Origen, for example, had thought in terms of a hierarchy of being in which God the Father was the ultimate one and the Logos was the mediating link between the ultimate and created essences."[56] Taking its impetus from the Council of Nicea, the later Athanasian Creed attributed complete coequality to the three persons of the Godhead. If Trinitarianism demands the "eternal Sonship" of Christ, the earliest post-

---

[52] Ibid., vi, 23.

[53] *Treatise on Prayer*, 15.

[54] "Origen," ed. Cross and Livingstone (Oxford University Press, 1974, second edition), 1009.

[55] C.C. Bunsen, *Christianity and Mankind*, 1:464, cited by Alvan Lamson, *The Church of the First Three Centuries*, 181.

[56] Frances Young, "Subordinationism," in *The Westminster Dictionary of Christian Theology*, ed. Richardson and Bowden (Philadelphia: Westminster Press, 1983), 553.

biblical writers were heretics, and even Origen fell short of what would be an acceptable creed in most Trinitarian circles today.

Conclusion

It appears that expert Trinitarian exegesis often weakens the attempt to base the Trinity on Scripture. There are no texts advanced in support of the orthodox understanding of the Godhead which have not been assigned another interpretation by Trinitarians themselves. Can the biblical doctrine of God really be so obscure? It may be simpler to accept the *Shema* of Israel and its belief in a unipersonal God. Since this was the creed spoken by Jesus himself, it would seem to have an absolute claim to be the Christian creed. Nothing of the glory of the Son is lost if he is recognized as the unique human representative of God, for whom God created the whole universe and whom the Father resurrected to immortality. His position as judge of mankind reflects the exalted status of his Messiahship, yet he derives all authority from the Father.

XII. HAVE WE BARTERED FOR ANOTHER GOD?

"In earliest Christianity, orthodoxy and heresy do not stand in relation to one another as primary to secondary, but in many regions heresy is the original manifestation of Christianity."
— *George Strecker*

If Jesus were God, then he must always have existed, and further discussion about his origin would be irrelevant. At Nicea, argument about the origin of Jesus was officially settled. Under the leadership of Constantine and the Greek theologians of the fourth century, belief in the consubstantial Deity of Jesus became a main plank in the doctrinal system of the Church, and so it has remained. But the emerging Trinitarian theory presented a considerable problem for the theologians. How were they to explain a Deity of two (and later three) persons and at the same time maintain that there was only one God? The unity which Constantine's council tried to foster became mired in endless debates about the nature of Christ. If Christ were God, and his Father were God, did not that make two Gods?

The point was a continuing source of irritation. The docetists advanced one solution. God was one, appearing as Jesus in another mode of being. Jesus, therefore, was not really a distinct person but God in another form. "As Christ's human body was phantasm, his suffering and death were mere appearance: 'If he suffered he was not God. If he was God, he did not suffer.'"[1]

Others reasoned that if the Father begat a Son, there had to be a time when the Son did not exist. The decision at Nicea in 325 AD, and later at the Council of Chalcedon in 451, was to

---

[1] Paul Johnson, *A History of Christianity*, 90.

declare Jesus *both* "very God of very God" and completely man at the same time. The technical term for this combination of natures was the "hypostatic union," the doctrine of the union of the divine and human natures in Christ, the two natures constituting a single person. The idea that Christ was both fully God and fully man, however, was self-contradictory to many. God, they objected, is by His very nature an infinite being, while man is finite. One person cannot at once be both infinite and finite. Moreover, the Jesus presented by the Gospels, especially in the records of Matthew, Mark, and Luke, is obviously a fully human person distinct from God, his Father. Not a word is said by these authors about his being God, nor of his having preexisted his birth.

The tortuous details of the dispute over the identity of Christ can be examined in any standard textbook of church history. The battle raged over the nature of the Messiah. How could his humanity be reconciled with the now deeply entrenched notion that he was also God? And how, since the Jesus of the Gospels was clearly a different person from his Father, could a charge of polytheism be avoided? The debate, although dogmatically resolved by church councils, has never been laid to rest. Both layman and scholar across the Christian world have continued to be troubled by the apparently contradictory terms of these conciliar decisions, not to mention the jumble of confusing words involved in the discussion. How can two separate individuals (as they obviously are throughout the New Testament records), Father and Son, both fully Deity, constitute in reality only one Deity? It has normally been safer to accept that it just is so.

Dissent from orthodoxy was met with an unaccountable harshness. Established religion apparently saw nothing unchristian about venting its wrath on objectors. One of many later opponents of Trinitarianism was "a Unitarian surgeon, Dr. George van Parris…[who] refused to abjure his faith. It was said of him at his trial before the Archbishop of Canterbury, Thomas Cranmer: 'that he believes, that God, the Father is only God, and that Christ is not very God.'" He was burned to death by leaders of the Church of England at Smithfield in England on April 25, 1551.[2]

Two hundred and fifty years later a British nonconformist minister, Joseph Priestley, saw a lifetime of scholarly work go up in flames at the hands of a mob in Birmingham, England. Priestley was the victim of the fire that had been ignited by the decision of the Nicene Council to suppress all objectors. He believed God to be only one person and Jesus to be mortal man, contrary to the Constantinian council's orthodox decision. This brilliant scientist and minister of religion, a Greek and Hebrew teacher, had come to the conclusion that much of what was taught as Christianity could not be supported by the Bible. His views brought him under attack. His home, library, laboratory, papers and chapel were destroyed by a rioting mob. Although a firm defender of the Bible against the attacks of critics and detractors, his deviation from the accepted beliefs of his clerical colleagues made him anathema.

What did these men, and many others who paid with their lives, find in the Bible which caused them to arrive at a different conviction about the nature of God? Why was this persuasion so powerful that they were willing to surrender everything for it? Why did religious leadership feel so threatened that they punished their opponents by putting them to death? Why even today, in many circles, does any questioning of the Trinity provoke such extraordinary alarm?

If there were even one unambiguous biblical statement to support the extraordinary idea that the previously existing Son of God, himself actually God, became man and was himself the creator of all that exists, would not those who believe in such an idea feel a quiet confidence accompanied by a sense of pity and charity for the ignorant unbeliever? Why does history record so much violence and intense anger roused in the Trinitarian believer in defense of what even he admits is largely a baffling mystery?

---

[2] G.H. Williams, *The Radical Reformation*, 779, 780.

It is hard to believe that assent to a proposition so impossibly difficult is the one great criterion for salvation. A seventeenth-century orthodox bishop of the Church of England seems to be caught in a trap against his own better judgment:

> We are to consider the order of those persons in the Trinity described in the words before us in Matthew 28:19. First the Father and then the Son and then the Holy Ghost; everyone one of which is truly God. This is a mystery which we are all bound to believe, but yet must exercise great care in how we speak of it, it being both easy and dangerous to err in expressing so great a truth as this is. If we think of it, how hard it is to imagine one numerically divine *nature* in more than one and the same divine *person*. Or three divine persons in no more than one and the same divine nature. If we speak of it, how hard it is to find out words to express it. If I say, the Father, Son and Holy Ghost be three, and every one distinctly God, it is true. But if I say, they be three, and everyone a distinct God, it is false. I may say, God the Father is one God, and the Son is one God, and the Holy Ghost is one God, but I cannot say that the Father is one God and the Son is another God and the Holy Ghost is a third God. I may say that the Father begat another who is God; yet I cannot say that He begat another God. I may say that from the Father and Son there proceeds another who is God; yet I cannot say that from the Father and Son there proceeds another God. For though their nature be the same their persons are distinct; and though their persons be distinct, yet still their nature is the same. So that, though the Father be the first person in the Godhead, the Son the second and the Holy Ghost the third, yet the Father is not the first, the Son the second and the Holy Ghost a third God. So hard a thing is it to word so great a mystery aright; or to fit so high a truth

with expressions suitable and proper to it, without going one way or another from it.[3]

If we confine ourselves to the plain statements of the Christian documents, what is the hard biblical evidence about the origin of Jesus? Is it not obvious that Jesus did not think he was the creator, when he referred to *God* who "made them male and female" (Mark 10:6)? In Hebrews 4:4 we learn that *God* rested at creation. The writer to the Hebrews means the Father when he refers to God (the term "God" is used, in a secondary sense, of Jesus in Heb. 1:8). Jesus is reported as saying that he was not God (Mark 10:18). Even a cursory reading of Matthew and Luke leads us to conclude that it was *at his birth from the virgin Mary* that Jesus came into being (Luke 1:35). This would also appear to be just what the Old Testament expected about the Messiah, unless we read back into the Hebrew Scriptures the idea of preexistence and mistakenly attribute it to the authors of the Bible.

Paul's short summary of the history of Jesus is not a Trinitarian statement: "And by common confession, great is the mystery of godliness; he who was revealed in the flesh [i.e., as a human being]...was taken up in glory" (1 Tim. 3:16). Paul holds that Jesus was revealed in the flesh — a plain statement of the way the Savior first appeared to man. It was as a human person. No hint of preexistence, as angel or as God, is implied in this concentrated picture of the Messiah. Some manuscripts have inserted the word "God" for the words "he who." The alteration is admitted by modern translators to be unwarranted. "God" is most unlikely to have been part of the older manuscripts. Such interpolations, like the famous spurious Trinitarian addition in 1 John 5:7, which is omitted by modern translations, suggest that someone was trying to force a new idea on the original text. Exactly the same violence to Scripture appears in the Vulgate

---

[3] Bishop Beverage, *Private Thoughts*, Part 2, 48, 49, cited by Charles Morgridge, *The True Believer's Defence Against Charges Preferred by Trinitarians for Not Believing in the Deity of Christ* (Boston: B. Greene, 1837), 16.

(Latin) translation of the Bible when it alters a prediction of the Messiah from "He is your lord" to "He is the Lord your God" (Ps. 45:11). The change symbolizes a fatal loss of Jesus' identity as Messiah.

Statements by theologians and historians who have recognized the tragedy that befell Christianity in the fourth and fifth centuries could fill an entire volume. A former professor of the history of philosophy at the University of Vienna wrote:

> Christianity today is like a tree, or a forest if you will, on a mountain top: uprooted by a storm, one suddenly sees how little soil it had to hold it up…The reason for this alarming fact is that Christianity is not rooted in the soil from which it stems — from Jewish piety, the Jewish fear of God, love of humanity, love of earthly pleasures, joy in the present and hope for the future. Christianity got itself into a dangerous position through its identification with the religio-political state of Constantine. Since Pope John XXIII, some real opportunities have arisen to break free of the Constantine influence.[4]

Unfortunately this Constantinian influence, unopposed except by a few dissenting voices, has proved to be the graveyard of true Christian unity. Can we call a body rallied around a synthesis of biblical truth and alien Greek philosophy, amalgamated with Gentile political systems, pagan customs and beliefs, truly Christian? Since the time when Constantine sponsored the church councils of the fourth century, history witnesses to the long agony of a divided Christianity, torn by sectarian strife, with lands shamed by some of the bloodiest struggles recorded in the annals of man. There is a deep irony in the fact that such warfare should have claimed the name of Christ. The baby wrapped in swaddling clothes, lying in a manger, was introduced to the world with an announcement by the heavenly host praising God, saying, "Glory to God in the

---

[4] Frederich Heer, *God's First Love* (Weidenfeld and Nicolson, 1970), xiv, xv.

highest, and on earth peace among men with whom He is well pleased [His chosen people]" (Luke 2:14). And yet the Christian community, which should have been an example to the world of peace among men, has failed miserably, even in its own house, to demonstrate that peace.

Jesus himself announced that he "did not come to bring peace but a sword" (Matt. 10:34). He was fully aware that his Gospel of the coming Kingdom, designed to instill in believers a love of peace, truth and respect for the one creator God, and to free our minds from the entrapment of fear and superstition, would not be integrated peacefully into a system rife with suppression and the control of human beings by fellow human beings. Under the banner of the prince of peace, some of the most vicious wars have been waged. The spectacle of Christian killing Christian and the Church supporting torture and violence against those deemed to be heretics gives point to Christ's prediction that "the time is coming for everyone who kills you [true believers] to think that he is offering service to God" (John 16:2). A heavy responsibility must lie on the shoulders of all those who have used the name of Christ to perpetuate systems of violence. Jesus' absolute ethic of love should have prevented believers from entering the machinery of warfare, which so often involved the slaughter of those whom they claimed as brethren in the faith. There is, after all, nothing complex about Jesus' message of reverence for the One God, his Father, and of love to all, even the enemy:

> The Gospel was addressed to plain and honest minds, and plain and honest minds can understand its important and practical lessons. The great principles of natural religion are so simple that our Savior thought men could gather them from the birds of the air, the flowers of the field, and the clouds of heaven; and he demanded of those who stood around him, why they did not of themselves judge what is right. The Gospel was addressed to the poor, the uneducated; and it was committed to unlettered men to teach it to others. It would be most strange, therefore, if only the learned could understand or explain it. In truth, its great and

> practical principles and character are most simple, as
> those will find it, who study it in the teachings and
> example of Jesus, rather than amidst the confusion of
> tongues, hypercriticisms, the presumptuous, or the
> frivolous conceits of uncompromising, prejudiced,
> bigoted, infuriate polemics; and enveloped in all the
> mystery and metaphysical abstruseness of theological
> controversy...[5]

Historians would be hard pressed to find a more striking example of confusion and bitter ecclesiastical struggle than the battles over what and who God and Jesus are, questions which formally surfaced in the centuries following the writing of the New Testament and which led to the tragic decisions made at the time of the Nicene Council. Today we refrain from killing dissenters. The law protects them. Nevertheless they may be punished in other ways. Those who disagree with accepted dogma are often ostracized and branded as heretics by others claiming to be the watchdogs of orthodoxy. Ears and minds are closed to what dissenters have to say, as though somehow a Satanic plot is unleashed when a contrary opinion is voiced. Few Christians can conceive the possibility that they may have embraced long-standing error. We have been well schooled by our teachers to wrap a protective armor round our imagined truth, even though it may be indefensible error. We are prone to give unquestioning assent to hallowed church tradition. We are often overawed by authority and title. Seldom do we pause to consider that religious leadership is in the hands of those who have conformed to a prevailing pattern or acceptable thinking and were rewarded for their orthodoxy. But can our present denominational systems, among which there exists serious conflict and disagreement, all faithfully represent God and truth? A British biblical scholar and author of journal articles on Christology admitted in correspondence that "my experience has been that Christology is a subject on which some are not as frank

---

[5] *Valedictory*, from sermons by Henry Colman (n.p., 1820), 322, 323.

as they should be, especially if as churchmen they are formally committed to the traditional creeds."

Theology's insistence that we must believe an unproved theory that three is one and one is three — a theory which it admits it cannot explain or understand — has imposed an intolerable burden on Christianity and has taxed the common sense of anyone who attempts to worship God with all the soundness that the mind can muster, as he is instructed to do. To impose an aura of sanctity on an unprovable and unbiblical concept because fourth-century theologians in league with a "Christian" emperor dictated the terms of the creed, elevates blind acceptance of dogma over the honest quest for biblical truth.

Christianity has rightly pointed a corrective finger at a secular world for its attempt to impose the unproven theory of evolution on mankind. Christians have with remarkable incisiveness exposed and warned fellow believers of the Oriental origins of the contemporary New Age movement. Yet Christianity has not recognized that it has harbored in its own doctrinal system a theory about God which alienates it from its roots in Hebrew theology and from Jesus, whose understanding of who God is was formed by the prophets of Israel, not by philosophy or church councils.

Christians have been told that Constantine, who is linked to the council which established Trinitarian belief, was converted to Christianity. What happened in fact was quite the opposite. This shrewd political giant took Christianity under his wing to further his own political aims. A vast number of Christians eventually sheltered under the protection of Constantine's system and have ever since enjoyed a working relationship with the political powers. Christianity became converted to Constantine and wedded to a religio-political coalition whose sponsor continued to have coins minted in honor of his God — Sol Invictus, the sun god, not the God of the early Christians. These are the verifiable facts of history, notwithstanding the attempts of apologists to reinterpret the facts in a way which enhances Constantine's Christian image. Few seem to be aware of the Church's accommodation to paganism and the compromise of true reverence for the God of Abraham, Isaac and Jacob. The resurrected Son of God has had to compete with the invincible sun god, Sol Invictus, the god of Constantine.

Christianity closed its eyes to biblical reality and simplicity when it decided that two or three persons compose the one God. The promotion of this multiple Deity has been one of the greatest ideological successes ever accomplished. It was achieved with the help of coercion, the sword, torture and the massive weight of pressure from a coalition of clergy and the state joined in an unholy alliance, and benefiting from a mysterious concept. Calling itself the Holy Roman Empire, however, scarcely reflected its real nature.

At the Council of Nicea, not only did Constantine excommunicate and exile anyone who refused to conform, he took the precaution of burning any letters of complaint and dispute. This was a tragic suppression of unwanted facts, and history is filled with parallel examples. Promoting Jesus as God — another, in addition to the Father — Christianity indeed "bartered for another God" (Ps. 16:4, NASV). It was to its shame and sorrow that it traded in the historical man, Jesus Messiah, whose desire, as God's unique human agent, was to lead men to the One God; in his stead it elevated the God-man. Greek mythology triumphed over Hebrew theology. Thus Christianity sold its birthright.

Established religion had failed to accept Christ or his message during his brief sojourn on earth. Nor has his Gospel message of the Kingdom of God found wide acceptance among the clergy since that time. Jesus has been transmuted into the God-man, a figure less than human, a metaphysical construct of the Greek speculative genius, not the man Messiah, King of Israel, described by the Christian documents. Lost in the theological confusion was the reality of the human Messiah who really died and was resurrected to immortality as an example to mankind, blazing the trail for others who might follow him on the path to immortality through resurrection into the Kingdom of God on earth to be inaugurated at Jesus' return.

When Christianity adopted a Godhead of more than one person, it unwittingly flirted with idolatry. It embarked on a course of lawlessness by embracing "another God" besides the only true God, the Father. Christianity thus broke the first commandment and has continued on the same troubled path, unaware of the source of its intractable problems. It could be argued that the sheer weight of numbers agreeing on the Trinitarian concept is sufficient evidence for the correctness of the belief. How could all these people be wrong? In reply it can be asked, when has the majority mentality been the judge of right and wrong? Is the earth flat or the center of our universe? Protestants allow that the whole Church had gone wrong for a thousand years before Luther called it back to Scripture. There is reason to believe that the Reformation needs to continue. Luther's adopting the doctrine of the sleep of the dead points to an element in the process of restoration that his followers found to be too radical for the times. Surely the doctrine of the Trinity is due for a thorough inspection to see if it might not be part of our heritage from the Fathers and councils rather than from the Bible.

Even the suggestion that Jesus is not God in the same sense as the Father appears to some as an unpardonable attack on Scripture. Yet Jesus himself made it clear that there is *only one true God*, and he named that one God as the Father. He always distinguished himself from God by claiming to be His messenger. He protested that he was not God but the Son of God (John 10:34-36). Jesus was continually referred to as a man by New Testament writers even after his resurrection. Not one writer ever refers to Jesus as "the one true God" or includes him in the phrase "one true God." Jesus and God are expressly distinguished whenever they are mentioned together. They are two separate and distinct persons. There are some 1350 unitarian texts in the New Testament, besides the thousands in the Old Testament. These occur every time the Father is called God. Jesus is called God (but in a different sense) for certain, only twice (John 20:28; Heb. 1:8). John 1:1, 14 state that the "word" which (not who) was fully expressive of God — *theos* — became a man, the man Jesus. The constant use of "God" for the Father hardly suggests that He and Jesus are to be thought of as "coequally God." In the Old Testament references to God with personal pronouns in the singular occur some 11,000 times, informing us that God is a single individual.

So vulnerable to attack is the Chalcedonian formula which declares Jesus "true God from true God, begotten not made, of one substance with the Father" and "the selfsame perfect in Godhead, the selfsame perfect in manhood, truly God and truly man," that a Roman Catholic scholar claims that "the demand for a complete reappraisal of the Church's belief in Christ right up to the present day is an urgent one."[6]

Baillie admitted "that a great many thoughtful people who feel themselves drawn to the Gospel in these days are completely mystified by the doctrine of the Incarnation — the idea that God merely appeared in Jesus in another form — far more than we theologians realize."[7] One of the leading spokesmen for fundamental Christian evangelism remarked on a nationwide television broadcast that no theologian had ever been able successfully to explain to him the doctrine of the Trinity. This seems to imply that one must simply place one's confidence in the decrees of fourth- and fifth-century Church Fathers that it is so. But we may ask the question: Who gave those Greek theologians the right to decide Christian theology for all time? Who invested them with the power to declare infallibly that the Godhead consists of three eternal persons?

Once belief in God as a single person was denied, speculation became rife. The single supreme God of the Hebrews no longer ruled without rival in the minds of believers. Paul documents the persistent tendency of the human mind to exchange the true God for other deities:

> For since the creation of the world...His eternal power
> and divine nature have been clearly seen, being
> understood through what has been made...For even
> though they knew God, they did not honor Him as
> God...but became futile in their speculations...They

---

6 Aloys Grillmeier, S.J., *Christ in Christian Tradition* (Atlanta: John Knox Press, 1975), 1:557.

7 *God Was in Christ*, 29.

exchanged the truth of God for a lie and worshipped and served the creature rather than the Creator (Rom. 1:20, 21, 25).

We now talk about how great Mother Nature is. We have removed Father God, the Creator, from our thinking. If some have their way it will no longer be acceptable to speak of God as Father, lest we appear sexist. The loss of a clear perception of the One God has opened the floodgates of so-called New Age thinking; every man declares himself god awaiting self-discovery. This philosophy is not really new. It is an ancient Oriental concept first introduced to Adam and Eve with the words, "For God knows that in the day you eat from it your eyes will be opened, and you will be like God" (Gen. 3:5). The pursuit of knowledge is proper, but it must be the true knowledge of the true God. All else is vain.

The drift into polytheism was inevitable, once the God of the Jews was rejected. Christianity has fulfilled the prediction of the Psalmist David when he said, "The sorrows of those who have bartered for 'another God' will be multiplied" (Ps. 16:4). As the Apostle Paul warned the first-century Church, "If one comes preaching another Jesus whom we have not preached...you bear this beautifully" (2 Cor. 11:4). It is impossible to find in Paul's writings a preexisting God/Son except by neglecting his primary creedal statements concerning the Son of God, "who was born of the seed of David according to the flesh" (Rom. 1:3; cp. Gal. 4:4). The verb used by Paul simply means "coming to be," "coming into existence," i.e., from a woman (Gal. 4:4), herself a descendant of David (Rom. 1:3). Paul holds firmly to his unrestricted Jewish monotheism, a creed which declares in the simplest terms that "there is one God and one mediator between God and men, *the man* Christ Jesus" (1 Tim. 2:5) and that there is no God but the Father (1 Cor. 8:4, 6).

When Christianity proclaimed "another Jesus" who was "very God," it automatically preached "another God" who became part of a divine triangle. The God of the Old Testament who said through Isaiah, "Understand that I am He. Before Me there was no God formed, and there will be none after Me...and

I will not give My glory to another" (Isa. 43:10; 42:8) was a single being in the mind of the Jews and the first-century Church.

Christianity began to worship *as God* one who was created. The faith thus fell into idolatry. Readers of the Bible neglected to note that Christ was called the Son of God *because of his supernatural conception* (Luke 1:35). Jesus came into existence in his mother's womb and was thus part of the creation, not the Creator. The official creeds sanctioned belief in "another Jesus" and "another God." On the flimsiest of evidence as, for example, Paul's belief that God sent His Son, the idea was propagated that Jesus existed before his birth. James Dunn puts his finger on the problem:

> It is possible that in the two passages where he speaks of God sending His Son (Rom. 8:3 and Gal. 4:4) he means to imply that the Son of God was preexistent and had become incarnate as Jesus; but it is as likely, indeed probably more likely, that Paul's meaning did not stretch so far and at these points *he and his readers thought simply of Jesus as one commissioned by God as one who shared wholly in man's frailty, bondage and sin, and whose death achieved God's liberating and transforming purpose for man.*[8]

It is clear that Trinitarians place considerable strain upon certain "proof texts" offered as evidence of the preexistence of Christ. *Elohim* gives no evidence of plurality in the Hebrew Godhead. "Sent from God" does not prove that you have enjoyed a life in heaven before coming to earth. In Scripture the prophets and John the Baptist were also "sent." Jeremiah was foreknown but not preexistent.[9] Jesus was first brought into being and then sent (Acts 3:26). This is commissioning after his birth, not arriving from a pre-human existence.

---

[8] *Christology in the Making*, 46, emphasis added.

[9] Cp. Jer. 1:5 with 1 Pet. 1:20 and see Jer. 1:7; 7:25; John 1:6.

An Entrenched Distortion of Monotheism

The hidden problem which faces the Church today is the error in its understanding of God which invaded it from Gentile philosophies. The early Church fought and lost the battle for belief in the unipersonal God. But with a determination to take an objective, fresh look at the hard evidence of the Bible we may find that the Triune God concept becomes little more than an adult theological myth. Trinitarians are at a loss to produce a single passage in the Bible in which the doctrine of the Trinity is clearly stated. If we accept the words of the founder of Christianity at face value, belief in the Trinity challenges his teaching about the most important law and the focal point of all true religion — belief in the God who is a single, undivided being. Before all other considerations comes the matter of the "foremost of all commandments," to "hear" and believe in the God of Israel who is "the one Lord" (Mark 12:29, New Jerusalem Bible). Paul follows Jesus when he states that there is no God but the Father (1 Cor. 8:4, 6).

This leads us to the important question: Does it really make any difference what we believe? One of the most devastating concepts to invade the modern Church is that a person's beliefs are insignificant as long as he loves God and his neighbor. After all, do not all versions of religion promote worship of the same God? The plain biblical fact is that Scripture insists on truth, as distinct from error, as the basis of worship and salvation itself. Paul expressly linked salvation to a correct understanding of the identity of God and Jesus: "This is good and acceptable in the sight of God our Savior, who desires all people *to be saved and to come to the knowledge of the truth.* For there is one God and one mediator between God and men, the man Messiah Jesus" (1 Tim. 2:3-5). The connection between correct, i.e., biblically orthodox belief and salvation is inescapable here, as also in Paul's statements in which "belief in the truth" is starkly contrasted with being wicked, and where salvation depends on receiving "the love of the truth" (2 Thess. 2:10-13).

The prophet Jeremiah was under no illusion about the importance of knowing the God of Israel when he said: "Let not a wise man boast of his wisdom, and let not the mighty man boast of his might...but let him who boasts, boast in this, that he understands and knows Me..." (Jer. 9:23, 24). He continued by stating that "The Lord is the true God" (10:10), a truth which was echoed by Jesus centuries later when he said: "This is eternal life, that they might know You, the only true God, and Jesus Christ whom You sent" (John 17:3).

With remarkable consistency the Bible insists on the unique personality of the One God, creator and Father, and the necessity of knowing this One God, the Father, and His Son, the Messiah. These strictly monotheistic texts dispel any idea that there can be more than one who is truly God. Scripture opposes the idea that we are at liberty to accommodate our conception of God to cultural environment, however well-meaning our intentions. To do so is to court paganism and inevitable polytheism, which is the ruin of true faith.

Christians throughout the world are challenged to face the age-old question, "What is truth?" Where two conflicting points of view present themselves, it is the truth-seeker's responsibility to determine which, if either of them, is true. We dare not escape the force of the challenge by asserting that truth is elusive or unobtainable. This would be to embrace the familiar approach of Pilate at Christ's trial when he asked Jesus, "What is truth?" (John 18:38). More than a genuine question, this was a philosophy, rejecting the belief that absolute truth is attainable. It implied, in true post-enlightenment style, that one opinion is as valid as another. It disregarded the claim Jesus had just made that he had come into the world for the very purpose of bearing witness to truth (John 18:37). To say that all truth is relative negates Jesus' promise that "you shall know the truth and the truth shall make you free" (John 8:32).

The Apostle Paul never for one moment conceded that someone else's error carried the same value as his truth. His somber warning to the church at Thessalonica about a great deception coming upon the world, which would cause the ruin of those who did not love truth, should not go unheeded. He clearly states that it is God Himself who will send upon them a strong delusion to make them believe a lie "because they did not welcome the love of the truth in order to be saved" (2 Thess.

2:10, 11). He repeated his warning to Timothy that there would "come a time when people will not endure sound teaching" but would listen only to those who pandered to human desires. As a result, they would turn away from listening to truth and wander into myths (2 Tim. 4:3-5). He was not talking about minor theological points, but about serious errors and myths leading to spiritual blindness, false goals, false gods, disobedience to God, and death. Nineteen hundred years later, a shrewd observer of the contemporary Church will want to know why there is such fragmentation over the major question of the identity of the One God and Jesus. We can trace the source of the problem to a fracturing of the most precious of all beliefs that there is *one God, the Father* and no other besides Him (1 Cor. 8:4, 6). John Locke thought traditional theology worthless because it was not primarily concerned with truth. He put the point powerfully in his essay *Concerning Human Understanding*, written in 1661:

> He that would seriously set upon the search for truth ought, in the first place, to prepare his mind with a love of it. For he that loves it not, will not take much pains to get it; nor be much concerned when he misses it. There is nobody in the commonwealth who does not profess himself a lover of truth; and there is not a rational creature that would not take it amiss to be thought otherwise of. And yet, for all this, one may truly say, there are very few lovers of truth for truth's sake, even among those who persuade themselves that they are so.[10]

Following Christianity's perceptive analysis and exposure of the dangerous New Age theology of our time, it is now the moment to direct the focus of its examination to its own camp and consider the invasion of paganism which dates from the second century. The influence of Greek philosophy which Canon Goudge described as a "disaster from which the Church has

---

[10] Cited by Paul Johnson in *A History of Christianity*, 355.

never recovered"[11] continues to go largely unnoticed by the majority of sincere Christians. Yet it affects the faith at its very heart. It is naive to suppose that we can translate the biblical, Hebraic concept of Deity, held as the foundation of true faith by Jesus, into Greek thought without the risk of disastrous damage.

It is fanciful to think that the Trinitarian and Binitarian systems, which claim to have roots in the Bible, can really be harmonized with the strict unitarianism of Jesus and the Scriptures. The persistent objection of the Jews that Christianity has betrayed its origins by corrupting the cardinal doctrine of God must be acknowledged.

Nor should the penetrating observations of contemporary historians be ignored. Historians have a way of seeing truth clearly, where theologians are prone to have their vision blurred by tradition. Ian Wilson is witness against the unreasonable way in which the Trinity still rules, despite Jesus' own ignorance of any such teaching. He wrote:

> If Jesus had wanted to institute a formula for the religion he taught, there is one moment, described in Mark's Gospel, when he had the perfect opportunity to do so. A scribe is reported as having asked him: "Which is the first of all the commandments?" It was an occasion to which Jesus could have imparted one of those characteristic twists, bringing in something new, something involving himself, if he wished us to believe that he was a member of a Trinity, on an equal footing with God the Father. Instead he looked unhesitatingly to his traditional Jewish roots.[12]

By quoting the "Shema" — "Listen Israel" — Jesus was affirming with the greatest possible emphasis the bedrock tenet of true belief. We are asked only to believe that the creed of Christ is the Christian creed, binding therefore on all Christian churches. If the *Shema* is incompatible with Trinitarianism, the

---

[11]"The Calling of the Jews," in the collected essays on *Judaism and Christianity.*

[12] *Jesus, The Evidence,* 176, 177.

creed of Jesus will not match our orthodox creed. Many churchgoers act as if Jesus (to parody the Sermon on the Mount) somewhere said, "You have heard that it was said, 'the Lord your God is one Lord,' but I say to you, He is three in one."

The first step towards the recovery of biblical Christianity would be an honest recognition that Jesus was a Jew, and that as such he confirmed the theology of the prophets of Israel. The story of Israel's failure to know God lay precisely in their inability to cling to the unipersonal God, the Creator of heaven and earth. Whereas Israel fell into the hands of Assyria and Babylon, the Christian Church was captured by the alluring world of Greek philosophy. It abandoned the God of Israel. The "Israel of God" (Gal. 6:16; cp. Phil. 3:3), the new Christian people, most unreasonably forsook the creed of Israel.

When Christianity modified its original creed and adopted belief in a God composed of three persons, it bartered for another God — to its multiplied grief. From that disaster, only a wholehearted recovery of biblical belief in One God, the Father, in Jesus as the Lord Messiah, and in his Gospel message about the coming Kingdom of God[13] can lead it to the glories of a new day.

---

[13] Matt. 4:17, 23; 9:35; 13:19; 24:14; Mark 1:14, 15; Luke 4:43; 8:1, 12; 9:2, 6, 11; Acts 8:12; 19:8; 20:25; 28:23, 31; 2 Tim. 4:1, 2. For an examination of the Christian Gospel about the Kingdom of God, see Anthony Buzzard, *The Coming Kingdom of the Messiah: A Solution to the Riddle of the New Testament* (Restoration Fellowship, 1988).

XIII. AN APPEAL FOR A RETURN
TO THE BIBLICAL CHRIST

"I should inform you, reader, concerning the origin of the Trinitarian doctrine: Thou mayest assure thyself, it is not from the Scriptures nor reason." — William Penn

John's Gospel Mishandled by Church Fathers

Much of traditional theological language about the nature of Jesus is based on a "reinterpretation" of the Bible, especially of John's Gospel. But it is a reinterpretation which alters the meaning of the original. John Robinson says that "it is clear that patristic theology of whatever school abused these texts [in John] by taking them out of context and *giving them a meaning which it is evident that John never intended.*"[1] Otherwise stated, John's Gospel was "'taken over' by the gnosticizers."[2] The tendency thus introduced is with us to this day.

The texts which suffered violence at the hands of the Church Fathers were those having to do with the origin of Jesus. John's words were given new meanings to lend support to the notion that Jesus was the eternal Son of God, rather than a human being supernaturally begotten as Son of God in the womb of his mother, as Matthew and Luke record. The transition occurred when Christology was restated in terms of Greek philosophy which was incompatible with the biblical documents. "Functional language about the Son and the Spirit being sent into the world by the Father was *transposed* into that of eternal and internal relationships between Persons in the Godhead and words

---

[1] *Twelve More New Testament Studies,* 172, emphasis added.

[2] "Dunn on John," *Theology* 85 (Sept. 1982), 235.

like 'generation' and 'procession' made into technical terms which New Testament usage simply will not substantiate."[3]

Augustine, when faced with John 17:3, where John's unitary monotheism is most clear, was forced to suggest an alteration of the text to include Jesus Christ within the phrase "only true God." He proposed to restructure the verse: "This is eternal life, that they may know Thee and Jesus Christ, whom Thou hast sent, as the only true God."[4] Augustine had inherited a tradition in which biblical monotheism became expanded to include a second person as Supreme Being.

Augustine's alteration of Scripture to fit his system is the inevitable result of trying to explain the essentially Hebrew Scriptures in terms of the alien thought-world of Greek philosophy. The attempt ought to be abandoned. Greek philosophy thinks in terms of "essence." Things are related because they are of the same "stuff." Objects that are green partake of the essence of "greenness." So, post-biblical theologians have argued, the Father, Son and Holy Spirit share a common quality of "Godness." This fact, of course, is quite obvious, but it is a sadly inadequate way of describing the richness of the biblical data. It blurs the sharp contours of the Bible's definition of the One God, His Son and the Holy Spirit. It seems to us as if the doctrine of the Trinity is like saying that a plane, a car and a tricycle are essentially the same thing. They possess the common quality of "conveyance." There is truth to this, but it is not the whole truth. Actually these three things are very different. It is that difference between Father, Son and Holy Spirit which is swamped by the dogma that they are all "one God." The fact that the Son of God has a beginning according to Luke has been overwhelmed by the teaching that the Son never had a beginning. The influence of Greek philosophy has been a disaster, especially because it has produced desperate attempts to

---

3 J.A.T. Robinson, *Twelve More New Testament Studies*, 172, emphasis added.

4 See his *Homilies on John*, tractate CV, ch. 17.

gerrymander the text of the Bible into the prescribed mold of the later creeds.

Documenting this post-biblical shift of opinion about the Godhead, another prominent New Testament scholar observes that "there is no basis in Johannine theology for the later scholastic theology of the procession of the Son from the Father within the Trinity by 'generation.'"[5] The idea of the Son of God generated in eternity is foreign to the Bible. Jesus in the Bible is Son of God because of the virgin birth (Luke 1:35) and further marked out as such "with power" by the resurrection (Rom. 1:4). Nevertheless, belief in the eternal generation of the Son was made the hallmark of orthodox belief and a requirement for salvation.

Raymond Brown admits that non-biblical language was forced onto John's language about Jesus coming from God. Commenting on John 8:42, "I proceeded forth and came from God" (KJV), he notes that:

> The phrase "from God" found its way into the Nicene Creed in the [unbiblical] expression "God from God." Theologians have used this passage as a description of the internal life of the Trinity indicating that the Son proceeds from the Father. However, the aorist tense indicates that the reference is rather to the mission of the Son.[6]

Similarly, Jesus says, "I came forth from the Father" (John 16:28). Brown cautions us that "'from' [*ek*] cannot be interpreted theologically in reference to the intra-Trinitarian relationship of Father and Son ('came out from the Father')." The phrase does not mean what "later theology would call the procession of the Son."[7] Moreover, Brown points out that in John 8:47 the phrase

---

[5] Edward Schillebeeckx, *Christ* (London: SCM Press, 1980), 875, fn. 57.

[6] *The Gospel of John, Anchor Bible* (New York: Doubleday & Co., Inc., 1966), 357.

[7] Ibid., 274.

"from God" (*ek tou theou*) is used "to describe an ordinary believer: 'the man who belongs to God.'"[8] The language used of Jesus applies also to Christians. So also in John 17:8, "I came forth from You" "refers to the earthly mission of the Son rather than to an intra-Trinitarian procession."[9] We may add that the "sending" texts which are sometimes used to support the eternal preexistence of the Son will not bear the weight put upon them. The same words are used of believers, who are also "sent," "just as" Jesus is sent (John 17:18; 20:21).

Despite this clear evidence, commentaries have continued to misread John's intention in the interests of promoting Nicene theology. Plummer says dogmatically, but without support from the text, "'I came out from' includes the Eternal Generation of the Son."[10] This appears to be an example of reading John within a post-biblical framework, instead of acknowledging that John did not have "one foot in the world of Greek philosophy and Nicene theology, as he is so often presented."[11]

The so-called Church Fathers of the third and fourth centuries changed the language of the Bible by reading their own philosophical meanings into biblical words instead of allowing the scriptural text to speak to them within its own Hebrew, Messianic context. The result was a reconstruction of the person of Jesus which turned him into an abstraction, contrary to Luke's transparently clear statement that Jesus is a new creation by means of Mary's supernatural conception: "Holy Spirit [*pneuma hagion*] shall come upon you [Mary] and the power of the Most High will overshadow you, and *for that reason* the holy thing being generated will be called the Son of God" (Luke 1:35).

This is sonship created in history, not in eternity. It perfectly fulfilled the great foundational text in 2 Samuel 7:14, the

---

[8] Ibid., 725.

[9] Ibid., 744.

[10] *Gospel of John, Cambridge Bible for Schools and Colleges* (Cambridge University Press, 1882), 296.

[11] J.A.T. Robinson, *Twelve More New Testament Studies*, 178.

promise to David that God would, in the future, become the Father of his descendant. The Messiah's Sonship is firmly grounded in a historical event of around 3 BC. His generation occurred when God brought the Son into existence (Acts 13:33, quoting Ps. 2:7).[12]

The result of the Fathers' misreading of the biblical language was the creation of the Trinitarian Jesus who is equal in "substance" with the One God. Yet it is clear in John's Gospel that:

> Jesus refuses the claim to *be* God (John 10:33) or in any way to usurp the position of the Father...Jesus is prepared to ignore the charge that by calling God his own Father he is claiming equality with God (John 5:18) and accepts that of being the Son of God (10:36), while vigorously denying the blasphemy of being God or His substitute.[13]

Jacob Jervell agrees: "Jesus is not God but God's representative and, as such, so completely and totally acts on God's behalf that he stands in God's stead before the world. The Gospel clearly states that God and Jesus are not to be understood as identical persons, as in 14:28, 'The Father is greater than I.'"[14]

Paradoxically, traditional theology has attributed to Jesus the claim to be God, a blasphemy which he discounted by asserting his claim to be the *Son of God*. Son of God is a legitimate title for a supreme representative of God, since the judges themselves had been addressed as gods (John 10:34; Ps. 82:6), *which for Jesus is equivalent to Son of God* (John 10:36). To be the Son of God was to demonstrate perfect obedience to the Father, the ideal status of Israel whose citizens are destined to be "sons of the living God" (Hos. 1:10). "Son of God" is also the recognized

---

[12] Acts 13:34 goes on to speak of the *resurrection* of Jesus.

[13] Ibid., 175, 176.

[14] *Jesus in the Gospel of John* (Minneapolis: Augsburg, 1984), 21.

title of the Messiah, God's chosen king.[15] And it was to prove the Messiahship of Jesus that John penned his entire Gospel (John 20:31). Everywhere in the New Testament Jesus is declared to be the "Lord Messiah" or "Lord Jesus Messiah."[16] The term "lord" does not, as so often mistakenly thought, mean that Jesus is the Lord *God* (thus creating the Trinitarian "problem"). Jesus is the "Messiah Lord," based on Psalm 110:1 where the second "lord" is the promised Messiah. Peter knew that this Psalm described the appointment of Christ as "Lord" (Acts 2:34-36). The enormous significance of Psalm 110:1 for New Testament Christology has been largely ignored by Trinitarians. The fact that this verse is cited by the New Testament more often than any verse from the Hebrew Scriptures should have alerted us to its critical importance. The use of *adoni*, not *adonai*, to designate the Messiah in this divine oracle should have prevented Bible students from thinking that Christ was to be God.

Jesus did, of course, claim to *function* for God as His agent. His words are the words of God. His acts are the acts of God; and the Father has conferred on him the right to forgive sins, judge the world, and even raise the dead. Thus it is that Old Testament verses which have Yahweh as their subject can be applied in the New Testament to the activity of the Son who acts for Yahweh. Trinitarians fail to understand the Hebrew principle of agency when they attempt to show from these verses that Jesus *is* Yahweh. He is not Yahweh but His supremely elevated representative. Jesus' equality of function with his Father does not mean that Jesus *is* God. Such an idea is an impossibility in John's Gospel which insists that the Father is "the only true God" (17:3) and "the one who alone is God" (5:44). "It should be noted," says Robinson, "that John is as undeviating a witness as any in the New Testament to the fundamental tenet of

---

[15] Ps. 2:6, 7; 89:26, 27, 35, 36; Matt. 16:16; 2 Sam. 7:14.

[16] See Luke 2:11 for the Messianic title *christos kurios* — Lord Messiah.

Judaism, of unitary monotheism. There is the one true and only God (John 5:44; 17:3); everything else is idols (1 John 5:21)."[17]

It seems only reasonable that Scripture should be read first of all within its own linguistic and cultural framework. Above all its bedrock foundation in the *Shema* of Israel must be recognized. At present Bible readers and commentators instinctively "hear" John in the way the creeds have taught them, and read him through spectacles clouded with Greek philosophy.

The Bible Dictionary and the Son of God

It is interesting to note the difficulty encountered by "orthodox" theology when it attempts to justify the new, non-biblical meaning assigned to the term "Son of God" by the post-biblical Fathers. Sanday discusses the title "Son of God" and asks the question whether the phrase as used by the New Testament anywhere implies preexistence. Does "Son of God" in the Bible refer exclusively to Jesus after his birth, or could it mean that he had existed as Son before his birth? The question is absolutely critical for the entire Trinitarian problem. Without an eternal Son there is no Trinity. What, then, are the biblical facts about the Son of God?

> Does it, or does it not, imply preexistence? What inference would be drawn from the Gospels? In regard to these there is no doubt that in the great majority of cases the words would be satisfied by a reference to Christ incarnate. All the instances in Matthew, Mark and Luke would come under this head. [Does John ever speak of Jesus as preexistent *Son*?] *That is more debatable. We have to look about somewhat for expressions which are free from ambiguity. Perhaps there are not any.*[18]

The admission that there may in fact be no certain references in John to Jesus as preexistent Son confirms how far later orthodoxy departed from the evidence of Scripture in its

---

[17] *Twelve More New Testament Studies*, 175.

[18] W. Sanday, "Son of God" in *Hastings Dictionary of the Bible*, 4:576, emphasis added.

definition of Jesus. The later dogma about belief in the "eternal Son," a title for which Scripture provides no support,[19] as necessary for salvation, was based, as we have seen, on a misreading of the words of John and the substitution of new meanings for key Johannine terms describing Jesus. The development of Christology might have been very different had exegetes remained within the meaning of Son of God as "the highest Christological designation, Jewish-messianic in origin."[20]

The Wisdom of James Denny

James Denny (1856-1917) was a distinguished theologian of the Scottish Free Church who sensed that there was something unbiblical about the statement that "Jesus is God," though he confessed to being a Trinitarian. In his *Letters to W. Robertson Nicoll*, he stated:

> "Jesus is God" seems to be one of those provocative ways [of describing belief in the Deity of Christ]. It has the same objectionableness in my mind as calling Mary the mother of God...In Greek, and in the first century, you could say "Jesus is God." But the English equivalent of that is not "Jesus is God" (with a capital G), but, I say it as a believer in His true Deity, "Jesus is god" (with a small g — not *a* god, but a being in whom is the nature which belongs to the one God)...A form of proposition which in our idiom suggests inevitably the precise equivalence of Jesus and God does some kind of injustice to the truth.[21]

---

[19] Cp. the observation of Buswell that "we can say with confidence that the Bible has nothing whatever to say about 'begetting' as an eternal relationship between Father and Son" (*A Systematic Theology of the Christian Religion*, Zondervan, 1962, p. 111). But without the doctrine of eternal Sonship the doctrine of the Trinity collapses.

[20] Matthew Black, *Romans, New Century Bible* (Marshall, Morgan and Scott, 1973), 35.

[21] *Letters of Principal James Denny to W. Robertson Nicoll*, 124, 125.

Denny's objection deserves close attention from those who insist that Jesus *is* God. A human being in whom the Deity dwells uniquely is well qualified to be the Savior. This is the Savior whom God has provided.

A Gnostic Tendency in the Traditional Doctrine of the Trinity

The facts of church history suggest that the Gnostic heretics misused the gospel of John: "John was adopted as 'their' gospel and the stress in the Johannine epistles on Jesus come in the flesh [i.e., as a real human person] (1 John 4:2; 2 John 7) must be seen as the reaction to the docetic impression his teaching evidently provoked."[22] A non-fully human Jesus was indeed constructed on the basis of a misunderstanding of John by the Gnostics. John's reaction to this misreading of his Gospel was to label such treatment as very "antichrist" (1 John 4:3; 2 John 7). "It was a misinterpretation of his intention."[23]

But did "orthodoxy" avoid the same trap when it transposed John's language into Greek philosophical terms? Many have complained that the creeds' definition of Jesus as "fully God and fully man" misrepresents what John wrote and overlooks the plain descriptions of the human Jesus given by Matthew, Mark and Luke. It must be significant that teaching about the "eternal Son" relies almost entirely on John's Gospel, even though the Bible dictionary admits that perhaps, even in John, there is no certain text to support a pre-human Sonship for Jesus.

Summary and Conclusion

Jesus' humanity is less than real once it is proposed that he did not come into existence in Mary's womb. The absence of any biblical evidence for Jesus being the *Son of God before his conception* suggests that the widely-held belief in his pre-human existence may not be soundly based in Scripture. We propose that it is based on a misreading of John's Gospel, by overlooking

---

[22] J.A.T. Robinson, *Twelve More New Testament Studies*, 142.

[23] Ibid.

the peculiar Jewish concept of foreordination found there. The fact that nothing is said about preexistence in Matthew, Mark, Luke and Acts (and Peter's epistles) ought to make us question whether John has really given us a picture of Jesus so different by attributing to him a conscious life before his conception. Did John really pose the "Trinitarian problem" which caused such trouble in the early centuries?

Texts in John which have been claimed as evidence for the literal preexistence of Jesus have been misunderstood, because too little attention has been paid to John's and Jesus' Jewish categories of thought. The phenomenon that past tenses do not always mean a reference to past events has been overlooked (John 17:5; cp. 17:22, 24). In John 3:13 Jesus said nothing of an eternal preexistence as "God the Son." He claimed rather to have been uniquely admitted to the divine counsels. He had not literally "ascended to heaven," nor had the Son of God been in heaven from eternity. He was destined to go to the Father, fulfilling Daniel's vision of the Son of Man (John 6:62). John 13:3, 16:28 and 20:17 have been mistranslated in the NIV to give the impression that Jesus was going *back* to his Father (see KJV, RSV). His glory had been prepared for him before the world came into existence (John 17:5; cp. Matt 6:1: future rewards are already secure), and he was chosen as God's supreme human representative, the Messiah, long before Abraham (John 8:58). It was as the *human Son of Man* that he had "preexisted" in the divine decree. Jesus is convinced that he must carry out God's predetermined plan: "Was it not necessary for the Christ to suffer?...All things written about me in the law of Moses, the prophets and the Psalms *must be fulfilled*" (Luke 24:26, 44).

The notion of real existence before conception led eventually to the fearful complexity and conflicts over the nature of Jesus which have never been resolved. Arguments were silenced by the imposition of a dogmatic Christology (at Nicea and Chalcedon), which dictated an official solution to the problem. The solution, however, attempts to settle the issue largely on the basis of John's very Jewish theology which was easily and tragically misunderstood by Greeks. The casualties in the dispute over the nature of God and Jesus were the cardinal biblical truths

about the unipersonal God and the real humanity of Jesus.[24]
Since the way to eternal life begins with a proper appreciation of
the Father as the only true God, and Jesus as Messiah (John
17:3), Bible readers should be alerted to the possible serious
damage done to the faith when philosophically-minded Greeks
read the Gospel of John without a sound basis in the Old
Testament, and with too little regard for the Christology of
Matthew, Mark, Luke and Acts, which was too hastily dismissed
as "primitive." In this connection the words of Karl Rahner are
an encouragement to return to the earliest stratum of Christology.
He confesses that:

> We often find traditional Christology difficult to
> understand...and so have questions to put to its source,
> the Scriptures. For example, let us take so central an
> assertion of the Scriptures as the statement that Jesus is
> the Messiah and as such has become Lord in the course
> of his life, death and resurrection. Is it agreed that this
> assertion has simply been made obsolete by the doctrine
> of the metaphysical Sonship, as we recognize it and
> express it in the Chalcedonian declaration, and that its
> only real interest for us now is historical...? Is the
> Christology of the Acts of the Apostles, which begins
> from below, with the human experience of Jesus, merely
> primitive? Or has it something special to say to us which
> classical Christology does not say with the same
> clarity?[25]

Karl Rahner's analysis of the New Testament use of the
word "God" bears repetition: "In no New Testament text is *theos*
[God] used in such a manner as to identify Jesus with Him who
elsewhere in the New Testament figures as *ho theos*, that is the
Supreme God."[26] "Nowhere in the New Testament is there to be

---

[24] John 17:3; 5:44; Deut. 6:4; Mark 12:29ff. 1 Cor. 8:4-6; Eph. 4:6; 1
Tim. 2:5; Jude 25.

[25] *Theological Investigations*, 1:155ff.

[26] Ibid.

found a text with *ho theos* [God] which has unquestionably to be referred to the Trinitarian God as a whole existing in three Persons."[27]

We suggest that a false distinction has been drawn between a so-called "high" Christology of John and the Christology "from below" of the Synoptics. Both John and the Synoptics present a Jesus who comes not only "from above" (Matthew and Luke by describing Jesus' divine origin in the womb of Mary), but also "from behind," by which Jesus is the culmination of the Old Testament promise that the greater son of David will appear. In fact, all New Testament Christology is Messianic. Each writer contributes, with different emphases, to the one portrait of Jesus as Son of God, *in that Messianic sense*. It is the transition from "Son of God" in the biblical sense to "God the Son" which has proved so devastating to the apostolic presentation of Jesus. Lampe makes the point forcefully that the introduction of the concept of literal preexistence throws into doubt the real humanity of Jesus:

> The Christological concept of the preexistent divine Son reduces the real, social and culturally conditioned personality of Jesus to the metaphysical abstraction "human nature..." Human nature, according to the classical Alexandrine tradition, was enhypostatized in the divine Person of the Son; it became the human nature of a divine personal subject...According to this Christology, the eternal Son assumes a timeless human nature, or makes it timeless by making it his own; it is a human nature which owes nothing essential to geographical circumstances; it corresponds to nothing in the actual concrete world; *Jesus has not, after all, really "come in the flesh."*[28]

A similar warning about the danger of turning Jesus into a being who had an eternal existence before birth comes from Paul van Buren:

27 Ibid., 1:143.
28 *God as Spirit*, 144, emphasis added.

there is no clear indication that the priority [of Jesus] was intended in a temporal sense. We may conclude that for the earliest Church, Jesus was accorded the priority in reality that the Rabbis assigned to the Torah. If one were to make the claim of priority in a temporal sense, one would be claiming that Jesus of Nazareth, born of Mary, had existed with God before the creation of the world. That claim would be worse than unintelligible; it would destroy all coherence in the essential Christian claim that Jesus was truly a human being, that the Word became *flesh*...Jesus of Nazareth began his life, began to exist, at a definite time in history: the Word became *flesh*.[29]

This present volume is prompted by a desire to avoid any such abstract Jesus and to urge a return to the historical Jesus, the promised Messiah of Israel. The reading of John which we suggest allows John's Jesus, however elevated, to be as human as that of the Synoptics.

Finding a preexistent Son in John will explain the disparaging way in which "orthodox" commentators sometimes dismiss Luke's Christology as "popular." The fact may be that Luke is representative of a common New Testament Messianic Christology which does not coincide with what became "orthodox" in post-biblical times. Referring to Luke 1:35, "That holy thing which is being generated...," Strachan says, "This belongs to the milieu where the theological idea of the preexistence of Jesus has given way to a more popular conception of his physical birth."[30] But this is a circular argument. Has Luke really relinquished the idea of Jesus preexisting for a more popular understanding? Instead, it seems that post-apostolic "orthodoxy" developed a point of view which replaced Luke's, and John's as well. The shift was more easily accomplished by working from John's Jewish-Christian

---

[29] *A Theology of Jewish-Christian Reality* (Harper & Row, 1983), 82.

[30] R.H. Strachan, "Holiness" in *Dictionary of the Apostolic Church*, 1:568.

language, and John was then thought to have portrayed a Jesus vastly different from the Synoptic picture. The reestablishment of a Messianic Christology and harmony between all four Gospel writers would do much to reunite believers around the central New Testament affirmation that Jesus is the Christ, the Son of God, herald of the coming Kingdom of God. This, after all, is what John set out to prove, declaring that life is to be found in the Jesus who is Son of God and Messiah (John 20:31; cp. Matt. 16:16). The invitation to believe and obey *that* Jesus remains as modern and as urgent as ever. A return to Jesus, the Messiah, will involve a rediscovery of the Synoptic Gospels and the Gospel about the Kingdom of God, the much-neglected saving message of the historical Jesus and the Apostles. Much contemporary preaching proceeds as if *all* that counts is selected sections or verses of the epistles of Paul and the cross of Jesus.

Some of the arguments advanced in favor of the doctrine of the Trinity are remarkably misleading. In the Bible, it is said, there is one called the Father who is God, one called the Son who is God and one called the Holy Spirit who is God. But we know that there is only one God. Therefore there must be three persons who compose the one God. This is an extraordinary way of presenting the evidence. In fact there is one in the New Testament called the Father who is said to be the One God (*ho theos*) over 1300 times. He is also designated "the only God" (Rom. 16:27; Jude 25), "the one who alone is God" (John 5:44) and "the only true God" (John 17:3). There is one called the Son, Jesus Christ, who is given the title God (*theos*) twice for certain (John 20:28; Heb. 1:8), but is never called *ho theos* (used absolutely), the "only God," "the one who alone is God," or "the only true God."

This data hardly suggests that there are two who are to be ranked equally as God, both being the one God. Add to this the fact that God in the Old Testament is said to be a single individual thousands of times, and it should be clear that Trinitarianism does not do justice to the biblical data. Moreover, the titles "only God," "one who alone is God" "and only true God," applied exclusively to the Father, point to a unique classification for Him as distinct from the Son. A mass of New

Testament texts present Jesus as subordinate to the Father, a fact not easily reconciled with the notion that the Son is coequal with the Father.[31] Paul believed that the Son would be for all time subjected to the Father, after he had handed back the (future) Kingdom to God (1 Cor. 15:28).

If the Trinity were taught in the New Testament, one would expect at least one verse somewhere stating that the one God is "Father, Son and Holy Spirit." Such a statement is absent from the pages of Scripture. When Father, Son and Holy Spirit are placed together in a biblical passage, they are never said to be "the one God" (Matt. 28:19; 2 Cor. 13:14). It is remarkable that greetings at the opening of Paul's epistles are never sent from the Holy Spirit. Nor is the Holy Spirit ever addressed or prayed to.

When Paul, however, defines monotheism as distinct from polytheism, he expressly says that there is one God, *the Father*, and that there is no other God but that one God, the Father (1 Cor. 8:4, 6).[32] That in its simple beauty is the biblical creed. It should lay all argument to rest. The Godhead has not been expanded. God is still the Father alone as in the Hebrew Bible. He is the Lord God of the creed of Jesus. The latter distinctly identifies himself as a "lord" who is not the one Lord God of the *Shema* (Mark 12:35-37). Jesus is the Lord Messiah and thus

---

[31] It is an encouragement to our thesis that the distinguished exegete I. Howard Marshall can write, "*All* New Testament Christology is subordinationist" (book review of Jervell, *The Theology of the Acts of the Apostles*, in *Evangelical Quarterly* 70:1, Jan. 1998, 76).

[32] Symptomatic of confusion over the Godhead is the fact that scholars sometimes inadvertently misquote Paul's own creed. Thus Klaas Runia states: "Paul writes to the Corinthians: 'For there is one God from whom are all things and for whom we exist'" (*An Introduction to the Christian Faith*, Lynx Communications, 1992, 114). But Paul actually wrote: "To us there is one God, *the Father*..." Runia adds that James and the other Apostles "say, with equal emphasis, that *Jesus Christ is also God*" (Ibid., emphasis his). But where did James or Peter say that Jesus is God?

constantly designated "the Lord Jesus Christ [Messiah]."[33] His Messianic title "Lord" is derived from Psalm 110:1. The constant confusion by Trinitarians of the supreme Messianic title "Lord" with "Lord" meaning "Lord God" is the cause of all the difficulty. There is no good reason to blur the clear difference between Lord Messiah (*adoni*) and Lord God (*Yahweh* and *adonai*) (Ps. 110:1, 5).[34] We may still fully acknowledge that Jesus operates on behalf of God. An important point was made by Caird when he referred to the Jewish practice of addressing an agent as though he were the principal:

> [In 2 Esdras 5:43-56]...God's spokesman, the angel Uriel, is questioned by Ezra as though he were both Creator and Judge. Ezra uses the same style of address to Uriel ("my lord, my master") as he uses in direct petition to God. This practice of treating the agent as though he were the principal is of the greatest importance for New Testament Christology.[35]

Many Trinitarians seem content to hold two contradictory propositions at the same time without trying to harmonize them: God is one and yet He is three. This is what the official creeds appear to ask of them. But the Bible requires no such mental feat. Some Trinitarians attempt to escape the charge that belief in three persons, each of whom is God, must involve belief in three Gods. They respond that God and Jesus are not persons in the way in which we customarily use that term. The obvious fact, however, is that every New Testament writer describes Jesus as a being self-consciously different from his Father. There is no mystification about the term Son and no word about "eternal generation." The contradictory proposition embodied in the Trinity is unnecessary, as well as unbiblical. It tends to

---

[33] Luke 2:11; Rom. 16:18; Col. 3:24. Cp. Luke 1:43 and the extra-canonical book Psalms of Solomon 17:32; 18:7.

[34] In the Greek of the LXX all three words appear as *kurios*.

[35] G.B. Caird, *The Language and Imagery of the Bible* (Philadelphia: Westminster Press, 1980), 181.

undermine both the cardinal biblical tenet that God is one and the foundation of all truth that Jesus is the Messiah, Son of God and son of David (Matt. 16:16; 2 Sam. 7:14; Heb. 1:5).

Christians are entitled to know what ideas have shaped the belief system which has been presented to them as the faith. Many are unaware of the crypto-Gnostic element which has been handed down to us in Trinitarian Christology. Throughout his ministry Paul struggled to fend off the menace of "knowledge [*gnosis*] falsely so called" (1 Tim. 6:20). In the post-apostolic Church the danger of Gnostic philosophy invading the faith was not averted. Though the Church claimed to be rejecting the blatant forms of Gnosticism, it failed to prevent a more subtle Gnostic influence from corrupting the original teaching about God and Christ. The attempt to proclaim the Deity of Jesus led to untold complexity over his "two natures" and a borrowing of pagan concepts which find no place in the Scriptures. The remark of a distinguished expert on early Gnosticism deserves the widest hearing:

> The early Christian Fathers, foremost Irenaeus and Tertullian, strove hard to find forms which make intelligible in a non-gnostic sense the prevailing division of the one Jesus Christ. Strictly speaking they did not succeed. Already Harnack was forced to say: "Who can maintain that the Church ever overcame the gnostic doctrine of the two natures or the Valentinian docetism?" Even the later councils of the Church which discussed the Christological problems in complicated, and nowadays hardly intelligible, definitions did not manage to do this; *the unity of the Church foundered precisely on this*...It has often been forgotten that gnostic theologians saw Christ as "consubstantial" with the Father, before ecclesiastical theology established this as a principle, in order to preserve his full divinity.[36]

---

[36] Kurt Rudolph, *Gnosis: The Nature and History of Gnosticism* (Harper & Row, 1983), 372, emphasis added.

If it be granted that Christians have as their aim to recognize and serve the Christ of Scripture and God, his Father, it must follow that they will want to possess the most accurate possible understanding of who that Christ is. Such understanding will confine itself to the portrayal of Jesus provided by the Christian documents. It is questionable whether traditional, orthodox definitions of Jesus pay close enough attention to the proportions of the biblical material. John's prologue has been so elevated in importance for the definition of Jesus that all the other evidence has had to bow to what was perceived as being the truth of that passage. Paul's famous Christological statement in Philippians 2 has likewise been taken as the norm for all his other references to Jesus, though many do not believe that Paul says anything in that text about a preexistent person. Rather, he exhorts the believers to imitate the self-sacrificing lifestyle of the Messiah Jesus, who, after all, is the subject of Paul's statement (Phil. 2:5).[37]

If full weight is given to the evidence of the Synoptics and Acts and the non-Pauline epistles, it becomes clear that their combined testimony is to Jesus as *Messiah*, not God in the

---

[37] Cp. A.H. McNeile's observation that "Many have doubted whether Paul would have appealed in such a context to a mystery so transcendent." In Phil. 2 Paul is "begging the Philippians to cease from dissensions and to act with humility towards each other. In 2 Cor. 8:9 he is exhorting his readers to be liberal in almsgiving. It is asked whether it would be quite natural for him to enforce these two simple moral lessons by incidental references (and the only reference he ever makes) to the vast problem of the mode of the incarnation. And it is thought by many that his homely appeals would have more effect if he pointed to the inspiring example of Christ's humility and self-sacrifice in his human life, as in 2 Cor. 10:1: 'I exhort you by the meekness and forbearance of Christ'" (*New Testament Teaching in the Light of St. Paul's*, Cambridge University Press, 1923, 65). The case for Phil. 2:5ff. being a description of the human Jesus may be examined in articles by C.H. Talbert, "The Problem of Preexistence in Philippians 2:6-11," *Journal of Biblical Literature* 86 (1967): 141-153; J. Murphy O'Connor, "Christological Anthropology in Phil. 2:6-11," *Revue Biblique* (1976): 26-50; G. Howard, "Philippians 2:6-11 and the Human Christ," *Catholic Biblical Quarterly* 40 (1978): 368-387.

Chalcedonian sense. The same may be argued for John. John's own summary statement about the purpose of his Gospel, that Jesus is to be believed in as Messiah (John 20:31), points to the fact that he is at one with his fellow witnesses to the faith. Even Hebrews 1:10, which of all texts might appear to ascribe the Genesis creation to Jesus, in fact does not do so.[38] The writer expressly says that it is about the "inhabited earth of the *future*" (Heb. 2:5) that he has been speaking; and it was God who rested at creation (Heb. 4:4), just as, according to Jesus, it was God who "made them male and female" (Mark 10:6; cp. 13:19). If with the NASV we read "when He again brings the firstborn into the world" (Heb. 1:6), it is clear that the author intends us to understand a reference to Jesus' function as founder of the coming world of the Kingdom (cp. Isa. 51:16, NASV). Occasional "difficult verses" must not override the plain evidence distributed throughout Scripture.

---

[38] For a detailed examination of Heb. 1:10, F.F. Bruce's analysis in the *New International Commentary* on Hebrews (Eerdmans, 1964) is essential. The writer to the Hebrews cites here a LXX text which differs significantly from the Masoretic Hebrew text.

XIV. EPILOGUE: BELIEVING THE WORDS OF JESUS

"The Lord our God is one Lord." — *Jesus Christ*

It is a most significant fact, often overlooked, that Jesus equates genuine faith with belief in his *sayings and words*. "He who hears my message and believes Him who sent me has life in the coming age" (John 5:24). This insistence on the message and teaching of Jesus is strongly emphasized by the Synoptics also, and it cautions us against divorcing Jesus from his own words and thus building for ourselves an image of another Jesus. John reports Jesus as saying, "He who rejects me and my sayings...will be judged by those very sayings" (John 12:48). "Believing Moses" is the same as "believing his writings" (John 5:46, 47), and in the same context "believing Jesus" is equivalent to believing *his words* (John 5:47). This seems to lay to rest any question about the importance of "doctrine" as compared with "practice," "for anyone who...does not remain in the teaching of Jesus does not have God" (2 John 9).[1] Jesus' own creed is central to all he said and did. But does our tradition faithfully reflect that "Jewish" creed? According to the Savior it is not possible to believe him if we are not prepared to believe Moses (John 5:46, 47). Failure to grasp the creed of Israel and what Moses said about the coming Messiah — notably in

---

[1] We are puzzled that Dr. James Kennedy seems to miss the enormous emphasis placed on the teachings of Jesus. He writes, "Many people today think that the essence of Christianity is Jesus' teaching, but that is not so...Christianity centers not in the teachings of Jesus, but in the person of Jesus as Incarnate God who came into the world to take upon Himself our guilt and die in our place" ("How I know Jesus is God," *Truths that Transform*, 11th Nov., 1989).

Deuteronomy 18:15-18 — will lead to disastrous results when it comes to believing Christ.

Christians are evidently supposed to believe everything that Jesus said, whether it be exhortation to Christian conduct or sayings relative to his own person. The two are inseparable in the Bible, so that "doctrine" may not be set in opposition to matters of conduct. A relationship with Jesus can be built only through his word. Christ's words are the vehicle of his self-impartation. By them the "atmosphere" and mind of the Spirit is transferred to the believer. It may be that Christians are breathing the contaminated air of Greek philosophy and would witness a striking improvement in their spiritual health if they tried breathing the pure atmosphere of the Hebrew biblical thought-world.

Successful Christianity depends on the Savior's instruction that "you abide in me and my words abide in you" (John 15:7; cp. 2 John 9). All false belief is dangerous, because it is built on a rejection of what Jesus said. No apology need be made, therefore, for trying to find out what, in fact, according to John and the other Gospels, Jesus did say about himself and his relationship to God. Throughout all the Gospels belief in Jesus is synonymous with belief in *what Jesus said* as well as in what he did and does — and indeed will do at his return in power and glory to establish his Kingdom on the earth. It matters very much, therefore, what a Christian understands and believes. Current opinion often tells us that "doctrine" divides and should be avoided. The very opposite is true: doctrine based on the witness of Jesus' words is the one hope for unity in the present chaotic division in the churches. The Church appears to have overlooked the core of Jesus' teaching: that repentance and forgiveness depend on the convert's intelligent reception of the Messiah's own Gospel about the Kingdom of God (Mark 4:11, 12; Luke 8:12).

Mark 12:28ff. presents Jesus as affirming his own belief in the unitary monotheism of the Jews. It is to that passage of Scripture that all discussion of the Godhead should refer. John's "Jewish" monotheism is never in doubt. The Father is still the "only true God" (John 17:3), "the one who alone is God" (John

5:44), and since Jesus is evidently a different person from the Father, Jesus is not God. He is the fully authorized agent of God, the ideal King of Israel for whom the Old Testament yearned. Jesus perfectly expresses the character of his Father and relays His message of the Kingdom (Luke 4:43). Thus it may be said that "the fullness of Deity dwells in Jesus" (Col. 2:9).[2] But this does not mean that he is himself God.

John's fully human Jesus is not only the Jesus presented by canonical Scripture, but also a more attractive model for imitation than some traditional versions of Jesus. One who is really God (in disguise?) would seem to be so far exalted above us that we would have no chance of living as he did. But John's Jesus, though he is unique by virtue of the spirit given to him "without measure" (John 3:34), does not distance himself from the disciples, as though they would be incapable of doing what he did. He constantly promises them that "just as" he has been sent into the world, they will be "sent into the world" to perform as great or even greater works than he (John 17:18; 14:12). And "just as" he is one with the Father, so also the disciples are to be (John 17:11, 21). Just as he was sent to announce the Kingdom of God (Luke 4:43), so are they.

The object of this book, therefore, has been to propose ways of believing more accurately what Jesus believed about God and himself and thus bringing our own doctrines into line with his. "The one who abides in the teaching [of Christ] has both the Father and the Son" (2 John 9). Every word spoken by the Messiah is precious, for the words that he speaks carry "spirit and life" (John 6:63). They are the only words, in fact, which can guide us to "life in the Coming Age," the life of the Kingdom of God. John does not differ in his understanding from the Synoptics by omitting frequent use of the term "Kingdom of God." John's Jesus speaks of the Kingdom as "everlasting life," properly rendered according to its Hebrew meaning, "life in the Coming Age." John's vocabulary, in his account both of the

---

2 Very similar language about the fullness of God dwelling in Christians is found in Eph. 3:19.

identity of Jesus and his message, must be translated back into its "Hebrew" original so that an unvarnished picture of Jesus may be recovered from beneath any distorting layers of tradition which may obscure him. It is with this in mind that we urge a reconsideration of some of the post-biblical ways of understanding John which hamper an intelligent reading of the Bible and obstruct faith in Jesus and obedience to what he believed and taught.

The recovery of belief in Jesus as the Messiah will dispel the fog of confusion which has enveloped the Gospel as it was proclaimed by Jesus. At present much contemporary evangelism proceeds as though there was no Gospel preaching until Jesus died. A glance at the Synoptics reveals this to be untrue. Jesus announced the Gospel *about the Kingdom* long before he made any reference to his death and resurrection.[3] It is misleading to build a theological system on certain texts in Paul's epistles without first taking into account the Hebrew Bible and the Synoptic accounts of the Gospel as it came from the lips of Jesus.

Loss of clear understanding about who Jesus is has been responsible for an entrenched theological tradition that Jesus somehow resented the title "Messiah" and that the New Testament struggles to replace Messianism with categories more congenial to Gentile converts. The doctrine of the Trinity is an unfortunate diversion which replaces the biblical focus on the Messiah and his coming Kingdom with questions of metaphysics and "relations" within the Godhead. Christians have for too long been looking in the wrong direction: backwards towards the descent from heaven of a so-called "eternal Son" instead of forward to the arrival of the Messiah in the glory of his Kingdom.

It is no longer sufficient to claim the simple equation "Jesus = God" as a valid reflection of the New Testament. Jesus is

---

[3] See for example Mark 1:14, 15; Luke 4:43; Luke 18:31-34.

nowhere called *ho theos*.[4] It seems quite amazing to us that there is no single case in Scripture of the word "God," in thousands of references to the supreme Creator, which can be shown to mean "the Triune God." If "God" nowhere carries the meaning "God in three persons," the case for the Trinity collapses. The evidence strongly suggests that the Triune God is foreign to the biblical revelation. Intelligent Bible study must search for a revised Christology which allows for the obvious and persistent subordination of Jesus to the One God. The category of Messiah, the supremely elevated divine agent of God, will be found adequate to account for everything the New Testament has to say about Jesus. Religious service as described by the Greek word *latreuo* is directed in its 21 occurrences to God the Father, while homage is paid to the Messiah as the agent of the One God.

A professor of theology remarked in a course on Christology that "our tradition dances best to a docetic tune."[5] In the interests of recovering the full humanity of Jesus, the glory of his Messiahship and the unmatched majesty of the One God, his Father, we propose that it should dance once again to a Hebrew, biblical melody. No one, perhaps, orchestrates that melody better than John.

---

[4] John 20:28 and Heb. 1:8 are apparent exceptions only. The definite article is used in these verses with a vocative meaning. In neither verse is Jesus addressed as God in the absolute sense. Cp. C.F.D. Moule, *An Idiom Book of New Testament Greek*, 116, 117.

[5] D.M. Scholer, Northern Baptist Seminary, winter quarter, 1986.

BIBLIOGRAPHY

Abbot, E.A. *Johannine Grammar*. London: A. & C. Black, 1906.

Addis, W.E. *Christianity and the Roman Empire*. New York: W.W. Norton, 1967.

Alford, Henry. *Greek New Testament*. London: Rivingtons andDeighton, Bell & Co., 1861.

Baillie, Donald. *God Was in Christ*. London: Faber, 1961.

Bainton, R.H. *Hunted Heretic: The Life and Death of Michael Servetus*. Beacon Press, 1953.

Barrett, C.K. *Essays on John*. London: SPCK, 1982.

Barrett, C.K. *The Gospel According to St. John*. London: SPCK, 1972.

Baur, F.C. *Church History of the First Three Centuries*. London: Williams and Norgate's, 1878.

Beasley-Murray, G.R. *John, Word Biblical Commentary*. Waco, TX: Word Books, 1987.

Beisner, E. Calvin. *God in Three Persons*. Tyndale House Publishers, 1984.

Bernard, J.H. *St. John, International Critical Commentary*. Edinburgh: T. & T. Clark, 1948.

Berkhof, Hendrikus. *Christian Faith*. Grand Rapids: Eerdmans, 1979.

Bevan, R.J.W. *Steps to Christian Understanding*. Oxford University Press, 1958.

Black, Matthew. *Romans, New Century Bible*. Marshall, Morgan & Scott, 1973.

Boettner, Loraine. *Studies in Theology*. Grand Rapids: Eerdmans, 1957.

Borgen, P. "God's Agent in the Fourth Gospel," in *Religions in Antiquity: Essays in Memory of E.R. Goodenough*. Ed. J. Neusner. Leiden, 1968.

Boyd, Gregory. *Oneness Pentecostals and the Trinity*. Baker Book House, 1995.

Brown, Harold. *Heresies*. Doubleday, 1984.

Brown, Raymond. *The Birth of the Messiah*. London: Geoffrey Chapman, 1977.

Brown, Raymond. *The Gospel According to John, Anchor Bible*. New York: Doubleday, 1966.

Brown, Raymond. *Jesus, God and Man*. New York: Macmillan, 1967.

Bruce, F.F. *The Epistle to the Hebrews, New International Commentary on the New Testament*. Grand Rapids: Eerdmans, 1964

Bruce, F.F. *Romans, Tyndale New Testament Commentaries*. Grand Rapids: Eerdmans, 1985.

Brunner, Emil. *Christian Doctrine of God, Dogmatics*. Philadelphia: Westminster Press, 1950.

Buswell, J.O. *A Systematic Theology of the Christian Religion*. Zondervan, 1962.

Buzzard, Anthony. *The Coming Kingdom of the Messiah: A Solution to the Riddle of the New Testament*. Restoration Fellowship, 1988.

Buzzard, Anthony. *Our Fathers Who Aren't in Heaven: The Forgotten Christianity of Jesus the Jew*. Restoration Fellowship, 1995.

Cadoux, C.J. *A Pilgrim's Further Progress: Dialogues on Christian Teaching*. Blackwell, 1943.

Caird, G.B. *The Language and Imagery of the Bible*. Philadelphia: Westminster Press, 1980.

Carey, George. *God Incarnate: Meeting the Contemporary Challenges to a Classic Christian Doctrine*. InterVarsity Press, 1977.

Cave, Sydney. *The Doctrine of the Person of Christ*. Duckworth, 1925.

Clarke, Adam. *Clarke's Commentary*. New York: T. Mason and G. Lane, 1837.

Colman, Henry. *Valedictory*. n.p., 1820.

Constable, H. *Hades or the Intermediate State*. n.p., 1893.

Cupitt, Don. *The Debate About Christ*. London: SCM Press, 1979.

Dana and Mantey. *A Manual Grammar of the Greek New Testament*. New York: Macmillan, 1955.

Denny, James. *Letters of Principal James Denny to W. Robertson Nicoll*. London: Hodder and Stoughton, 1920.

Dewick, E.C. *Primitive Christian Eschatology, The Hulsean Prize Essay for 1908*. Cambridge University Press, 1912.

Dosker, H.E. *The Dutch Anabaptists*. Judson Press, 1921.

Dunn, James. *Christology in the Making*. Philadelphia: Westminster Press, 1980.

Dunn, James. *Romans, Word Biblical Commentary*. Dallas: Word Books, 1988.

Ehrman, Bart. *The Orthodox Corruption of Scripture*. Oxford University Press, 1993.

Eliot, W.G. *Discourses on the Doctrines of Christianity*. Boston: American Unitarian Society, 1886.

Erickson, M.J., ed. *Readings in Christian Theology*. Baker Book House, 1967.

Fackré, Gabriel. *The Christian Story*. Grand Rapids: Eerdmans, 1978.

Filson, F. *The New Testament Against Its Environment*. London: SCM Press, 1950.

Flesseman, Ellen. *A Faith for Today*. Transl. J.E. Steely. Mercer University Press, 1980.

Fortman, Edmund J. *The Triune God*. Baker Book House, 1972.

Friedmann, Robert. *The Theology of Anabaptism*. Herald Press, 1973.

Gesenius, H.F.W. *Gesenius' Hebrew Grammar*. Ed. E. Kautzsch. Oxford: Clarendon Press, 1910.

Gilbert, G.H. *The Revelation of Jesus, A Study of the Primary Sources of Christianity*. New York: Macmillan Co., 1899.

Gillet, Lev. *Communion in the Messiah: Studies in the Relationship between Judaism and Christianity*. Lutterworth Press, 1968.

Gore, Charles. *Belief in Christ*. London: John Murray, 1923.

Goudge, H.L. "The Calling of the Jews" in the collected essays on *Judaism and Christianity*. Shears and Sons, 1939.

Green, F.W. *Essays on the Trinity and the Incarnation*. Longmans, Green & Co., 1928.

Grensted, L.W. *The Person of Christ*. London: Nisbet and Co. Ltd., 1933.

Grillmeier, Aloys. *Christ in Christian Tradition*. Atlanta: John Knox Press, 1975.

Hanson, A.T. *Grace and Truth: A Study in the Doctrine of the Incarnation*. London: SPCK, 1975.

Harnack, Adolf. *History of Dogma*. Trans. Neil Buchanan. London: Williams and Norgate. 7 vols. 1895-1900.

Harnack, Adolf. *What Is Christianity?* Trans. T.B. Saunders. Gloucester, MA: Peter Smith, 1978.

Harrison, Everett F. *Romans, Expositor's Bible Commentary*. Grand Rapids: Zondervan, 1976.

Hart, Thomas. *To Know and Follow Jesus*. Paulist Press, 1984.

Harvey, A.E. *Jesus and the Constraints of History*. Philadelphia: Westminster Press, 1982.

Hay, David. *Glory at the Right Hand: Psalm 110 in Early Christianity*. Nashville: Abingdon, 1973.

Heer, Frederich. *God's First Love*. Weidenfeld and Nicolson, 1970.

Hertz, J.H. *Pentateuch and Haftorahs*. London: Soncino Press, 1960.

Hick, John, ed. *The Myth of God Incarnate*. London: SCM Press, 1977.

Hill, Christopher. *Milton and the English Revolution*. New York: Viking Press, 1977.

Hillar, Marian. *The Case of Michael Servetus (1511-1553) — The Turning Point in the Struggle for Freedom of Conscience*. Edwin Mellen Press, 1997.

Hodgson, Leonard. *Christian Faith and Practice, Seven Lectures*. Oxford: Blackwell, 1952.

Hodgson, Leonard. *The Doctrine of the Trinity*. Nisbet, 1943.

Humphreys, A.E. *The Epistles to Timothy & Titus, Cambridge Bible for Schools and Colleges*. Cambridge University Press, 1895.

Inge, W.R. *A Pacifist in Trouble*. London: Putnam, 1939.

Jervell, Jacob. *Jesus in the Gospel of John*. Minneapolis: Augsburg, 1984.

Johnson, Paul. *A History of Christianity*. New York: Atheneum, 1976.

Knight, G.A.T. *Law and Grace*. Philadelphia: Westminster Press, 1962.

Knox, John. *The Humanity and Divinity of Jesus*. Cambridge University Press, 1967.

Kuschel, Karl-Josef. *Born Before All Time? The Dispute over Christ's Origin*. Transl. John Bowden. New York: Crossroad, 1992.

Lampe, Geoffrey. *God as Spirit*. London: SCM Press, 1977.

Lamson, Alvan. *The Church of the First Three Centuries*. Boston: Houghton, Osgood & Co., 1880.

Lapide, Pinchas. *Jewish Monotheism and Christian Trinitarian Doctrine*. Philadelphia: Fortress Press, 1981.

Lindbeck, George. *The Nature of Doctrine and Religion: Theology in a Postliberal Age*. Philadelphia: Westminster Press, 1984.

Lockyer, Herbert. *All the Divine Names and Titles in the Bible*. Zondervan, 1975.

Loofs, Friedrich. *Leitfaden zum Studium der Dogmengeschichte* (1890). Halle-Saale: Max Niemeyer Verlag, 1951.

Lyonnet, S. "L'Annonciation et la Mariologie Biblique," in *Maria in Sacra Scriptura*. Acta Congressus Mariologici-Mariani in Republica Dominicana anno 1965 Celebrati. Rome: Pontificia Academia Mariana Internationalis, 1967.

Mackey, James. *The Christian Experience of God as Trinity*. London: SCM Press, 1983.

MacKinnon, James. *The Historic Jesus*. Longmans, Green and Co., 1931.

Marshall, I. Howard. *Acts, Tyndale New Testament Commentaries*. Grand Rapids: Eerdmans, 1980.

Mattison, M.M. *The Making of a Tradition*. Ministry School Publications, 1991.

Metzger, B.M. *A Textual Commentary on the Greek New Testament*. United Bible Society, 1971.

Meyer, H.A.W. *Commentary on the New Testament: Gospel of John*. New York: Funk & Wagnalls, 1884.

McLachlan, H.J. *Socinianism in Seventeenth-Century England*. Oxford University Press, 1951.

McNeile, A.H. *New Testament Teaching in the Light of St. Paul's*. Cambridge University Press, 1923.

Milton, John. *Treatise on Christian Doctrine*. Reprint. London: British and Foreign Unitarian Association, 1908.

Morey, Robert. *The Trinity: Evidence and Issues*. World Publishing, 1996.

Morgridge, Charles. *The True Believer's Defence Against Charges Preferred by Trinitarians for Not Believing in the Deity of Christ*. Boston: B. Greene, 1837.

Morris, Leon. *The Gospel According to John, New International Commentary on the New Testament*. Grand Rapids: Eerdmans, 1971.

Mosheim, J. *Institutes of Ecclesiastical History*. New York: Harper, 1839.

Moule, C.F.D. *An Idiom Book of New Testament Greek*. Cambridge University Press, 1953.

Moule, H.C.G. *Romans, Cambridge Bible for Schools and Colleges*. Cambridge University Press, 1918.

Moulton, J.H., ed. *Grammar of New Testament Greek*. T&T Clark, 1963.

Mounce, R.H. *The Book of Revelation*. Marshall, Morgan and Scott, 1977.

Mowinckel, S. *He That Cometh*. Transl. G.W. Anderson. Nashville: Abingdon, 1954.

Murray, J.O.F. *Jesus According to St. John*. London: Longmans, Green, 1936.

Neusner, J., ed. *Religions in Antiquity: Essays in Memory of E.R. Goodenough*. Leiden, 1968.

Norton, Andrews, ed. *General Repository and Review*. Cambridge, MA: William Hilliard, 1813.

Ohlig, Karl-Heinz. *Ein Gott in drei Personen? Vom Vater Jesu zum "Mysterium" der Trinität*. Mainz: Matthias Grünewald-Verlag, 1999.

Olyott, Stuart. *The Three Are One.* Evangelical Press, 1979.

Ottley, C. *The Doctrine of the Incarnation.* Methuen and Co., 1896.

Paine, L.L. *A Critical History of the Evolution of Trinitarianism.*
Boston and New York: Houghton Mifflin and Co., 1902.

Pastor, Adam. *Underscheit tusschen rechte und falsche leer.*
Bibliotheca Reformatoria Nederlandica.

Pittenger, Norman. *The Word Incarnate.* Nisbet, 1959.

Plummer, Alfred. *Gospel According to S. Luke, International Critical
Commentary.* Edinburgh: T & T Clark, 1913.

Plummer, Alfred. *Gospel of John, Cambridge Bible for Schools and
Colleges.* Cambridge University Press, 1882.

Priestley, Joseph. *History of the Corruptions of Christianity.* J. & J.W.
Prentiss, 1838.

Purves, G.T. *The Testimony of Justin Martyr to Early Christianity.*
New York: Randolph & Co., 1889.

Quick, Oliver. *Doctrines of the Creed.* Nisbet, 1938.

The Racovian Catechism. Transl. T. Rees. London: Longman, Hurst,
Rees, Orme and Brown, 1818.

Rahner, Karl. *Theological Investigations.* Baltimore: Helicon Press,
1963.

Reese, Alexander. *The Approaching Advent of Christ.* Grand Rapids:
International Publications, rep. 1975.

Richardson, Alan. *Introduction to the Theology of the New Testament.*
London: SCM Press, 1958.

Robinson, J.A.T. *The Human Face of God.* London: SCM Press, 1973.

Robinson, J.A.T. *Twelve More New Testament Studies.* London: SCM
Press, 1984.

Rogers, J.B. and Baird, F.E. Introduction to Philosophy. San Francisco:
Harper & Row, 1981.

Rubenstein, R.E. *When Jesus Became God: The Struggle to Define
Christianity during the Last Days of Rome.* Harcourt, 1999.

Rudolph, Kurt. *Gnosis: The Nature and History of Gnosticism.* Harper
& Row, 1983.

Runia, Klaas. *An Introduction to the Christian Faith.* Lynx
Communications, 1992.

Runia, Klaas. *The Present-Day Christological Debate.* InterVarsity
Press, 1984.

Sanford, C.B. *The Religious Life of Thomas Jefferson.* University Press
of Virginia, 1987.

Schaff, Philip. *History of the Christian Church.* Grand Rapids:
Eerdmans, 1907- 1910.

Schillebeeckx, Edward. *Christ.* London: SCM Press, 1980.

Schonfield, Hugh. *The Politics of God.* London: Hutchinson, 1970.

Schurer, Emil. *The History of the Jewish People in the Age of Jesus Christ.* T&T Clark, 1979.

Schweitzer, Albert. *Paul and His Interpreters.* London, 1912.

Scott, E.F. *The Fourth Gospel.* T & T Clark, 1926.

Selwyn, E.G. *First Epistle of St. Peter.* Baker Book House, 1983.

Simon, Morris. *The Soncino Chumash.* London: Soncino Press, 1947.

Snaith, Norman. *The Distinctive Ideas of the Old Testament.* London: Epworth Press, 1944.

Stott, John. *The Authentic Jesus.* Marshall, Morgan and Scott, 1985.

Sumner, Robert. *Jesus Christ Is God.* Biblical Evangelism Press, 1983.

Tasker, R.V.G. *John, Tyndale New Testament Commentaries.* Grand Rapids: Eerdmans, 1983.

Temple, William. *Foundations.* London: Macmillan & Co., 1913.

Torrey, R.A. *The Holy Spirit.* Fleming Revell Co., 1977.

Turner, Nigel. *Grammatical Insights into the New Testament.* Edinburgh: T&T Clark, 1965.

Van Buren, Paul. *A Theology of Jewish-Christian Reality.* Harper & Row, 1983.

Vaucher, Alfred. *Le Problème de l'Immortalité.* n.p., 1957.

Wainright, Arthur. *The Trinity in the New Testament.* London: SPCK, 1962.

Walvoord, John F. and Zuck, Roy B., eds. *The Bible Knowledge Commentary.* Victor Books, 1987.

Watson, David. *Christian Myth and Spiritual Reality.* London: Victor Gollanz, 1967.

Wendt, H.H. *The Teaching of Jesus.* Edinburgh: T&T Clark, 1892.

Wendt, Hans. *System der Christlichen Lehre.* Göttingen: Vandenhoeck und Ruprecht, 1907.

Wenham, G.J. *Genesis 1-15, Word Biblical Commentary.* Waco, TX: Word Books, 1987.

Werner, Martin. *Formation of Christian Dogma: An Historical Study of Its Problems.* A & C Black, 1957.

Westcott, B.F. *The Gospel of John.* Grand Rapids: Eerdmans, 1981.

Wiles, Maurice. *The Remaking of Christian Doctrine.* London: SCM Press, 1974.

Williams, G.H. *The Radical Reformation.* Philadelphia: Westminster Press, 1962.

Wilson, Ian. *Jesus: The Evidence.* Harper & Row, 1984.

Wilson, John. *Concessions of Trinitarians.* Boston: Munroe & Co, 1845.

Wilson, John. *Unitarian Principles Confirmed by Trinitarian Testimonies.* Boston: American Unitarian Association, 1848.

Wright, C.J. *Jesus: The Revelation of God.* Book 3 of *The Mission and Message of Jesus.* New York: E.P. Dutton and Co., 1938.

Wuest, Kenneth. *Great Truths to Live By.* Grand Rapids: Eerdmans, 1952.

Yates, James. *Vindication of Unitarianism.* Boston: Wells and Lilly, 1816.

Zweig, Stefan. *The Right to Heresy.* Beacon Press, 1951.

SCRIPTURE INDEX

Luke 1:4 — 185
Luke 1:17 — 228, 238
Luke 1:31, 32 — 70
Luke 1:31, 35 — 189
Luke 1:35 — xiii, 60, 70, 72, 76, 163, 228, 235, 277, 278, 303, 312, 321, 322, 331
Luke 2:11 — 53, 56, 89, 179
Luke 2:11, 26 — 276
Luke 2:14 — 305
Luke 2:52 — 82
Luke 4:43 — 32, 66, 202, 204, 341
Luke 6:35 — 71
Luke 8:12 — 340
Luke 9:20 — 63
Luke 11:20 — 229
Luke 12:28 — 169
Luke 20:42 — 57
Luke 21:14, 15 — 232
Luke 21:15 — 232
Luke 22:20 — 110
Luke 23:50-52 — 67
Luke 24:21 — 64
Luke 24:26, 44 — 328
Luke 24:49 — 229

John
John 1:1 — 128, 172, 245, 246, 249, 260, 292
John 1:1ff. — **174–78, 190–200, 283–88**
John 1:1, 14 — 309
John 1:1-3 — 129
John 1:1-4 — 182, 183
John 1:6 — 202
John 1:9 — 204
John 1:9-14 — 132
John 1:14 — 129, 172, 259, 260, 287
John 1:14, 18 — 132

John 1:15 — 204
John 1:15, 30 — 205
John 1:18 — 206, 207, 260, 292
John 1:39 — 194
John 1:45 — 47
John 1:49 — 63, 276
John 3:2 — 202
John 3:11 — 206
John 3:13 — **205–10**, 328
John 3:14 — 208
John 3:34 — 236, 341
John 3:35 — 214
John 4:6 — 82
John 4:22 — 161
John 4:22, 23 — 17
John 4:25 — 219
John 4:26 — 219, 220
John 4:40 — 194
John 4:49 — 222
John 5:18 — 42, 44, 290, 323
John 5:19 — 44
John 5:24 — 339
John 5:27 — 214
John 5:28, 29 — 208
John 5:38 — 132
John 5:44 — 40, 41, 45, 85, 126, 133, 174, 212, 220, 284, 325, 332, 341
John 5:45 — 41
John 5:46, 47 — 339
John 6:15 — 66
John 6:20 — 218
John 6:27 — 41
John 6:33, 38, 50, 51, 58 — 204
John 6:62 — 166, **205–10**, 213, 328
John 6:63 — 194, 237, 341
John 7:1-5 — 59
John 7:18 — 41
John 7:37 — 110
John 8:24 — 219

AUTHOR INDEX

SUBJECT INDEX

Abraham, 218–23
Adam, 81, 102, 311
address, forms of, 60, 63–65, 78–
   79, 88–89, 176–77, 220,
   275–76, 289, 323–26
adonai (Lord God), 23n, 30, 48–
   57, 324, 334
adoni (lord Messiah), 48–57,
   104, 179, 324, 334
adoptionist Christology, 187, 242
Alogi, 242–43
Anabaptists, 128, 183, 188–89,
   217, 248–49, 259
angels
   as agents of God, 48, 75, 108–
      9, 140, 184, 227, 230
   Gabriel, 70, 73, 159
   Michael, 76, 78n
   preexistence and, 67, 76, 158,
      171, 173
   titles of, 42, 54, 76, 88n, 89,
      166, 334
   Uriel, 334
anhypostasis, 73, 260
   See also hypostasis;
      impersonal humanity
Apocrypha, 198
Apollinarianism, 255n, 256
Apostles' Creed, 30
Arian Christology, 149, 164, 168
   See also preexistence
Athanasian Creed, 30, 128, 134,
   177, 250, 297

Athanasius, 134, 151, 263
atonement, 263, 288–89, 299–
   300
Augustine, 10, 38–39, 134, 170,
   320

baptism language, 235–36
belief. *See* faith
benediction language, 236
Bible
   authentic faith source, 14, 30–
      32, 112, 115–20, 127–28,
      158, 294, 309
   errors and alterations
      additions, spurious, 235, 303
      Jesus equated with God, 38–
         39, 47–57, 83, 139–40,
         303–4, 319–20
      Jesus' origin, 168n, 174n,
         277–79
      in secondary sources, 49,
         53–54, 107n, 280n
      spirit, meaning of, 226
      through non-Jewish modes
         of thought, 116, 192–93,
         198 (*See also* Greek
         thought patterns)
   See also Bible translations;
      disputed Bible passages;
      language issues; *separate*
      Scripture index

Binitarianism, 7, 15, 21, 57, 61,
    138, 171, 316, 320
blasphemy, 36, 43–46, 152, 250,
    290–91, 323
    See also coequality of the Son
Buzzard, Anthony, 250n, 317n

Calvin, John, 143, 154–58, 178n,
    234, 248, 290
Chalcedon, Council of, 80, 86,
    120–21, 128–30, 149, 266,
    294, 299, 310
Christ. *See* Jesus
Christologies
    adoptionist, 187, 242
    Arian, 149, 164, 168
    conception (*See* conception
        Christology)
    Trinitarian (*See* Trinitarian
        Christology)
    unitarianism, 31, 37–40, 56,
        128, 252, 290, 300–303,
        309
    See also under heresies
Church of England, Articles of,
    228, 261, 295
Codex Ephraemi, 282
coequality of the Son
    blasphemy, 36, 43–46, 152,
        250, 290–91, 323
    in extra-biblical literature, 49,
        112, 198
    effect on God's oneness, 20,
        25–28, 139–40, 272–74,
        289–91
    effect on Jesus' humanity, 134,
        170–78, 246–47, 253–68,
        309–12, 327–32
    Justin Martyr on, 296–97
    Origen on, 296–97

unbiblical, 35, 52–54, 93, 183,
    271, 279, 294–98
coeternal Son. *See* Eternal
    Sonship, doctrine of
Colwell's rule, 284
conception Christology
    defined, 174, 242
    discussion, 31, 60, 69–72, 76,
        129, 168, 242, 327
    divine sonship, 70, 188, 276,
        312, 322
    Mackey on, 257–58
    Mary and, 59–60, 70–73, 166–
        68, 184, 188–89, 228,
        247–49, 277, 303, 322
    Menno Simons on, 249
    Pastor on, 248–49
    Paul of Samosata on, 245–47
    preexistence and, 184–89, 328
    Servetus on, 248
    See also humanity of Jesus
Constantine, 144, 146–52, 307–8
Constantinople, Council of, 30,
    94, 237, 297
consubstantial. *See* coequality of
    the Son; substance
councils. *See* Chalcedon, Council
    of; Constantinople, Council
    of; Nicea, Council of;
    Toledo Synod
Cyril of Alexandria, 176–77

death, 82, 161, 208, 288–89, 309
definitions. *See* language issues
Deity of Jesus, 30, 54, 60, 121,
    253–54, 261, 279–81, 288–
    89, 296
"descent" language, 203–4, 258